Africa Emerges

Africa Emerges

Consummate Challenges, Abundant Opportunities

ROBERT I. ROTBERG

polity

First published in 2013 by Polity Press

Polity Press
65 Bridge Street
Cambridge CB2 1UR, UK

Polity Press
350 Main Street
Malden, MA 02148, USA

ISBN-13: 978-0-7456-6162-9
ISBN-13: 978-0-7456-6163-6 (pb)

A catalogue record for this book is available from the British Library.

Typeset in 9.5 on 12 pt Swift Light
by Toppan Best-set Premedia Limited
Printed and bound in Great Britain by Clays Ltd, St Ives PLC

The publisher has used its best endeavours to ensure that the URLs for external websites referred to in this book are correct and active at the time of going to press. However, the publisher has no responsibility for the websites and can make no guarantee that a site will remain live or that the content is or will remain appropriate.

Every effort has been made to trace all copyright holders, but if any have been inadvertently overlooked the publisher will be pleased to include any necessary credits in any subsequent reprint or edition.

For further information on Polity, visit our website: www.politybooks.com

In Memory of Great Leaders
Aleke K. Banda (1939–2010)
H. B. Masauko Chipembere (1930–1975)
Dunduzu K. Chisiza (1930–1962)
Eduardo Chivambo Mondlane (1920–1969)
Eddison J. M. Zvobgo (1935–2004)

and for Joanna H. H. Rotberg (1935–2008)
Who lived and experienced it all, and greatly led and inspired all with whom
she interacted.

Contents

Acknowledgements

I am grateful to Polity Press, especially Louise Knight and David Winters, for asking me to write this book, and encouraging me throughout the process of doing so. After many years devoted to Leadership, Governance, Failed States, Genocide, Corruption, and similar cross-cutting and more theoretical scholarly pursuits, it was a welcome challenge to return to compelling first concerns – Africa and its future.

Many Africans – friends and colleagues – have over many years and in myriad telling ways of friendship and collaboration contributed to this book and made it possible: the late and much missed David T. Hatendi, Selma and Jules Browde, Johnnie Carson, Caty Clement, Firle Davies, Sue Drummond Haley, Rachel M. Gisselquist, Allan Hill, Francie and Jeffrey Jowell, Calestous Juma, Raymond and Jean Louw, Frances Lovemore, Justin Malawezi, Moeletsi Mbeki, Greg Mills, Ben Rabinowitz, Christopher Saunders, and Thomas Tieku. During the course of intensive research for this book each added – as several have done for many years – important insights that have enriched the book. Several, too, were generously hospitable, providing important refuges amid the competing vortexes of Africa. I also appreciated and profited from the thoughtful suggestions of two anonymous readers for Polity Press. Leigh Mueller's precision and exact wordsmithing greatly enhanced the final prose of this book; her efforts are celebrated by me as they will be by readers. I also thank Erin Hartshorn for producing such a full index.

Many of the strands in this book were brought together and woven more tightly at a remarkably evocative dinner in Lusaka, presided over graciously by Ambassador Mark Storella, in 2012. Elias Chipimo Jr., Mark Chona, Lishomwa Lishomwa, and Sikota Wina were among the friends and participants who spanned the succession of sub-Saharan Africa's challenges and opportunities that all of us share. Their sometimes wry, sometimes trenchant, and always well-informed commentaries on past and present inform this book's message. Cornelia C. Johnson helped to enliven that dinner, just as she has helped magnificently to make this book as relevant and game-changing as possible.

Ottawa, Madison, and Cambridge, October 15, 2012

Introduction: A Continent on the Move

Africa no longer is the fabled, deeply troubled, dark continent. Most of its constituent countries are growing economically, delivering significant social enhancements to their inhabitants, and progressing politically. A number of the region's nation-states are increasing their per-capita Gross Domestic Products (GDPs) more rapidly than their Asian counterparts. Poverty is diminishing. Trade between sub-Saharan Africa and the rest of the world has tripled since 2000 and attracted more private foreign investment than official aid handouts since 2005. Its share of global foreign direct investment has quadrupled since 2000. Almost everywhere in the sub-continent there is the exciting bustle of improvement and take-off. Its much-lamented infrastructural deficits are being erased, thanks to China. Furthermore, Africans are much healthier than they were, with startling improvements in child mortality being recorded across half of the sub-continent; dictators are fewer, democrats more common; the intrastate wars of the sub-continent are claiming fewer lives; and almost everywhere in sub-Saharan Africa there is hope for the future and an upwelling of pride. Sub-Saharan Africa is no longer the "basket-case" of yore, about whose future the rest of the world once despaired. Africa is ready at last to play an increasingly important role in the affairs of the world. Major positive changes, in sum, have already transformed what once was a chilling outlook for most of the sub-continent into a future potentially much more warm and uplifting.

Many, including the International Monetary Fund (IMF), various consultancies, and experienced analysts, strongly believe that sub-Saharan Africa has turned the corner: "Something deep is at work. These countries are on a different path from the one they were on in the past. . . ." This "turnaround is neither cyclical nor temporary. It is not just a blip on the screen. . . ." Nor, Radelet assures us, is this resurgence of Africa a result merely of high commodity prices. It has been long in the making, at least in the 17 successful-country cases that he examined thoroughly, and results in part from fundamental shifts in governance and leadership.[1]

President Ellen Johnson Sirleaf of Liberia echoes this analytical optimism. What is going well in Liberia, she writes, is similar to a transformation occurring across a number of other sub-Saharan African countries: "Dictators are being replaced by democracy. Authoritarianism is giving way to

1

accountability. Economic stagnation is turning to resurgence. And . . . despair is being replaced by hope – hope that people can live in peace . . . that parents can provide for their families, that children can go to school and receive decent health care, and that people can speak their minds without fear."[2]

A rapidly swelling, ambitious, and globally conscious middle class is among the key drivers of this new momentum almost everywhere south of the Sahara, as it was a few decades ago in Asia. Twenty years ago, Africa's middle class was much smaller, and powerless. Now there is a coterie of entrepreneurs and executives that is much less dependent than before on governments for favors, beneficial regulations and permits, and contracts. The rise of middle-class independence and an independent mind-set are signs of an Africa – as Radelet and Johnson Sirleaf proclaim – very much on the rise.

This is the new Africa that has begun to banish the miseries (and the miserable public relations) of the past. Whereas many observers in times past despaired of sub-Saharan Africa, and murmured that bad news seemed to overwhelm anything else coming out of Africa, now there are true success stories, demonstrable improvements in governance and democracy, and a brighter outlook all around. Twenty-five years ago, only Botswana and Mauritius were full democracies. Today there are elected democracies in a large proportion of the sub-continent's states. Additionally, in many sub-Saharan African countries, formal rules are better respected and political institutions are taking hold.

Propelled to some important extent by significant drivers of economic uplift such as the dramatic spread of mobile telephone capabilities and China's pulsating appetite for African resources, sub-Saharan Africa, almost for the first time in more than 60 years, has a golden interlude in which it and its peoples can take advantage of abundant new opportunities. The African renaissance could be at hand, propelled as it will be by a new generation of gifted leaders, by a new emphasis on strengthened governance, by a new willingness and desire to play a central role in the global commons, and by a determination to overcome the ethnic and acquisitive challenges that have for too long held back its states from becoming nations.

But, as we rightly emphasize the new positives, the road ahead for sub-Saharan Africa is not obstacle-free. The challenges are many, and serious. There are long-standing and several surprising, even alarming, new barriers that could derail this long-overdue great leap forward.

Sub-Saharan countries are about to expand their populations exponentially. Many small and weak states will double or triple their inhabitant numbers in the next 30 years. Several of the sub-continent's now more populous nations will take their places among the largest countries on the planet. Cities will mushroom. Youth numbers will surge and dominate country after country.

As one sub-Saharan African state after another becomes much larger than could hitherto have been imagined or envisaged, so existing challenges will be neither erased nor avoided. Sub-Saharan Africans will still have to contend with the scourge of disease and reduced life expectancies and productivities, with massive educational deficits at secondary and tertiary levels, with an absence of potable water, with energy shortfalls, with being landlocked, and with weak road and rail infrastructures. Together with its burgeoning population, these are sub-Saharan Africa's key natural, physical, and geographical challenges.

There are man-made challenges, too: the remaining civil conflicts and simmering wars in some parts of the sub-continent detract from development as well as creating worsening outcomes for the civilian populations directly affected. Everywhere, in nearly all countries, corruption prevails and hinders developmental progress. Weak rule of law regimes, internal insecurities, inhibited political participation, limited transparency and accountability, and a widespread disrespect for fundamental human rights all contribute to poor governance and its counterpart, slower economic growth. A legacy of irresponsible leadership (military coups and despotic adventurism) has brought about this lack of good governance and a deepening of the policy challenges that the sub-continent must now overcome if its future is going to remain strong.

This book is squarely about the onrush of positive change south of the Sahara amid consummate challenges and abundant opportunities for growth. It focuses on the heady, new emergence of the sub-continent and its countries, on the remaining obstacles and possible stumbling points of its coming decades.

This book sets out the chief challenges in some robust detail. After a pithy elaboration of these challenges in the first chapter, together with a discussion of economic prospects and the exercising of political voice, the second sets out the major, unanticipated, demographical hurdles over which much of the sub-continent must jump. The third chapter discusses the sub-continent's tropical and geographical legacies, its health and disease challenges, and how those deficits are being overcome. The fourth chapter focuses on the region's educational weaknesses, especially its paucity of university-trained personnel, its shortages of artisans, and the consequences for Africa of its "brain drain." The fifth chapter sets out the sub-continent's formidable need for peace, explaining the great extent to which war has mortgaged development and destroyed productive livelihoods. The sixth examines those factors of weak accountability and transparency which plague most of the countries of the region and hinder their progress. The seventh shows how sub-Saharan Africa is beginning to cope with its vast under-served need for electrical energy, and how it must start to build and maintain arteries of commerce – roads, rails, and harbors.

The concluding four chapters of the book are about the abundant opportunities which are available – if policy makers and their voters wish – to help to resolve challenges and enhance the progress of the countries of the sub-continent. Chapter 8 analyzes the communications revolution that promises, through the harnessing of mobile telephone capabilities, to vault sub-Saharan Africa over many of its developmental hurdles. Chapter 9 looks at the compelling Chinese contribution to the sub-Saharan African renaissance now and over the next decade. The tenth chapter sets out the benchmarks that will turn sub-Saharan Africa's weak existing modes of governance into a strong, deeply rooted pattern of governance of the kind that the new middle classes desire and demand. The eleventh chapter is about leadership, and how the countries of the sub-continent can nurture the kinds of effective, modern leaders that they have largely long lacked.

Sub-Saharan Africa is emerging from its chrysalis of despondent, conflicted, corrupted, and ill-led decades. Tyranny and despotism are largely scourges of the past. This book celebrates the meeting of challenges and the triumph of human will and ingenuity over both natural and man-given adversity.

* * * * * *

This book is intended to be an intensely analytical, dispassionate, examination of the African condition. It is thoroughly grounded in empirical reality. Little is meant to depend upon conjecture or hope. At the same time, readers should understand that this book also represents an intensely personal attempt to come to terms with Africa's future from the perspective of someone whose adult life has been involved intimately in the politics, the political and economic development, the governance, and the leadership of Africa and Africans.

In my public and private life I have attempted to support beneficial outcomes over the denigration of their peoples by African despots and dictators. I have tried to employ the power of the pen to right wrongs done to Africans by their own kind and by post-colonial outsiders. Having devoted an academic and public policy lifetime to Africa, having lived (and researched and taught) for long periods in Africa, having an abiding affection for all things African, and having a fervent desire to observe the uplifting of the peoples of Africa, in the writing of this book I have tried to employ the strongest possible scholarly skills of objectivity and data-mining. But the writing has also drawn on a deep well of compassion for the disparate peoples of the sub-continent.

The peoples of sub-Saharan Africa have much about which to rejoice. But they also have much about which to worry. The future of their region and the respective countries in which they live is fraught with the innumerable challenges discussed in this book. Unless they and their leaders recognize their abundant opportunities, and seize them appropriately, they may prove unable to claim what is rightly theirs. This book, and my effort, is meant to set out the obstacles ahead clearly so that sub-Saharan Africans can overcome them, and so that they may emerge triumphant as modern Africa achieves goals that until now have proved mostly unattainable.

1
Myriad Challenges and Opportunities

Africa, especially the 49 countries south of the Sahara that belong to the African Union, is poised to grow and mature – to begin rapidly catching up with progress and modernity in the rest of the developing world and, soon, with advances everywhere. Its 900 million people, much more urbanized and urbane than before, and much more driven than in past decades by middle-class aspirations similar to those voiced everywhere around the globe, seek to transform the missed opportunities of the era from 1960 to 2000 into the sustainable successes of an Africa newly emergent and newly ready to triumph over the myriad geographical, material, and human vicissitudes that have for far too long prevented Africa from meeting the lofty expectations of its peoples and its more responsible rulers. Africans now seek to reclaim the promise of their independence years. They not only wish to assume their rightful place in the corridors of world diplomatic and political power but also want gradually to achieve parity of opportunity and prosperity with Asia and Latin America.

Africa has lagged the rest of the world for decades, failing overall to deliver to its numerous peoples the improved incomes and life chances to which they have long aspired. Compared to East Asia, Southeast Asia, the Caribbean, and Latin America, Africans today remain under-educated; more afflicted with deadly tropical and other diseases; deficient in preventive and curative health care and facilities; particularly susceptible to the periodic stresses and strains of global warming and climate change; prone to low crop yields; desperately poor; malnourished; bereft of water; short of power; under-served by road and rail; and limited by flimsy Internet connections. Yet Africa is rich in potential, with vast supplies underground of critical industrial minerals, gems, and gold. Off or near its coasts there are substantial quantities of newly discovered deposits of oil and gas, many already productive and others awaiting exploitation. Only a few countries are now densely populated on the land, although those densities are about to increase exponentially. For the most part, Africa's countries enjoy abundant sunshine to compensate for deficient soils and erratic rainfalls, and their indigenous farmers are endlessly inventive, conservative, and hard-working. Moreover, and significantly, in 2013, Africa is much better led and much better governed than it was during the first post-colonial period. Overcoming its deficits and bringing all of the positive attributes and possibilities together is the challenge of Africa's next era of growth and development. Yet, policy makers must lead responsibly if Africa is to emerge healthy and strong in 30, and then 50, years' time.

Middle-class expectations

Sub-Saharan Africa's middle class has emerged as a critical driving force of positive change. Before this decade, Africa lacked a substantial middle class just as it had long lacked a meaningful hegemonic bourgeoisie. Now Africa's middle class (defined by the World Bank and the Asian and African Development Banks as persons earning between $2 and $20 a day) has grown since 1990 from 117 million to over 200 million (in 2012). Thus, of Africa's 900 million people, nearly a quarter are "middle-class" in wealth and, presumably, attitude and aspiration. About 60 million households now have yearly incomes equivalent to $3,000. (Nevertheless, this is a new middle class that has much less disposable income than comparable middle classes elsewhere. Most are still very poor by the standards of industrialized countries. Few are able to afford the "white goods" – appliances – on which middle-class households elsewhere dote. They do not routinely carry credit cards.) A Pew Foundation poll of 13 emerging markets confirms anecdotal evidence that the new middle classes in Africa and the rest of the developing world are more politically engaged than the poor for whom popular politicians in African states have long catered. Members of the middle class "consistently" care about such values as free speech and free elections; the poor seek primarily to improve their incomes. As it grows, the middle class acts on abstract ideas about governance and thus demands improved political leadership and service delivery. The middle class mobilizes via the new social media and the Internet, and uses mobile telephones more innovatively than do others. Sub-Saharan Africa has about 500 million mobile telephone users, and more everyday.[1]

The new urban middle-class Africans are members of the global village. They have largely thrown off traditional or "tribal" attitudinal shackles. They want jobs, but hardly ever on farms, and now try to hold their rulers to standards of responsible governance and transparency that are refreshingly novel for Africa. Too long in thrall, these middle classes are the driving forces of change and modernization in an Africa that has seen the rest of the world race far ahead across several dimensions; Africa's citizens, now more empowered than ever before, intend to catch up. These newly empowered citizens are what Ayittey calls the new "Cheetahs" – swift, assertive, accountable, and technologically sophisticated.[2] Active stakeholders, they demand enlightened and responsive policies from their ruling classes.

Africa's renaissance

This renaissance has been a long time coming. In the 1960s, when most of Africa cast off the chains of colonial domination, several West African and

East African nations boasted per-capita GDPs higher than similarly new former colonies in Asia, notably Singapore and Malaysia, but also Taiwan and South Korea. Those outposts became economic wonders – the Asian Tigers – while the economically leading countries of Africa slipped inexorably into decades of intense impoverishment. Most of the rest of post-colonial Africa joined them in perpetuating this immiserating condition. Some of the new African countries, forgetting fundamental economic rules, attempted to surge to prosperity through import substitution, protection of infant industries, and neglect of traditional agriculture. But grasping at grandiose panaceas gained them little. The experiments largely failed. Many countries forfeited their previous ability to feed themselves. Many went heavily into debt as they attempted massive uplifts of their educational and health services, created their own airlines, expanded their armies and purchased tanks and aircraft, opened diplomatic missions across the globe, and naturally attempted to become big players on the world scene.

These lost decades – modern Africa's dark ages, corresponding in time to the era of the Cold War and reflecting many of its Manichaean absolutes – were desperate ones for many of Africa's peoples. They mostly lost the representative institutions that they had inherited from departing colonial rulers. Almost everywhere, democracy was replaced by Afro-socialism and single-party rule, or by a succession of military dictatorships. The "big man" – the ruling individual hegemon, rule giver, autocrat – became the norm. Rejecting democracy as a "Western" invention and a product of "imperialist dogma," these new leaders "established Soviet-style one-party states and declared themselves 'presidents for life.'"[3] Citizens became objects rather than subjects and were preyed upon by rulers and ruling classes as their individual standards of living declined dramatically and those of the overweening potentates exploded exponentially. Even in those few countries governed by well-intentioned autocrats, benevolent dictatorship deprived most citizens of opportunities to achieve relatively higher levels of prosperity, improved educational attainments, and modern social advances. Almost everywhere, Africa fell backwards, missing opportunities to grow and progress with the rest of the developing world. For the most part lacking responsible leadership and good governance, and mired in a morass of spreading corruption, Africans also found themselves engaged in bitter, seemingly interminable, civil wars. Diseases spread, too, and large swathes of Africa suffered from periodic famines as the rains failed and the new national social safety nets proved nonexistent or inadequate. Whole generations lost hope while their leaders ostentatiously paraded around the world and grandly neglected their long-suffering subjects.

Nigeria, Africa's largest nation and among its very wealthiest per capita in 1960, spent most of its first 40 years of independence in turmoil and tragedy. Military officers ousted the post-independence elected regime in 1966, and continued to plunge the country back into military dictatorship regularly until 1999. There was a bitter civil war between the eastern third of the country and the rest for three years in the late 1960s, mostly fueled by discoveries of oil. Petroleum-derived revenues and rents have fueled internecine battles over spoils ever since, exacerbating the corrupt practices that had plagued Nigeria for centuries and depriving ordinary citizens of rightful services and entitlements normally expected from governments. Nigeria squandered its new oil-derived riches, failed even to refine sufficient petroleum to fuel its own automobiles and tractors or to power its electricity grid, made farming unprofitable, and drove many Nigerians into crime. (Aviation fuel was in short supply throughout the country, even in 2012.) Nigeria effectively lacked responsive governing bodies for decades, its millions having to suffer under and make do with a shifting array of greedy regimes unable to share spoils with the mass of its dependents. Nigerian generals, mostly from the Muslim north of the country, ate the land and left little that was edible for those unfortunates who tried to go to school, obtain medical services, or make their way economically.[4]

Africa had many Nigerias, if always on a smaller scale and not always based on rents from oil. But some tightly run satrapies had mountains of bauxite, warehouses of cocoa, vast reserves of copper, piles of uranium, or mines that yielded diamonds, gold, cobalt, cadmium, iron, and other precious minerals. Unhappily, the returns from such resources were usually deployed to benefit new ruling classes, not to uplift the women tilling maize or manioc or the men beating metal in an urban foundry. In places like Zaire (Congo), Uganda, Equatorial Guinea, Togo, and the Central African Republic, rulers became the state, with each country's large or small resources existing mostly to serve the needs of the tyrant in charge and his entourage.[5]

Not all of Africa was so despotic during the Cold War, but even in places like Tanzania and Zambia, where the bosses were humanists at heart, people possessed little voice, there was hardly any transparency, and very few attempts were ever made to ascertain what the people preferred. Even in those relatively benign states, there were political prisoners, little freedom of speech or press, and more attention paid to what was deemed politically or socialistically/humanistically correct than to what might uplift and advance the lives of citizens. Conformity, even some attempts to collectivize agriculture, trumped individual initiative; the all-knowing state decided what was permissible.[6]

The result of all of these missed opportunities to join the global marketplace, embrace international trade, and float currencies was economic decline and social sclerosis. Africa's emergence was retarded throughout much of its first 30 or 40 years of independence by the greed and obstinacy of its rulers and ruling classes more than by any colonial legacies and hangovers. Leaders were concerned with enriching and advancing themselves and their families, clans, and lineages, not with strengthening the foundations of their states (most were not yet fully fledged nation-states) or uplifting and ennobling their peoples. Mobutu Sese Seko of Zaire/Congo purchased chateaux in Switzerland. He and other patrimonial despots obtained private jet aircraft with state money, distributed funds from the national treasuries to retainers and close followers, and created large and well-equipped armies and even air forces to cow their citizens and display their personal might. Rulers of less well-off or less extravagant African countries might have cried out against the opulence and oppression of their fellow African rulers, but few did. The Organization of African Unity (OAU) did nothing as a regional body to curb or even to complain about the excesses and depredations of some of its members.

Africa slipped farther and farther behind in the race for human advancement. That was the result of the forsaken opportunities, the civil war mayhems, the predatory oppressions, and the mismanagement of Africa by so many of its rulers and ruling classes during the dark decades.[7] In Sierra Leone, for instance, a small but well-run ex-colony in West Africa was transformed by the perverted greed of its elected president into a kleptocratic stew of civil conflict and retaliation. Beginning in the late 1970s, President Siaka Stevens gained personal control of his country's diamond and agricultural wealth and thus systematically benefitted himself and his family at the expense of the nation and its people. "Over the course of one year in the mid-1980s," Stevens and his financial partners "gained a windfall . . . [of] . . . about 3 percent of recorded GDP. . . . Almost no aspect of the state escaped Stevens' mania for personal appropriation."[8] Emasculating the state bureaucracy, willfully destroying the formal institutions of the state, and bankrupting the nation by stealing its revenues, Stevens militarized politics, sponsored armed gangs that enforced his predations, and consequently propelled Sierra Leone into a cauldron of conflict and, after his own death, into a civil war of unspeakable depravity. Blood diamonds were his legacy.

Fortunately, two small states in Africa resisted the common tendency to deprive citizens of their rightful deserts. Two leaders, Sir Seretse Khama in Botswana and Sir Sewoosagur Ramgoolam in Mauritius, believed in the responsibilities of leadership, in uplift, in stewardship, and in bucking the common single-party and Afro-socialist preferences of the very best of their peers in the OAU. Being hostile to dictatorship was natural and easy for leaders who were instinctive democrats. But it was harder to hew to a distinctive democratic path when even such well-meaning fellow leaders as Julius Nyerere (Tanzania) and Kenneth Kaunda (Zambia) believed that tight, authoritarian control delivered better results.

Khama inherited a dirt-poor land from Britain and, despite being surrounded by apartheid South Africa, transformed it into mainland Africa's most well-managed, most thoroughly democratic, and most prosperous land (diamonds were mined and exported only ten years after he had begun to run the new Botswana).[9] He even accomplished something which few others have yet done. He built a nation from a collection of tribes and ethnic groups united only in part by a (mostly) common language. He led in such a gifted and honest way, without the taint of corruption, that good governance (the delivery of quality services) is now taken for granted throughout Botswana, and solid institutions now hold its rulers in check and provide such luxuries – for Africa – as a consistent and independent rule of law, an energetic and committed civil service, a self-sufficient private sector, and strong educational and health services.

First forging a lonely, determined, course as a democracy distrusted by the autocracies and military dictatorships of Africa, the Botswanan model pioneered by Khama emphasized strict adherence to the rule of law, an independent judiciary, dedication to free speech, freedom of assembly and religion, widespread citizen participation, prudent management of human and financial resources, and a close attention to the needs of the nation and its people rather than to the demands of the ruling class and its families. Khama was modest and unostentatious – a rare combination in a Cold War Africa of "big men," self-styled potentates who declared that they knew what was best for their subjects.[10] Possibly as much because of Khama's attention to incentives and honest management, and also because Botswana was strictly well governed, the country prospered (avoiding Dutch disease – overvalued currency and marginalization of all other enterprises) as supplies of gem diamonds were discovered and carefully exploited. In time, Botswana became the only country on the mainland with a non-stop history of good governance.[11] It therefore grew faster than any other African country throughout the 1980s and 1990s and into this century. Despite high HIV/AIDS numbers, Botswana consequently was able to deliver consistently more social services and better opportunities to its citizens. Aside from a small, autocratic, oil producer, Botswana in 2013 is the wealthiest country per capita in Africa and has been for several decades.

Mauritius is the third-wealthiest African country per capita. Although an Indian Ocean island sharing few cultural or historical affinities with mainland Africa, it now belongs to Africa and the African Union by political choice, its leadership and governance example remaining influential within any discussions of Africa. Part (27 percent) of its population is descended from slaves shipped from Africa to the successively Dutch-, French-, and British-controlled island during the eighteenth and nineteenth centuries. A majority of Mauritians, however, are descended from Hindi-speakers who were brought to Mauritius from India to cut sugar cane under British rule. Others speak Creole, Chinese, French, and English as a mother tongue. Intermarriage and broad waves of assimilation ever since have blurred the personal or family links to Africa, or even to nearby Indian Ocean island nations such as Madagascar, the Comoros, or the Seychelles. But this blurring has led to very successful post-independence experiments in ethnic and cultural pluralism and in democratic tolerance and free expression that provide a model for the rest of Africa.

Ramgoolam, the first Prime Minister of Mauritius, understood at independence that he had inherited a small country rife with racial antagonisms. Earlier, it had suffered periodic ethnic riots. He thus had a leadership choice: to maintain Hindu hegemony and feather his own nest, possibly by copying single-party modes of rule from the African mainland, or to join Khama in rejecting Afro-socialist mantras and taking his and his community's chance on the gradual development of an island-wide ethos of democracy. Ramgoolam chose the second course, but he knew it would be unsustainable if he could find no means of enhancing prosperity for all Mauritians. He thus opted to reduce the island's dependence on sugar cultivation and rapidly to turn to labor-intensive light industry based on the creation of export processing zones. Textiles, wool fabrics, electronic goods, and other value-added products became Mauritius' contribution to world trade. Standards of living rose rapidly throughout the island.[12]

From the 1970s onward, Mauritius under Ramgoolam and his Hindi-speaking and non-Hindi-speaking successors, crafted a durable democracy capable of providing acceptable quantities and qualities of important political goods. Free expression in the three official national languages, an unabashed free press and radio, fair play, and an unshakeable rule-of-law framework, plus strong and unhindered economic growth, contributed to this happy outcome. With its empowered middle class, vigorous politics, and robust institutions, Mauritius has become a model for its fellow members of the African Union.

The power of numbers

Sub-Saharan Africa's emerging middle class desperately seeks life-enhancements such as those that are available to all Botswanans and Mauritians. But as they look expectantly forward, the middle classes – and all sub-Saharan Africans – must wrestle with major new and unforeseen challenges as well as conquer a series of tough additional obstacles left over from the dark decades.

Sub-Saharan Africa's largest opportunity and foremost challenge is demographic. The inexorable laws of population dynamics indicate that the countries of sub-Saharan Africa will continue to expand their populations just as the rest of the world, even China, contracts. Sub-Saharan Africa is exploding demographically beyond all but expert expectations. It is growing much faster than any other part of the world. This coming bulge of people could create the kinds of population dividends that came decades ago to Asia. Productivity of all kinds could increase as educational attainments grow, fertility gradually shrinks, diseases are conquered, foreign and domestic firms invest to supply burgeoning local markets, and outsiders (and the world's media) recognize and celebrate sub-Saharan Africa's new-found potential. Or the coming potential demographic advantages could be forfeited. Most of sub-Saharan Africa's 49 nations could then be saddled with immense unmet social needs, innumerable unrequited aspirations, painful intrastate conflict, crime, corruption, and cascading degradation.

Populations throughout sub-Saharan Africa will double, in some cases triple and quadruple, all by mid-century or before. Crowded cities and whole countries will become more packed, in some places to surprising degrees. There will be no way to avoid coming to terms with vast numbers; literally, there will be no places to hide, especially for would-be leaders. This unexpected and, for Africa, unprecedented revelation depends on estimates of fertility and the conquest of disease about which no one can be certain for a few years, at least. But the women who will be fertile are all born and, unless they suddenly become very well educated or become very wealthy, they will tend to give birth to future generations just as their mothers and grandmothers did. Sub-Saharan Africa consequently needs to prepare for the kinds of overall total numbers, and some startling national numbers, which have the capacity to transform sub-Saharan Africa either for immense good or disastrously.[13]

Africa's population is the youngest and most fertile anywhere. Most of the 10 fastest-growing countries in the world are African, as are the majority of the fastest-growing 40. In 2015, sub-Saharan Africa's median age is expected to be 19 years. Half of almost every national population is under 35. Aside from Palestine, all of the world's 33 countries with the largest percentage (between 42 and 50 percent) of people aged 14 and under are African. This youth bulge leads to educational deficits, high levels of unemployment and underemployment, large and chaotic informal economies, and incessant normlessness and restlessness.

Whether or not sub-Saharan Africa benefits from its coming demographic surge depends almost entirely on whether its attributes of leadership and governance continue to strengthen rapidly, and whether its leaders can improve what are still weak rule-of-law institutions, enhance transparency and accountability (and media freedom), reduce rampant corruption, and deliver key political goods to their citizens, more of whom today consider themselves middle class with accompanying desires to have governments serve their needs, not the other way round.

In sub-Saharan Africa, the wealthiest and best-governed countries will increase in population size much more slowly than the others. The possibility of poverty in other countries will intensify if, as is likely, their population numbers grow faster than jobs are created in the cities or on the land. Unless the weaker nations of sub-Saharan Africa manage to educate their peoples in greater numbers and to higher standards than today, skills shortages will worsen, and the educational advances that helped to create Asian tigers and widespread Asian prosperity in the twentieth century will escape southern Africa and its youth bulge for much of the twenty-first century. Dealing with demographic realities is sub-Saharan Africa's most pressing, most enduring, and most profound concern.

Wealth, health, and schooling

But there are others. The existing deficits and deficiencies cannot be ignored. Sub-Saharan Africa's GDP average per capita was only $4,000 at PPP (Purchasing Power Parity) in 2010, well behind the European Union's $34,000. Four years earlier, when sub-Saharan Africa's GDP per capita in then current US dollars was only $920, comparable GDPs per capita for other continents were: Asia, $2,900; South America, $5,100; the Caribbean and Central America, $6,000; North America, $43,000; and Europe, $22,500.[14] Even though sub-Saharan Africa's extreme poverty was reduced in 2011, with only 47 percent (down from 56 percent in 2002) of the sub-continent's peoples falling below the World Bank's $1.25-a-day line of absolute poverty, some individual African countries are still strikingly poor: The Democratic Republic of Congo (per capita GDP of $328), Liberia ($392), Zimbabwe ($434), Niger ($755), Malawi ($827), and Ethiopia ($1,016) are among the desperately destitute. Somalia is off the charts and not measurable. Moreover, according to its own statistics, in 2012 there were more, not fewer, Nigerians living in "absolute poverty"; 61 percent, up from 55 percent in 2004, were so listed despite the country's large oil holdings and its $2,600 GDP per capita (PPP). Only a few African countries are rich: Equatorial Guinea (tiny but with oil) at $18,143; Botswana (diamonds) at $15,489; Mauritius (an island outlier) at $14,097; and South Africa at $10,498. Even this last number is about four times the sub-Saharan African average; the gap between rich and poor still vast even though South Africa's total GDP, once half that of all of sub-Saharan Africa, is now less than one-third of the sub-continent's GDP.[15]

Sub-Saharan African average literacy rates lag behind those of the rest of the world, at 62 percent in 2009 versus more than 83 percent world-wide, 99 percent in Europe, 96 percent in North America, 93 percent in Oceania, 92 percent in South America, 82 percent in Asia, 68 percent in the Caribbean, and 63 percent in Southwest Asia. In sub-Saharan Africa, country literacy rates range from the 90th percentile down to the 20th. The fourteen least-literate countries in the world are African, all falling below Bhutan (53 percent) and Timor-Leste (50 percent), the least-literate countries in Asia.[16]

Life expectancy at birth statistics illustrate the health deficit that Africa must overcome. The world-wide weighted average life expectancy is 70 years, Japan and Singapore have average life expectancies of 82; Canada, Sweden, and Switzerland 81; the United Kingdom 80; and the United States 78 years. Sub-Saharan Africa's average national life expectancy is 53. The longest-living Africans, on average, reside to an age of 73 in the tiny Seychelles and to 70 in Cape Verde. After India and Russia at 66 years, and Burma at 64, come Madagascar and a host of other sub-Saharan polities with diminished life chances. Once again, almost all of the bottom-ranking countries on this sug-gestive list are sub-Saharan African.[17]

Maternal and child mortality outcomes comprise part of the life expectancy rankings. The countries in the world with the worst outcomes for maternal mortality (where the world average is 207 maternal deaths per 100,000 births) are sub-Saharan African (average 640, as compared to South Asia, 290, and Latin America and the Caribbean, 85), with Sierra Leone (1,800), the Democratic Republic of Congo (1,300), Chad (1,100), Eritrea (1,000), Guinea (980), and the Congo-Brazzaville (780) reporting devastating numbers of maternal deaths per 100,000 births. The figures for the United States are 8, the United Kingdom 7, Singapore 6, Israel and Sweden 5, and Grenada 1. Cuba has a 33 per 100,000 result, Costa Rica 29, Chile 23, and New Zealand 15. Africa has far to go in just this one area of human health outcomes.[18]

These and other medical results show how much African countries trail other developing nations. Poor outcomes curtail productivity and limit economic performance. Additionally, aside from being disease-ridden – HIV/ AIDS, malaria, tuberculosis, cholera, waterborne diarrhea, schistosomiasis, and other parasitic infections overwhelm Africans – too few citizens have been vaccinated against measles (72 percent) and other common afflictions. Nutrition is often deficient; kwashiorkor and marasmus, indications of food insufficiencies in children, are common. In the Democratic Republic of Congo, "sure [the small ones] . . . ask for food, but we don't have any," said one mother. Or, "today we eat, tomorrow we'll drink tea."[19]

In a dozen or so African countries, a full 50 percent of children under five are severely stunted, significantly wasted, and critically underweight.[20] In Algeria and Barbados, for comparison, only 1 percent are underweight. Preventive care in sub-Saharan Africa is rare. So is access to curative medicine. Africans can depend on a mere 0.09 physicians per 1,000 citizens, compared to Europe's 3.6 per 1,000, the United States' 2.3 physicians per 1,000, and Asia's 0.5 per 1,000. In 2008, Malawi had 1 physician per 356,000 people.[21]

Likewise, Africa has fewer kilometers of paved roads per capita and per square kilometer than South Asia.[22] Whereas Germany has a total of 644,000 km of paved roads, physically larger African places, such as the Côte d'Ivoire (6,500 km) or Zambia (20,000 km) have many fewer paved road kilometers and therefore greater transportation and commercial challenges. Nigeria counted only 29,000 paved km in 2004 and the entire (old) Sudan a mere 4,320 in 2000. In the vast Democratic Republic of Congo, geographically the size of Western Europe or the United States east of the Mississippi River, there are many fewer kilometers of paved roadway (2,250 km) today than there were at independence, and many more potholes. But Botswana, a well-governed desert country, became independent with nearly no paved roads and now has a solid network of 26,000 km, nearly 9,000 km of which are paved.[23] It is harder to grow economically if the arteries of commerce are weak.

Many fewer Africans (a mere 60 percent in 2008, both urban and rural) than South Asians (88 percent) or Latin Americans (93 percent) have ready access on a daily basis to potable water. Only 31 percent of sub-Saharan Africans in 2008 enjoyed ready access to improved sanitation facilities, compared to 60 percent in South Asia and 80 percent in Latin America and the Caribbean. The availability of water and sanitation remains an enormous challenge for Africa. According to the World Health Organization (WHO) and UN International Children's Fund (UNICEF) Joint Monitoring Programme of 2008, only 6 African countries were expected to meet their Millennium Development Goals for the sanitation target, and 26 for potable water. For example, 93 percent of South Africans and Namibians had access to water, but only 46 percent of Congolese (Brazzaville), 42 percent of Mozambicans, and 29 percent of Somalis. Sanitation access results ranged from 59 percent in South Africa, 50 percent in Angola, and 45 percent in Mali to 28 percent in Senegal, 23 percent in Somalia, and 11 percent in Sierra Leone.[24]

There are a number of other essentials of modern developed life to be obtained if Africa is to prosper and grow. For example, although a country like South Africa can count on 0.85 kilowatts of electric power per capita, countries attempting to industrialize like Angola (0.05), Botswana (0.07), Ghana (0.06), and Mali (0.02), must make do with much less. Although Mauritius could boast complete landline and mobile telephone coverage as far back as 2007, Ethiopia (2.66 per 100 inhabitants), Malawi (8.49), and Uganda (14.22) had to make do with far fewer.[25] In terms of Internet usage, Africa, as late as 2011, lagged far behind other continents. Fortunately, however, in 2011 new fiber-optic cables reached East Africa and South Africa from Europe, potentially quadrupling capacity and, in time, coverage and usage.

The scourge of insecurity

Africa, at about 50 percent, is becoming almost as urbanized as Asia and Latin America, both about 70 percent.[26] That is a startlingly major change from decades ago, and Africa (not necessarily as a result) also suffers from much higher rates of crime (especially homicide and rape) than Asia and most of Latin America. Although Honduras endured the highest murder rate in the world in 2012, with 86 persons killed (mostly in drug-related violence) each year per 100,000 residents, with Guatemala and El Salvador closely behind, South Africa (39 per 100,000) is almost as homicidal. The numbers for most of sub-Saharan Africa are lower: Botswana (15 per 100,000), Kenya (7 per 100,000), Mauritius (4 per 100,000), and Zambia (2 per 100,000) show the spread of results for 2008 for homicides. In the United States, only 5 persons are killed per 100,000.[27]

Narcotics trafficking has only come to Africa, largely from Latin America, in the past decade. For South American drug-running organizations, parts of West and Equatorial Africa sit athwart the shortest routes from Venezuela and Colombia to Europe. In 2012, the UN Office on Drugs and Crime asserted that nearly 1 billion dollars'-worth (21 tons) of cocaine was passing through

Nigeria, Benin, Togo, Guinea-Bissau, Senegal, South Africa, and Mali each year, en route to markets in Western Europe. The South African Medical Research Council concluded in 2012 that Cape Town was one of South Africa's largest and most troubling drug markets. In the twelve months from April 2010 to March 2011 there were 70,000 drug-related crimes in South Africa's Western Cape Province alone.

South American cartels, said the head of the UN Office, were exploiting West African poverty, but also taking advantage of lax border controls, weak law enforcement, and widespread corruption. The UN Office also believed that illegal narcotics consumption was growing along with the trade; there were an estimated 2.5 million drug users in sub-Saharan Africa in 2012. Al-Qaeda in the Maghreb may, additionally, have formed an alliance of convenience with several of the South American cartels.[28]

Africa has more internal wars, too; perhaps 10–15 million African civilians and fighters have been killed in the crossfire of combat and from attendant disease and hunger since 1990, dwarfing numbers in Asia or Latin America. Sudan's wars may have consumed about 3 million persons; the Democratic Republic of Congo's continuing combat, about 5 million; Angola's internecine conflict, about 1 million; and the various battles in Somalia, Sierra Leone, Liberia, Côte d'Ivoire, and Burundi, another 3 million.[29] In 2013, the killing and pillaging fields of the Congo persisted, 14 years after Laurent Kabila's insurgency ended the venal reign of Mobutu Sese Seko and supposedly ushered in a period of more responsive and more caring governance. In 2013, too, the Sudan and South Sudan both remained at war internally; the Central African Republic experienced continued strife; Chad was uneasy; there were small groups of rebels opposing the governments of Angola and Senegal; fractured Somalia harbored Muslim extremists and pirates, both at war with Western-backed regimes and with the West; Ethiopia fought ethnically inspired dissidents; Mauritania still battled al-Qaeda of the Maghreb; Niger and Mali contended with similar forces based originally in the Sahara, and the northern two-thirds of Mali was controlled by three insurgent groups; and giant Nigeria harbored at least six or seven antagonisms that regularly enflamed the Niger Delta, the Middle Belt between northern and southern Nigeria, Benue and other Plateau towns, different additional sectors and cities in the north, and population centers where tensions between locals and supposed interlopers were periodically violent. Additionally – and more persistently deadly – an Islamic group (Boko Haram) friendly to al-Qaeda created havoc throughout northern Nigeria in 2013. In 2013, Africa was still not at peace.

Economic growth prospects

But there is hope, and much about which to be positive. Africa in 2013 is beginning to overcome its statistical and very real human deficits. Just in the past year or two, many African countries have begun to grow rapidly, thanks in part to a new determination to open their economies to international trade. Sections of Africa are growing at 6 and 7 percent per year, thanks to China's relentless feeding frenzy, newly unleashed Chinese infrastructural construction activity, and continuing high global prices for oil, copper, diamonds, gold, and so on. In oil-rich, autocratic, Angola, for example, massive Chinese investments and concessional lending mightily contributed to 7.8 percent annual growth in 2011 and 10.5 percent growth in 2012.[30] Other sections of the continent are growing more slowly, but the lethargy and autarchy of earlier decades have been superseded by a willingness to embrace global economic realities and seek new accommodations with the forces of international commerce and competition. Africa now trades with its old partners in Europe and the United States, but also with China, India, and Brazil. Chinese state capital is the impressive driver of this expanded two-way trade, but India's private firms in 2012 were seeking to follow and compete with the Chinese thrust into Africa.

According to the IMF, the last 10 to 15 years have been "the best ever" for sub-Saharan Africa. Spurred by the mining of minerals and growth in the telecommunications, tourism, and construction sectors, the region, in 2011 and 2012, was growing at more than 5 percent per year – largely propelled by a commodities boom. Indeed, the IMF believes that today's African economic advances compare very favorably to Asia's 20 or 30 years ago. Rwanda and Mozambique, to name two of several rapidly emerging African economies, are "taking-off" faster than India, Vietnam, Korea, or Thailand decades ago. Admittedly, not all of this new wealth is being shared equitably with the poor, and several countries in conflict are hardly growing. Additionally, says the IMF, for all or most of sub-Saharan Africa to emerge definitively from poverty, the current high rates of per capita income achievements must be sustained for decades.[31] That is a key task for the sub-continent's new leaders.

Since 1995, median real incomes in sub-Saharan Africa have risen more than 20 percent. Labor productivity has been growing at nearly 3 percent a year. In 17 countries, average incomes have improved by 50 percent or more; another 6 countries are growing more slowly, but promisingly.[32] Yet 17 states, mostly poorly managed and internally conflicted, have not displayed such changes despite (in some cases) significant resources. The remaining 9 – the oil exporters – show both high rates of growth (Equatorial Guinea and Angola) and mediocre growth (Cameroon, Chad, Nigeria, the Sudan, among others) with little trickle-down effect or major social improvements. In these latter countries, inequality has increased, while in the more successful countries it has stabilized or decreased.

The statist economic policies of the 1970s and 1980s are now largely gone, certainly in the better-performing countries of the region. Openness – free trade without import and export restrictions – largely prevails and has contributed to the strengthened economic results of the success stories in sub-

Saharan Africa. Except in a few still benighted countries, overvalued currency exchange rates (which hinder investment and export profits) have disappeared, being replaced by flexible, or at least more competitive, rates. Shortages of foreign exchange have eased and black markets for foreign currency have vanished. In about a third of sub-Saharan Africa, reserves of foreign currencies have doubled since the dark days of the 1980s, although a few countries still are virtually bankrupt. Inflation is more widely held in check. Tariffs have been lowered substantially and made more uniform and less complicated (enhancing trade flows and hindering corruption). As a result, trade and investment have both increased, as have real incomes. Overall, there is a broader (but still incomplete) awareness of the advantages of following sensible, practical economic pursuits.

Africa's citizens have become serious consumers, no less than their counterparts in Southeast Asia and beyond. They also depend on remittances (up to $40 billion a year) as much as do other parts of the world; their diasporas are on the move and successful, whether as professionals in Europe or America or as traders in China, India, and Russia. In 2010, 30 percent of Lesotho's GDP derived from remittances (mostly from laborers in South Africa), 20 percent of Nigeria's GDP came from remittances, 5 percent of the GDP of the Sudan and Uganda, and nearly 1 percent of the GDP of Niger, Ghana, and Botswana.[33]

Although declining, agriculture remains both a substantial source of income within each sub-Saharan African country and a critical well of employment. It accounts for 12 percent of GDP overall and 64 percent of labor force occupation. (Other shares of GDP in sub-Saharan Africa in 2010 were resources, 24 percent; wholesale, 13 percent; retail, 13 percent; transportation, 10 percent; and manufacturing, 9 percent.) Juma suggests that agriculture's GDP share will grow substantially by 2030 from $280 billion to $880 billion if barriers to productivity – shortage of finance, lack of title or rights, the absence of technical assistance, trade hindrances, and seed shortages – are eased or removed.[34] Already, the development in recent years of sub-regional economic groupings such as the Southern African Development Community (SADC) and the East African Community (EAC), together with the initiative represented by the Common Market for Eastern and Southern Africa (COMESA), have begun to encourage trade in agricultural and other commodities across national boundaries. Farmers are beginning to take advantage of wider markets, just as they are of higher world prices for many of the cash crops that they grow.

Exercising political voice

On the back of this refreshingly welcome economic opportunity, many – but hardly all – African regimes now seek to satisfy the pent-up social, educational, and medical demands of their newly assertive citizens. Meaningful participation in politics has become more widespread as democratic aspirations have more and more been translated into practice. The people, not everywhere but in more places than before, have gained political voice. In opinion polls, Africans reject being ruled by autocrats and demand open and honest contests for power. Elections are freer and much more competitive. More countries that were once judged "not free" are now judged "partly free."[35] There is somewhat less tolerance for military coups, as the 2012 African response to coups in Guinea-Bissau and Mali demonstrated. Even in those few countries still ruled by old-fashioned despots, indigenous demands can frequently be heard. The battle is now more joined than ever before between repression and freedom, rather than between timid acquiescence and restricted autonomy.

The other not-yet-full nation-states of Africa are now poised to become more and more governed in the manner of Botswana and Mauritius.[36] Their middle classes want what the citizens of Botswana and Mauritius now take for granted. They are eager to embrace for themselves the good leadership and good governance that both countries have long enjoyed. Admittedly, many of the states of mainland Africa are much larger than Botswana and Mauritius and all kinds of important governing issues may therefore be, or have become, more complex. Immense countries such as Nigeria, Ethiopia, the Sudan, or the Democratic Republic of Congo each harbor ethnic and religious differences and sectional antagonisms that are more fearsome and chilling than those within some of Africa's smaller or more compact polities. Yet, at least among the medium-sized nations on the continent, several have overcome military and autocratic legacies and, in very recent years, have emerged, like Benin, Ghana, and Senegal, as well-governed plural democracies devoid of significant internecine conflict and excessive ruling-class greed. South Africa, Zambia, Tanzania, Sierra Leone, and Liberia may already have joined Ghana and the other well-run, but smaller, states – such as the Seychelles, Cape Verde, and Namibia – in this era's democratic surge. Everywhere there is pent-up demand – a desire for political systems and regimes that deliver good individual outcomes and enable Africa and Africans to hold their collective heads proudly aloft.

As former British Prime Minister Tony Blair told a conference of corporate executives, "I am noticing in my frequent visits [to Africa] that there is a new generation of leaders in politics, business, and civic society who don't simply have a new competence about how they approach their tasks; but a new attitude, a new frame of thinking, a new way of looking at their own situation."[37]

The road ahead

Unfortunately, just as Africa's real roads are laced with potholes, so Africa's metaphorical road toward a favorable future is strewn with massive boulders and other man-made and natural impediments. In order for Africa to catch up with Asia and for Africa's peoples to enjoy greatly improved social, medical, educational, and economic outcomes, sub-Saharan Africa must contend effectively with the demographic surge that will soon turn it into the second most populous continent on earth, and countries such as Nigeria, Tanzania, and the DRC into vast reservoirs of people. In order to transform this population opportunity into a demographic dividend, as Southeast Asia did in the 1980s and 1990s, sub-Saharan Africa must begin to do much more to strengthen its prevailing modes of governance, benefit from better leadership, reduce its predilection to conflict and mayhem, dispel dictators, elevate transparency over corruption and rent-seeking in political and economic life, strengthen the rule of law, enshrine freedom of expression and assembly, conquer the many diseases that burden Africa unconscionably and reduce its productivity and economic growth, educate its people much more effectively than at present, buttress and improve its inadequate physical and communications infrastructures across many dimensions, become energy- and water-sufficient – a daunting and critical task – and restore hope and a faith in progress to millions who no longer readily believe in the possibility of African miracles.

There are many tough challenges to be overcome if Africa in the twenty-first century is finally to meet the uplifting expectations of its founders and of the several generations who have seen global progress pass them by. This book is about how sub-Saharan Africa will reorganize and reenergize itself to cast aside the deficits of its first 40 years in order to forge ahead in this and succeeding generations. The nations of sub-Saharan Africa are ready to advance. But first they must separately and collectively accept and overcome the consummate challenges discussed in the six succeeding chapters. Then they will be in a good position to take advantage of the abundant opportunities charted in the final four chapters. There is much to do, and little time.

2
A Demographic Dividend or Just More People?

Africa has always depended on its people. Their industry, their intrinsic innovativeness, and their resilience in the face of the challenges of debilitating diseases, limited educational opportunities, poor soils, challenging rainfalls, and intense poverty have permitted many unexpected triumphs over adversity. But until now their total people numbers have not been worryingly large, compared to the rest of the world. Nor have those ascending numbers threatened to diminish the past decade's healthy per capita economic growth advances. Sub-Saharan African fertility rates hitherto have not greatly exceeded those of the rest of the globe, their youth proportions not grown exponentially, nor their urban inhabitant percentages equaled those of Asia. Nor have their probable pressures on available national resources ever seemed stark. Yet over the next decade, and for the remainder of the twenty-first century, all of these relatively comforting expectations will shift. How Africa takes advantage of its new demographical opportunities and realities will determine how Africa emerges, and how Africa's peoples prosper.

Half of all of the persons born in the world from now until 2050 will be Africans. Sub-Saharan Africa is growing faster than any other part of the world, despite HIV/AIDS, malaria, tuberculosis, diarrheal and many other ailments, drunk drivers, high rates of infant and maternal mortality, civil wars, and the rest. Fertility rates have fallen considerably, but at a sub-Saharan average of more than 2.2 children per woman, African fertility now exceeds that in every other section of the globe. Its families are larger, with more dependent children, than anywhere else. Its median age is younger, at 20, than in other continents or parts of continents. Even at mid-century, sub-Saharan Africa will have the globe's youngest population, with a median age in 2050 of 38. By then, sub-Saharan Africa may have realized a beneficial demographic dividend – or not.

If the growth of the planet's peoples follows today's official predictions, in 2100 there will be 10 billion of us. About 4.6 billion will be Asian, 3.7 billion African, 0.7 billion living in Latin America and the Caribbean, another 0.7 billion in Europe, 0.5 billion in North America, and under 0.1 billion residing across the scattered islands and continents of Oceania. Those numbers represent a major shift in percentages of the total from today, when Asians, Europeans, and North Americans are much larger percentages of the whole.

Africa's small population size will swell, and nearly all of the major explosion in new peoples will come from a sub-Saharan Africa that will burst its own seams.

Whereas Africa in 1975 had half the population of Europe, it exceeded Europe's entire population in 2004 and will have doubled Europe's total numbers by 2020. By 2050 (based on 2010 figures), Africa should contain 2 billion people, Europe just 720 million. This will mean major shifts in the sizes of Africa's countries. Nigeria, now with 162 million people and the seventh-largest nation-state in the world, will grow and grow, until at the end of the century it holds 730 million people and becomes the third-largest polity on the planet. Kenya will expand from 40 million to 160 million. Ethiopia is expected to swell from 83 million in 2010 to 150 million in 2100. Little Malawi, a poor sliver of a narrow country in southern Africa, will expand from 15 million to 129 million. Guinea will increase from 10 million to 37 million over the same period. Even the Gambia, a tiny place along the river of the same name, will increase from 1.7 million in 2010 to 6 million in 2100.[1]

Population growth estimates

Within Africa, population numbers will show important and, in some cases, surprising fluctuations, decade by decade. In southern Africa, for example, South Africa will hardly grow over the century, from 50 million in 2010 to 54 million in 2100, Botswana will increase from 2 million to 2.4 million, Namibia will only enlarge from 2.2 million to 3.7 million, but Zimbabwe will almost double, to 21 million, Mozambique will increase from 23 million to 77 million, Zambia will zoom from 13 million to 140 million, Malawi will show the burst of people already noted, and the Democratic Republic of Congo will increase from 66 million to 212 million and become the globe's eighth-largest entity, preceded by Pakistan and Indonesia and followed by the Philippines and Brazil.

These numbers are still productive in this one sub-region if, instead of projecting UN figures to 2100, we look ahead only to 2020 or 2030. Congo will not quite have doubled in size, from 66 million to 105 million, but still over the next twenty years there will be 50 million more Congolese mouths to feed, clothe, educate, and care for medically. Malawi will almost double to 28 million – desperately poor now, can it cope? Madagascar, in a situation similar to Malawi, will grow from 20 to 35 million. Will there be a government in place in Madagascar that can plan appropriately for so many more people? Zambia will nearly double, to 24 million. If China flourishes and copper supplies do not run out, Zambia might be well placed to become much more advanced than Malawi, Madagascar, and Congo. If not, its prospects are problematic. Mozambique and Zimbabwe will both grow marginally, to 35 and 17 million, respectively, over the same period. If democracy breaks out in time, Zimbabwe might be able to resume its one-time position as the best-educated, and therefore potentially the most prosperous, country in Africa, proportionally. If not, not. For South Africa, Namibia, and Botswana, the increases from 2010 to 2030 are about the same as they are from 2010 to 2100; in other words, they will not experience the fertility splurges that their poorer neighbors will display. And the rich ought therefore to get richer, proportionally, and profit accordingly from the demographical transition. Even though the last three countries, and Zimbabwe, will lose size proportionally in Africa, they should become relatively more prosperous per capita, working from an already high potential.

In Eastern Africa and the Horn of Africa, high fertility rates and medical care improvements will bring about large upward shifts and several surprises for policy makers, given the estimated future population sizes of nearly all of the components of this combined sub-region. Tanzania, in 2010 a nation-state with a mere 45 million people, grows to 82 million by 2030, 138 million by 2050, and a huge (for Africa) 316 million in 2100. It will then be the fifth-largest nation-state in the world. Compact Uganda, startlingly, begins with 33 million people and then swells rapidly by 2030 to 60 million, to 94 million by 2050, and then to a crowded 171 million by 2100. Next-door Kenya grows at the same time from 41 million to 66 million, then to 97 million, and finally in 2100 to a projected 160 million. (Note that only a third of Kenya's land is truly arable.) Ethiopia, in 2010 about 83 million, will grow to 119 million by 2030, 145 million by 2050, and only to 150 million by 2100. The Sudan's estimates for the same years are: 44, 67, 91, and 128 million respectively (including South Sudan, not independent at the time that the projections were developed). In 2012, South Sudan's population was estimated at 9 million; it will likely grow much faster than its northern neighbor so, rather than tripling, South Sudan could quadruple in people to 32–36 million by 2100. Somalia's comparable numbers (including Somaliland and Puntland) are: 9, 16, 28, and 73 million. Tiny and already densely peopled Rwanda increases over the same time frame from 11 million to 18, 26, and 42 million for the respective years. Burundi, with a comparably volatile ethnic mix, increases more slowly from 8, to 11, 14, and 15 million over the same period. Eritrea grows from 5 million to 8, 12, and 15 million. Djibouti, the smallest polity in the combined region, goes from 0.9 million to 1.2, 1.6, and 1.9 million over the century.

The East African Community, now embracing five countries and poised someday to enroll Somalia and South Sudan, will grow much larger than its northern Horn of Africa neighbors. At the same time, with so many new people, arable resources will remain limited, except in South Sudan, and climate change could wreak havoc and marginalize drier areas now used for grazing. Unless the swelling cities of these combined regions can absorb vast legions of incomers, and employ them (a major question), the per capita economic and social prospects of Ugandans, Kenyans, Ethiopians, Rwandans, and the rest will remain at serious risk.

In West and Equatorial Africa, Nigeria, as already noted, becomes over the period to 2100 the third-largest polity on the planet, up from seventh place. In the nearer term, it grows from 162 million now to 258 million in 2030, 390 million in 2050, and 730 million in 2100. (India is projected to hold 1.6 billion persons and China only 941 million in 2100. The United States will be the fourth most populous country, with 478 million.) That is, Nigeria will have approximately seven-eighths as many Africans in 2100 as all of sub-Saharan Africa holds now (900 million). No other country in Africa will be so densely peopled over the century. More than one-fifth of all sub-Saharan Africans (3.4 billion in 2100) will be Nigerian, compared to fewer than one-fifth now. (In 2030 there will be 1.3 billion sub-Saharan Africans, in 2050 nearly 2 billion.) This massive growth is based on the assumptions that local fertility rates per woman will decline only slowly, from 5+ to 4+ in the next twenty years, dipping under 4 per woman after 2035, and that the yearly percentage of population growth, now well over 2.5 percent, shifts to under 2.1 percent (the replacement rate) annually only in the decades after 2045. (In Nigeria now, northern women give birth to 7.2 children on average, southern women to 2.2.) Demographers further base their predictions for Africa on enduring falls in infant, child, and maternal mortality rates, a slowing of the HIV/AIDS epidemic, only a very gradual spread of modern contraceptive use from its current low base, and no new dramatic threats to African survival. Implicitly, for Nigeria and the rest of Africa and the world, the UN Population Division presumes that natural disaster, increases in literacy and educational attainments, the results of catastrophic climate alterations, the spread of new and old diseases, intensive population planning, and major interstate wars and intrastate conflicts will not slow population growth severely.

The median age of Nigerians is predicted to remain between 18 and 20 until 2040. Ten years later it will be 23. At that point, 420 Nigerians will inhabit the average single sq. km of the country, contrasted with 173 now. (Rwanda, Africa's most densely populated place, will have increased from 403 persons to 987 persons per sq. km over the same period – a density five times that of Japan. Sub-Saharan Africa's average density of people across the entire region will grow from 35 per sq. km in 2010, to 45 in 2020, 56 in 2030, 81 in 2050, and 138 per sq. km in 2100 – not impossibly high concentrations compared to Asia, but very congested for a continent with large deserts and comparatively limited arable land.)

By contrast, all of Nigeria's West and Equatorial African peers will remain relatively limited in size. Niger, to Nigeria's north, the home of uranium deposits and with empty semi-desert spaces leading to its northern border with Libya, will more than double its population in fewer than 20 years. So will Liberia. Niger moves stridently from 16 million to 31 and 55 million and then to 139 million in 2100. Mali expands rapidly from 15 million in 2010 to 27 million in 2030, 42 million in 2050, and 81 million in 2100. Ghana will increase from 24 million in 2010 to 37, 49, and 67 million in 2030, 2050, and

2100, respectively. Côte d'Ivoire, the world's premier cocoa producer, swells comparatively slowly from a 2010 size of 20 million to 30 million, 41 million, and 57 million. Chad, largely consisting of shifting desert and much dry land, surprises by growing from 11 million in 2010 to 18 million, 27 million, and 44 million. Senegal increases from 12 to 20, 29, and 44 million. Guinea accelerates from 10 million to 16, 23, and 37 million. Sierra Leone increases in size from 6 million only to 9 million, 11 million, and 14 million. The forlorn Central African Republic starts at 4 million and becomes 6 million in 2030, 8 million in 2050, and 11 million in 2100. Guinea-Bissau's progression over the same years is from 1.5 to 2.3, 3.2, and 5.5 million. Gabon's 2010 baseline is the same: 1.5 million. That becomes 2.1 and 2.8 million in 2030 and 2050, and only 3.8 million in 2100.

All of sub-Saharan Africa, even some of the smaller countries not listed or discussed here, will experience significant population growths according to the estimates advanced by the UN Population Division. Sub-Saharan Africa will be larger than Europe and Latin America and more than half the size of Asia. Will the Africans who now feed themselves still be able to do so? Will agricultural pressure of people on the desiccated lands of the Sahel, combined with the probable effects of global warming, mean a rapid creep southward of Saharan desertification across Mauritania, Mali, Niger, Chad, and the Sudan? Will the larger places, such as Nigeria, which have relied for decades on trading oil revenues for food imports, still be able to import foodstuffs and other consumables in the quantities necessary for such expanded populations? Will the poorest countries in the world, on average, manage, while growing rapidly, to provide education and health services for their ever larger populations? How will they manage the inevitable social stresses of enhanced populations characterized by prominent youth bulges? How and when will the necessary jobs be created? If they are not, what is in store for Africans?

The cities

More Africans than ever before will live in towns of over 5,000 people, and in much larger and much more crowded cities and metropolitan areas. In coming decades their numbers will triple, and sub-Saharan Africa will no longer be predominantly rural, with much of daily life focused on success in an urban surround rather than on subsistence or commercial farming. Today's African population is already very heavily urbanized, at more than 40 percent of the total. In 2030, according to UN Habitat, half of all sub-Saharan Africans (900,000) will be city dwellers. In 2050, 1.2 billion sub-Saharan Africans, or 60 percent of the total, will be born, nurtured, schooled, and socialized in large urban environments. Indeed, sub-Saharan Africa is growing urbanized at a higher rate – 3.4 percent a year – than any other part of the globe.

In 2010, Luanda and the Luanda urban conglomeration included more than 4 million people. Kinshasa exceeded 8 million, and Lagos 10 million. In 2015, Lagos will count 12 million inhabitants, Kinshasa more than 10 million, and Luanda 6 million. By 2020, Kinshasa will comprise more than 12 million people, Luanda 7 million, and Lagos 14 million. Both Lagos and Kinshasa will by then have overtaken Cairo to become the most populous cities on the African continent. Between 2010 and 2020, Kinshasa and Lagos will add 4 million people. Dar es Salaam, Nairobi, Ouagadougou, Abidjan, Kano, and Addis Ababa are all expected to increase their urban numbers by at least 1 million people over the same ten years.

In terms of percentage growth, Ouagadougou (Burkina Faso) sets the projected record. By 2015, it will have grown from its present 839,000 by an astounding 81 percent; Dar es Salaam (Tanzania), Kampala (Uganda), and Mbuji-Mayi (central Congo) will expand by more than 50 percent; and Abuja (Nigeria), Bamako (Mali), Luanda, and Lubumbashi (southern Congo) will be increasing by more than 47 percent. Almost all of the sizable urban areas of sub-Saharan Africa will be growing by at least 32 percent over the period. As UN Habitat says poignantly, whereas in 2010 African cities held 410 million people, by 2050 they must find a way to include an additional 517 million, some in intermediate as well as capital cities.[2]

In 2010, the 26 sub-Saharan African cities additional to Lagos, Kinshasa, and Luanda with 1 million or more inhabitants in their central cores included Abidjan, 3.3 million; Kano, 3.2 million; Ibadan, 3.0 million; Cape Town, 2.7 million; Addis Ababa, 2.6 million; Nairobi, 2.5 million; Dar es Salaam, 2.4 million, Dakar, 2.3 million; Durban, 2.3 million; Harare, 1.8; Accra, 1.6; Conakry, 1.6; Johannesburg, 1.6 (but greater Johannesburg had more than 5 million residents); Omdurman, 1.6; Kaduna, 1.4; Douala, 1.2; Pretoria (Tshwane), 1.2; Soweto, 1.2; Khartoum, 1.2; Lusaka, 1.2; Mogadishu, 1.1; Yaounde, 1.1; Port Harcourt, 1.1; Maputo, 1.0; Benin, 1.0; and Freetown, 1.0. Several more were listed at almost 1 million. Another approximately 280 sub-Saharan African cities hosted between 100,000 and 1 million inhabitants in 2010.[3] All will, at a minimum, double in size by 2020; many will triple.[4]

Some sub-Saharan African countries were already heavily urbanized by 2010. Thanks to the location of massive copper deposits and a historic rail line that drove rails across its central waist, Zambia's mining centers and its colonial administrative entrepôt early attracted rural migrants from every direction into its embryonic cities. Later, during the post-independence decades, work opportunities, ill-advised subsidies, and unwise pricing policies induced Zambians to flee their farms for the new urban (and more urbane) establishments. By 2010, whereas the rest of the sub-continent was at least 40 percent urban, Zambia was probably 65 percent urban. In a country of 13 million citizens, 1.2 million people lived in Lusaka, the capital. Two major copper-dependent towns, Ndola and Kitwe, boasted 348,000 and 305,000 people, respectively. (Greater Lusaka included 1.7 million people, greater Kitwe 786,000 and greater Ndola 590,000.) Other Zambian mining towns of significant size in 2010 were Kabwe, with 213,000 people; Chingola, 150,000; Mufulira, 131,000; and Luanshya, 124,000. Livingstone, Zambia's old anchor town in the far south of the country, counted a further 108,000 inhabitants. Together, these many sizable places that had grown up along a rail line amid ancient subsistence settings of maize and manioc testify to the surprising urban experience of but one medium-sized sub-Saharan African country. In 2010, at least 3 million of Zambia's citizens were dwelling in cities bigger than 100,000 people. Another 6 million inhabited tinier settlements that had mushroomed into small cities: Chinsali, Chipata, Choma, Kasama, Mbala, Mongu, Monze – to name but a few.

Adjacent Malawi, without much industry, a country-spanning railway, or city-favorable policies, was roughly the same size in terms of total people nationally in 2010. But it had only two cities over 100,000 people: Blantyre included 533,000 and Lilongwe, the capital, another 486,000. Neither had additional concentrations of people beyond their city cores. Malawi was much more rural (and much poorer per capita) than Zambia in 2010. But the UN predicts that it, too, will grow (and therefore urbanize) with great rapidity. Its modestly sized cities will swell as fertility rates stay high (but ultimately fall in the municipalities) and people are forced off the land into the existing conurbations (and towns that will become new cities) by 2020 and 2030. Once-quiet rural places like Balaka, Karonga, Malindi, Mzuzu, Nkhotakota, and Zomba will become bigger, with attendant urban social and economic problems as displaced farmers and descendants of farmers flock into these new peripheral trading and service destinations. Likely, none will have much industry, so jobs could be scarce as a weak country like Malawi tries to stretch its existing governance capabilities to match its people's new demands and expectations.

Ghana, despite its wealth and centuries of commerce with the world, resembles Malawi much more than it resembles Nigeria. It is a cocoa producer, so the rural area in the southern half of the country is vibrant. Gold mining provides employment and income away from the historic coastal cities. Accra, the country's busy capital, holds 1.6 million people and greater Accra a total of 2.7 million. Kumasi has another 627,000 people within the city limits and almost a million in its surrounding zone. Tamale is a municipality of 269,000 and Obuasi holds 122,000 dwellers, but no other urban center includes more than 100,000 people.

In contrast, Nigeria has for centuries been a big state with an active urban tradition. Heinrich Barth, the German explorer, saw how industrious, vital, and populous northern Nigeria's Muslim cities were in the middle of the nineteenth century, when they were hubs of a far-flung trading network. Others were impressed by the Nigerian city-states of the south, especially Benin.[5] Not only are Lagos, Ibadan, Kano, Kaduna, Port Harcourt, and Benin today overflowing with millions, but beleaguered Maiduguri holds almost 1 million persons, Zaria 899,000, and less-celebrated entities such as Aba, Ogbomosho, Onitsha, Ilorin, Jos, Abeokuta, Warri, and Sokoto all count more than a half-million people within their jurisdictions. Bauchi, Calabar, Akure, Ife, Iseyin, Minna, and Okene are not far behind, trailed by 40, mostly southern, cities with populations of more than 100,000. Nigeria is obviously urban, and becoming more so by the day. No end to this process of citification is in sight, at least not in this century. Since Nigeria now has many problems meeting the expectations of its vocal and long-suffering citizens, it is not yet clear how Africa's largest nation-state will manage to satisfy them, and everyone as yet unborn, as they expand the country's major cities and turn small towns into major new metropolises. Despite its almost limitless petroleum wealth, Nigeria today provides poorly for its citizens. When their ranks are swelled, in 2020 or 2030, how will Nigerian governments perform and provide?

Additionally, throughout nearly all of sub-Saharan Africa, capital or major commercial cities will continue to draw migrants from distant and near rural areas and from smaller towns and cities. Most African nation-states have dominant commercial centers (Nairobi, Lusaka, Accra, and Dakar, for example) that attract people like giant magnets and suck the commercial air out of the countryside. Even when their slums are fetid and notorious, their jobs limited, and their infrastructures underwhelming, these central cities usually dominate the political and economic horizons of those who enter them and choose to reside in their midst. Transport is easier, markets fuller, and services more available. There is access to television, to the Internet, and to credit.

People, even the poorest of the poor, often choose unwisely. But in coming to central cities they are implicitly calculating a cost–benefit outcome that favors the city (with its promise or myth of comparative prosperity) over a stagnant or decaying village environment. Cocoa growers can stay on their farms. So can coffee growers and those raising vegetables and fruits for local markets. But the subsistence maize, manioc, or yam provider, dependent as she and he is on quixotic drops of rain and inputs of costly fertilizers, often feels unable to remain at home. He or she migrates along with the petty village trader fearing competition directly from Chinese entrepreneurs, or from their low-priced merchandise offerings.

The conurbations will spread, suffocating what is left of sub-Saharan African rural vitality. Some forests and the occasional tangled, vine-encrusted jungle will remain in out-of-the-way corners, and there will still be Africans eking out success from the soil, herding sheep and goats, fishing in inland waters, guiding or supplying services to tourists, and generally pursuing traditional paths of rural endeavor. But those opportunities will become more constrained as the century wears on and the pressure of people on the land, on the cities, and on governments becomes increasingly severe.

Clearly, sub-Saharan Africa has already undergone a little-known transition from villages and small rural trading centers to great agglomerations, with their myriad celebrated and uncelebrated square miles of shacks – "misery villas" – and their social service problems (water and power), their overloaded or nonexistent utilities, absent or overwhelmed sewage systems, their high rates of crime, their deficient and potholed roads, and their massive dependence on informal economic pursuits. All of these challenges will double and re-double in intensity if sub-Saharan African demographical projections prove accurate. Even if those projections are only realized imperfectly, sub-Saharan Africa's problems will have multiplied enormously. Again, can the resilient peoples of Africa cope with these additional stressors? Major cities will become more over-crowded with squatters – perhaps half of the total everywhere, and intermediate cities will escalate in size – as predicted for Ouagadougou, Mbuyi-Maji, Abuja, Bamako, and many other once small and little-challenged medium-sized entities. Insignificant towns will become important urban places. By 2050, if not before, much of sub-Saharan Africa will be urban to its very core. With very large youth bulges, insufficient school and employment opportunities, inadequate and unprepared infrastructures and a profound lack of housing stock, the challenges for the governments of Africa could become overwhelming.

The youth bulge

In the decades ahead, Africa's cities will feel the massive unsettling effect of its projected preponderance of young people. There will be many more people aged 15 to 35 than on any other continent, and that youth bulge will endure for many more years than elsewhere. Policy makers in Africa (and beyond) will perforce become conscious of the powerful influence of youthful elements for much of the remainder of this century. The median age of sub-Saharan Africa rises to 19.1 in 2015, 19.6 in 2020, 21.1 in 2030, and 24.9 in 2050. In 2010, there were 92 million sub-Saharan Africans aged 15–19, 81 million aged 20–24, 68 million aged 25–29, and 56 million aged 30–34 – a total of 297 million in an overall population of 856 million. As those cohorts move upwards over time, and are replaced at the earliest ages, their numbers advance to 103 million, 90 million, 78 million, and 66 million (337 million in aggregate) in 2015. Five years later these cohorts are expected to number 116 million, 101 million, 88 million, and 75 million, respectively: a total of 380 million. In 2030, the anticipated appropriate numbers are 142 million, 127 million, 112 million, and 96 million – or a total of 477 million.[6] As a bulge, these combined clusters of young people will thus surely represent massive proportions of both their overall regional and each country's national populations. As a succession of age-designated groups pulsing through the sub-Saharan African state-based system, their potential political importance will only be equaled by their societal significance. If their nations are capable of educating them and providing sufficient health care, and if the states and private enterprise can together offer employment opportunities that equal net new jobs to match the bulges, the impact of these vast population bursts could become less sharp and disruptive. If not, if the aspirations and expectations of these young men and women are less than fully satisfied – if their disillusionment and sense of rejection becomes the norm – Africa by mid-century, if not well before, will find itself under intolerable strains from its surging, possibly aggrieved, people pressures.

For example, a modestly sized country like Zimbabwe counted about 5 million persons, or nearly half of its total population, in the 15–35 age cohort in 2010. In 2020, nearly 8 million Zimbabweans will be in that age bracket. Ten years later, 9 million people, more than half of its probable population, will be distributed across those same years. Tanzania, with its dramatically burgeoning numbers, faces a similar impact of population growth. In 2010 there were 20 million people in the 15–35-year distribution sequence, less than half of its 45 million population size. In 2030, when its total population is expected to be 82 million, there should be 38 million young people – closer to half of the total. Guinea provides one more example: in 2010 there were about 5 million persons aged 15–35 in a country of 10 million. In 2030, there should be 7.5 million young people in a state then expected to include a total of 16 million people.

Policy makers in each of sub-Saharan Africa's strong, weak, and failing states need now, and steadily over time, to understand to what extent these large youth bulges, approximating half or more of a country's total population in 2012 and for the remainder of this century, will, might, and should influence the absolute contours of national responses and initiatives. Wealthier small nations like Botswana and Mauritius might be able to respond more fully to such demographical realities. But can Congo (Kinshasa), tightly ruled Ethiopia, or sprawling and contentious Nigeria, with their outsize, unruly, ambitious, youthful populations, do so satisfactorily? Will they be able to channel the energies and ambitions of their young peoples over the next several decades into constructive, productive, pursuits? Or will these youth bulges in one or more nations prove destructive and the fodder of intensified civil conflict, crime, and social unrest?

The demographic dividend

As fertility begins to fall and family size shrinks, so the share of working-age adults in a country increases. With fewer mouths to feed, parents invest proportionally more in each child's education, thus enhancing human capital. Families save more, so more total national investment is likely. Women may also enter the work force. With more people working, more money circulates. These are the components of an ideal demographic dividend.

Asia benefitted significantly from growing population numbers in the 1980s and 1990s, and from the wedge of working-age citizens that naturally accompanied that surge. Asia was poised to educate its new young people, and did so to dramatic effect in Singapore, Malaysia, South Korea, and Taiwan.

Investment in the upcoming generations of their young people enhanced productivity, attracted foreign investors, boosted personal incomes and consumer spending, led through a healthy multiplier effect to great advances in national GDPs and consequent continuous improvements in the living standards of a succession of youthful cohorts, and finally caused lowered fertility rates that boosted per capita incomes and improved dependency ratios (the ratio of children and pensioners to the entire national population). In the 1960s, Africa's dependency ratio was 10 points higher than East Asia's; 50 years later the dependency ratio in East Asia was 40 points lower than Africa's. That, for East Asia, was the happy demographic dividend: more and more workers could support those younger than 15 and older than 35, leading to well-received and prosperous outcomes because official policies were put in place nearly everywhere in Asia to take full advantage of the dividend's potential. The tigers (and some near-tigers, like Indonesia) did so, and prospered as nations together with their many young citizens.

Africans could claim the same opportunity, and make it their own. The nations of sub-Saharan Africa could well follow Asia, and ride high anticipated population waves toward the long deferred goal of higher real incomes and social attainments. But transforming that claim into a substantive opportunity is far from guaranteed. What will make a major difference between success and failure is a replica, or at least a near-replica, of the serendipitously wise policy solutions devised in Asia. Those included sensible macroeconomic decisions regarding the openness and stability of economies, meaningful attacks on prevalent patterns of corruption, the considered reduction of conflict and war-mongering, transparent elections and political stability, overall good governance, and – critically vital – responsible and far-sighted leadership.

A plethora of young people of working age capable of boosting production and providing an engine of growth for an entire country and an entire subcontinent offers the great hope. But, in order to take full advantage of the potential productive capacities of this youth surge, new jobs are critical. Yet accomplishing employment creation seems an unusually difficult recipe for Africa in 2013, when the continent is awash with unemployment and underemployment. Hardly any sub-Saharan African country has a real unemployment rate lower than 25 percent per year. Some particularly wretched places, like Zimbabwe, have fewer than 30 percent of their populations gainfully employed. Thus to provide even low-waged positions for new waves of job seekers seems a tall order unless Africa's politicians can replicate the Asian formula. To have any hope of meeting the needs of people in the bulge, and their nations more generally, they must seek ways to grow even faster than many sub-Saharan African countries grew in the 2005–2011 period, i.e. at 6 percent and more annually. Much will depend on China's enduring appetite for African products and resources, on improving the skills of Africa's young people, on measurably strengthening governance in the weaker sectors of

Africa, on dodging Dutch disease, and on avoiding intrastate tensions that roil the prevailing peace. Otherwise the dividend could become a disaster.

The downside of the many opportunities presented by this decade's population explosion is the numerous challenges ahead: the vast array of new de-ruralized mouths to feed, to house, to educate, to care for medically, and to socialize. Still inchoate states are fractured in ways that Asia's polities were not; modern nations are still to be built. Governments in Africa, by providing conditions attractive to investors, must help to create net new jobs sufficient in number to address most of the needs of their expanding worker pool. Alternatively, the policies of unenlightened governments may well discourage industries and service entities from employing more and more of the newly minted workers, and they may frighten foreign investors. The countries in sub-Saharan Africa that need employment growth the most now, and in the near future, include some of the very countries where the population surge will soon have the greatest impact and where cities will explode in size beyond comprehension.

Bigger populations, year after year, will demand infrastructural improvements of all kinds – more and better-equipped schools and hospitals, paved roads and better bridges, deeper ports, longer airport runways, stronger and faster railways, storage depots, potable water and sanitation system upgrades, telephonic and Internet connections, and much more. They will demand assistance to work the land more effectively, especially in those sections of sub-Saharan Africa that have yet to be farmed intensively. Policies that help farmers stay on their farms, profitably, will have positive returns; those policies that drive farmers and their offspring into the cities will exacerbate existing urban problems and conceivably sabotage the realization of a demographic dividend.

Feeding the huddled masses

Somehow, the new urban masses will have to be fed. As the developed world urbanized in previous centuries and farmers left their distant agricultural holdings to crowd the industrializing cities, so the remaining people working the land became more productive. Malthus was wrong and the cornucopia believers right. But absent sensible new credit and modern tenure policies, favorable inputs, and enhanced security for their lonely operations, the viable opportunities for African agriculturalists could prove limited. Credit is everywhere scarce, and seeds and fertilizer, like other essential inputs, are either hard to obtain or wildly expensive. Agricultural extension or assistance services, widely available in colonial times, now hardly exist. The Asian tigers were able to feed their urban populations by raising incomes generally, so the proceeds of industrialization easily purchased essential staples and other comestibles from abroad, or from their own productive farming sectors. To do so, they managed to offer their own farmers incentives sufficient and real prices high enough to encourage continued agricultural growth. Africans over the last few decades have done the opposite, many subsidizing urban consumers for political purposes and devaluing and under-compensating farmers. If the urban masses are to be food-sufficient, country after sub-Saharan African country will need to adopt more sensible and more effective policies. Otherwise the potential demographic dividend will indeed become a disaster.

Already there are serious periodic food crises all across the Sahel and eastwards across northern Kenya into drought-prone Somalia, where famines are frequent and devastating. Unusually low rainfalls are the precipitating cause, probably exacerbated by the vagaries of climate change and poor harvests, and deepened and extended by misguided national political decisions harmful to rural productivity. Irrigation in this region is limited and grain reserves practically nonexistent. When that combination occurs, critical supplies of cereal grains shrink, prices rise severely, and pastoralists and agriculturalists go without, or starve. Naturally unable to provide sufficient quantities of edible food for themselves, they also cease supplying urban dwellers. And some of those who are still rurally based head for the cities, to relatives, or to take advantage of charity feeding operations.

The inhabitants of Mauritania, Mali, Niger, Chad, and the middle Sudan – together comprising the Sahel, just south of the Sahara – were at particular risk in late 2011 and throughout 2012, echoing similar crises in 2005 and 2010. The best estimates suggest that 19 million Sahelians were severely short of food in mid-2012. More than 1 million children were close to death; 3 million additional children were acutely malnourished.[7] So were southern Ethiopians, northern Kenyan pastoral communities, and southern Somali. Until it finally rained in late 2011, Somali fled to refugee camps in Kenya and Ethiopia, or found themselves herded into local detainment centers run by the fundamentalist al-Shabab movement. Al-Shabab in turned banned most external relief agencies from helping, further exacerbating a deep existential divide and leading, in part, to attacks in 2012 on al-Shabab from Kenya, Ethiopia, and African Union forces backing the Transitional Federal Somali government.

Certainly, to boost the potential for effective demographic dividend returns, the rest of Africa must try to avoid preying upon its most productive agricultural producers, as Zimbabwe under Mugabe has done, relentlessly. He and his colleagues in the first decade of this century systematically destroyed, for spurious and invidious political purposes, its once successful and fully diversified farming operation, losing 400,000 waged employees, ready supplies of consumable food, and abundant export earnings and tax payments in the process. South Africa could gradually fall into the same trap, sacrificing productivity, food supplies, and income generation in order to attempt to gain a hard-to-achieve appeasement of a mythical indigenous hunger for land, often articulated among nostalgic residents of cities. Zimbabwe and other countries must also attempt to resist selling or leasing agricultural opportunities and vast tracts to outsiders, prominently Chinese and South Koreans; Madagascar, Mozambique, Angola, the Sudan, Uganda, and Ethiopia have already succumbed to this Chinese temptation along with Zimbabwe, thus reducing their own indigenous potential food security over the long term.

Since sub-Saharan Africa's people numbers will almost inevitably be immense, and since sub-Saharan African leaders have no real way to stop the population juggernaut from pulsing through the coming decades, overwhelming their nation-states, it obviously behooves leaders to pay attention – quickly crafting sensible and far-sighted policies to harness the engine of population rather than trying, Canute-like, to hold back population increases or wish them away. Good leadership gives the demographic engine appropriate fuel and steers it well. Only by developing that leadership in the appropriate political, economic, agricultural, and educational arenas will Africa be able to make the promised dividend pay, and pay well. The future social and economic betterment of sub-Saharan Africa and its disparate citizens depends on leaders and governments coping effectively with the demographic juggernaut. That is sub-Saharan Africa's greatest and most enduring challenge.

3
Tropical Dilemmas: Disease, Water, and More

Most of sub-Saharan Africa is unavoidably tropical and many of its countries are irredeemably landlocked. Those bald statements may seem irrelevant or incidental, but some economists have shown a clear correlation between total tropicality (not mere latitudinal distances from the equator) and slow economic growth. Sheer climatic effects are important, too, in influencing productivity. So are deficient tropical soils. The availability of potable water in much of tropical Africa is also limiting. Likewise, some economists have demonstrated a strong association between being landlocked – without access to navigable waterways – and lower GDPs per capita. Sub-Saharan Africa as a whole therefore enters the developmental sweepstakes well behind others globally, whatever are its coming demographic challenges or its long-existing governance and leadership weaknesses. Additionally, when countries are located in the tropics, especially the low-lying ones, they naturally are prone to serious health challenges that stem from conditions prevalent more commonly in that region: mosquito-borne malaria and yellow fever, fly-carried afflictions of the eyes, snail-hosted parasites of the liver, various specialized cancers, deadly HIV/AIDS, and on and on.

Geographical realities

These many challenges will not go away. Certainly, the geographical realities are seemingly constraining, requiring policy reforms to overcome nature and location. Of Africa's 54 nations, 49 are sub-Saharan. Of those 49, a full 47 fall almost entirely between the tropics of Cancer and Capricorn (23.45 degrees N and S latitudes): only South Africa and Lesotho are excluded. (A tiny portion of northern South Africa is tropical, as are the upper halves of Namibia and Botswana. "Tropical" can be defined as at least 50 percent of a country being situated in the tropics.) A pioneering cross-country regression analysis found that simply being "tropical" cost a typical African country 0.85 percent in likely per capita GDP growth per annum.[1] Possibly this disputed tropical penalty reflects the impact of human disease, crop pests, and epizootic ailments – all more common in tropical than in temperate climes and all capable of reducing labor productivity. Lower productivity also results from poorer soils, a feature of the geology of the tropics, and the limited and erratic rainfall patterns prevalent throughout much of tropical Africa – a consequence of the low-pressure inter-tropical convergence zone that determines much of Africa's weather. But the lack (for many reasons) of the spread of technology and knowledge from temperate to tropical locations has also inhibited real growth. Other researchers assert that there is almost nothing to sustain the "tropical" geographical argument in all of its permutations – it is simply "wrong." For these persuasive revisionists, politics and politically inspired leadership explain far more than supposed differences between temperate and tropical outcomes.[2] Either way, sub-Saharan Africa enters the developmental catch-up sweepstakes with severe handicaps.

Whether or not "tropicality" is a fully sustainable explanation, 16 of these tropical states of Africa – many more than on any other continent – are also cut off from the sea or from navigable rivers: Ethiopia, South Sudan, Uganda, Rwanda, Burundi, Zimbabwe, Malawi, Zambia, Botswana, Swaziland, Lesotho, the Central African Republic, Chad, Burkina Faso, Mali, and Niger. (Rivers have to carry ocean-traveling vessels to be considered truly navigable.) Mozambique and Zimbabwe's Limpopo and Zambezi Rivers do not permit sea-going vessels to ascend very far. Malawi's Shire River, the Nile in South Sudan, and the mighty Niger River in Niger and Mali do not count, for the same reasons. (Contrast Southeast Asia's Mekong River, or the River Danube in Europe, with their steady and abundant sea-going traffic.)

Globally, most tropical countries are poor. Most wealthy nation-states are found in northern and southern temperate zones. Furthermore, coastal states – those with ready access to the sea and to sea-borne transport – boast higher incomes than comparable places that are geographically landlocked. (Clearly Switzerland, Luxembourg, Andorra, San Marino, and Liechtenstein, connected by historical low-cost trade to the countries of the European Union, are special exceptions.) Globally, the GDPs per capita of the non-tropics are three times those of the tropics. In the late 1990s, economists calculated that countries situated in the tropics lost almost $5,000 per head simply by being situated there (off an annual average of $18,000), and another $5,000 for being landlocked.[3] Since these comparisons were calculated in the 1990s, population surges in Africa have meant a major widening of the difference between the incomes of those who reside in the high and middle latitudes and those who inhabit the tropics, especially Africa.

Of the 32 landlocked nation-states in the world, nearly all are poorer than their neighbors. Only diamondiferous Botswana, of the African countries cut off from the sea, is prosperous. Average incomes in coastal states are four times higher than those in states with no access to the coast. Average annual per capita incomes in landlocked states are 57 percent of those in nearby maritime polities. That is, persons in landlocked states lose about half a percentage point of growth yearly just because they reside in such locations. Life expectancies are lower, as are educational scores. UN Development Programme

Human Development Index ratings in land-locked states are characteristically below those of coastal states.

These findings do not mean that geography determines outcomes. Rather, these data and correlations imply that improving citizens' lives is tougher in those places. Transport and freight insurance is more costly (in Africa, about double) than in coastal countries, where there is readier access to global advances. Modern communications, such as the Internet and mobile telephony, may begin to overcome the disadvantages of geography. But so far they have not, and sub-Saharan Africans must continue to contend with the vicissitudes of the geographical hand that they were dealt. Those realities also trump any colonially delivered impediments. Arbitrarily drawn borders, bifurcating ethnic groups or creating small entities, matter less today than the sheer fact of making one's way in the post-colonial world from within the tropics, and/or from within a country cut off from easy and inexpensive shipping access to the rest of the globe.

Landlocked countries must rely on neighbors for the transit of goods to ports on oceans. That transit is more costly, subject to delays, and politically fraught with obstacles than the trade of coastal polities. The Central African Republic must export through Cameroon, often a month-long journey. Rwanda's main transport route through Kenya and Tanzania to the Indian Ocean is 1,867 km long. Malawi and Zimbabwe must import petroleum products and consumer goods and send their own wares through Mozambique (or South Africa). Zambia likewise relies on transportation routes through the Democratic Republic of Congo to Angola, through Zimbabwe and Botswana to South Africa, and to Tanzania's main port, worlds away. Ethiopia lost its own opening to the Red Sea when it helped Eritrea gain independence; now Eritrean hostility largely forces Ethiopia to export through Djibouti, a longer and more tortuous route. Moreover, whenever the maritime countries are at war with themselves, traffic from the interior suffers or is blocked. Even at the best of times, there are customs to pay and border posts (and guards) to navigate. Landlocked states cannot easily control their destinies.

International trade provides a path of growth; it is easier to conduct, even in the air-travel age, by sea. Bulk exports of agricultural and mineral products are obviously less expensive if they can travel in slow steaming vessels. Copper and maize, say, can really travel no other way. Air transport is only suitable for commodities that are perishable or of high value, such as cut flowers or gem diamonds.

Beyond the logistics of trade are issues concerning the diffusion of innovation and the infusion of technological advances. The barrier of the Sahara may thus have inhibited the transfer of European knowledge north to south, or even Chinese and Asian advances east to west across the seas into the historically isolated interiors of eastern and central Africa. Sub-Saharan Africa in pre-colonial times was kept apart from global movements of innovation. The colonial exploration and occupation of Africa reduced much of that enforced separation. But it also rationed how sub-Saharan Africans interacted with the modern world. Colonial rule hardly encouraged Africa to overcome its tropical disadvantages. Moreover, the coming of independence fractured larger entities (French West Africa and French Equatorial Africa) into smaller and more fragile states, with poorer transportation routes and limited outlets to the sea. Equally, as a bevy of macroeconomic studies has noted, African countries, whether tropical or not, landlocked or not, have prospered when they opened their economies to international trade – when they followed liberal policies that promoted competition, efficiency, and the mobility of physical capital.[4]

Climatic factors

Prime Minister Lee Kuan Yew of Singapore intuitively realized in 1982 that his humid, hot, equatorial city-state was less productive than it could be because of its climatic and geographical handicaps. So he ordered the city-state to become the world's first fully air-conditioned metropolis. And productivity increased for that and many other reasons.[5]

None of the equally hot and humid capitals and commercial cities on Africa's west coast, where intrinsic conditions are no better than were Singapore's, took such drastic steps to enhance productivity in an era before air-conditioning was common. Yet economic research shows that the heat and precipitation of the tropics do deter growth, conceivably by about 1 percent per annum on average GDP per capita. Countries in the tropics (defined as zones of high year-round temperatures and without winter frost) between 1960 and 1990 grew 1 percent less rapidly than those in temperate zones. From another perspective, the temperate zone globally was 4.5 times richer in income than the tropics. Productivity per hectare in temperate climate zones was 51 percent higher than in non-temperate climate zones on average, reflecting increases in productivity per unit of input.[6] Cereal grains grow more readily in temperate than in tropical zones. In the tropics, plant respiration is higher and more costly; photosynthesis is less productive. Clearly, Lee understood more quickly than contemporary African leaders how to strengthen the competitiveness of his state, and how to cope with a weakness of its geographical location.

This is not to recommend that rural Africa should air-condition itself, an obvious impossibility. Rather, existing research suggests that there is something very real about torrid, damp conditions that slows much of Africa's growth and, together with its other geographically induced constraints, compels entrepreneurs and well-intentioned politicians to work that much harder for positive results in at least the low-lying areas of tropical Africa. There, it rains regularly for ten or so months a year; Limbe (Victoria) in southwestern Cameroon receives more than 120 inches (3,500 mm) a year, on average. The arid tropics (deserts and Sahel) – about 30 percent of sub-Saharan

Africa by area – and the upland savannah tropics – another 30 percent – both receive heat without steady rainfall. Indeed, even more dramatically since the advent of rapid global warming, 92 percent of most of Africa (bar the humid tropics) has too little water most of the time, or too much episodically. Ironically, about half of the continent is regularly short of water, a situation worsening as climate change intensifies and populations grow exponentially. Drought is increasingly common. Scientists blame the failure of the rains of 2011 in East Africa, for example, on the oscillations of El Niño and La Niña, far away in the eastern Pacific Ocean.[7] Whatever the cause, food security from Djibouti to Tanzania and Rwanda was imperiled by the drying-up of the atmosphere, and more such variations around the old stable norm are Africa's destiny.

Even conditions in the arid and the savannah zones (as well as in the wet tropics) have historically restrained rapid growth and deterred productivity, possibly because mobilizing human energy in such circumstances has always been more costly and more difficult than in temperate zones. Given what we know about CO_2 emissions and global heat gradients, Africa is likely to suffer more rather than fewer climatic upsets in coming decades. Together with its geographically ordained traditional climatic deficits, sub-Saharan Africa should expect tougher times ahead. Indeed, children in sub-Saharan Africa will suffer especially: children are unusually vulnerable in the tropics to the spread of malarial, diarrheal, and other diseases, all of which influence impoverishment and malnutrition.[8] Paradoxically, urban sub-Saharan Africa is also beginning to experience an epidemic of type-2 diabetes, affecting young adults and, increasingly, children. In many other ways, too, especially in those parts of the continent where GDP per capita still depends on agricultural and pastoral livelihoods, Africa will remain the continent most vulnerable to the adverse effects of climate change. Temperatures are expected to increase more in Africa than elsewhere. Low-income countries (the majority of sub-Saharan Africa's states) will suffer more than those with higher incomes. Sub-Saharan Africa as a whole, and the poorer countries particularly, will find it both very difficult and very expensive to adapt.[9]

Soils and forests

Only 8 percent of Africa is truly arable. Another 10 percent is suitable for cattle, camels, sheep, and goats. In terms of agricultural (not pastoral) productivity, sub-Saharan Africa's original GDP backbone, all of its tropical growing areas suffer from classically poor soils and insufficient rainfall. Africa lacks the rich loams and deep black earths of the American Midwest and Western Europe. Instead, its lot – especially in the tropical sections – is thin, fragile, friable, and nitrogen-poor, with unworkable heavy clay soils; African farmers have not enjoyed the more easily ploughed ecologies of their East Asian and northern European counterparts. Nor, because of tsetse-fly-borne equine sleeping sickness and other epizootic challenges, can all African smallholders prepare their soils with animal assistance. Back-breaking labor is the norm in much of tropical Africa.

African soils are weathered by heavy precipitation and rapid mineralization and leaching of organic compounds as a result of high temperatures. In temperate climes, regular frosts prevent mineralization and thus the attendant locking-up of soil values. In the tropics, heavy rains wash away valuable nutrients; fertilizer, even where it is affordable, cannot keep up with persistent mineral losses. Moreover, when these soils are worked, year after year, they lose whatever little nutrient values they once had; Africans almost everywhere, generations ago, learned to let their lands lie fallow for years at a time. This shifting cultivation and the pastoral reliance on transhumance practices were African answers to declining productivity and soil exhaustion.

Even where shifting cultivation has been practiced successfully, soil degradation has remained a constant reality because of the frequent planting of nutrient-draining cash crops such as coffee or subsistence grain crops like maize and teff. Livestock overgrazing (an accompaniment of population explosion) also degrades the soil. Nomadic practices harm the land as grazing animals strip vegetation and trample thin soils. Subsequent rains (when they come) cause heavy erosion. Even irrigation (only 6 percent of Africa's farmland is irrigated) can harm soils: rapid water evaporation allows salts to build up to levels harmful to plant growth. Many of these processes, especially the intensified exploitation of marginal lands, accentuate desertification. As soil fertilities decrease, so the loss of vegetation to hungry herds and desperate farmers often allows once-productive districts to join the Sahel ecologically, and dry lands north of the Sahel to become desert.[10] When the harsh Harmattan wind sweeps south from the Sahara, for example, it blows sand and fine dust across all kinds of terrain, and is capable of killing vegetation across thousands of miles.

Much of tropical Africa is surprisingly treeless. Three-quarters of Africa's traditional forest cover has been lost, and nearly 1 percent more is disappearing each year. Western Africa is less than 14 percent forest-covered now, and East Africa under 7 percent. Ethiopia since 1960 has decreased in tree-covered hectares from 40 percent to 3 percent; its remaining forests will be gone by 2020. Kenya has trees on only 1.7 percent of its land surface.

As sub-Saharan Africa's population numbers spiral, so tree numbers will collapse. Historically, even in the poorer sections of sprawling cities, and certainly in rural areas, most trees have been lost to firewood cutting. But climate change is also having an impact. Across the Sahel, one in six trees died in the last half of the twentieth century as average rainfall decreased by at least 20 percent and vegetation zones moved south. Global warming effects were the main cause.[11] By 2025, there may be no forests at all from Mauritania to Ethiopia across the wide belt of land usually described as Sahel and savannah. But, in addition to cutting trees for fuel, Africans have converted their forests to cropland or pastureland; traditional slash-and-burn practices, moreover, mean that trees are cut down and burned in order to let tree ash fertilize the otherwise poorly endowed gardens and fields of such subsistence cultivators. In Madagascar, the world's fourth-largest island, less than 15 percent of the land still has its original forests. Rice is cultivated instead.[12]

Without forests, soils erode. Where there are still trees, their roots can help keep soils soft and porous and assist in maintaining the quality of aquifers, streams, rivers, and wells. Without forests, water is often lost in massive amounts to evaporation. CO_2 can hardly be absorbed if there are fewer trees, thus forest loss means not only loss of habitat but also the intensification of global warming. As Africa's cities inevitably grow and as farmers flee the rural areas, so many more trees will be cut, water availability and quality will degrade, agriculture will contribute less to average GDPs, and the quality of life for many Africans will inevitably worsen unless political solutions are engineered.

Water and not a drop to drink

Water, even before the loss of still more forested land, is a scarce commodity in much of Africa. It often falls in sudden deluges that overwhelm catchment basins and holding ponds. In the heat, ambient water also evaporates rapidly. Thus, even where it should be readily available, water supplies are thin, stretched, and beyond reach. Women and girls (never men!) have to travel increasingly longer distances, even on the outskirts of many cities and within some too, to find water. More than a third of sub-Saharan Africa's population lacks easy access to good water sources. Around 70 percent of sub-Saharan Africans have no access to proper sanitation facilities. About 2,000 children die each day from diseases attributable to dirty water and bad sanitation.

The Index of African Governance found in 2009 that 100 percent of Mauritians had ready access to drinking water; 98 percent of residents of Botswana, and 93 percent of South Africans likewise could find clean water easily. But, elsewhere on the mainland of Africa only 42 percent of Ethiopians, Nigeriens, and Mozambicans, 46 percent of Congolese (Kinshasa), and 48 percent of Chadians could count on such supplies of water. In Somalia the comparable figure was 29 percent.[13] The WHO/UNICEF Joint Monitoring Program for Water Supply and Sanitation (JMP) in 2012 noted that, although Millennium Development Goal 7c – halving the proportion of people globally who lack sustainable access to clean water and basic sanitation by 2015 – had already been met, they did not necessarily have access to good-quality, "safe" water. Moreover, in sub-Saharan Africa, close to 40 percent (as many as 400 million people) – mostly rural dwellers and the poor – still lacked good sources of potable water. The JMP report also said that 750,000 sub-Saharan

African children were dying every year from unsafe water.[14] Bottled water, obviously, is too expensive to substitute for readily available groundwater from wells or boreholes, or from rain-filled cisterns.

Inadequate clean water inhibits health and nutrition, prevents good hygiene, and imperils sanitation. The World Health Organization calculated that sub-Saharan Africa's absence of sufficient potable water cost the region more than 5 percent of the sub-continent's GDP, much more than the $48 billion that the region receives annually in foreign assistance. Studies in Ghana confirm the GDP estimate. According to WHO, this large amount includes output forfeited because of child mortality, water-borne tropical diseases, reductions in educational achievement due to illness and the reduced time in school of girls, and the sheer time and opportunity cost devoted to collecting water on foot daily.[15]

According to the Executive Secretary of the African Ministers' Council on Water, investing $1 in enhancing supplies of water brings a $4 to $12 return: "Over 60 percent of hospital beds are occupied with water borne disease." People drink from contaminated boreholes. "So if you invest in water," he said, "and give them clean water, you are going to reduce your medical bill." Moreover, at the village level, making drinkable water available locally prevents the necessity of long treks to find it. Since children are key water fetchers, they go to school instead, and become productive.[16]

As wetlands and mangrove swamps have been lost to human settlement and agricultural conversion, so water has ceased being purified naturally and supplies have been lost or degraded. The growth of cities and the absence of suitable industrial purification machinery have caused and will cause interminable further problems because of untreated waste, pollution, and the consequent forfeiting of large supply potentials. As a result, as populations grow, so Africa predictably becomes increasingly short of water. Only Windhoek, a national capital situated in Namibia's near-desert, has responded to natural scarcity by massive recycling – treating its effluent so that it can be purified and reused for human consumption.

Other advanced methods employed in industrial societies to purify water that depend on modern reverse osmosis technologies consume enormous amounts of energy. So do desalination plants. But a possible hope for Africa's water needs could come from new experiments in purification using nano-membranes or magnetic nanoparticles, new kinds of filtration systems, and the perfection of inexpensive plastic membranes. Managing rainwater more effectively than now and enhancing methods to conserve existing groundwater sources could assist, too. There are many schemes along these lines being considered by one or more African countries, and by some of the sub-regional compacts. But very little policy leadership in this critical area has emanated from and been articulated as governmental direction. As populations swell, water will become increasingly a prime commodity, and a source of competition and contention.

While awaiting the perfection of these new attitudinal and technical fixes, a pilot program in Kenya promises to provide rural families with abundant supplies of affordable potable water. Employing an inexpensive and widely available chlorine solution and a plastic dispenser, about 400,000 Kenyans were obtaining disinfected water from communal sources in 2012. The new innovation is also being tested in areas without water purification and sewage systems in Swaziland and Somalia. Rather than relying on the distribution of bottles of cleaned water to individual homes, the key to the new approach's success and reduced expense is its communal base. Large volumes of treated, chlorinated, water are dispensed from existing communal water sources, thus minimizing unit costs and continuing traditional village involvement in water affairs. Given the critical importance of water for health betterment, maintaining daily activities, and agricultural improvements, these and similar future creative technologies for enhancing its availability, affordability, and quality may be able to make major transformations in the way in which Africa's poor and remote inhabitants are able to respond to their harsh and dangerous environmental settings.[17]

Those are the water realities as we know them on the ground in sub-Saharan Africa in mid-2012. But, according to a startling new scientific discovery, sub-Saharan Africa may literally be sitting on vast as yet untapped resources capable of supplying fresh water to the countries and exploding cities of the sub-continent for eons to come. Two large recently assessed underground aquifers hold a volume of water estimated to be 100 times that of the currently available freshwater of Africa: "For many African countries appropriately sited and constructed [deep] boreholes [could] support hand-pump abstraction . . . and contain sufficient storage to sustain abstraction through inter-annual variation in recharge."[18] However, the aquifer contents have yet to be tested and proved, and their contents may be tapped in future only with ingenuity and difficulty.

Pests and animal ailments

Most African tropical agriculture systems have been monocultures – maize, manioc, millet, sorghum, sugar, tobacco, yams. Such systems suffer unusually harshly from plant diseases and pests of plants, neither of which are killed off by winter frosts and all of which flourish in warm, humid climates. Africa's animal husbandry is also limited because of the prevalence of tsetse-fly-borne equine sleeping sickness, East Coast fever, rinderpest, and other epizootic diseases. In 2012, for example, already stressed Congo (Kinshasa) was suffering a major epidemic of ovine rinderpest; its sheep and goats, the poorest farmer's moveable bank accounts, were dying in droves. In certain areas, too, elephants trample village gardens and lions and leopards take cattle. A farmer's life is never easy. In Africa, subsistence farmers and cash croppers exist in perilous times.

Whether it is because of leaf borers on maize or fungus on manioc, sub-Saharan Africa endures a continuing developmental deficit because of where it sits – squarely athwart the tropics. Heat and equatorial rainfall make bananas grow plentifully, and so the Baganda and other Ugandans have always felt fortunate. But despite what outsiders might regard as bountiful, easy conditions conducive to happy and prosperous livelihoods, the burden on Africans in the tropics is heavier than on their temperate cousins. Most plant and cereal crops grow with more difficulty and at greater cost, animals thrive with much more effort, water is less easily available than outsiders would imagine, and forests are receding and deserts advancing. Concerted, analytically innovative policies are necessary, together with the kind of smart leadership capable of transforming sub-Saharan Africa despite its unavoidable and debilitating geographical and climatic legacies.

The human disease burden

The GDP gap between temperate and tropical zones may be explained by resource and productivity differences that are climatic in origin, by water shortages, by absences of available arable land, by landlockedness, and by major transportation and other logistical impediments. But many of the observable and researchable comparisons between temperate and tropical outcomes, especially in sub-Saharan Africa, are also health- and disease-related. Being productive while riddled with parasites is difficult. It is similarly challenging to surmount high health barriers stemming from one or more common and a number of exotic tropical afflictions, most of which thrive in (indeed, require) warm, moist climates.

Malaria is a threat throughout nearly all of sub-Saharan Africa; 21 countries – the lower-lying and more tropical – are heavily impacted.[19] *Plasmodium falciparum*, the most deadly of the five forms of parasite genus that affect humans, predominates in Africa, where transmission occurs as a result of the bites of infected female mosquitoes. Of a worldwide total of 3.3 billion people infected by malaria in 2010, a full 600 million were African and at high risk (more than 1 case per 1,000 population).[20] Of the 216 million episodes of malaria illness in 2010, approximately 81 percent, or 174 million cases, were African. About 655,000 persons died globally in 2010 from malaria; 91 percent or roughly 468,000 were African, at least 86 percent of whom were children under the age of five.

These high numbers mask the downward trend everywhere in malarial incidence. Globally, malarial occurrences have declined by 17 percent between 2000 and 2010. In Africa, malaria-specific mortality rates declined during the first decade of this century by an encouraging 33 percent. This reduction in mortality was associated with a rapid spread of insecticide-treated mosquito bed-nets and increased indoor residual spraying. By mid-2011, 50 percent (up from 3 percent in 2000) of Africa's households possessed (not necessarily were using) treated bed-nets and 11 percent of households had been sprayed. A full 27 African countries had adopted the WHO recommendation to provide treated bed-nets for all persons at risk of malaria; 38 African countries were distributing bed-nets free of charge but not necessarily to all persons at risk. Longer-lasting nets are being manufactured, so costs should fall per household and coverage should grow in the future. More nets could be distributed free by African nations, too, if their health budgets were increased and devoted proportionately more to prevention than to in-patient hospital care.

Indoor spraying reduces and interrupts malarial transmission through effective vector control; in 2010, 36 African countries were engaged in such spraying, 13 with DDT. Protected by such spraying were 78 million people – up from 10 million in 2005 – or about 11 percent of the at-risk population. Most of the spraying is of pyrethroids, synthesized from a plant base. Only 13 percent is carried out using DDT. Growing resistance to pyrethroid-based insecticides has also been widely reported in Africa.

In Africa, most *P. falciparum* cases are treated with artemisinin-based combination therapies, although chloroquine is still being used. Unfortunately, treatment of malarial cases has been compromised in recent years by the parasite's growing ability to resist the effects of the artemisinin-based combination therapies. Moreover, to the chagrin and concern of the World Health Organization, twice as many artemisinin combination treatments were being administered as infected persons were being tested fully to see if their infections merited such medicines.

All of these several interventions led to the major reductions listed in overall African mortality from malaria, and its daily incidence. The biggest gains were made in the better-governed (and least tropical) countries – the nation-states with a greater focus than elsewhere on service delivery and the responsibility to perform for citizens. Botswana, Cape Verde, Namibia, Rwanda, São Tomé and Príncipe, South Africa, and the Zanzibar region of Tanzania made more progress in combating malaria than other African countries. Swaziland, with low governance attainments, also joined their ranks in 2011. The World Health Organization reported that, in those places, the decreases in confirmed malaria cases were associated with "intense malaria control interventions," especially much-increased surveillance efforts and more thorough diagnostic utilizations.[21]

Dengue fever and yellow fever are also transmitted by mosquitoes, albeit a different variety (primarily *Aedes aegypti*) than that responsible for malaria. Neither disease, fortunately, poses as much of a threat to the health of Africans as does malaria. Indeed, dengue fever is found primarily in coastal eastern Africa – Mozambique, Kenya, Somalia, and Djibouti – and affects far fewer people than malaria. Dengue fever usually presents itself as an ailment reminiscent of influenza. Few die from it. Yet, when children are attacked repeatedly by dengue, especially the hemorrhagic variant, it can be fatal.

Although yellow fever is present in 32 African countries, it is largely found in the equatorial African belt; a small percentage of victims suffer very high fevers, jaundice, and dangerous deterioration of kidneys, liver, and heart. If it, too, progresses to a hemorrhagic form and patients bleed from their mouths, eyes, and other organs, coma and death often follow. Of approximately 30,000 deaths from yellow fever world-wide each year, about three-fifths are African. (Viral hemorrhagic diseases like Ebola, Lassa, Marburg are often fatal as well, but outbreaks occur infrequently – largely in the northern Congo (Kinshasa) in the case of Ebola, in Uganda and the Congo for Marburg, and in Nigeria, where it is spread by rats, in the case of Lassa.)

Tuberculosis (TB) has long debilitated Africans and Africa, no less so in recent years and in close association with HIV/AIDS. Pulmonary tuberculosis causes chest pains, the coughing up of blood or sputum, fatigue, weight loss, reduced appetites, chills, and fevers. The numbers who are infected with this bacterial invasion of the human lungs has been growing rapidly across the continent, both separately and in association with HIV/AIDS. Between 1995 and 2005, the incidence of TB in Africa tripled. In 2010, for example, of more than 8,800,000 new cases across the globe, and compared to 3 million in India and China, there were 490,000 new cases in much smaller South Africa, 220,000 each in Congo (Kinshasa) and Ethiopia, 210,000 in Nigeria, 130,000 in Mozambique, 120,000 in Kenya, and 80,000 each in Zimbabwe and Tanzania. Those are alarmingly high numbers, especially given the recent spread of highly treatment-resistant forms of TB in southern Africa.

About a third of all HIV-infected persons world-wide also have TB, and TB is the leading cause of death among those with HIV because of compromised immune systems. The highest rates of TB incidence among HIV-infected persons are in Africa, with Swaziland topping the list with 1,056 per 100,000 of total population. (The global average is 16 per 100,000.) The other southern African countries – South Africa (591), Lesotho, Zimbabwe (480), Namibia, Mozambique, Botswana (326), and Zambia (302) – follow. This additional list of countries with TB complications continues with Gabon and the nations of East Africa.

Mortalities attributed primarily to TB are also exceedingly high in most of Africa. Of the 1.1 million who die globally every year, about 36,000 are Congolese (Kinshasa), 33,000 Nigerians, 29,000 Ethiopians, and 25,000 South Africans.[22] A combination of directly observed and monitored treatment with four effective antibiotics prevents death and usually brings about a cure. But innumerable afflicted patients, too many in Africa, never take their pills consistently. The infection may hence continue, and kill. Additionally, multi-drug-resistant TB and extreme drug-resistant TB strains have become more common, especially in southern Africa. The usual drugs do not work well, and death rates for those with these two newer forms of TB are very high.

Of the 34 million persons living with HIV/AIDS in 2011, fully half were Africans – including 6 million South Africans, 3 million Nigerians, 1.5 million Kenyans, and 1 million Mozambicans, Zimbabweans, Ugandans, and

Tanzanians. Although the global adult prevalence rate for HIV/AIDS is just under 1 percent, 10 to 25 percent of southern Africans were afflicted with the disease in 2010. So were up to 10 percent of East Africans and West and Equatorial Africans (including those in massive Nigeria). These numbers are much lower than estimates a decade ago. Moreover, antiretroviral treatments, where and when available, have turned an always-fatal disease into a chronic one. (The only African countries showing more than 50 percent antiretroviral coverage in 2009 were Rwanda, Botswana, Namibia, Swaziland, Benin, Senegal, and Mali.) Of the 1.8 million persons who died from AIDS across the globe in 2010, about 330,000 were South Africans, 220,000 Nigerians, and about 80,000 each in such countries as Tanzania, Mozambique, Kenya, Zimbabwe, Uganda, Malawi, Zambia, and Cameroon.[23]

A plague of worms and flies

Intestinal and urogenital worms and flukes are other major tropical African afflictions. The World Health Organization estimates that 40 percent of the global tropical disease burden results from various kinds of internal worm infestations and other ailments spread by flies and mosquitoes. In Africa these include:

(1) Schistosomiasis (bilharzia), for which snails in slow-moving freshwater (behind dams or in irrigation canals, and sometimes in lakes and streams) are the vector; they host a fluke or parasitic worm that penetrates the skin of humans and migrates to blood vessels, producing eggs. The eggs then move into various organs, impairing growth and causing fever and other complaints. There are about 75 million new cases a year in Africa. Of the 207 million persons with schistosomiasis, 85 percent live in Africa. Schistosomiasis is found everywhere in sub-Saharan Africa bar Somaliland, South Africa, Namibia, and the Kalahari desertified parts of Botswana.

Chronic schistosomiasis often results in anemia, kidney lesions, stunting, reduced ability to learn, and infertility. About 200,000 Africans die each year from complications of schistosomiasis.

(2) Soil-transmitted helminthiasis – round worms, hook worms, and whipworms – is found in the humid tropics where sanitation is poor; there are about 300–400 million cases a year in Africa, about half of whom are children.[24] The absence of careful sanitation means that parasite eggs, transmitted from the feces of infected humans, seep into land and water sources. These intestinal worms can lead to anemia, Vitamin A deficiency, stunting, malnutrition, impaired development, and intestinal obstructions.

(3) Lymphatic filariasis (elephantiasis) cripples numerous Africans. Mosquito-borne, its worms block human lymphatic systems, swell breasts and limbs, damage genitals, and harden skin. Nigeria and Congo (Kinshasa) are the primary African countries affected, with 30 million persons at risk overall in tropical Africa.

(4) Trachoma is a highly contagious, chronic, inflammation of the mucous membranes of the eyes. A bacterial infection spread by flies attracted to the eyes, it also is infectious through human contact. It occurs in densely populated areas with poor access to clean water. Repeated infections and the scarring of the upper lids often cause blindness, especially in women and children. About 30 million Africans are affected and many more millions are at risk. Fortunately, powerful antibiotics have brought infected cases down to manageable numbers and virtually eliminated the disease in Ghana and Mali. Further anti-trachoma action and investigation are being pursued in Niger and Nigeria, and latrines are being constructed in Ethiopia to enhance sanitation in the trachoma areas. About a third of the numerous cases of blindness in Ethiopia are attributed to trachoma. About 44 percent of children in Niger once suffered from trachoma. South Sudan and the Sudan are other states with serious trachoma. Corrective surgery has also restored eyesight to as many as 300,000 Africans with trachoma.

(5) Onchocerciasis (river blindness) comes from a microscopic worm carried by small black flies that swarm around fast-flowing rivers and streams. When a fly bites a human it releases tiny larvae into the host's bloodstream. The larvae become worms that in turn produce more larvae and are in turn spread again by biting flies to someone else. These onchocerca larvae cause intense itching, ugly lesions, and – ultimately – destroy eye-tissue and cause blindness. The disease also compels Africans to avoid useful sources of water. Fortunately, the distribution of antibiotics in the affected areas of West Africa, especially along the Niger and Volta Rivers, has largely eliminated this once merciless disease of Africa's tropical rivers.

(6) Dracunculiasis (guinea worm disease, or the disease of dragons), comes from a parasitic roundworm that is ingested by humans from stagnant water sources contaminated with aquatic fleas (corepods) or aquatic crustaceans carrying the worm's larvae. Once inside the human abdominal cavity, the larvae multiply and become 2- or 3-foot-long thread-like worms. Once the worms are mature, after about a year, they release another cycle of larvae through a large blister – the worm's exit point – at the edge of a human's lower extremities. Intense itching and burning occurs at the blister site. Victims cannot easily attend school, tend their crops or other activities, or care for their families. Extracting the worm or worms from humans through the blister site takes many weeks.

Once more widespread, with 3.5 million cases in 1986, in 2011 only 1,710 cases of guinea worm disease were reported in tropical Africa, mostly in what is now South Sudan. Ethiopia, Mali, and Ghana also harbored less intense outbreaks of the disease in 2010.[25] The use of an effective larvicide and water filtration equipment has gradually reduced or eliminated guinea worm contaminations from stagnant water sources.

(7) Human trypanosomiasis (sleeping sickness), a parasitic disease transmitted by the bite of the tsetse fly, no longer achieves the 300,000 or so African victims it claimed as recently as 1995. In 2010, thanks to African Union and World Health Organization efforts of surveillance, concerted eradication of the vector by host governments and international donors, and new combination drugs, only 7,100 new cases were reported. These were the fewest cases reported in 50 years, and a decrease in case numbers of 63 percent since 2000. Of Africa's 15 countries with sleeping sickness, only the Central African Republic and the next-door Congo (Kinshasa) reported more than 1,000 cases each in 2009.[26]

(8) Visceral leishmaniasis (kala azar) is among the least-known but the most debilitating of Africa's neglected diseases, primarily affecting the poor. A zoonotic infection spread from rodents by protozoa transmitted by female sandfly bites, *Leishmania* are intracellular parasites infecting mononuclear phagocytes. They cause self-healing, localized ulcers and dangerous progressive lesions of the skin, mucus membranes, and the entire reticuloendothelial system (the spleen, liver, and bone marrow). Leishmaniasis is also responsible for acute peripheral neuropathy. Present in Africa since at least the eighteenth century, and common wherever there are sandflies and no frost, in recent years it has become more virulent in Africa because of HIV/AIDS, and immunal weaknesses. Consequently, it has followed HIV/AIDS into urban Africa. Sharing of unsterilized needles by intravenous drug users has also exacerbated the spread of leishmaniasis. Of the 500,000 cases of leishmaniasis that are found world-wide in a typical year, the African countries of the Sudan and South Sudan, Ethiopia, Kenya, Cameroon, Mali, Mauritania, and Burkina Faso are the worst afflicted.[27] Visceral leishmaniasis is particularly acute along the Blue Nile River in the Sudan and Ethiopia, and among the Nuer along the White Nile River in South Sudan.

Much of the reduction by 2012 of the specialized diseases of Africa – onchocerciasis, trachoma, guinea worm disease, elephantiasis, and schistosomiasis – has been organized by the World Health Organization, UNICEF, the Carter Center, the Bill and Melinda Gates Foundation, and other important, targeted, external efforts. Major pharmaceutical companies have donated drugs and research expertise. In early 2012, 13 large drug firms, the Gates Foundation, and the British and American aid agencies pledged to "conquer" many of the deadly tropical diseases, including those discussed above, plus leprosy. Together, they would spend at least $785 million and supply more than 1 billion "treatments" to poor countries in the hope of further eradicating easily remedied diseases that have afflicted Africa and other parts of the tropics.[28] Even before the announcement of the coalition effort in London, the battle against neglected and other diseases has been a grand team effort. Polio and measles vaccination projects have also been organized and promoted from outside Africa. The battle against HIV/AIDS was originally largely sponsored from offshore, too, by the UN, the United States, Europe, and Japan.[29] But now the wealthier African nations have largely taken charge.

The other killers

Diarrheal diseases are big killers of Africans, along with pneumonia and three other preventable sometime scourges. Diarrheal diseases (including dysentery, gastroenteritis, rotavirus, typhoid, and cholera) cause about 4 million deaths each year among African children under five, a number that has finally begun to drop. Whereas, in the rest of the world, the public health battle against such diseases was won because of improved sanitary measures, Africa until recently showed the smallest reductions in mortality and morbidity per 1,000 births; the under-five mortality rate in Africa was until about 2005 seven times that for Europe. In 1980, this difference was only a factor of 4. But, in 2012, a World Bank review of child mortality statistics since 2005 revealed that 16 of 20 sub-Saharan African countries surveyed in a detailed manner showed startlingly favorable falls in deaths of children under five years of age, per 1,000 live births. Senegal, Rwanda, and Kenya reported improvements of more than 8 percent a year and states as disparate as Madagascar, Nigeria, Mozambique, Zambia, Ghana, and Uganda showed better than 4 percent a year improvements. Of the 20, only Zimbabwe, Lesotho, Namibia, and Liberia went backwards – by as much as 2 percent a year.[30]

These significant life chance improvements can plausibly be explained by the increased use of treated bed-nets to reduce malarial infections. But rising GDPs, accompanied by better governance, more accountable bureaucracies, heightened middle-class expectations, improved nutrition, more readily available potable water, reductions in fertility, and enhanced clinical practices also seem to have played an important role in another African success story.

The battle for child survival, however, is not yet won. HIV/AIDS is a complicating issue, but compromised sanitation and potable water shortages are also major contributing factors in the persistence of diarrheal diseases among adults as well as young children in Africa. There was a major typhoid outbreak in 2012 in Harare, Zimbabwe's capital, caused by unrepaired municipal water mains, and a shortage of funds with which to purchase chlorine and other standard disinfectants. The frequent unavailability of common remedial measures, like oral rehydration salts and solutions, also contributes to the continued high death rates in Africa from diarrheal diseases.

Pneumonia and related afflictions caused by the *Streptoccus pneumoniae* bacterium infect the bloodstream and cause acute respiratory infections of the lungs. There are other bacterial and viral forms of pneumonia, and one found largely in infants with HIV/AIDS. All forms of pneumonia are together the largest single cause of deaths among children under age five, world-wide, and in Africa. As many as 400 million Africans may die each year from pneumonia or related severe influenzas. Indeed, it is believed that pneumonia-related afflictions are responsible for more deaths of sub-Saharan African children under age 15 than HIV/AIDS, tuberculosis, and malaria combined. Moreover, if a child has both pneumonia and HIV/AIDS, her/his chances of dying are six times greater than if she/he has pneumonia alone.[31]

Fortunately, in Malawi in 2012, a pilot Child Lung Health Programme organized by the International Union Against Tuberculosis and Lung Disease demonstrated that "standardized case management" for severe and very severe pneumonia in under-age-five children reduced case fatalities by more than 50 percent, thus saving thousands of lives. The International Union ensured adequate supplies of key antibiotics, monitored cases thoroughly, and persuaded the Malawian government to commit its available resources to modern treatment strategies. Three refinements were critical; all could be applied to improving acute pneumonia care elsewhere in Africa: (1) "An initial financial commitment by a donor agency can support the government in their efforts to provide the necessary services for those most at risk of dying;" (2) at the district hospital level, donor-supplied staff could assist local pediatricians and nurses, demonstrating the latest "standardized" techniques; (3) ample and regular supplies of antibiotics could make a major difference in outcomes.[32]

Epidemics of the related meningococcal disease (for which Type A *Neisseria meningitis* is responsible) erupt infrequently, but have caused thousands of deaths from Senegal to Ethiopia – across the Sahel belt. Children succumb more readily than adults.

Additionally, measles, a disease easily vaccinated against, was particularly dangerous in Africa in 2010 in Malawi (118,000 cases of 327,000 world-wide), Zambia, Zimbabwe, Nigeria, and the Congo (Kinshasa). Although, globally, measles deaths were reduced between 2000 and 2010 by 74 percent, India and Africa remained resistant to such improved outcomes largely because of a failure to reach large populations with vaccines. Of all measles mortality in 2010, 36 percent was African, despite a very large decrease in deaths from the disease from the year 2000.[33] Infantile paralysis (polio) was a serious problem in 2010 in the two Congos, in Nigeria, Angola, and Chad.

Malnutrition and food security

Given sub-Saharan Africa's heavy disease burden, it is no wonder that malnutrition – protein and micronutrient deficiencies, plus missing energy ingredients – accompanies it, and adds mightily to the obstacles that African development has to surmount. The populations of the Congo (Kinshasa), Eritrea, Burundi, the Comoros, Zambia, Angola, Ethiopia, and the Central African Republic are all strikingly undernourished, ranging from 69 percent to 40 percent malnourished in the first decade of the twenty-first century within their countries.[34] The global average was 13 percent. Malnourishment means that infectious diseases have an easier time when attacking human populations. The reduced immunities that accompany deficient nutrition enable diseases to flourish.

In early 2012, after the failure of the winter rains once again plunged the swath of states that comprise the immediately sub-Saharan region of the Sahel into drought (following severe droughts in 2009, 2010, and 2011), between 10 and 23 million Africans were believed to be hungry and facing potential starvation. Niger, Chad, Mali, Burkina Faso, Mauritania, and Senegal had all experienced lack of rainfall, poor harvests, pest attacks, and, ironically, some localized flooding. The International Red Cross Federation estimated that 50 percent of the populations in those countries were living on the edge of crisis; food prices had shot up as much as 85 percent in the five years from 2006. With widespread hunger, shortages of clean water, and a lack of basic health care, diseases such as cholera, meningitis, and measles flourished.[35]

Conditions of depressed nutrition and "hunger" inhibit productivity and contribute to many other tropical deficits. According to the Global Hunger Index, 2011, 26 African countries have "levels of hunger" that were "extremely alarming" or "alarming." Burundi (40 of 100), Chad (30), the Democratic Republic of Congo (39), and Eritrea (34) were the most worrying. (Somalia could not be measured.) Only "alarming" were conditions in Sierra Leone, Liberia (22), Togo (20), Niger, the Central African Republic, Angola (despite its oil wealth, 24), the Sudan (22), Ethiopia (29), Djibouti (23), Rwanda (21), Tanzania (21), Zambia (24), Mozambique (23), Madagascar (23), and the Comoros (26). Indeed, because of incessant conflict and instability, the Congo's Hunger Index score deteriorated by 63 percent between 1990 and 2011 and, because of data lags, did not even include the worsening famine and high food prices found there in 2010–11. Burundi's ratings slumped by 21 percent, the Comoros by 17 percent, and Swaziland by 15 percent in the same period. Ghana improved by 59 percent. Yet, Ghana's rating was only 9 on the same 100-point scale. Botswana was 13, South Africa 6.The Hunger Index measures the proportion of a country's population that is undernourished, i. e. the proportion whose calorie intake is below standard norms; the proportion of children under five years of age who are underweight and/or stunted in a population; and the mortality rates for children under five in a national population. In 2011, the International Food Policy Research Institute (the maker of the Index) rated 122 countries.[36]

Another index, Save the Children's thirteenth annual Mothers' Index, in 2012 put Niger at the very bottom (165) of its rankings, after Afghanistan. It was "the worst place in the world" to be a mother. Chronic malnutrition in Niger, said Save the Children, threatened the lives of up to 1 million youngsters. Hungry mothers produce stunted, underweight, and vulnerable babies.

Niger's 2011 food affordability and supply crisis obviously accentuated existing motherhood issues in one of the sub-continent's poorest places. Moreover, in addition to Niger, seven of the bottom ten countries on Save the Children's list were sub-Saharan African.[37]

Higher commodity prices for cocoa and pineapples greatly helped Ghanaians become less hungry. The country also nearly halved its poverty rate between 1991 and 2006, from 51 percent to 28 percent. But in addition to improved global prices, Ghana benefitted from much better governance, a strengthened macroeconomic and fiscal system, better policies toward investors and investment, intensified land use, and – possibly most of all – from greater productivity by growers. In Uganda, over roughly the same period, poverty was reduced by 6 percent on the back of a 10 percent improvement in coffee prices. In deeply poor Malawi, thanks to subsidized innovative seed and fertilizer inputs, increased official spending, better roads, backing for very small irrigation schemes (including pumps powered by foot treadles), support for new crops, improved marketing, and innovative low-cost storage alternatives (to keep rodents at bay), hunger levels fell and poverty was reduced, starting with the 2007–2008 period and continuing into 2012.

In combating malnutrition, hunger, and poverty, these three countries on either sides of the sub-continent, and many others, are beginning (but very slowly) to overcome the traditional weaknesses (in addition to poor soils and episodic rainfall) of African agriculture. Yet from the 1960s to 2010, accounting in large part for the gap between Asian and African incomes per head, African food production decreased by at least 10 percent. This fall reflected the globe's lowest adoption of yield-enhancing practices and techniques, the least mechanization, very limited applications of fertilizers and pesticides, and sparse irrigation. Crop yields in Africa are "far below" average yields elsewhere in the world, possibly two-thirds behind. Only 2 tractors (50 percent lower than in 1980) plough 100 sq. km of arable land, compared to a global average of 200 tractors per 100 sq. km. Only 3.6 percent of sub-Saharan African arable land is irrigated, as compared to 18.4 percent world-wide, and 39 percent in South Asia. Fertilizer use is 9 kilograms per hectare in Africa, and 100 per hectare globally.[38]

In order for the rest of sub-Saharan Africa to foster farmer productivity as in Ghana, Uganda, and Malawi, attention will have to be paid to policy changes that permit higher world commodity prices to be translated quickly into earnings growth for smallholders. Additionally, the availability of fertilizers and pesticides will need to be improved, global advances in crop modification and pest prevention will have to be examined and adopted, roads and other transport arteries (in and out) will have to be extended and maintained (roads with too many potholes impede the smooth delivery of inputs and the easy conveyance of farm products to local and global markets), the spread of readily accessible information about sale opportunities and prices through mobile telephone text messaging will need to be made routine, and governments will have to nurture their subsistence and cash-cropping farming sectors with appropriate and forward-looking policies and attention. The road to African food security, poverty alleviation, and freedom from hunger is paved with informed and active political leadership, a willingness to increase expenditures supportive of agricultural innovation (as in Malawi), some technological leapfrogging, strengthened governance that attends to the myriad needs of rural subsistence and cash-growing dependents, and a realization that the peoples of Africa merit the kinds of agricultural advances that have helped elevate incomes and self-respect in Asia and Latin America.

A continuing struggle

Despite all of this successful deployment of talent and cash, and the winning of many of the special disease battles, Africa is still not well. Infant mortality is much lower in the temperate as compared to tropical zones, and life expectancies are 8 percent higher, controlling for income differences. Human productivity is lower, and cognitive and physical capacities are reduced, in the tropical areas. Economic performance naturally suffers.[39] As this chapter has demonstrated, winning, or at least starting to win, the developmental struggle still awaits the perfection of vaccines, the provision of adequate supplies of clean water and improved sanitary facilities, and attention by the better governments and leaders of Africa to decisions about how best to attack Africa's heavy burden of disease. When joined to the geographical and climatic handicaps from which Africa already suffers, the disease and health penalty still mightily constrains Africa's progress. With growing populations, there is an ever more pressing need for national policy decisions and reallocations of scarce revenues to cope with a tropical health and disease challenge that will not vanish. These are the tasks of Africa's new leaders.

4
Educating Future Generations

The future of Africa depends on advances in educational opportunity, on greater and greater access to enhanced schooling chances, and on ensuring that more and more of Africa's young – especially girls – are well educated. There are innumerable reasons why Europeans, Americans, later Japanese and Southeast Asians, and now Chinese ascended the commanding global economic, social, and political heights. The acquisition of knowledge was a key element, as were the greater skills and scientific and technological innovations that made use of and advanced such knowledge. Singapore's rapid progress, for example, from a pirate swamp controlled by Chinese-speaking gangs to an economic powerhouse of stability and prowess could not have been achieved without a concerted emphasis on the importance of schooling, together with a broadening of the city-state's educational opportunity base, a mid-course shift from instruction in local vernaculars to English as a medium, and the subsequent official tracking and support of gifted students from primary school to university and beyond, into gainful employment. Likewise, in neighboring Malaysia, the opening-up of higher schooling chances, especially technical training, in Penang in the 1980s propelled a learning explosion that contributed mightily to rapid advances economically and socially throughout the young nation.

Sub-Saharan Africa awaits such a revolution in capability and accomplishment despite populations that have yearned for many years for just such a possibility. Africans know that everything is realizable in life with better schooling and that nothing is attainable without such openings. They also know that, compared to the developed world and places such as Singapore, China, Chile, or Barbados, their primary, secondary, and tertiary schools and universities are overcrowded, under-resourced, poorly provided with libraries and computers, staffed with dedicated but weakly accredited teachers, and generally inferior. As populations expand throughout the continent, conditions and ratios may even worsen. Africa's political leaders will need to redouble their attempts to cope with the existing pent-up schooling demand if their nation-states are to flourish and conceivably to manage to catch up economically and socially with the rest of the world. Otherwise, they will fail their nations and their peoples by missing a key and critical developmental opportunity to nurture and mobilize nascent talent.

As the Director-General of UNESCO wisely concluded, "There can be no escape from poverty without a vast expansion of secondary education. This is a minimum entitlement for equipping youth with the knowledge and skills they need to secure decent livelihoods in today's globalized world. It is going to take ambition and commitment to meet this challenge. But it is the only path towards prosperity."[1]

Barriers to opportunity

The contours of the problem are clear. Sub-Saharan Africa is not meeting the ever rising demand for schooling, particularly the clamor for places in secondary school. Whereas in prior years in many of the weaker African countries the problem was persistence – keeping pupils in primary school long enough to complete their basic education – now the issue is providing places and teachers for those who complete their primary education and want – nay, demand – to become more fully educated in secondary school. Girls, as usual, are especially disadvantaged.

Sub-Saharan Africa, with an overall adult literacy rate of 62 percent, has two very lettered and well-educated offshore island populations. The Seychelles boasts 92 percent adult literacy and Mauritius is 88 percent literate. On the mainland, Gabon, Botswana, Kenya, Namibia, and South Africa all show results almost as promising as those for the Seychelles and Mauritius, but for the rest of mainland sub-Saharan Africa the relevant numbers are much more distressing. In Angola, Cameroon, Malawi, Rwanda, the Sudan, Tanzania, Uganda, and Zambia, literacy percentage rates are all in the low 70s. Ghana and Nigeria only report literacy levels for adults in the low 60s. In Benin, the Central African Republic, Côte d'Ivoire, and Togo, those rates are in the 50s, and in Senegal and Sierra Leone they are in the high 40s. Chad and Guinea show levels in the 30s. For Burkina Faso, Ethiopia, Mali, and Niger only 20+ percent of adults are functionally literate.[2]

Effective or functional literacy among adults is difficult to measure, especially in countries with weak statistical services and little devotion to measuring literacy in local languages, much less imported languages. More informative are primary school enrollment rates, reports on the number of children who actually complete all of primary school, secondary-level enrollment numbers, and persistence (completion) figures for secondary school. Between 1999 and 2009, during which years the school-age population in sub-Saharan Africa increased by 25 percent, primary school enrollments grew by a full 59 percent. The average national adjusted net enrollment rate indicated, moreover, that in sub-Saharan Africa in 2009 about 77 percent of eligible children were in school, compared to 90 percent globally. Of that enhanced number of students, only 67 percent in Africa completed primary school satisfactorily in 2009 (the last year available) as contrasted to 88 percent globally.

Gross enrollment rates differ considerably from, and are less accurate than, adjusted rates. (Gross enrollment is defined as the total enrollment, regardless of age, expressed as a percentage of the official or notional school-age population within a given country.) Nevertheless, it is instructive that the average gross primary enrollment rate for sub-Saharan Africa is a nominal 100 percent whereas the average gross secondary enrollment rate is only 35 percent. Even accepting the 100 percent average in terms of national primary enrollments, there are some striking deviants: the Sudan, 74 percent; Côte d'Ivoire, 73 percent; Djibouti, 54 percent; and Eritrea 48 percent.

At the secondary level, the enrollment percentages range from a low of 12 percent in the Central African Republic and 13 percent in Niger upward to figures in the 20th percentile for Angola, Burkina Faso, Burundi, Mozambique, Chad, Côte d'Ivoire, Equatorial Guinea, Liberia, Malawi, Rwanda, Sierra Leone, Tanzania, and Uganda. Madagascar, Nigeria, and Senegal report that 30 percent of eligible children attend secondary school. In Ghana and Kenya, nearly 60 percent of eligible pupils are in secondary school. In Gabon, despite high literacy levels, only 50 percent of eligible pupils are in secondary school. Higher percentage enrollments occur in Namibia, Botswana, Mauritius and South Africa, where nearly 94 percent of potential students attend. The Seychelles reports more than 100 percent of the potential primary population attends secondary school, i.e. that students beyond the usual primary ages are also enrolled in some number.[3]

Another way of conceptualizing the numbers of eligible students who graduate from primary school and do or do not continue their educations by going on to enroll in secondary education is the persistence or progression rate. In Botswana, 96 percent thus progressed; in the Seychelles, 94 percent did so, as did 92 percent in the (old) Sudan; and 85 percent in South Africa. But only 14 percent of Burundians, 26 percent of Nigeriens, 30 percent of Ugandans, and 32 percent of Burkinabes persisted in the same manner. The rate for Côte d'Ivoire was 36 percent, for Mali 38 percent, for Senegal 39 percent, for Togo 42 percent, for Mozambique 48 percent, for Tanzania 49 percent, for Madagascar 51 percent, and for Guinea 56 percent.[4] These progression performances, as well as gross secondary enrollment rates in Africa, are all much poorer than they are for any other continent. Even Nepal and Burma, very low-ranking Asian countries on the UNDP's Human Development Index (at 157 and 152 respectively, of 176) report reasonable secondary enrollments of 43 and 53 percent respectively.

These arrays of numbers show that much of sub-Saharan Africa is failing to satisfy the pent-up educational demand of young people (and their parents). Even though there have been huge gains in providing access to secondary-school opportunity since 1999, from 28 percent to 43 percent of the student catchment, there are now secondary school places for no more than 36 percent of the students clamoring for entry. In other words, two-thirds of all eligible young people must be turned away. Or, according to UNESCO's 2011

Global Education Digest, in the 20 most educationally weak countries in sub-Saharan Africa, a pupil in her or his last grade in primary school has at best only a 75 percent chance of finding a lower secondary school place. Nearly 22 million potential pupils are hence turned away and will never spend one day learning in a secondary setting. Furthermore, 40 percent of all girls and 33 percent of all eligible boys were not attending school in 2009.

Making these disparities somewhat more central to sub-Saharan Africa's future, no other region in the world displays such an educational gender gap. Established research shows that developmental prospects are influenced significantly and positively when girls are well educated, certainly as well educated as boys.[5] Fertility rate declines are correlated closely with educational advances. So are health advances and the conquests of disease. National productivity grows. Ultimately, GDPs per capita rise. Yet, despite the various improvements in African prospects generally, even at the primary level sub-Saharan Africa shows poorer results for girls' schooling than countries elsewhere in the world. In the Central African Republic, Chad, and the Democratic Republic of Congo, fewer than 69 girls enter the last grade of primary school for every 100 boys. In Tanzania and Nigeria, the worst performers in Africa, in 2009 fewer than 44 percent of all girls who finished primary school entered lower secondary school. Despite the opening of universal primary education to girls in countries such as Burundi, Kenya, Lesotho, Malawi, and Tanzania and the subsequent improved flow of girls everywhere in those states into lower secondary schools, by the time that these populations reached upper secondary school, only 76 girls persisted for every 100 boys.[6]

The Ghanaian case is instructive, particularly since Ghana is among sub-Saharan Africa's best-governed and most highly ranked countries according to the Index of African Governance and other measures. In 2005, Ghana abolished school fees for all children and instituted an annual $2.50 grant per pupil to cover learning materials, sports equipment, sanitation, and building repairs. Seven years later, more than 90 percent of all children aged 6 to12 – a total of 3.2 million – attended primary school. Of all those attending, 10 percent received free meals each day, thus reducing the impact of hunger on retention and persistence. But, despite or because of these enrollment successes, there are critical shortages of teachers; according to the African Union, in 2015 Africa will need 2 million new teachers. In 2012, Ghana lacked 20,000 teachers and so could not fill 15,000 classrooms. Pay was low in Ghana, averaging $300 a month, and half of all teachers receiving higher training each year failed to return to the classroom. About 38 percent of teachers were untrained. Moreover, there were too many teachers in Accra, the capital, and too few in the rural areas where many teachers refused to serve. As a result of all of these compromising factors, even in a comparatively wealthy country like Ghana – which spends a whopping 10 percent of GDP and 31 percent of its annual budget on education, only 40 percent of the students in basic primary schools were deemed proficient in English and mathematics, and too many failed to qualify for secondary school entrance.[7] Given Ghana's long history as an educational leader in West Africa, the schooling crisis elsewhere among its neighbors cannot be any less desperate.

In some of the more advanced educational environments in sub-Saharan Africa, such as South Africa, secondary schools may indeed be full of eligible students. But in their final year, South African students also sit national school-leaving "matriculation" examinations. Those who receive high scores on these "matric" exams are deemed ready for tertiary education. Those who simply pass the examinations are considered to have thus completed their secondary schooling and are classified as employable. Unfortunately, even in South Africa, 400,000 or so young South African men and women fail their "matric" every year and are effectively "discarded." During the decades of apartheid, African pass rates were well below 50 percent, whereas white students achieved 90 percent pass rates or higher. After the apartheid yoke was lifted and official efforts to enhance secondary results were redoubled, scores for black South Africans improved to 60 percent and higher. But blacks were still, as late as 2012, not passing their matric examinations in the kinds of high numbers that would qualify them for university entrance, or even for gainful employment. In 2011, about 16 percent of age-eligible black South Africans qualified for university entrance and another 50 to 60 percent failed their matriculation requirements. As many as 3 million South Africans aged 18–24 were considered "outside education," based on several years of failing for various reasons to have completed their secondary schooling. Indeed, the total numbers of matric-successful students (roughly 80,000) in South Africa has not improved significantly since the 1980s. According to South Africa's National Planning Commission, an African female teenager today has a 46 percent chance that she will drop out of high school and only a 4 percent chance that she will qualify for university entrance. She has an 80 percent chance of being unemployed five years after leaving school. If so, her probability of earning enough to cross from below to above the national poverty line of $53 a month is nil.[8]

Even the secondary schools in comparatively wealthy South Africa are crowded and poorly maintained because of budget restrictions. But among the larger problems in South Africa and many other countries are the paucity of trained teachers, high pupil–teacher ratios, low pay (and low standards), and – notably in South Africa – the sheer absence of teaching personnel. In the poorer state schools in South Africa, teachers only appear on average about 3.5 hours a day. On Fridays, hardly any teachers show up. Those who teach in the more rigorous, wealthier, former white schools, instruct more than 6 hours a day. Moreover, 1,700 South African schools in 2012 were without water, 15,000 had no libraries, and thousands of schools were without textbooks. A High Court judge indeed ruled in 2012 that the government's failure to provide textbooks to all pupils in state schools arrogantly "violated their constitutional right to an education." South Africa's Education Minister admitted that 80 percent of his schools were "dysfunctional."[9] Even so, South Africa's educational system is among the most highly regarded on the continent, and among the best funded.

Vocational education is in no better shape in sub-Saharan Africa, not even in South Africa, where there has long been a shortage of indigenous artisans. In 2012, despite high national unemployment rates of about 40 percent, there were an estimated 800,000 unfilled positions available in South Africa for highly skilled artisans, accountants, nurses, and social workers. At the same time, recognizing its large pool of failed school leavers and its paucity of post-secondary training alternatives, South Africa decided to expand its "Further Education and Training" sector in order to produce artisans and others with "mid-level" skills. It proposed to strengthen existing colleges specializing in the training of engineers, construction workers, tourism and hospitality industry employees, business administrators, early childhood care workers, nurses, farmers, and policemen. Beyond the colleges, it proposed creating Community Education and Training Centres to offer general education and basic training to out-of-school young people. The government also promised to enhance distance learning possibilities. A shortage of properly accredited lecturers was recognized as a limitation hindering all forms of such expanded training. Indeed, South Africa has acknowledged that teachers for all subjects at all levels have been trained with too little rigor and without a broad range of teaching skills.[10]

That South Africa, at or near the top of the educational attainment pyramid in Africa, should in 2013 still be suffering from such critical and difficult issues in the schooling and training sectors, speaks to sub-Saharan Africa's overall weaknesses and to the decades that it will presumably take before any remediation efforts succeed. Except in the better-governed places such as Botswana and Mauritius, and possibly Kenya, schooling accomplishments and abilities overall do not yet match citizenry aspirations or needs. Private academies take up some of the slack and handfuls of capable artisans are being trained on the job, but citizens still look appropriately to their capitals for educational opportunity advances. If wealthy states like South Africa cannot provide what citizens demand, consider how in deficit the poorer African countries must be in this sector.

Furthermore, if sub-Saharan Africa is going, Asia-like, to realize its demographic dividend between now and 2050, its nation-states must all begin relentlessly to expand educational opportunity. Juma makes the significant further observation that major improvements to Africa's essential agricultural productivity require educational attention in specialized settings.[11] One of the critical keys to Malaysia's success in the 1980s was its attention to technical and vocational training and its willingness to meet the skill requirements of foreign and local investors. But how will Africa make that same forward leap? Even in the fast-growing oil-producing countries, schooling budgets are still constrained and teacher-training facilities are still under-funded. Their graduates are poorly paid and have reduced reasons to devote themselves to insufficiently supervised, overcrowded schools lacking modern textbooks or computer-age facilities. For the students, even those in most secondary establishments, the incentives to learn are less strong than they might be. With so few secondary school students being able to enter university because of poor results and limited tertiary-level openings, and with paid jobs even for university graduates scarce – 600,000 such South African graduates were without employment in 2012 – becoming an educated African is both difficult and potentially unrewarding. Moreover, even if a South African overcomes all obstacles and qualifies for entrance into one of his country's many universities and colleges, she/he may not find a place. In late 2011, when the University of Johannesburg advertised that it might have a few openings in its 2015 classes, beginning in 2012, a large crowd tried to enter its campus, with a mother and son being trampled to death in the ensuing mêlée.[12]

Universities and colleges

Despite the fact that expanding university educational opportunities and technological advances go together, and despite the fact that Africans increasingly want fully to join the rest of the world in enjoying higher standards of living and increased global progress, only about 6 percent of potential enrollees can find university places. (Some of Africa's countries only enroll 1 percent of eligible students.) This is the lowest gross enrollment ratio in the world by a factor of at least 5, and further poignant testimony to the extent of the gap between sub-Saharan Africa and other regions of the world. Even the Middle East and the North African and South and Central American regions show higher educational enrollment ratios of more than 30 percent.[13] "We are told we need to at least double [Africa's higher education gross enrollment ratio] to 12 percent if we are just to get the human resources that we need," said Beatrice Njenga, head of the African Union's Education Division. "One reason we might not meet [Millennium Development Goals] . . . is because we don't have human resources," she continued; "Where do human resources come from? Not basic education." The head of UNESCO's East Africa office, in the same vein, argued that the key to progress in basic education was the strengthening of higher education: "Teachers come from higher education."[14]

Additionally, only a few of Africa's mostly state-run universities are world-class; many have deteriorated in quality thanks to shrinking government grants, pressure to teach more and more quantities of students with reduced staffs, and poor salaries and facilities. As a consequence of the quantity and quality factors, the senior ranks of politicians and civil servants in one sub-Saharan African country after another operate without the benefit of university-level training. In Mozambique, for example, a decade ago only 3 percent of the country's officials had graduated from a university. In Rwanda, where skilled labor is very scarce, less than 6 percent of the domestic work force has tertiary qualifications. As a result, a Legatum Institute report declared, most locally educated Rwandans "have never learned how to think independently and critically, and they do not understand what is expected of them in the business world."[15]

UN Secretary-General Kofi Annan, a decade ago, urged the leaders of Africa to rebuild and strengthen their universities. "The university must become a primary tool for Africa's development in the new century," he said; "Universities can help develop African expertise; they can enhance the analysis of African problems; strengthen domestic institutions; serve as a model environment for the practice of good governance, conflict resolution and respect for human rights, and enable African academics to play an active part in the global community of scholars."[16] Research shows that university graduates in the developing world enhance their personal incomes, their employment prospects, and their nation's economic growth prospects. Possibly more significantly, university training increases "the speed at which a country adopts technology and raises its total factor productivity." Thus, "increasing tertiary education appears to raise the rate of technological convergence toward a country's production possibility frontier."[17]

Nations that are now established leaders in quality of life and economic growth per capita measures consciously sought some years ago to emphasize enhanced higher educational opportunities, information technology acquisition, and knowledge accumulation as the cornerstones of a development strategy for this century. Australia, Denmark, Finland, New Zealand, Singapore, and South Korea embraced this path and joined earlier European and American models in appropriately transforming themselves and their peoples. China and India have also followed congruent paradigms, to outstanding success. In Africa, where citizens clamor for educational advances, no country has yet enunciated such a plan. Only a few states would be able easily to marshal the necessary resources (with or without donor support); even so, no leader has yet urged his followers to create such a local or African renaissance based on the strengthened acquisition and local dissemination of technical and other knowledge. Despite its wealth compared to other sub-Saharan African nations, Botswana has not constructed a strong science and technology platform at its national university. Across Africa, this reluctance, inability, or lack of awareness flies in the face of the now well-accepted linkage of higher educational attainments and societal progress. Even South Africa in 2011 had no vision of higher education in development. "The speed and extent to which developing countries are able to absorb, utilise and modify technology developed mainly in high-income countries, will determine whether they will be able to realize a . . . rapid transition to higher levels of development and standards of living." The Finlands and Singapores "leap-frogged" important stages of development by investing lavishly and intelligently in robust forms of higher education.[18] Will Africa follow?

The Cape Town Centre for Higher Education Transformation (CHET) found that in the eight relatively high-income nation-states that it studied in 2009–10, none "had a clearly articulated development model or strategy" that encompassed a role for higher education. Only Mauritius seemed cognizant, officially, that "knowledge drives economic growth." Kenya and Mauritius exhibited the strongest awareness of the significance of knowledge accumulation in economic development. Even in the ministries of education across the eight countries examined, except for Mauritius, the "concept of the knowledge economy" was largely absent.

Sub-Saharan Africa was contributing in this century to global scientific (published) output only 0.7 percent, less than it had 15 and 20 years before. Of the flagship universities in the eight countries, only those of Botswana, Mauritius, and Uganda (Makerere) explicitly articulated their roles in ensuring a "knowledge economy" and maximizing higher education's contribution to economic growth. The University of Mauritius was the only one of the eight institutions studied with an "engine of development" as a dominant discourse, shared in that case with its national government.[19]

Only 3 million or so sub-Saharan Africans today find places in the region's approximately 235 universities or college equivalents. About 1 million (or 10 percent of the potential total) are Nigerians attending one of that country's 169 nodes of higher education. About 0.5 million are South Africans enrolled in one of the country's 23 universities or equivalents. About 150,000 of the 3 million+ are Ethiopians, who mostly attend their country's main university in Addis Ababa. After that, the individual national numbers are much reduced. Unfortunately, as in many other countries, about half of the enrollees never graduate, many dropping out during the first year for academic, financial, or personal reasons. Very high attrition rates have also been reported from the Central African Republic (95 percent in mathematics), Madagascar (85 percent in mathematics), Niger (75 percent overall), and Uganda (60 percent overall).[20]

Doubling access to higher education in sub-Saharan Africa, from the current 3 million+ to 6 million would require $10 billion a year in new funding, some of which could come from students and some from donors, if any can be found. Now, according to the UNDP, university education in Africa costs about $2,500 to $3,750 per student per year, or between $10,000 and $15,000 for a full four-year course. Hence, the total expenditures now are about $7.5 to $11 billion, of which about $2 billion is paid by the students themselves and their families.[21] As the population of sub-Saharan Africa grows exponentially in coming decades, educating greater numbers of tertiary students will, naturally, prove even more expensive.

Although the quality of teaching and research, and therefore "education," in African universities is widely regarded locally and externally as at best mediocre, sub-Saharan Africa does celebrate at least a handful of world-class universities. According to rankings published by the *Times Higher Education Supplement*, the long-established University of Cape Town, ranked 103rd globally, and two other South African universities, Stellenbosch and the University of the Witwatersrand, both with global ranks of between 251 and 275, are the leading institutions. The Consejo Superior de Investigaciones Científicas, the largest public research institution in Spain, ranks the world's universities largely on their informal and formal scholarly attainments: its Africa list of 100 institutions north and south of the Sahara is topped by Cape Town, followed by the Universities of Pretoria, Stellenbosch, and Witwatersrand, the University of KwaZuluNatal, Rhodes University, the University of the Western Cape – all in South Africa – Cairo University, the University of South Africa (a prime distance-learning establishment), and, in tenth place, Makerere University in Uganda. The Kwame Nkrumah University of Science and Technology in Ghana is ranked 13th and the main higher education institutions in Senegal, the Sudan, Ethiopia, and Botswana are ranked 16th, 17th, 21st, and 23rd, respectively. The majority of the remaining rated universities and equivalents are in North Africa.[22]

CHET ranked the institutions that it investigated according to their academic cores, essentially reviewing the results of the years 2001 to 2007. Cape Town was strong on all eight indicators (enrollments at various levels, student–teacher ratios, teacher qualifications, research publications, and the like); the second echelon included Mauritius, Makerere, and Nelson Mandela Metropolitan University (South Africa); the third grouping included Dar es Salaam, Nairobi, and Botswana; and, the fourth, Ghana and Eduardo Mondlane University in Mozambique.[23]

In the case of Botswana, here singled out because of the nation's high level of governance, very high GDPs per capita, and general lack of turmoil in its political and educational experiences, its attainments in higher education were regarded as "weak" compared to the other seven less prosperous countries examined. Science and technology enrollments as a percentage of total numbers enrolled in 2007 were a minimal 22 percent. Only 9 percent of all students were studying at the post-graduate level, a low figure, and 0.3 percent of the enrollment total was pursuing doctorates. (Botswana remained a traditional undergraduate teaching establishment.) The average teaching load for undergraduates was 17 per instructor. Just 31 percent of faculty held doctorates. Research productivity was low, amounting to 0.16 publications per year per instructor, well below the 0.50 rate in South Africa.[24] If Botswana's numbers are at all representative of sub-Saharan African universities – and they probably are better than most – the continent's institutions of higher education are serving the needs of their nations and their potential students only to a limited extent.

In the Ugandan case, where Makerere University – another establishment focused almost exclusively on undergraduate instruction – has been a leading higher educational institution since the 1930s, the comparable numbers in 2007 were: 32 percent of all students were learning in the science and technology area; 9 percent of all students were studying for postgraduate degrees, and there were proportionately fewer doctoral candidates even than in Botswana; the average student–teacher ratio was 18:1(but 96:1 in the business area); 31 percent of the academic staff held doctorates; and the research output per instructor ratio was 0.20.[25]

According to rectors and principals of British universities who previously ran African universities, the "trajectory" of higher education in sub-Saharan Africa is "quite depressing, and the prognosis is not particularly good."[26] The CHET study found that the (better) universities that it studied transmitted established knowledge rather than undertaking new research and thus adding to scholarship. Only three (Nairobi, Cape Town, and Dar es Salaam) of the better universities in the CHET study in 2007 boasted more than 50 percent of their permanent academic staff with doctorates. Even in South Africa, 50 percent of the instructional roster of only 3 of the 23 universities held doctorates. These universities are also graduating only small handfuls of doctoral students, with Cape Town, graduating over 100, the exception. Unless African universities produce their own doctorates, they cannot easily replace their teaching faculties. Aside from Cape Town, the academics based in the universities in the study produced, on average, one published research article every ten or more years. "It is evident," the analysis concluded, that these output variables of the universities were not strong enough "to make a sustainable knowledge production contribution to development."[27]

Furthermore, as Juma argues, farming will remain central to sub-Saharan Africa's rural emancipation as well as to the sub-continent's food security as its population swells. But nearly all of sub-Saharan Africa's educational focus is on training young persons for employment in urban areas. Little attention has been paid to fostering agricultural innovation through university research and training: "Most of the strategies to strengthen the technical competence of African farmers will entail major reforms in existing universities and research institutions."[28] Such major reforms will flow from the policy initiatives of leading politicians and educators.

African universities are chronically under-resourced, and have been for 50 years. According to a University of Dar es Salaam official, "we have deteriorating students' hostels, we don't have enough teaching facilities, the laboratories are dead, the workshops are dead."[29] Few universities can afford books and journal subscriptions for their libraries. Most are overcrowded (especially on business courses), with even highly ranked Makerere University being forced to hold classes virtually around the clock and at weekends, with lecturers almost constantly in the classroom. The University of Zimbabwe runs its business administration courses fully over weekends because most of its students are employed during the normal week. Only South African universities, because of stronger governmental support over longer periods, still hold their own as places of scholarship and teaching in international competition. But even South African universities are facing more under-prepared students than ever before in an era of declining budgetary support. Graduation rates there and elsewhere in Africa are low; typical percentages of an entering cohort graduating within six years are about 50 percent. At Eduardo Mondlane University earlier in this century, the graduates in science and technology were exceedingly few, proportionately. Until and unless Africa is able to afford higher-quality higher education, sub-Saharan Africa will find it almost impossible to reap any measure of the much-anticipated demographic dividend. Nor, despite the influx of new foreign investment, will it be able to begin to catch up with the remainder of the world. Education generally, no less higher schooling, is a critical element in sub-Saharan Africa's race to the top, economically and socially. Political leadership in this and related areas is essential.

The brain drain

The countries of sub-Saharan Africa produce too few university graduates each year to transform their nations' needs for ever-increasing knowledge acquisition, or for the timely up-take and absorption of technological innovations from the rest of the globe. Africa is estimated to require at least 1 million researchers and medical personnel to meet its current (not its future) scientific and treatment needs. Yet, each year, sub-Saharan Africa loses legions of its best-trained minds to nations who need such talents less – the nations outside of Africa, particularly those in Europe and America. The emigration of skilled personnel – the brain drain – removes accomplished researchers, scholars, physicians, nurses, engineers, chartered accountants, and many more from the sub-continent, where they are in unusually short supply. Africa also forfeits the funds that it has spent to educate and train those skilled individuals. The brain drain creates a two-fold deficit in sub-Saharan Africa and shifts knowledge and the purveyors of knowledge from an environment of scarcity to one where such skills are comparatively abundant.

What some have called the hemorrhaging of professionals from the sub-continent has in many cases stripped the poorer countries of Africa of the ability to meet their own medical, instructional, or other needs. The International Organization for Migration (IOM) estimates that 100,000 well-trained professionals leave sub-Saharan Africa yearly. Of this total, 75 percent has attended an African university, and 10 percent of the total has graduated with a degree. IOM suggests that this represents a loss of at least $1 billion and perhaps $1.5 billion a year for sub-Saharan Africa.[30] Since such an amount exceeds the total funding that the sub-continent receives by way of donor assistance for education each year, sub-Saharan Africa ends up subsidizing the production of physicians, nurses, and other professionals for the developed world.

The Network of African Science Academies reports that fully one-third of all African scientists live and work in the developed world. "Universities in

Africa," it says, "have been hollowed out by decades of brain drain and now find themselves severely handicapped by dilapidated facilities and inadequately trained staff."[31] Obviously, trained personnel migrate to those locations where they believe that the best opportunities exist, where they believe that they can make the best contribution, and where their abilities will be most appreciated. Given the mayhem in some countries, and the oppression in others, it is hardly a wonder that African professionals go elsewhere. Moreover, corruption and sheer criminality also drive educated Africans out of Africa.

The UN Economic Commission for Africa estimates that 27,000 Africans emigrated to industrialized countries between 1960 and 1975. Another 40,000 departed from 1975 to 1984. More loss estimates include 30 percent of all Ghanaian and Ethiopian trained physicians, 90 percent of the physicians trained in Zambia between 1978 and 1999, 90 percent of all economists trained in Ethiopia, and 30 percent of all Ph.D.s from the University of Cape Town.[32] More Malawian-trained nurses work in Britain than at home, and Zimbabwean midwives populate British cities and towns. Senegalese and Côte d'Ivorian professionals are numerous in Paris and provincial French municipalities. Ethiopia, Nigeria, and Ghana have lost the largest numbers of professionals. A 2008 study indicated that only 20,000 scientists remained in Africa, 3.6 percent of the world total of advanced scientific personnel. Ethiopia in 2008 supposedly had 1 full-time economics professor at home, while 100 Ethiopian economists held comparable positions in the United States alone. Half of all Ghanaian-trained physicians were abroad; Kenya was losing 20 doctors a month. At least 30,000 Nigerian physicians were healing people elsewhere, about 21,000 in the United States. The Zambian state sector retained only 50 of the 600 doctors produced in its national medical school between 1978 and 1999. There were more Ethiopian-trained doctors in Chicago than in Ethiopia in 2008. There are many more Liberian-trained surgeons outside the country than the 10 who remain to cope with the medical needs of Liberia's 5 million people. Half of Zimbabwe's 3,000 trained social workers were employed outside their home country. In large part because of emigration, Malawi in 2008 could count only 17 nurses per 100,000 people, whereas many Western countries average 1,000 nurses per 100,000 population.[33] An end to this persistent flight of better- trained African persons in search of enhanced opportunities elsewhere is difficult to ensure, however, especially given the enduring political and social problems and weak finances of the countries of the sub-continent.

A 2011 study indicates that sub-Saharan African countries lose about $2 billion annually when physicians migrate to Australia, Britain, Canada, and the United States, making up local shortfalls in the receiving states. South Africa and Zimbabwe send the majority, and thus lose the most from having previously trained doctors for more prosperous lands. But other big losers are Ethiopia, Kenya, Malawi, Nigeria, Tanzania, and Uganda.[34]

There is one major redeeming feature of this steady exodus. Well-paid professionals, and even less well-off individuals, remit reasonable proportions of their incomes in the new nations back to the sending countries. Africa is enriched substantially by such cash transfers even if it subsidizes the skills needs of industrialized countries: "The present value of remittances more than covers the cost of educating a brain drainer in the source country." One report estimates that professionals in this century were remitting to their home states amounts equivalent to 81 percent of foreign aid received, 13 percent of exports, and 3.2 percent of GDP – almost $9 billion in all for sub-Saharan Africa in 2005. In many respects, the authors conclude, the brain drain benefits Africa more than it subtracts from development.[35] If some of the overseas sojourners eventually return to their home countries, or even if they only visit periodically, another argument can be made that this skills diaspora actually grows professional qualifications and transfers science and technology learning back home through periodic visits and eventual returns. In other words, the exodus is not always unidirectional in its effect, and the accumulation of knowledge can return to the sending countries in multiple beneficial ways.

The task ahead: boosting the knowledge base

The nations of sub-Saharan Africa will have many priorities in the decades ahead, especially as their populations increase exponentially. At the forefront must be educational advances. No part of the world has ever developed without intensified attention to schooling enhancements, particularly to high-quality secondary educational and then higher educational opportunities. Most of the nations of the sub-continent are vastly behind Asia in the provision of secondary and university-level places, graduation rates, Ph.D. production numbers, scientific and other scholarship per capita, and awareness at political leadership levels of what countries are missing or not doing. Africans and their governments want to join the knowledge environment; major policy shifts and budgetary reallocations will be essential if sub-Saharan Africa is to catch up in this century to its peers in the developing world.

5
To War Rather than to Prosper

Africa has endured decades of war. From Western Sahara and Mauritania on its northwestern flank to the Sudan, Ethiopia, Eritrea, and Somalia on its northeastern periphery, and south through the Democratic Republic of Congo, Zimbabwe, and South Africa (mostly before independence in 1994), only some of the peoples of Africa have tasted the sweet fruits of sustainable peace and harmony within their own countries and across neighboring borders. Even Madagascar and the Comoros, offshore, have known intermittent civil war, as have many of the countries in 2013 that are now free from fratricide. The legacy of this intrastate mayhem still hampers the development and curtails the prosperity and enhanced standards of living of countries as disparate, and at one or more points in time "failed," as have been Angola, Burundi, the Central African Republic, Chad, Côte d'Ivoire, Kenya, Liberia, Niger, Sierra Leone, South Sudan, and the Sudan. Then there is the "collapsed" geographical entity of Somalia (but not Somaliland or Puntland) – in a class of its own, with civil war, potent non-state actors, and piracy.[1]

In 2013, hot conflicts of great danger persist: in the eastern districts of the DRC; in Darfur and in two other southern provinces of the Sudan; in South Sudan as a result of conflict with the old Sudan and internally; in Mauritania (against al-Qaeda of the Maghreb, which also threatens Mali and Niger); in Mali from a fundamentalist Tuareg insurgency that captured the country's entire northern two-thirds in mid-2012; in southern Somalia from remnants of al-Shabab, once in full control of most of south Somalia; and locally and devastatingly across much of Nigeria from Boko Haram, the Movement to Emancipate the Niger Delta (MEND), and a host of others. Finally, there are those nation-states where another attempt to rig an election or distort the democratic process could re-ignite internal fires – in Guinea, Ethiopia, Kenya, Madagascar, Swaziland, and Zimbabwe, to mention only six among a number of likely possibilities.

Whether or not each of these capsule diagnoses is widely shared, the transformation of Africa from a region where hostilities between ethnic, geographical, linguistic, or religious groups are always raw and contentious into a region where everyone feels an integral part of and a valued contributor to the nation-state project is still ongoing. Distrust (political more than ethnic) across communities is rampant and widespread. Grievances are legion.

Resource avarice abounds. So do zero-sum approaches to wealth and political advantage. The inability of many of the nation-states of Africa to keep their citizens safe and secure or to provide them with reasonably adequate quantities and qualities of essential political goods means that minorities often feel oppressed and ethnicity or some other separate identity often trumps national solidarity. People feel threatened, especially when they believe that they and peoples similar to them are being preyed upon rather than protected by a central government – or by a ruling cabal that constitutes a regime in power. Likewise, if wealth opportunities are shared unequally or are channeled to a preferred group, anger intensifies and fuels antagonism.

Anywhere an African polity does not fulfill the functions of a modern nation-state and discriminates against some of its own people; anywhere African leaders look after themselves, their lineages, and their kin rather than their entire citizenry; anywhere leaders appear to steal from their people; anywhere in Africa that is consumed by flamboyant corruption and criminality; anywhere in Africa dominated by greed without a social conscience; and anywhere lacking strong separation of powers and rule of law, plus a military subordinate to civilians – any of these locales is at prime risk of a countervailing popular reaction and cataclysmic civil conflict. That is precisely what has happened so many times already in sub-Saharan Africa (as well as in 2011 and 2012 in North Africa and the Middle East). Those are among the realities that hold Africa back. Without close leadership attention to the new approach to peacemaking that Africa's emergent middle class now demands, even China's warm economic embrace of Africa will be unable to create proper foundations for a new progressive African order.

Human agency brought Africa to its current state of disarray. Human agency must, equally, provide the wisdom and energy to meet Africa's critical challenges and to chart a successful path forward. Those are the striking conclusions of an analysis of the determining role of leadership in all developing societies, as well as of a broad understanding of Africa's history since 1960. Leaders clearly make a difference; the smaller and the more fragile the state, the more leadership actions are substantial and critical. Hence, the failed states of Africa never failed by themselves or on their own. They were driven to failure and thus to internal warring by purposeful leadership actions. Equally, those few African states that have never known internal conflict, those few states that have long been fully participatory, those few states with high incomes and high social returns per capita, and those polities today seeking to emulate Botswana and Mauritius are all well led, with strong political cultures and well-established political institutions.

Intrastate conflict occurs in Africa and elsewhere not primarily because of colonial legacies or poorly drawn borders, not because of ancient hatreds between peoples, not exclusively because of competition for scarce resources, and not completely because of innate avarice. Instead, it is the failure of the modern nation-state in Africa and elsewhere to perform adequately – to deliver the essential political goods that are fundamental to the existence of a nation-state and that satisfy the expectations of its citizens – that causes ruptures of trust, the breaking of the implicit social contract between the state and its citizens, and outbreaks of reactive war. Conflict also is protective. Minorities (sometimes majorities) strike back against authority when they fear for their lives and their rights, or anticipate perpetuated assaults by the state. Conflict, in Africa and elsewhere, is rarely anomic, offensive, or without a recognizable trigger – real or perceived state-delivered discrimination, deprivation, and oppression.

Conflict follows from state failure

Nation-states exist to supply adequate quantities and acceptable qualities of essential political goods to their citizens. From the Westphalian epoch to the present, as monarchs were succeeded by early and then more mature forms of the modern nation-state, the role of the state was to exchange the provision of security and safety, rule of law, forms of participation, incipient and later more robust civil liberties and civil rights, opportunities for persons to prosper economically, roads and other arteries of commerce, Human Development (nowadays access to educational and improved health chances), and a sense of belonging to a noble and fulfilling larger enterprise for the wherewithal (taxes) to fund first the monarchs and then states, their executives, their legislators, their bureaucrats, and their diplomatic and martial adventures at home and abroad. These provisions, the political goods citizens or inhabitants expect of their own political entities – their nation-states – collectively constitute the test of good governance. If governments of any kind of jurisdiction (nation-states, provinces, states, or municipalities) show that they are unable or unwilling to supply several or many of the requisite political goods, or if they supply hardly any of some of the more critical political goods, they could fail both objectively (according to determinations of comparatively low GDP per capita or high crime rates, etc.) and subjectively (according to the polled sentiments of their citizens).[2]

The many nation-states in Africa that have in recent decades endured massive bouts of intrastate conflict have all been collapsed, failed, or nearly failed polities. Conflict indeed has followed the breakdown of the nation-state in every case, from the Siaka Stevens era in Sierra Leone to the vicissitudes of today's Sudan and Congo (Kinshasa).[3] Thus it is the strengthening of the state – improving governance – and the building of the nation (creating a robust democratic political culture) that prevents and will prevent the sliding of African states from weakness (or strength) toward failure, and hence into internal war and the denial of higher standards of living and advances in the human welfare of citizens. Think how Côte d'Ivoire in this century moved from an enviable position of strength as compared to its neighbors into a decade of nasty civil war, forfeiting the benefits that its citizens had long enjoyed as a result of decades of comparatively good governance and adequate supplies of political goods – security, safety, and the rest.[4] Note also how a rigged election in Kenya in 2007 led to outbreaks of rural and urban ethnic violence and to a perilous slide toward civil war and state failure. Kenya has since struggled to recover from its near-plunge into failure and all-out intrastate conflict.[5]

Failed states are those states that fall below a threshold of political goods supply; always, they fail to satisfy the Safety and Security minimums. That is, when a state's citizens are preyed upon by state-controlled operatives or by outsiders crossing its borders, when the state loses its monopoly of violence within its borders and non-state actors (warlords) gain primacy within disaffected regions, then the state is insecure and failed. A state's prime function is to eliminate attacks on the national order or social structure and "to enable citizens to resolve their differences with the state and their fellow inhabitants without recourse to arms or other forms of physical coercion."[6] Likewise, even if a state is otherwise secure, if high levels of crime make its citizens unsafe, it can become weak and unstable. High levels of crime, especially murders, rapes, ransomings, and carjackings, indicate that the state is unable to perform appropriately for its peoples. Weakness ensues and breakdown can follow.

Without security and safety, citizens cannot easily go about their daily pursuits – whether schooling, urban work, or farming – without fear. Productivity naturally suffers, as does the pursuit of human happiness. Moreover, only where there is adequate security, perceived or real, is the delivery of other desirable political goods possible. That is, for the modern nation-state in Africa to deliver reasonable accumulations of political goods it must be both secure and safe. When the African state cannot perform in this manner, civil war often is a consequence, followed in some circumstances by outside intervention and the introduction of international security substitutes.

Once a nation-state is safe and secure it can – if capable – provide a predictable, systematized method of adjudicating disputes between individuals or groups, or between individuals and groups and the state. This constitutes an enforceable rule of law and also implies an effective and independent judicial system. Once citizens observe that they can obtain justice from the courts without ruling-party or presidential interference, citizens smooth their differences or reduce their antagonisms without resort to arms. Within Nigeria, in part because the rule of law is viewed as partial and subject to flows of money, competition between ethnic groups for land, for employment, for residence (in Bauchi or Jos, say, or even in distant Zamfara), for schooling, for medical attention, and so on is too often decided with weapons rather than by reason or adjudication. If the state is seen as weak or incapable, citizens default to their ethnic solidarities and defend themselves against others perceived to be threatening their livelihoods or their opportunities.

A third essential political good permits – indeed, in the more advanced polities, encourages – free and open participation in a national political arena. This is the ability of individuals and all peoples to express their views and their grievances freely, to participate in the ongoing affairs of the state without hindrance, to compete for public office without barriers, and to vote for their own preferred candidates without undue interference. Integral to this political good is respect on the part of the state for essential human rights and liberties and the basic freedoms – of assembly, of expression, of religion, of language, and of community. Where the citizens of African nation-states enjoy this political good to the full, when they consider themselves free to be critical of their rulers and to campaign against perceived wrongs, there is a welcome absence of strife. Moreover, there may even be a strong sense of belonging to a nation-state that is fulfilling its social contract. If so, and if the nation-state (like modern Ghana) has the leadership or means to perform well, then Ghanaians, for example, can maximize their individual educational and economic opportunities and, conceivably, begin to enjoy improved social attainments of the kind that are impossible when a state is mired in conflict.

Nation-states enable individuals to prosper through individual initiative or group effort. If their supplying of this fourth political good is energetic, GDPs per capita will grow, inflation rates will stabilize, macroeconomic indices will be robust, a central banking system will be sound, the local currency will be fairly valued, relative equality across groups and classes will prevail, and the regulatory environment will enable individuals to transact commerce without undue interference or delay. Nation-states which score well according to this category of political good have invested in extensive and well-maintained modern arteries of commerce and have embraced and extended their Internet and mobile telephone networks. Nation-states in conflict invariably have neglected the provision of modern infrastructures or have destroyed inherited road networks (as in the Congo [Kinshasa]). By plunging into conflict, too, they often undermine their macroeconomies and, inevitably, reduce GDPs per capita.

Africans individually and in groups look first to their states for security and safety and, only when the state fails to provide, look to non-state actors for these same provisions. Only states supply fair rules of law (despite al-Shabab and other pretenders); only well-functioning states nurture "voice" and respect human and civil rights and enshrine freedoms. Only states that are at peace and are well governed can offer stable macroeconomic frameworks, solid currencies, a supportive regulatory environment, and the rest.

Likewise, the developmental bundle that comprises the fifth political good is rarely deliverable when the state is failing, failed, or collapsed. And for most Africans, beyond security and safety, the fifth political good is the one that most concerns and interests them. Africans, so long deprived, seek from their states as much educational opportunity as they can possibly obtain.

They also look to the state for medical services, especially in this dire era of rampant HIV/AIDS, malaria, tuberculosis, and so on. The better states further provide increasing access to clean water. International research demonstrates that among the more robust contributors to rapid GDP growth are the availability of potable water, improved sanitation, and the widespread education of girls (plus reduced fertility, a result of educational advances).[7] The avoidance of conflict or, more positively, the attainment of sustainable widespread peace flows from these strengthened social conditions. No African nation-states suffer civil conflict when the delivery of political goods is strong and their citizens believe that their lives are improving and their dreams are being fulfilled.

According to these criteria, strong states are those which deliver a broad range of high-quality political goods and show up well on all of the standard indices of economic, political, and social performance.[8] All strong states are secure and comparatively safe (South Africa being an exception because of high rates of crime). Weak states, however, may be inherently weak for structural reasons, or fundamentally strong but situationally or temporarily compromised. Weakness, moreover, need not be derived from weakness, but rather from performance or delivery inadequacies that are quantifiable, and rarely artifacts of exogenous variables. Often such weak states display ethnic or other inter-communal tensions that are incipient rather than already overtly violent.

Most weak states – and Africa contains more weak nation-states than any other continent – are badly led and poorly governed. Even the nominal democracies may be run by tyrants, as in Zimbabwe. Thus such states have a diminished ability (not a diminished capacity) to supply some or many of the basic political goods, and they signally often honor rule of law in the breach. Such weak states show declining economic and social attainments; their physical infrastructures betray neglect. Weakness in such states may persist for decades. Or, precipitated by the misadventure of rulers or unexpected natural disasters, an enduringly weak state might plunge (as Malawi did briefly in 2011) into overt internal conflict and the edge of failure. Because so many of Africa's nation-states are "weak" (or "fragile" as some donor agencies prefer), because they underperform, because they frequently disappoint their citizens or, at worst, foster ethnic or linguistic-derived discrimination, Africa's legion of weak states always lie at the cusp of failure, and conflict.[9]

The final descent into outright failure comes when the nation-state loses legitimacy – when it forfeits the "mandate of heaven." When citizens finally realize that their rulers are running the nation-state as a criminal enterprise for themselves as the sole beneficiaries – when citizens become persuaded that the state no longer cares for or about the fate of most of its inhabitants – then nearly everyone appreciates that the social contract binding rulers to ruled, and vice versa, has been sundered irreparably. At this point citizens frequently transfer allegiances to non-state actors, and resort to arms.

The failed states of Africa (and its one collapsed state, now a mere geographical expression) and the world are those that are replete with insurgencies, civil unrest, and heady mixtures of discontent and dissent. Those kinds of states are incessantly violent, but it is not the absolute intensity of violence that identifies a failed state. Rather, it is the enduring character of that violence and the crescendos of antagonism that are directed ceaselessly at the regime in power that identify the failed state. These civil wars are rooted in ethnic, linguistic, or other intercommunal enmities, but are almost always propelled, as in the Congo (Kinshasa) and the Sudan, by power and avarice. Pools of mineral or similar wealth opportunities entice poor scramblers and rich entrepreneurs alike, with the latter almost always unrelenting in their quest for zero-sum gains. Crowds in cities within failed states may riot against the state, but civil war itself is pursued by purposeful non-state entities anxious to gain advantage (or to equal another's advantage) and access to wealth.

Failed states victimize their own citizens. Rulers (whoever wields the power of a big gun) oppress, extort, and control their own compatriots while privileging favored ethnic, religious, or linguistic cohorts. Failed states rarely can exert themselves beyond capital cities. They cannot readily control their own hinterlands and usually dispute the control over whole regions (as in the Sudan's Darfur, Blue Nile, and Nuba Mountains provinces and states).

Maximum leaders and their close cohorts in failed states subvert democratic norms, restrict participatory processes, coerce civil society, and override such institutional checks and balances as may theoretically exist. They curtail whatever is left of judicial independence, harass remaining media, and suborn or co-opt security forces. Rulers show more and more contempt for their own nationals and surround themselves with family, lineage, or ethnic allies. Many of these arrogant leaders grandly drive down national boulevards in massive motorcades, commandeer national commercial aircraft for foreign excursions, and put their faces prominently on the local currencies. In private and in public they persuade themselves that the state and the riches of the state are theirs personally to appropriate.

In failed states inflation grows, rampant corruption flourishes, and economic growth shrinks. Social services wither. Officials loot what remains of state supplies. Consumer goods grow scarce. Sometimes, as in Zimbabwe from 2005 to 2012, segments of the population are deprived of food and go hungry or starve. Criminal violence increases. Lawlessness spreads beyond the cities. Criminality and criminal gangs proliferate. Arms trafficking and narcotics trafficking become common. Regarding protection, citizens naturally realize that the state can no longer offer them security and safety, or even social services. So they turn for succor to incipient warlords. Open combat follows.

Weak states exhibit flawed communication and transportation infrastructures. In the states that fail, especially in Africa, these inconvenient blemishes and hindrances become catastrophes, with paved roads turning into tracks and highways becoming ribbons of potholes. Outages overtake electric power. Educational and health systems become dysfunctional because of shortages of cash and foreign exchange. Teachers stop teaching and children eventually stop coming to class. Literacy rates fall. Simultaneously, hospitals run short of medicines and bandages, even sutures. Infant mortality numbers soar and life expectancies plummet from the 60s to the 40s, as they have in this decade and the last across large swaths of Africa. Eventually, citizens, especially rural inhabitants, realize that the distant central government has abandoned them to the capricious and harsh forces of nature. To survive, they must align themselves with winners against losers, with non-state actors and other war-lords against what is left of the state (and any international support that the failed state can muster).

As states fail, as the downward spiral accelerates, only a concerted, deter-mined effort can slow its momentum. Corrupt autocrats and their equally corrupt associates usually have few incentives to arrest their state's slide. They themselves discover clever ways to benefit from their state's impoverish-ment and misery; the ruling elements are not the ones to suffer as state services rapidly decay and shooting begins. As foreign aid and domestic investment dries up, jobs vanish, and per-capita incomes fall, leaders and their venal associates profit from food and fuel shortages, from arbitraging foreign exchange, from skimming state treasuries and from drugs-running. They also send money out of the country into secret European and Caribbean hiding places.

Ethnicity as a cause

Weakness, failure, and collapse in Africa are often ascribed to ethnicity run amok, to arbitrary colonial national demarcations that put tribal groups on the wrong side of borders or that separated peoples who belonged together. As much as the colonial powers acted in the nineteenth century and after without considering the impact of their actions on disparate ethnic groups, the modern descendants of these ethnic groups have learned to assert them-selves and to battle for their rights within contemporary borders. Moreover, ethnic strife is neither inevitable nor immutable in today's Africa. Sub-Saharan Africa is the home of thousands of linguistically and ethnically dis-tinct groups, but the sheer number and existence of so many entities hardly prove or imply that conflict is unavoidable.[10]

Although it is true that Hutu slaughtered Tutsi in 1994 (and before) in Rwanda, that Congolese persist in killing other Congolese on account of antagonisms usually expressed ethnically, that Nigerians periodically attack Nigerians who come from other ethnic backgrounds, and that Kenyans from one set of ethnicities went to war after the rigged 2007 elections against Kenyans from supposedly opposed ethnicities, these damaging occurrences were examples of politically inspired competition for scarce resources and limited power much more than they were atavistic outbursts against peoples who were "different."

Zambia, encompassing 13 million people, has 70 distinct language and ethnic groups and 4 dominant ethnicities and languages. Since independence in 1964, Zambia has known only very occasional and minor clashes fuelled by ethnic hostility. Some of the very same groups that battle to the death in next-door Congo live peacefully together in Zambia.

Internal harmony, as in Zambia, and civil war as in the Congo, Côte d'Ivoire, Kenya, and the Sudan, are explained not by the absence or existence of primordial enmities but by egregious failures of national leadership and governance. When the regime in charge in a state is perceived as behaving fairly and even-handedly to all of its citizens there is an absence of ethnic strife. When a state behaves unfairly, favoring chosen ethnic groups over others, the "others" become restless.

The civil wars of sub-Saharan Africa

Civil mayhem results from the failure of states to perform. Since the early 1990s those internal disturbances, politely described as intrastate conflict, have resulted in massive numbers of innocent civilian deaths (and a plethora of rapes and other brutalizations) from direct combat, from collateral damage and collateral attacks, and from disease and starvation incidental to the battles themselves.[11] Of the estimated 10–15 million Africans who have lost their lives in and incidental to these several intrastate wars since about 1990, many millions succumbed in the massive Democratic Republic of Congo, the Sudan, and Angola; 800,000 or more in Rwanda; 300,000 or more in Burundi; and comparatively fewer but still large numbers died as a result of the intense civil conflicts in Liberia, Mali, Sierra Leone, Côte d'Ivoire, Kenya, Guinea, Chad, Mauritania, the Comoros, Togo, Niger, and Nigeria. Others – about 80,000 – lost their lives as a consequence of Africa's only significant interstate conflict – the still smoldering "brothers'" war between Eritrea and Ethiopia (begun in 1998 and nominally concluded in 2000).[12]

In each instance, hostilities deterred economic growth and social progress in the countries concerned. This conclusion is obvious when the experiences and outcomes of countries at war or once at war are matched against those of neighbors or peers who never fought against their own, and prospered. Indeed, internal war saps the vital core of any state and weakens both its government and its governmental performance. Until a state can be resecured it cannot govern, it cannot supply meaningful political goods, and it cannot meet the needs of its citizens. The killing fields of Africa pose serious obstacles for all manner of development. They constitute one of the most massive, if not the most massive, obstacles to Africa's successful modernization.

Two case studies well illustrate the depths of Africa's misery: the Congo and the Sudan.

The War in the Congo

When Mobutu Sese Seko, a soldier during the last years of Belgian occupation of the Congo, emerged with US backing to rule what he called Zaire in 1965, his subjects numbered about 18 million, of 250 different ethnic groups speaking their diverse languages but conversing nationally in French, Lingala, and Swahili. They spread over a vast area equivalent to most of Western Europe or the US east of the Mississippi River. The Belgians had constructed railways and roads, and used the Congo River as a major artery of commerce from the far eastern interior through Stanleyville (now Kisangani) downstream and southwestwards to Léopoldville (now Kinshasa), the country's capital.

Mobutu's Zaire was greatly rich in resources, boasting quantities of copper, cadmium, cobalt, gold, diamonds, tin, and zinc. Belgian companies mined these minerals, especially in far-off Katanga (adjacent to Zambia), and the young African state paid for its rudimentary educational, medical, and social services from the royalties and taxes supplied by Belgian and other foreign companies. Under Mobutu, Zaire became an American ally – in some significant respects, a client. Push-back there was, but largely from Marxists who would have preferred to situate Zaire in the Soviet sphere and from those who had supported Patrice Lumumba, Congo's first leader, before his assassination.

Ultimately, Mobutu governed repressively and autocratically. More and more, as his rule stretched from the 1960s into the 1990s, he denied voice to Congolese, ran a patrimonial patronage system that enabled him for some years to rely on an obedient and orderly army, and gave more and more preference to relatives and fellow Ngbandi from the north-central section of his vast country. Mobutu stole too, robbing Zaire/Congo over his 32-year tenure of at least $13 billion, purchasing chateaux in Europe, giving and taking perquisites to and away from cronies and opponents, respectively, and always doing as little as possible for his subjects. By 1985, if not before, Zaire/Congo had become a state failed by Mobutu despite its riches, despite its potential, and despite (not because of) its legacy. That failure meant that ordinary Congolese had very little access to schooling or health clinics. A per capita income that might have been middle-income (for colonial Africa) had plunged under Mobutu (despite copper and the rest) to impoverishment. Roads deteriorated. Railways hardly functioned. Even the riverboats on the Congo were little better in the time of Naipaul than they had been a century before in Conrad's day.[13]

When Mobutu's despotic and latterly bumbling days were almost over, a force of Congolese, Rwandans, and others, under Laurent Kabila, inspired and funded by Rwanda and Uganda and militarily supported, liberated the Congo and ended Mobutu's reign in 1997. Mobutu had harbored thousands of Hutu genocidaires fleeing from Rwanda after the Tutsi victory there in 1994, defying President Paul Kagame and his Rwandan Patriotic Front. Although based in refugee camps, the genocidaires raided Rwanda, further angering Kagame. Ample gold, uranium, tantalite, columbite, tin, and timber in the eastern Congo, especially in the two Kivu provinces, also attracted Rwandans and Ugandans.

But Kabila was hardly a stable improvement on Mobutu. He shut down the press and outlawed opposition political groups. He failed to reconstruct the country's shattered infrastructure and did nothing to lessen poverty. He also refused to deliver Hutu mercenary refugees and soldiers to Rwanda and angered his sometime patrons by siding with Angola, Namibia, and Zimbabwe against Rwanda and Uganda. Another rebellion, this time inspired by Rwanda against Kabila, took place in 1998, but Kabila senior was protected by the armies of Angola and Zimbabwe. Then, after ruling ineffectively for another three years, Kabila was killed by one of his own bodyguards in 2001. Joseph, Kabila's 29-year-old son, was quickly installed by his father's close associates as successor, despite Joseph's youth, his limited acquaintance with the Congo (he grew up in Tanzania, speaking Swahili), questions about his real lineage, and his profound political inexperience.

The Congo, never having recovered from failure, has been at war with itself ever since. A mélange of non-state actors – greedy warlords, ethnic rivals, criminal mafias, local and quasi-national militias, and a variety of chancers who had purchased weapons from illicit dealers or had gained patronage from wealthy Congolese, Rwandan, Ugandan, and other financiers – began to fight against each other for control over tangible resources and territory containing tin and the magical coltan – a heat-resistant combination of columbite and tantalite that, when refined, holds high electrical charges. (Coltan is essential for creating capacitors controlling current flows in mobile telephones, laptops, and other electronic devices. It is found in major quantities in the eastern Congo.)[14]

With no effective nation-state to contain the warring opportunists in eastern Congo, indeed with no nation-state to adhere to and thus with no national army that could even begin to attempt to keep order, the Congo descended rapidly into the throes of swirling civil mayhem. Congolese Tutsi (emigrants from decades ago) battled other ethnic groups for control over potential riches. So did Hutu, many originally from Rwanda. Warlords arose everywhere in what had become the lawless eastern frontier of the Congo, as well as in Kasai and northern Katanga. From Laurent Kabila's invasion to 2012, millions of Congolese, nearly half of whom were under five years of age, lost their lives.

Most of those forfeited lives were only indirectly attributable to combat. The majority of the killings constituted collateral damage. War prevented farming. War brought disease in its wake. Without the ability to grow crops and without access to health services, eastern Congolese starved, certainly went hungry for long periods, and could not recover in their debilitated state from the ravaging diseases of tropical Africa – from malaria, pneumonia, kwashiorkor, marasmus, and diarrhea – all preventable conditions. Not even the arrival of about 22,000 UN peacekeepers (19,000 soldiers from dozens of countries plus about 1,000 police personnel, and civilians), first in 2000 as the UN Mission in Democratic Republic of the Congo (MONUC), then as the UN Stabilization Mission in Democratic Republic of the Congo (MONUSCO) in 2010, could stanch the spread of death. How many died is still disputed, but whether or not the estimated 5.4 million total overall death figure should be reduced to 3.5 million (based on a different methodology) or increased to 6.9 million – because of the passage of time and the continuing death toll in 2010 and 2011 of about 45,000 a month – may matter less than the callousness and waste to which these large numbers testify.[15] Additionally, literally millions were forced from their homes, some propelled deep into surrounding forests.

In 2013, after the late 2012 battles between the upstart March 23 (M23) militia and the inept Congolese army, at least 2 million Congolese were still internally displaced, with another 450,000 having fled across borders to neighboring nations.[16] Atrocities always abounded. In the streets of Bunia in 2007, aid workers found 200 bodies of women and children, some decapitated, some with their hearts, livers, and lungs ripped out. About 1,000 people in nearby Drodro in the same year were raped, maimed, and hacked to death. Mutilation and plunder was everywhere in that year, in the five years from 2002, for much of the time from 2007 to 2011, and again in late 2012. Water sources, health clinics, and farms were everywhere destroyed in the process by marauding gangs. Although directed by adults and young adults from 1 or more of 25 rebel groups, many of the "warriors" perpetrating these atrocities on their fellow Congolese were children carrying AK-47s, Kalashnikovs, and machetes – teenagers and kids as young as seven and eight, mostly high on hashish and other drugs.[17]

Gang rape against women as a form of power-mongering and as a weapon of war was common. The number of sexual violence victims in the Congo by 2011 was reputedly about 3 million between ages 15 and 49, with 1.8 million having been raped and the remainder having experienced "intimate partner sexual violence." (Boys and men have been raped, also.) In 2010 and early 2011, there were notorious mass rape occurrences in North and South Kivu when hundreds of women were victimized at once. Women were assaulted in those incidents and in others because they were from an ethnic group being attacked by a rebel group from an opposed ethnic group, because they were poor and simply in the way, because they went outside of displaced persons camps to collect firewood, or because they worked alone in their distant farming fields. "I went out to look for my children," one victim reported in late 2011, "and on the way back I met three armed [rebels]. They raped me and my friend."[18] The rapists were equally soldiers of the official Congolese army and fighters from rebel groups. Most of the rapes occurred in the troubled eastern provinces of South and North Kivu and in Orientale, but Equateur, in the far northwest of the Congo, also reported very high rape rates.[19]

In 2013, even after a national election in late 2011, Joseph Kabila's Congolese state lacks the qualities of nationhood that would end renewed spasms of violence. There is limited security and safety, especially in the eastern Congo but also in many other sections of the country. Throughout 2012, rebel groups – some backed by Rwanda – continued to operate, to kill, to maim, to rape, as the M23 did at the end of the year.[20] Sometimes rebel groups simply sought to maintain their hard-won power. Sometimes they sought control over coltan, tin, timber, or gold. Sometimes their pillaging appeared to out-siders to have no basis in economic or political sense. But non-state actors and their leaders often perceive their personal or group self-interests in idio-syncratic or asymmetrical ways. Plunder is self-perpetuating, especially when the nation-state has failed and power to keep the peace (even with UN force assistance) is severely limited.

Neither the Congo nor Africa can advance amid such all-out mayhem. Developing and growing Africa is difficult enough, but when one of its largest pieces of real estate and population is mired in conflict, people everywhere suffer. Those inside Congo suffer directly, but so do the poorer inhabitants of the nine countries that surround the Congo. Foreign investment and even donor assistance are slowed. So are domestic investment and, ultimately, the productive forces of ordinary workers and citizens. In the far reaches of the eastern Congo, subsistence and commercial farming remain unsafe and dif-ficult. Exploration for new minerals and legitimate mining are curtailed. Transport services are restricted, along with schooling and preventive health efforts. Africa cannot move forward with the Congo in its current chaotic state.

The Sudan

Nor can Africa prosper and raise living standards for its peoples with the Sudan, once Africa's largest country, still at war with itself. The 2005 peace agreement between north and south Sudan, now the separated countries of Sudan and South Sudan, and the 2011 referendum that confirmed South Sudan's breakaway status and independence, were supposed to end one of Africa's longest-running internal wars (from 1981 to 2011). After all, about 3 million soldiers and civilians, some in combat and many more from hunger and disease, had lost their lives in interminable battles across the territory of what is now South Sudan.[21] The discovery of oil was the initial trigger for a war based on religious and ethnic differences, on earlier enslavements of southerners by northerners, and on a desire by southerners to escape long decades of discrimination by Arabs and northerners against themselves, mostly Christian converts and animists speaking different languages and enjoying distinctly different cultures.

After 2011, with the South's independence recognized by the Sudan, the African Union, and the UN, all should have been well, and propitious for rapid nation-building in the south and a peace dividend in the north. But parallel to the war between north and south and influenced by the south's relative success in gaining autonomy and holding off the north, in 2003 war between Arab-speaking Sudanese and ethnically distinct African groups in Darfur, the Sudan's westernmost province, broke out after decades of discrimination against the non-Arabs (but Muslims nevertheless) and because of the rumor of the discovery of oil. From about 2004 to 2010, forces of the government of Sudan attempted brutally to contain and then to obliterate the non-state actors who rebelled and were as a result massacred by government aircraft and soldiers and, especially, by marauding Arab mercenaries on horseback loyal to the Islamist government in Khartoum. President George W. Bush's State Department declared that this repression of Darfuri civilians amounted to genocide; nearly 300,000 African (as contrasted to Arab) inhabitants of Darfur, 80 percent of whom were civilians succumbing to disease, lost their lives between 2003 and 2007.[22] Another 2.7 million fled into local camps for the internally displaced or across the Chadian border to become official refugees. Rape was used as commonly in Darfur as it was in Congo as an instrument of war.

In 2012, the Darfur conflict was much more muted than before, without being resolved.[23] The main rebel groups negotiated for many months with the Khartoum government, just as they had in earlier years, to resolve differences. They failed to do so over and over again, but reduced repression and intense conflict fatigue, plus the participation of more than 23,000 African Union and UN military and police peacekeepers (the African Union / United Nations Hybrid Mission in Darfur – UNAMID), limited the numbers of persons killed or attacked in 2012 to a few thousand. Yet, without a final resolution of the conflict, and with continued rumors of oil deposits, Darfur was still neither integrated into the Sudan nor autonomous within it. Thus, reconstruction and resuscitation could hardly proceed. The camps for displaced persons were still mostly full in 2013, with only limited, tentative, movement for most internally displaced and refugee citizens back to farming or other productive pursuits.

The partition of the Sudan into its northern and southern components has now focused the military-junta-ruled state of the Sudan on its remaining conflicts, first in Darfur and – after the South's secession – on the province of South Kordofan and the states of Abyei and Blue Nile – all entities on the southern fringe of the Sudan. Abyei straddles the north–south border and supplies about 20 percent of the petroleum that the Sudanese pipeline once pumped north from the now southern oilfields and the northern wells in

Abyei to waiting Chinese and Malaysian tankers at Port Sudan on the Red Sea. Abyei's borders were supposed to have been demarcated early in 2011, as part of the final settlement of disputes between north and south. But that issue, and thus the precise dividing line through the oil-producing region between north and south, remains contentious and unresolved. even after the 2012 "peace" agreement between the new entities supposedly ended hostilities over oil (and transit fees) and the Abyei ambiguity.

Likewise, the easterly Blue Nile state and the Nuba Mountains district of South Kordofan both harbored detachments of the South Sudan Southern Peoples Liberation Army (SPLA-North) throughout 2012. Most of the peoples in both regions were aligned to the Southern Peoples Liberation Movement (SPLM) that now rules South Sudan. In both areas, most of the indigenous populations long resented the heavy-handed overrule of the Arab-dominated government of the Sudan. Hostilities occurred in both regions in late 2011, after the South's secession, and conflicts there remain unresolved in 2012 after serious Sudanese bombings of its own civilians. Once again, the two small southerly parts of the north resent decades of repression by Arabs and seek greater freedoms and autonomy. There are also rumors of abundant oil in South Kordofan, which exacerbates resource avarice on both sides.

Peace, and thus the holistic development of the new Sudan, depends mightily on the resolution of these separate Darfuri, Blue Nile, and Nuba Mountains conflict situations, but it also depends significantly on the future of the ruling regime in Khartoum. Since coming to power by a military coup in 1989, General Omar al-Bashir has presided over an all-powerful Islamist officers' junta. Bashir, now indicted as a war criminal by the International Criminal Court and subject in theory to global arrest, rules the junta and the Sudan as an authoritarian commander. But in recent years he has increasingly been challenged by younger officers, a group of whom have allegedly dictated policy in the new border areas. Hence it is Bashir's weakness, not his strength, that bedevils the resolution of these remaining post-secession conflicts. He cannot afford to preside over policies that would meet the new rebels (or even the older ones) part-way. Compromise is hard, meaning that Bashir and his associates have focused on renewed repression and conflict.

Likewise, despite South Sudan's independence from the north, issues which could cause renewed war are abundant. Even after the brokered agreement between the two Sudans in late 2012, there was still no complete accord on the just net share of oil proceeds between north and south. That is, exactly how much should the south pay to ship its oil through the north's pipeline? The north has wanted to capture from transit revenues dollars sufficient to make up at least partially for the oil proceeds now transferred to the south. The south has naturally resisted such extortionate demands, mirroring traditional natural gas transit disputes between Russia and Ukraine. Indeed, South Sudan stopped shipping oil northwards in early 2012, preferring to renounce its own revenues until the Sudan negotiated fairly. South Sudan also initiated talks with Uganda and Kenya regarding the construction of a prospective pipeline across the territories of its southern neighbors from Juba to Lamu.

The brokered agreement in late 2012 promised to ease the flow of oil north again through the Sudan, and to demarcate much of the Sudan–South Sudan border. But the thorny question of Abyei's status remained unresolved, as did the fate of the oppressed peoples of the Nuba Mountains (within the Sudan). And, as of the first days of 2013, no oil flowed.

Further, the south has its own internal conflicts between ethnic groups. The dominant Dinka believe that they won the war against the north and deserve its beneficial results. But the Nuer, South Sudan's second-largest ethnic group and historic rivals of the Dinka, want fully to share the victory dividend. The Nuer also have ongoing disputes over grazing lands and cattle with the Murle; both raid each other and each other's cattle frequently, with severe loss of life.

Being Africa's newest and poorest country, with an untested political leadership under President Salva Kiir, South Sudan also has a difficult process of nation-building and physical and administrative organization ahead. Battles within and renewed contests with the north over bordering lands and vital petroleum revenues could hinder the modernization of the South, no matter how generously outside donors attempt to assist South Sudan to recover from its brutal war with the north.

Other Incipient Conflicts

Those are Africa's most deadly and most long-running current conflicts. Other once equally vicious intrastate imbroglios, such as those within Angola and Côte d'Ivoire were resolved in 2002 and 2011, respectively, after the loss of nearly 1 million lives in the Angolan civil war (over 20 years) and about 5,000 (over 10 years) in the Ivoirian controversy. Kenya's internal fracas in 2008 cost about 2,000 lives, and at least 500,000 were driven from their homes.[24] Zimbabwe's repression of President Robert Mugabe's presumed opponents probably caused 1 million deaths from disease, hunger, and direct assaults by security personnel on villagers and townspeople from 1999 to 2010. The depredations of the non-state actor Lord's Resistance Army in Uganda, and then in South Sudan, the Congo (Kinshasa), and the Central African Republic, probably resulted in 3,000 killings of innocent civilians along with the kidnapping of boys and girls, property damage, and widespread anxiety from 1990 to 2012.

In 2012, the Somali war between the Western- and African Union-backed Transitional Federal Government (TFG) and the al-Qaeda-linked al-Shabab movement continued, with the TFG, now backed by Ethiopian and Kenyan troops as well as UN peacekeepers from Uganda and Burundi, slowly gaining the upper hand in 2013. Casualties in the Somali wars since about 1992 probably number fewer than 100,000, including those brought about by piracy.

Such estimated mortality numbers and ancillary casualties in the myriad millions suggest the horror and enormous waste to which Africa has been subjected. Missing limbs and disfigured bodies testify today to the mind-numbing brutalities of the distant (1990s) and more recent episodes of combat in Africa. Likewise the numbers of children in Africa with stunted statures and distended bellies are a result of long-running animosities or sudden bursts of violence against out-groups. In some countries and regions, insecurity is the norm and anxiety almost always prevalent. Villages in Africa are often less peaceful than they appear to casual observers, and some urban African population centers are dangerous, tense, and unsafe.

Much of Africa, in other words, remains a tinderbox – latent, volatile, frequently explosive, often deadly, and always on edge. In the absence of a governmental apparatus capable of providing the key political good of security, and absent a predictable and independent rule of law and police who intervene fairly and open-handedly, minorities and majorities have learned to revert for protection to their ethnic, linguistic, or religious default affinities and to resolve disputes themselves, frequently by force. When they do so – when some of them give up on the state – internal wars and overthrown regimes may result, as in Côte d'Ivoire. Or sections of the state, as in Congo (Kinshasa), the Sudan, and Somaliland, may – in effect or in law – secede, breaking apart the fabric of the older order. In the dozen or so collapsed, failed, and failing states, combat trumps development and the people suffer as mercilessly as they have done in Congo (Kinshasa) and southern Somalia, where the clutches of impoverishment are hard to escape and the path to development has been lost.

Note that the mere existence of ethnic divisions does not foreordain ethnic clashes. Similarly, the existence of land or water that could become scarce, or resources that might produce great wealth, does not in and of itself lead Africa into conflict. It is the politicization of ethnicity and the politicization of differential access to resources that produce resentment, antagonism, and, sometimes, a reversion to chauvinist solidarity and ethnic battles. If the regime that runs the state in question is perceived as dealing with access fairly; if it educates everyone equally; if it provides medical or other facilities without favoring or discriminating against ethnic, linguistic, or religious groups; if the state is perceived as even-handed in its everyday dealings with its diverse citizens; if the state's leaders seem to understand that they are responsible to all citizens, not just to their own *confreres* – then, and only then, can a weak (and sometimes a strong) state remain free from inter-ethnic tension and, in time, conflict. In Kenya, for example, it was easy, after the results of the rigged 2007 elections were released, for those who had been cheated to mobilize their fellow Luo and Luhya against the establishment Kikuyu and Kamba. In Côte d'Ivoire, all it took was the southern-dominated ruling regime's dismissal of the presidential candidacy of a northerner to mobilize fellow northerners to protect those participatory rights, and thus to commence an all-consuming civil war to reassert their inalienable prerogatives.

But, as tragic as is Africa's descent into intrastate conflict, not all of the sub-Saharan states have succumbed. Botswana and Mauritius, the best managed, offer security, rule of law, and the other essential political goods. The mandate of heaven blesses both places; in those states there has been no major marginalizing of outgroups and no rise of communally based competitors to the state. Likewise, Zambia has known no strife of this kind and in 2011, thanks to responsible leadership, even enjoyed a governmental transition from one president to his opponent without rigging, or bloodshed.

Ethnicities in many countries, despite competition for scarce resources and some historic enmities, do not necessarily act on ethnic impulse. Ethnic or linguistic clashes have not been typical in Ghana, Namibia, Tanzania, or South Africa. Nor have the inhabitants of Cape Verde, the Seychelles, Lesotho, and other well-managed African nation-states defaulted willy-nilly into chauvinistic combat. Recurrent civil wars do not have to be Africa's pattern. Better leadership and governance, the creation of strong national political cultures, and the gradual strengthening of institutions ought to prevent renewed mayhem. With a little assistance from African and international organizations, sub-Saharan Africa could end its warring ways and help its peoples prosper.

The remedial role of African and UN organizations and institutions

Even if the reduction and prevention of conflict within Africa largely depends on improving responsible national leadership and strengthening national governance so that states become nation-states and perform adequately for their constituents, Africa-wide and African sub-regional organizations could have a significant role to play in boosting the possibilities for peace in troubled times and troubled countries. Certainly the African Union (AU), representing all of Africa, south and north, should be able to intervene on behalf of the African people to ameliorate cross-border and internal conflicts. So should sub-regional entities such as the Southern African Development Community (SADC), the Intergovernmental Authority on Development (IGAD), the Economic Community of the West African States (ECOWAS), and the East African Community (EAC) be important interlocutors in their own areas. Likewise the African Peer Review Mechanism (APRM) of the New African Partnership for Africa's Development (NEPAD) should have a sensible role to play by bringing cohort pressure to bear on African countries governing dangerously or poorly, or abusing their own peoples and thus inciting conflict and inhibiting economic growth.[25]

But in the field of conflict reduction or conflict resolution, all of these entities are known more for their inadequacies than their triumphs. The AU has deployed peacekeepers to southern Somalia (from Uganda, Burundi, Kenya,

Djibouti, and Sierra Leone) to protect the floundering Transitional Federal Government in Mogadishu; has sent peacekeepers from 21 African and many non-African countries to protect internal refugees in Darfur; in 2008 dispatched a small military force from Tanzania to quell an insurgency in Anjouan, one of the Comoros islands; and refused to recognize Laurent Gbagbo's usurpation of power in Côte d'Ivoire after his defeat in the 2010 presidential elections. It acted in a similar fashion when President Mamadou Tandja in Niger clung to power in 2010. In 2012, the AU and ECOWAS were active in protesting against coups d'état in Guinea-Bissau and Mali, and in attempting to end Mali's Tuareg rebellion. In 2013, French and ECOWAS troops, assisted by European and American nations, pushed al-Qaeda affiliated warriors out of northern Mali and seemed poised to end the threat of a widespread Tuareg-initiated insurgency.

These were all exemplary expressions of the AU's mandate to preserve the peace and extend justice throughout Africa. But, largely because the AU is an organization that acts mostly by consensus and thus expresses the political will of all of its 54 member countries, it has been woefully unable to intervene politically and diplomatically (much less militarily) to curb (or even verbally to condemn) the excesses of Africa's most mendacious leaders – Robert Mugabe in Zimbabwe and Isaias Afewerki in Eritrea.[26] The AU would not criticize Omar al-Bashir's regime in the Sudan, despite his and its war against what is now South Sudan and its attacks on civilians in Darfur. Nor will it deliver him to the ICC. The AU is absent from the Congo (Kinshasa), leaving peace-making there to the UN and foreign powers. It left the heavy lifting in Côte d'Ivoire and Mali to France, and in Libya to NATO.[27]

The AU cannot bring itself, despite the secession of South Sudan, to consider and recognize the well-functioning quasi-nation of Somaliland. When there was famine in Kenya and Somalia, the AU, in 2011, called a conference. But few of its members showed up and the resulting monetary pledges of assistance were derisory.[28] The AU even showed its weakness palpably before the world when it permitted Teodoro Obiang Nguema Mbasogo, the notoriously corrupt and authoritarian ruler of Equatorial Guinea, to become its elected President in 2011 and to convene the AU's annual summit in his well-guarded capital of Malabo.[29] Because many of the member states of the AU are poor, and frequently withhold or are late in paying their annual assessments, the AU is also weak bureaucratically and administratively. Its many organs have significant mandates, but accomplish little because of financial weaknesses and because offending member states, especially the more powerful and wealthy ones, would be imprudent.

Not only do nearly all of the intrastate conflicts within Africa continue without much attention – not even any hand-wringing – from the AU, but also the vast majority of interventions to reduce mayhem in Africa have largely come from individual African countries acting mostly alone (e.g. Kenya intervening in Somalia, as Ethiopia did earlier, returning in 2012 for more action), or with individual countries supplying peacekeepers at the request – or not – of the AU (as, for example, Ethiopia in South Kordofan, and the assorted African brigades in Darfur and Somalia).

Sub-regional organizations like ECOWAS have helped to restore order after the 2012 Malian coup and, earlier, to dampen hostilities in Liberia and later in Côte d'Ivoire. National mediators (such as South Africa in Burundi) have undertaken exercises of conflict resolution. So have individual mediators such as Kofi Annan in Kenya and Thabo Mbeki in the Sudan. These are all very positive developments, but, alas, Africa cannot look first to the AU to strengthen peaceful pursuits or to ensure that human development trumps internal combat.

The sub-regional organizations, closer to hostilities in many cases, have refused to recognize coups, as in Madagascar in 2010, Niger in 2010, and Guinea-Bissau and Mali in 2012, but they have been unable in most cases to return rightful heads of state to their capitals. Except in the very limited cases of the Comoros and Lesotho (where South Africa acted on behalf of SADC), the sub-regional organizations have had neither the will nor the troop power to do much. The major exception was Nigeria's massive military intervention on behalf of ECOWAS to separate the warring sides in Liberia, beginning in 1990. IGAD in 2011 endorsed Kenya's military involvement against al-Shabab in southern Somalia, but in many other cases the relevant sub-regional organization has been silent. Only in 2011, after many years of camaraderie and embarrassed tolerance for the despotic antics of Mugabe in Zimbabwe, did SADC finally begin to pull back its welcome mat. It has since insisted that proper and free elections be held, and demanded that Mugabe respect the rule of law and honor commitments made to Prime Minister Morgan Tsvangirai and the government of (supposed) national unity. But SADC has not had the means or the political will to do more. Nor, in the best tradition of the AU and the other African sub-regional organizations, can it bring itself publicly to criticize Mugabe or others like him for overstepping civil norms, brutalizing civilians, rigging elections, and the like.

When Mbeki was President of South Africa and helped to establish the APRM in 2003 to promote and reinforce high standards of governance, it had lofty aspirations. All of the nations of Africa were to self-monitor themselves according to those standards and were further to submit themselves to periodic peer review in order to assess how much each country was accomplishing for democracy and development and in order to provide a scorecard that could suggest areas needing improvement. That was an impressive initiative, but it began its existence with insufficient funds (and limited staffing) and without a mandate for rigor. Most of the initial national peer reviews (and there were 16 through the beginning of 2012) were easy and gentle affairs. They were intended to measure democracy and good governance, economic governance and management (including transparency), corporate governance (including promoting ethical principles and values), and socio-economic development (progress toward the elimination of poverty). Only the Ghanaian and Mauritian self-assessments were sufficiently broad-based and inclusive of all sectors of local society. South Africa's self-assessment, like a few of the others, was heavily manipulated by its existing (Mbeki) government. The outside assessors – an integral part of each overall assessment in addition to the self-assessment – in almost every case examined were unable to express themselves toughly; it soon became clear inside and outside Africa that the point of the APRM was largely to provide cosmetic whitewash. The final reports also had to be approved by the presidents of the countries being scrutinized. Most of all, the APRM never tackled any of the difficult country cases where candid outside assessments might have called official attention to tyrannical regime behavior or wild abuses of transparency. Zimbabwe was not subjected to the APRM. Nor were Madagascar, the Congo (Kinshasa), Nigeria, Equatorial Guinea, Gabon, Cameroon, Guinea or any of the other jurisdictions in Africa where rulers preyed on their people and thus precipitated conflict or hindered development and growth. Indeed, only 30 of Africa's 54 states had adhered to APRM by early 2012.[30]

The United Nations, through the Security Council, the Department of Peacekeeping, and the Department of Political Affairs, plus the specialized agencies, has often taken the initiative when the AU and African sub-regional organizations could not or would not. Africa's bloodshed since the end of the Cold War would have been much more sanguine without UN peacekeeping and peace enforcement missions in Angola, Burundi, the Central African Republic, Congo, Côte d'Ivoire, Liberia, Mozambique, Sierra Leone, Somalia, and the Sudan, among others. The mandates of those missions in many instances have been too limited or carried out poorly by supplying countries in Africa and beyond. But there has been no substitute for the UN in some of these conflicts, particularly in the Congo and Liberia where as many as 23,000 soldiers and police have in each place tried to keep the peace. The UN and the Secretary-General personally have actively promoted talks between contending sides in the internal wars, and also in Africa's sole serious cross-border conflict between Ethiopia and Eritrea in 1998–2000. The UN has done what Africa collectively could not.[31]

The ICC was established by the Rome Statute in 2002 to prevent future crimes against humanity by bringing those responsible for such crimes to international justice. Most of its accused in its first decade have been African, including warlords from the Central African Republic and Congo, state actors and non-state actors from Côte d'Ivoire, politicians from Kenya charged with fomenting ethnic violence in 2008, Sudanese operatives allegedly responsible for atrocities in Darfur, and the leaders of the Lord's Resistance Army, originally from Uganda. But its most celebrated indictment has been that of Bashir, the Sudan's president. Bashir is accused by the ICC of authorizing war crimes against hundreds of thousands of innocent civilians in Darfur; persuading Bashir to come before the ICC, or persuading countries where he has visited to arrest him on behalf of the ICC, proved impossible through 2012. Thus the ICC has not been able to demonstrate that it has the ability to bring very high-level alleged miscreants to justice. If it cannot, then other heads of state who might equally be accused of warring against their own people (such as Mugabe) will continue to enjoy impunity. One potential weapon against tyrants will thus be hard to employ, making Africa less secure.[32]

Improved governance

Improved governance will strengthen the weaker countries of Africa and enable them to prosper and to avoid state failure and the clash of arms that depresses individual standards of living and reduces the social safety net. If the leaders of Africa can begin to condemn despotism amid their ranks, if they can at least shun those among their fellow heads of state who compromise the rights of citizens, if they can thus bolster the chances that democracy will take root in more rather than fewer countries, then, and only then, will the civil wars of Africa diminish in number, frequency, and lethality. Otherwise, Africa will continue to struggle to catch up with Asia and Latin America, where the good governance battle has largely been won and internal wars are now rare.

Africa, especially its emerging middle class, wants to free itself from conflict so that it can truly banish intrastate conflict and consequently join the global village of economic growth. There is no other path to prosperity.

6
Accountability and the Wages of Corrupt Behavior

Corruption is an enduring human condition with ancient global roots. In Africa, public notables have ceaselessly abused their offices for personal gain for centuries, if not eons. Well-born and common citizens alike, we may assume, have always sought advantage by corrupting those holding power or controlling access to key perquisites. Critically, the exercise of discretion, especially those forms of discretion that ease or bar opportunity, sparks a magnetic impulse that attracts potential abusers. Claimants of all strata have for centuries sought favor from authority (pre-colonial, colonial, and post-colonial). Likewise, authority, appreciating the strength of its position, has always welcomed inducements.[1]

Until avarice and ambition cease to be dominant human traits, corruption will continue to flourish in Africa and globally. Self-interest and family or lineage interest dictate the demanding and granting of special favors. Only in a minority of African nations does merit determine outcomes, personal advancement, and contractual awards. Thus, in sub-Saharan Africa and elsewhere, the riptide of corruption exists as a steady undertow; in Africa even more than on other continents, citizens presume that desirable outcomes are secured primarily, possibly only, by means of illicitly pressed influence or hard-purchased privileges.

Least and most corrupt

Almost no African nations and no assemblages of African leaders are immune to the temptations of corruption, the abuse of public office for private gain.[2] Indeed, in many of Africa's nation-states corrupt practices are egregious and obscenely excessive. As one noted economist concluded ruefully, "the leaders of many of the poorest countries in the world are themselves among the global superrich."[3] Nigerians believe that their country has forfeited $380 billion to various methods of graft since independence in 1960.[4] Transparency International's (TI's) annual ratings (based on subjective surveys by experts) of corrupt countries regularly place nearly all of sub-Saharan Africa's polities in the bottom half of its 176-country global list. Indeed, year after year, Somalia, the Sudan, Chad, Burundi, Angola, Equatorial Guinea, the Congo (Kinshasa), Guinea, and Zimbabwe fill the lowest ranks, along with such global pariahs as North Korea, Iraq, Burma, Uzbekistan, Turkmenistan, and Afghanistan. The Seychelles, Rwanda, Mauritius, Cape Verde, and Botswana are the only African countries that rank in the top 51 of Transparency's least corrupt world nations at 51, 50, 43, 39, and 30 respectively. New Zealand, Denmark, Finland, Sweden, and Singapore are the globe's least corrupt polities. The United Kingdom rated 17th and the United States 19th in 2012.[5] Of all the nations of Africa, Transparency International's complementary 2011 Bribe Payers' Index only included data on South Africa. It ranked in the middle of the 28 states assessed.[6]

Global Integrity, which uses a somewhat different and more qualitative/anecdotal methodology than TI, also lists 11 sub-Saharan African countries among its bottom 31 most corrupt states world-wide through 2010. Nigeria, Zimbabwe, the Sudan, Tanzania, Mozambique, Cameroon, Burundi, Liberia, Congo (Kinshasa), Angola, and Somalia (from least to most corrupt) were the egregious 11, clustered with the likes of Sri Lanka, Ukraine, Armenia, Algeria, Jordan, Egypt, Iraq, Lebanon, the Yemen, and Syria. Tanzania was the African country where corruption results had worsened most dramatically between 2008 and 2010. (The UN concluded that leaders of Somalia's Transitional Federal Government of 2004 to 2008 embezzled seven out of every ten dollars they received from the UN and other donors.[7]) The African nations at the more benign end of the Global Integrity scale included Benin and South Africa (above Canada), Malawi and Rwanda (ahead of Bangladesh and India), and Ethiopia and Uganda (above Russia, Namibia, Papua New Guinea, and Sierra Leone). Global Integrity has not measured all of the states of Africa or the world; nor does it rate every country every year. Its aim is to evaluate the anti-corruption legal frameworks and the "practical enforcement of those frameworks" across the globe.[8]

But it is less the moral stain and more the economic consequences that make these two comprehensive, if not completely quantitatively measured, indictments of large-scale corruption consequential for the emergence of modern Africa. Corruption of all kinds, especially the venal large-scale corruption that prevails so widely in Africa, distorts national priorities, increases national inefficiencies, inhibits or deters foreign direct and domestic investment, substitutes patronage rewards for honest political activity, and reduces mass confidence in governmental legitimacy. In some cases, the pursuit of corrupt gains may actually lead to widespread hunger, the spread of disease, and diminished life chances. Studies show that, on average, corruption reduces annual GDP increases by at least 1 percent.[9] Thus, the profits from the jobs and the accompanying multiplier effect that impoverished Africans desperately need are in numerous cases swallowed up by thefts from the public exchequer, the awarding of large construction contracts to over-priced vendors promising nice rents (kick-backs), and a pervasive criminalization of the offices and functions of the state. Furthermore, well-meant local and international efforts to improve the health outcomes, educational attainments, general welfare, and human rights of the citizens of Africa are inhibited, or at least reduced, by the prevalence of corrupt practices.

Oil and natural gas riches have long distorted African (and global) economies and led to paroxysms of greed and, hence, the kinds of graft that have dwarfed most ordinary forms of corrupt practice. The bonanza of unexpected and suddenly abundant sources of wealth in much of Africa has resulted in unbridled avarice on the part of those fortunate enough to be in power at the time of discoveries or exploitation. Without so much as lifting an entrepreneurial finger, the regimes in charge have embraced their "gifts" and found ways to channel the resulting petrodollars into private rather than national accounts. In Angola – along with Nigeria, Africa's largest producer of petroleum – President Jose Eduardo dos Santos and the men around him have pocketed $3 or $4 billion a year; very little trickles down to the mass of deprived Angolans. Angola rates toward the bottom of Transparency International's annual Corruption Perceptions Index, Global Integrity's list, and the UN Human Development Programme's Human Development Index. In 2009, the Index of African Governance placed Angola 46th of 53 countries.[10]

In Equatorial Guinea, growing on the back of oil at the rate of 5 percent a year, only President Teodoro Obiang Nguema Mbasogo and his family and associates enjoy the resulting largesse, possibly $3 billion a year. As Africa's fourth-largest petroleum exporter, Equatorial Guinea's tiny population of subsistence farmers might have been expected to have become better educated, better cared for medically, and better fed. Instead, social conditions and medical outcomes have deteriorated since oil has been pumped in large amounts. As many as 70 percent of its inhabitants fall below the African poverty line of $1.25 a day. "Here is a country," said Human Rights Watch, "where people should have the per capita wealth of Spain or Italy, but instead they live in conditions comparable to Chad or the Democratic Republic of Congo." Its report continues: "This is a testament to the government's corruption, mismanagement, and callousness to its own people."[11] Freedom House calls Equatorial Guinea "highly corrupt."[12]

Nigerian military oppressors made sure that they appropriated for themselves the bulk of offshore oil receipts before 1999 and the installation of the country's first civilian ruler since 1965. Only after the election of President Goodluck Jonathan in 2011 has Nigeria begun, very tentatively, to utilize its oil wealth to resuscitate local agriculture and industry and to create the beginnings of a social safety net for the millions of Nigerians who are poor. But whether Jonathan can win the battle against deeply ingrained corrupt practices is, in 2013, unclear.

Gabon's President Omar Bongo and his successor son thrived and now enjoy hefty revenues from the steady pumping of oil. Ghana began exploiting oil finds only in 2011, and Mozambique has not yet brought its gas onshore for local use and export.

In Uganda, where 40 percent of the population survives on $1.25 a day or less, the $2 billion or so that the exploitation of waxy oil deposits near Lake Albert will produce in 2013 could transform the fortunes of its largely agricultural people. But Uganda is already regarded as a small country wallowing in corrupt practices. So will the proceeds from the new oil finds simply flow into high-placed pockets? Apparently, Uganda's hitherto tame parliamentarians worried that they (not necessarily the people, their constituents) would lose out. Preemptively, in 2011 they accused Uganda's prime minister and other senior government officials of taking lavish bribes from the British petroleum company that controls the discoveries. To have thus taken bribes would not have been exceptional. Indeed, the British company pointed a finger at an Italian rival concern, claiming that it had spent more than $200 million in bribing the nation's President and other prominent officials in order to subvert its own oil rights. President Yoweri Museveni, in power since 1985, said that he "can never be given money by anybody." To suggest otherwise, he continued, was "contempt of the highest order."[13]

Nevertheless, in late 2012, Ireland suspended its attempt to help uplift impoverished northern Uganda under a Peace, Recovery, and Development Programme run by Uganda's Office of the Prime Minister after more than €4 million of Irish funding had found its way into a personal bank account controlled by the Prime Minister. The *Daily Monitor* (Kampala) reported that billions of shillings meant to help northern Ugandans rebuild their lives after decades of war ended up constructing mansions for officials in the Prime Minister's office.[14]

Zimbabwe, another despotism, has diamonds rather than oil. But the results are largely the same – unsurpassed looting of the nation's new resource wealth by President Robert Mugabe and his closest cronies and a refusal to share more than a tenth of the proceeds of diamond stripping (perhaps $2 billion a year?) with the nation through taxes, royalties, or normal fiscal methods. After the likely bonanza of the Marange diamond fields in eastern Zimbabwe was first fully appreciated in 2008, military and police leaders, Mugabe's wife, the Minister of Defense, and the government's Central Intelligence Organization forcibly pushed local miners off the prosperous grounds, committing unspeakable human rights and physical abuses and shooting 200 hapless prospectors from helicopters. Then they gave concessions to themselves, fenced out others, including one of the rightful owners of a large portion of Marange, and proceeded to smuggle uncut stones out of Zimbabwe without paying anything to the central government. "The people who are mining are [Mugabe] faithfuls," reported an opposition politician; "They are not mining for the government. They are mining for their leaders."[15] The generals and Mugabe's family are now much richer, the nation still poor. Whereas Zimbabwe was regarded before the discovery of diamonds to have become noticeably corrupt under Mugabe since at least 1995, diamond-fueled corruption (and violence) has proliferated from 2008, with no end in sight.[16]

When Mugabe unexpectedly crossed the Zambezi River in late 2011 to chat with Michael Sata, the newly elected President of Zambia, he arrived with 50 aides and accomplices. Sata came with his press person and 2 or 3 others, and he came by bus (not in a motorcade) from the local airport. Mugabe and Sata talked for an hour at a hotel in Livingstone, Zambia's tourist city. When Mugabe and his entourage departed, Sata startled the hotel staff first by demanding a bill for the services rendered and, second, by paying it himself, personally.[17] The contrast in behavior with his predecessors, and with Mugabe, was pointed.

Congo (Kinshasa) has diamonds, but is primarily resource-abundant in copper, cobalt, cadmium, coltan, and gold. Mobutu Sese Seko, President from 1965 to 1997, profited personally from export revenues and special deals with the state-owned mining companies. Before national elections in late 2011, Congo's government secretly sold off a broad array of mining licenses to cabinet ministers and their nominees, inexpensively. This was privatization Russian-style, with favored friends and associates of President Joseph Kabila grabbing (through nominees) about $5.5 billion worth of Congolese assets for far less than they were worth, and via shell companies located in the British Virgin Islands.[18]

A more typical tale of Congolese rapacity involves the "circulation" of sealed "envelopes." "If you want to buy votes in Parliament to squelch the audit of your state-run company, you pass around envelopes. When you want to obtain a lucrative contract to supply the police with beans and rice, you make sure the officials on the procurement board all get envelopes delivered to their home." No one, in other words, receives cash openly. That would be unseemly. They receive "anonymous" stuffed envelopes, sealed, instead.

An opposition parliamentarian told Stearns that, after a meeting at the presidency to discuss a pending vote, he was given "something" for his "transport costs." Inside were ten $100 bills. An operative in Joseph Kabila's executive office ran this off-the-books payroll and managed to keep operatives of many tendencies loyal.[19]

An American-backed dictator who ruled Chad from 1982 to 1990 apparently stole millions from his country's central bank and from the provincial administrations in his impoverished land. When he fled to Senegal to avoid arrest, he purchased a luxurious villa in Dakar and used some of his ill-gotten funds to try to buy protection against extradition and media criticism. According to press reports at the time, a bank in Dakar had to close temporarily "to count the cash that arrived in suitcases" on the airplane carrying Hissene Habre from N'jadmena, the capital of Chad.[20] Although charged in a Senegalese court in 2000 for crimes against humanity, torture, and barbarity, Senegal for many years refused to put Habre on trial, or to send him back to Chad or to Belgium, which had also sought since 2005 to try his case. According to the 1992 Chad Truth Commission, Habre's regime had killed 40,000 opponents and tortured many others. In 2012, the International Court of Justice decided that Senegal should try him without delay. At the end of 2012, Senegal's parliament legislated in favor of bringing Habre before an especially created African Union tribunal presumably similar to the one that jailed Charles Taylor for crimes against Sierra Leone.

"Corruption," President Paul Kagame of Rwanda admits, "is clearly, very largely, behind the problems [that] African countries face. It is very bad in African or Third World countries . . . [and it is hard to change because] it has become a way of life in some places." As Archbishop Desmond Tutu of South Africa told a local university audience, "Our country with such tremendous potential is [being] dragged backwards and downwards by corruption, which in some instances is quite blatant." Even in Botswana, by far mainland Africa's acknowledged least corrupt nation, its second President was often offered access to secret bank accounts in Switzerland. Local businessmen tried to entangle him in lucrative conflicts of interest by offering him shares in their businesses.[21]

As if to reinforce Archbishop Tutu's exasperated jeremiad, in 2012 the South African government began investigating several of its provinces for wildly overspending their official budgets. In Limpopo Province, in the far north, the politicians in charge exceeded their annual allocations by $250 million, much of the expenditure being doled out in the form of contracts and special payments to persons with close ties to local bigwigs. Provincial leaders made $360 million worth of unauthorized payments, many lucrative contracts were awarded without competitive bidding, and 200 of the province's 2,400 teachers drew salaries but did not exist. At least $80 million worth of purchases of various kinds were ordered improperly. Meanwhile, 62 percent of the residents in Limpopo live below the local poverty line and 40 percent of all eligible workers are unemployed. Water is short, recently paved roads are mostly ribbons of potholes. "We thought that South Africa could be different," said the head of Limpopo's branch of the South African Communist Party. Yet, according to businessman Moeletsi Mbeki (the younger brother of the former President), these corrupt dealings are not unique to Limpopo. "It is all over the country," he said; "It is a general form of self-enrichment by the politically connected."[22]

In Africa's newest nation, South Sudan, President Salva Kiir in 2012 resorted to an unusual tactic: he wrote letters to 75 current and recent officials of his own government, and later suspended them from office, requesting that they return the monies that they had stolen from state resources. (About $60 million were recovered soon after his letter was sent out.) He accused his own personnel of misappropriating at least $4 billion from the nation – all well within the year that South Sudan had become independent.

"People in South Sudan are suffering and yet some government officials simply care about themselves," he wrote; "Most of these [peculated] funds have been taken out of the country and deposited in foreign accounts. Some have purchased properties, often paid in cash." Furthermore, "Once we got to power we forgot what we fought for and began to enrich ourselves at the expense of our people."[23] More than $2 billion apparently went missing in a scheme that "purchased" sorghum, the local staple, from bogus companies that never delivered the grain to the government.

Venal corruption

Venal corruption – the large-scale stealing of state revenues or resources – is far more directly antagonistic to national economic, social, and political progress than lubricating or petty everyday corruption. In Nigeria's Abia State, for example, when one fortunate agricultural entrepreneur became the Director of a World Bank-funded development program, he immediately gave a substantial contract to a relative to supply equipment for palm-kernel processing. The relative profited substantially, and, almost equally, so did the Director. Normally, the person awarding the contract expected a standard 10 percent of the total value of the contract. Sometimes, too, in the heady degenerative atmosphere of the late 1990s Nigeria, they demanded even more. One military administrator in Abia was nicknamed "Where My Own."[24] In another fairly typical Nigerian (and African) instance, the head (soon to be the ex-head) of the nation's tax authority reported that he had tried for two years to persuade the chair of a key legislative committee to propel a small, technical, clean-up bill through parliament. "How much?" was the chair's response. "No bribe, no law," was the rule.[25] The entire state machinery, according to the *Economist*, "exists to siphon off cash." Indeed, "Nigerian politics is one big bun fight over oil money," suggests a prominent consultant.[26]

In Zambia, President Frederick Chiluba was convicted in a British court of stealing $46 million from the people of his country. His wife was jailed by a Zambian court for 3.5 years for receiving and obtaining stolen properties and for taking 300,000 dollars'-worth of cash and goods that Chiluba had pilfered from State House.[27] President Robert Mugabe of Zimbabwe made sure in 2001 that the contract for the construction of Harare's new international airport was awarded to his nephew. In 2011, the Nigerian High Court heard testimony that the former Speaker of Nigeria's House of Representatives unilaterally authorized the increase of allowances for members per quarter from 17 million naira to 42 million naira, amounting to a 42 billion unbudgeted naira expense. The Speaker and his deputy, being tried for criminal breach of trust, were alleged cleverly to have borrowed 60.4 billion naira, however, from the allowance account, personally pocketing the 18.4 billion naira difference.[28]

In Gabon, a close aide to the late President Omar Bongo claimed that the former Gabonese strong man generously sent "briefcases stuffed with millions in cash" to French politicians, including President Nicolas Sarkozy. "When a French politician comes to Gabon," the aide said, "we say 'He's come for his briefcase.'" President Jacques Chirac, Sarkozy's predecessor, also supposedly received millions of dollars from a range of Francophone African political leaders, according to "a notorious [French] bagman for France's interests in its former African colonies."[29] At the very least, there was lots of loose cash available to French Africa's big men. They obviously used it, as we would imagine, in order to ensure that France, "the mother country," regarded them and their interests well. These allegations about African monies finding their way to France, partially for French political campaigns, further demonstrates that the corrupt use of state resources knew few bounds. In Bongo's case, he ran his small oil-rich nation authoritatively for 41 years (1967–2009), having "shamelessly" looted its wealth.[30] Transparency and accountability were lacking, even laughable, in his country's case, as in so many others across Africa.

Burundi, next door to staunchly anti-corruption Rwanda, has all the laws and rhetoric in place to extirpate corrupt practices. President Pierre Nkurunziza launched a fervid campaign against all forms of corruption when he took office in 2005. He articulated a "zero tolerance" campaign and outlined a national strategy including all of the technical ingredients of a comprehensive attack plan – strong laws, independent monitoring, civil society accountability, transparent tendering, and merit promotions in the civil service. Instead, corruption levels accelerated. The ruling party of the President arrogated virtually all national resources to itself and to elites close to the President, turned appointments to bureaucratic positions into a cash cow, and did the same regarding the many important "commercial" entities controlled by the government. The public procurement process became a vehicle for the immense enrichment of cabinet ministers and other persons of privilege. A local assessment of the situation declared that the award of public contracts in Burundi was "based on bribes and personal contacts with members of the government." Burundi remains among the poorest countries in sub-Saharan Africa, with a GDP per capita of about $170 per annum. But political leaders and the politically connected have grown immensely wealthy, almost – as a Congolese observer said – to levels "prevalent" in his home country.[31]

Petty corruption

Petty or lubricating corruption, as typified by the policeman who overlooks a vehicular offense in exchange for "a consideration," is more visible and thus more annoying to the general public than is venal corruption, no matter how destructive larger-scale corruption may be to the national interest. In nearly all of Africa, petty corruption – the "contribution" of relatively minor amounts of rands, shillings, or dollars to obtain permits, licenses, and important documents that should by right be available freely – is a daily ordeal undergone by nearly everyone. It may be less developmentally destructive in aggregate than venal corruption, but the overall cost to society in cash and time may still be significant and damaging economically, and harmful dramatically to the very fabric and trust of local society and local politics.

It is arguable, too, that compared to the baleful consequences of venal corruption, the moral legitimacy of all affected societies is rent equally, if not more, by the inescapable nature of petty corruption. Where there have been country and household studies, as in Kenya, the toll on ordinary household incomes attributed to bribes can be immense.[32] "The entire state has been captured to a certain extent by corrupt interests," Transparency International's Kenya Executive Director reported. "Nearly every institution of governance and service delivery is working in the interest of a small group of people who profit from it."[33] In Sierra Leone, offenders on trial routinely negotiate lighter punishments by paying fees to clerks and magistrates. In government hospitals, nurses' handbags become illegal pharmacies from which prescription drugs are sold to patients. Extra payments to officials in government departments obtain faster processing for various theoretically free public services. "People have little option but to pay [such] incentives."[34] There are no complaint mechanisms and no way, really, of protesting against such "speed" or "lubricating" mechanisms.

In Nigeria, touts will sell access to airport fast-track security channels for $10, working in cahoots with personnel who know when to go slow. Smith concludes: "people commonly pay extra money for basic services such as the issuance of licenses, passports, and birth certificates." But they think of each of these bribes as a "dash" – a "sociable and socially acceptable" way of gaining favor in exchange for cash. However, heavier payments for preference for jobs or education, to employ public vehicles for private use, to run a private health operation within a public health facility, to employ university resources for private consulting, to overlook vehicular defects, or to ignore the expropriation of public building materials for private use or sale, are viewed in Nigeria as "outright extortion."[35] In Zimbabwe, as late as 2012, government ministers, senior civil servants, military and police officers, and anyone with power brazenly appropriated fertilizer destined for poor farmers, some of it given by donors.[36]

Bribes in exchange for release or freedom from arrest are common. Police on the Zimbabwean–South African border "confiscate, destroy, or refuse to recognize valid documents in order to justify an arrest for the purposes of extortion." The police have been in cahoots with people-smuggling rings, accepting payoffs for directly facilitating their operations or looking the other way when migrants crossed the Limpopo River frontier. About 18 percent of undocumented non-South-African nationals interviewed in 2007–2008 reported paying a police officer or some other governmental person to avoid arrest or detention. Among documented interviewees, 16 percent bribed the same kinds of individuals for the same reasons.[37] Almost every border crossing in the developing world would doubtless report similar kinds of behavior.

In 2012, South Africa's police chief and his head of the police crime intelligence unit were both discharged by President Jacob Zuma for "corruption, dirty tricks, political machinations, and even [alleged] murder." In 2011, nearly 6,000 complaints were laid against South Africa's police for assault and attempted murder. Nearly 600 persons were shot by the police in 2009–2010; nearly 300 more died in custody. Transparency International reported that 68 percent of urban South Africans questioned asserted that the police were "extremely corrupt." More than half of South Africa's motorists had been shaken down by police in 2010–2011. A police chief in Gauteng agreed that police graft was among its biggest causes of crime. His officers had arrested 600 of their own from 2011 into 2012 for murder, assault, blackmail, and burglary.[38]

Within countries, when times are tough, police (and thuggish "entrepreneurs") set up roadblocks, use regulations or supposed regulations to find fault with vehicles or licenses, and demand payment immediately. A car's mandatory reflective triangle may be the "wrong size" or a mirror may be broken: a handy small payment will suffice to permit the automobile to proceed, especially if it is dark and the police or pseudo-police are menacing. Everywhere in the rougher parts of sub-Saharan Africa, and even in some of the supposedly more law-abiding countries, such practices occur. Citizens thus endure humiliation, annoyance, peculation, and, now and then, physical harm.

Rewards of limiting corruption

Leaders cannot uplift their nations and enhance stability and prosperity without eliminating the scourges of venal and petty corruption. Equally, as the sub-Saharan African cases of Mauritius, Botswana, and Cape Verde show, wealth increases correlate with the absence or the minimal nature of corrupt practice. In Africa, Botswana and Mauritius, both without oil and absent Dutch disease, grew more rapidly in the 1980s and 1990s and in this century than any other African country. Their average GDP increases of 7 percent per year made them the only African tigers. (In recent years, petroleum drillers like tiny Equatorial Guinea have experienced even more rapid growth, but without distributing it widely among their people.) Cape Verde has been growing at an annual average of 5 percent for ten years. The Seychelles grew slowly for much of the last decade but achieved an annual GDP growth of more than 6 percent in 2010. Globally, Singapore's example of massive GDP per capita wealth attainments since 1965 also demonstrates the saliency produced by greatly reducing corrupt temptations of all kinds.[39]

Sub-Saharan Africa's small handful of countries boasting limited corruption and high growth (all ranking in Transparency International's blessed top 51) are highly participatory, open economically, well-managed administratively, and typified by sustained good governance (as indicated by the findings of the Index of African Governance and other sources). Remarkably effective leadership enabled these results; such countries did not emerge from colonial rule more advantaged than their neighbors and cohorts. Other than being small, two had mostly desert as their legacy. A third had mixed and contentious ethnicities and a history of discord. As in Singapore, their leaders decided to shape a political culture antagonistic to corrupt practice, an approach that Rwanda in recent years has been attempting to emulate.

Almost at the same time as Singapore began to crack down on corruption, so Botswana and Mauritius understood that the best – if not the only – way to curb corruption was by example, starting at the top. Where previous policies, even colonial oversight, were generally permissive of at least mild levels of corruption, Lee Kuan Yew in Singapore, Seretse Khama in Botswana, and Seewoosagur Ramgoolam in Mauritius knew that they must prevent its spread if they wanted their democratic governments to be respected, to be sustained, to prosper, and, over time, to uplift their peoples. They also appreciated that transparency and accountability went hand in glove with a successful anti-corruption strategy. Thus, judges and courts had to be independent and free of executive or legislative interference. A free media was also important, the better to keep governments honest and accountable. Universities supported by the state but allowed to follow global academic norms, with little regime involvement, were also crucial. A merit-based bureaucracy was seen to strengthen the ability of these new states to manage themselves well. Welcoming an engaged civil society was another plus.

In Botswana, Mauritius, Cape Verde, and the Seychelles; more recently in a few additional countries such as Rwanda, Ghana, Lesotho, Namibia, and Zambia; and partially in larger nations such as South Africa, Nigeria, Kenya, and Tanzania, an awareness has spread that accountability and transparency are two of the critical bases of improved governance. Africa's emerging middle class campaigns for such ameliorations, but has a major battle ahead in those states still saddled with authoritarianism and the practice of corruption, lack of transparency, intolerance of dissent, and kinds of oppression that characteristically accompany such denials of fundamental human rights.

Battling corruption

Fortunately, those countries which have over decades demonstrated a willingness, and thus an ability, to stanch corruption provide a model for others, and thus for an Africa still largely mired in rent-seeking, favoritism, nepotism, and a blatant disregard for the integrity of the public purse. That positive model is based on a proven syllogism. Lesser officials and politicians steal from the state and cheat their fellow citizens because they can – because everyone else does. If their immediate superiors cheat, lower-ranked bureaucrats and security officials assume that they, too, have a license to enrich themselves. Middle-ranked officials look to their cabinet ministers and their presidents and prime ministers to see what they, too, "can get away with." Almost all of us are self-maximizers. So are those in high or low-level positions in Africa capable of seizing available opportunities to use public positions for private gain: "Whatever one's views of human nature and human fallibility, if the prevailing political culture tolerates corruption, nearly everyone will seek opportunities to be corrupt."[40] Leadership actions in turn determine those political cultures and thus signal by their own greed and permissiveness (or the reverse) how others learn to behave.

The nation-states that traditionally occupy the top (more favorable) spots on Transparency International's Corruption Perceptions Index are all either long-established developed or industrial nations with political cultures and institutions that safeguard against corruption or the few newly emergent nations in Asia and Africa that have managed to create similarly effective political cultures and political institutions. In other words, it is not that the human spirit is more refined or less greedy in the world outside of Africa but rather that greed has been tempered in such places by leadership assertiveness and positive action.

Some observers will continue to aver, however, that corrupt practices in sub-Saharan Africa are merely outgrowths of traditional forms of culturally sanctioned gift-exchanges that respect kinship obligations. As in so much of Africa, loyalties do run to the family and the lineage before the nation or the public. Lineage values trump public values in many polities and situations. But not in all circumstances or all countries. Botswanan presidents never received "back-handers" from international favor-seekers or distributed patronage to relatives and friends. And can Nigeria's 10 percent rule on contracts, or the purchasing by Congo's Mobutu Sese Seko of chateaux in Switzerland, with state funds, be considered culturally approved gift-exchanges?

In Singapore, Lee inherited a small entrepôt state dominated by Chinese triads, Mafia-like gangs. The British colonial police kept order, but without undermining the raffish criminal culture of the place. Lee knew that he had to break the power of the gangs and also to keep the Chinese-dominated Communist movement under control if his reform government were to prosper. So establishing a strict anti-corruption ethic was essential. He signaled his determination by firing the first dozen or so of his associates (deputy prime ministers, cabinet ministers, parastatal corporate bosses, et al.) who were even slightly compromised. Most were subsequently punished by the courts. Those actions together helped to remove the temptation for lesser officials to use their public offices for private gain, especially when punishment was always severe and unforgiving. Lee's leadership gradually triumphed, turning a one-time pirate swamp into an oasis of rectitude (and social conformity).

Khama (1966 to 1980) had an easier task than Lee, for the Bechuanaland Protectorate (now Botswana) under British rule was too poor and too isolated to ever be considered as a particularly corrupt locale. Yet Khama well appreciated the temptations of nearby black-ruled and apartheid-dominated white Africa. He was aware of the destructive nature of the loose practices common in Ghana, Nigeria, Senegal, and even in next-door Zambia. He saw that the "big men" in those contemporary African nations abused their positions to enrich themselves and their cronies, sometimes to an obscene degree. Khama was hence determined from the very beginning of his presidency to follow Lee and to extirpate the notion that African nations necessarily needed to be corrupt. He tried to impose a new paradigm by demonstrating a strong Personal example and by ensuring that his Vice-President and cabinet ministers joined him in setting a proper tone of abstinence. Independence was not, for him or them, to be the route to personal or family enrichment. As his Vice-President and successor wrote, "we worked hard to avoid" being tempted by corruption. Together, they also shamed and prosecuted any high politicians or officials who strayed. (One was Khama's cousin, another was his Vice-president's brother.) Botswana under Khama and Quett Masire consciously continued the British tradition of "properly accounting for things." It fostered open discussion and welcomed complaints from citizens about abuses.[41]

Khama and his successors had also to create a rule-of-law regime that was fair and perceived to be fair. They tried to establish judicial practices that were even-handed and not beholden to dictates from State House. Real power had to be transferred to legislatures since obedient or obsequious parliamentarians would have operated against the nation-building project and severely compromised the message against corrupt dealings. Doing so, and being transparent and accountable, meant for Botswana, as for Mauritius, Cape Verde, the Seychelles, and others, that national resources could be allocated efficiently and managed with a focus on economic growth rather than on personal or family enrichment.

Khama, unlike virtually all of his contemporaries in the then young Africa, lived modestly and avoided motorcades or other forms of ostentation. In impoverished Malawi, by contrast, first under President Hastings Kamuzu Banda and then under his democratic successors, presidential motorcades of extreme length forced ordinary motorists off the streets and highways of their impoverished country for hours at a time. Banda's ministers and most African leaders and officials employed government chauffeurs and insisted on flying first-class. But in Botswana, cabinet ministers traveled by air in economy, not first-class, and initially drove their own automobiles. Masire recounts how, as Vice-President, he arrived for an important meeting in Ethiopia but was so far to the rear of the aircraft that the red carpet that had been rolled out for his reception had been rolled up again by the time that he had emerged at the front of the plane.

Botswana and Rwanda: positive examples

Indeed, what Khama (and Ramgoolam) communicated so well to their constituents was that he and his colleagues were not in office to accrue wealth or power. The motives of other leaders in other African countries could, in contrast, have been misconstrued. Unlike them, Khama and his team were there to serve, to build a new nation from the poverty of the Protectorate. Thus, by way of anti-corruption efforts, a fetish for transparency and accountability, and a firm belief in the efficacy of multi-party democracy, Khama sought to implant values (a political culture) that respected the inherent norms of traditional Botswanan society and religion and rejected the despotic tendencies of so many of his fellow African heads of state. Khama affirmed that he had sought the presidency of Botswana in order to offer "a strong moral and practical compass for the nation."[42] Doing so meant the elimination of corruption.

Khama did more. He established a professional civil service protected by a strong and independent Public Service Commission even when it meant only the gradual application of "affirmative action" for local Botswana. His successors eventually stimulated the printing of the country's first indigenous newspapers, helped to nurture civil society, built an independent university, and tried (sometimes unsuccessfully) to rule temperately and tolerantly over a state that slowly became a nation, with strong, vibrant political institutions. Those institutions now buttress Botswana's democracy and are there to check corruption and other lapses in accountability. Unfortunately, too few of sub-Saharan Africa's countries have reached that level of political maturity. That is the task of this decade.

Rwanda is attempting, rather late, to emulate Botswana and Singapore. Kagame asserts that "You can't fight corruption from the bottom. You have to fight it from the top." He prohibits the employment of his own relatives or relatives of cabinet ministers. He has prosecuted several friends and cabinet ministers for abusing their positions. The police, critical in any catch-up against corrupt practice, are regarded as more professional than in many other African countries. Throughout Kigali, the country's capital, Kagame's administration has erected hoardings opposing corruption, bearing slogans such as "He Who Practices Corruption Destroys His Country." Public officials are required to file annual statements of net worth, to be examined by the embryo nation's ombudsman.[43]

Kagame runs a tightly controlled country; his attempt to stamp out corruption may therefore work, gradually revamping what had been a more common and more African approach to serving oneself while serving the people. Already, ordinary crime levels in Kigali have been vastly reduced and venal corruption is a pursuit of the past. But Rwanda still lacks fully free media and an independent judicial system, so achieving transparency and accountability are jeopardized. Rural big men still demand their due, and dole out favors. In Liberia, too, where President Ellen Johnson Sirleaf has been attempting to dismantle the edifice of corruption that was constructed by the country's Americo-Liberian rulers and then greatly expanded by President Charles Taylor, the battle is difficult even with a vibrant civil society, a mostly free press and radio, and judges who attempt in vain to remain independent.

Although Johnson Sirleaf discharged senior and allegedly corrupt civil servants from key ministries and persuaded Liberia's legislature to pass a Code of Conduct bill regulating behavior of officials, international non-governmental organizations collected credible reports of the persistence of corruption throughout the country. Ghost workers turned up in Grand Cru, finance ministry officials solicited bribes in Nimba, judges and jurors accepted payments in Bomi, well-placed civil servants embezzled in Grand Geddeh, and police everywhere demanded "gifts" from motorists. Liberia's own General Auditing Commission noted the country's "speedy torpedo-like" public thefts.[44] Finally, in late 2012, Leymah Gbowee – the winner of the Nobel Peace Prize along with Johnson-Sirleaf in 2011 – accused her fellow Laureate of herself indulging in corrupt and nepotistic practice. (Johnson Sirleaf's three sons held prominent government posts.) Gbowee resigned as head of the Liberian Peace and Reconciliation Commission and accused Johnson Sirleaf of doing too little to lift Liberia out of poverty and of condoning continued corruption.[45]

Transparency and the media

Transparency and accountability depend on leadership and juridical action. They are enhanced dramatically if a free media helps to disclose possible abuses of the public purse. In Africa, many radio broadcasting stations, from which most Africans obtain their news and views, are tightly controlled by governments. The press is only free, and vigorous in its reporting, in a handful of countries. Yet, no matter how vibrant press and radio reporting might be in those few African countries, without the kinds of financial backing that are still mostly enjoyed in the developed world, editors and journalists often find themselves inhibited and self-censoring. Fairly often, too, they are subject to arrest and torture (as in Zimbabwe and the Sudan), or officially censored.

In South Africa, a mature African country with a history even during apartheid of investigative reporting, in 2011 and 2012, parliament considered new legislation making it a crime to reveal information that the government wanted to keep secret. Despite howls from the official opposition and civil society, the ruling African National Congress (ANC) persisted in wanting to restrict the ability of journalists to report any information that any state agency deemed to be a government secret. That means that South Africa's hitherto active press and private radio could find its politicians and officials much less easy to challenge and hold to account. Critics said that the Orwellian-entitled Protection of State Information Bill was primarily intended to shield corrupt officials from media scrutiny. Nobel Laureate Archbishop Desmond Tutu said that it was "insulting to all South Africans to be asked to stomach legislation that could be used to outlaw whistle-blowing and investigative journalism."[46] Leading independent commentators viewed the bill as just one more attempt by the ANC to curtail media freedom and free expression. Raymond Louw, a veteran anti-apartheid editor, called the law a betrayal of the ANC's commitment to press freedom: "The intention of this bill is to stop the media from disclosing corruption, malpractice and misgovernance, and inefficiencies," nothing less.[47]

In 2012, artistic freedom, or at least the freedom to display art critical of the ruling regime, was again heavily compromised when the ANC went to court to compel a leading Johannesburg art gallery to remove a painting implicitly critical of President Jacob Zuma. The focus of the ANC's complaint was a 6-foot-tall acrylic representation of a man in a Lenin-like heroic pose with his genitals exposed – part of a white artist's exhibition of several new works collectively entitled "Hail to the Thief II." Another canvas featured the ANC logo, with the words "for sale" across it. The gallery in question said that it routinely provided a "neutral space" in which to encourage dialogue and free expression. Gwede Mantashe, an ANC senior leader, called the painting "rude, crude, and disrespectful." An African commentator in a leading Johannesburg newspaper suggested that Zuma's "outsize" sex life made the topic "fair game."[48]

Already there is heavy pressure within all sectors of South African society to conform to the needs of the ruling ANC. The rampant corruption that the country knew after Mandela may have been marginally reduced, but its leaders set no good example and permit everyone of influence, no matter how minor, to take advantage of their public offices and positions. In 2011, the national police czar was found guilty of going easy on high-level drug traffickers. A successor was accused of abusing contract and bid regulations, and removed from office. A cabinet minister with whom he was conspiring was also discharged. President Jacob Zuma is still widely suspected of having received millions of dollars, when he was Deputy-President, from a French firm trying to sell frigates and aircraft. Several of his ministers and the cabinet's official spokesman have been implicated in the same potential scandal. When an influential newspaper tried to run an article in late 2011 about the spokesman's possible bribe-taking, it was suppressed. Mandela's legacy of openness and integrity cannot easily be sustained in a government allegedly dominated by politicians seeking to maximize their opportunities for personal enrichment.[49]

The nature of media freedom in Africa is heavily compromised. It is largely free in Botswana and Namibia; under attack, but still lively, in places such as South Africa, Ghana, Senegal, Liberia, Zambia, Malawi, Tanzania, and Kenya; vibrant and often wild in Nigeria, where corruption flourishes regardless; heavily controlled at a minimum in Burundi, Côte d'Ivoire, Guinea, Rwanda,

Sierra Leone, Togo, Angola, Gabon, Zimbabwe, the Central African Republic, Chad, the Sudan, Ethiopia, Djibouti, South Sudan, and Swaziland; and nonexistent in Cameroon, Equatorial Guinea, the Gambia, and Eritrea.

Reporters without Borders' Press Freedom Index for 2011–12 rates 179 of the world's 194 countries. Eritrea finished dead-last on its list, but a number of other African countries also rank in the bottom fifth: Swaziland (144th), the Congo (Kinshasa), Malawi, Rwanda, Djibouti, Côte d'Ivoire, Equatorial Guinea, and the Sudan. Cape Verde (9th), Namibia (21st), Mali (25th), and Niger (29th) were the highest-ranking African countries. Africa also saw the biggest falls in the index from the previous year. South Africa and Botswana were both rated 42nd. Djibouti, "a discreet little dictatorship" in the Horn of Africa, fell 49 places to 159th. Malawi (146th) fell 67 places because of the totalitarian tendencies of President Bingu wa Mutharika. Uganda fell 43 places to 139th. Finally, Côte d'Ivoire slipped 41 places to 159th because the media were badly hit by the fighting between the supporters of rival presidents Laurent Gbagbo and Alassane Ouattara.[50]

In a far-ranging interview with the Voice of America, President Isaias Afewerki of Eritrea said that he was not interested in preventing people from expressing themselves. But he had to protect his country from "external aggression" by those media people "who take money from outside governments to create chaos and spread misinformation." They were perpetrating "organized sabotage." So-called "democracy" was less important than building up his country.[51]

According to Freedom House and the Committee to Protect Journalists, only a few African countries have a free media: "Many governments are intent on suppressing in-depth journalism."[52] Or, "When you send interview questions, instead of a response, you get contemptuous silence"; "When we publish something, the people concerned will call us not to deny [the details], but to ask who gave us the information. Threaten us."[53] In 2010, the chairman of Cameroon's state petroleum company ordered intelligence agents to arrest four newspaper editors for sending him a series of questions about possible "commissions." One of the editors was tortured, another died in detention, and the remaining two spent nine months under preventive arrest.

In the Gambia, where President Yahya Jammeh was re-elected with 72 percent of the thoroughly orchestrated national vote in 2011, promising to rule for "one billion years," Reporters without Borders says that there is "absolute intolerance of any form of criticism." Death threats and arbitrary middle-of-the-night arrests are the lot of any would-be reporters who "do not sing the government's praises."[54] A journalist who failed to sing properly was killed in 2004.

Even in a usually peaceful and stable country like Senegal, journalists in recent years worked under the threat of lawsuits or newspaper seizures. In 2010, police raided the premises of a leading daily, confiscating printing materials. Journalists at other dailies were convicted of libeling presidential advisors; one served a six-month prison term. Ghanaian and Liberian journalists operated in 2010 and 2011 under some of the same constraints. Burundi arrested journalists in 2010, imprisoning one on a charge of treason. In Rwanda, in the same year, an editor was killed, three journalists were imprisoned for "invasions of privacy," several radio stations and newspapers were shut down, and a number of media workers were imprisoned on criminal charges. In late 2011, a dissident Rwandan journalist was killed by rifle fire late at night in a bar in Uganda, presumably having been hunted down. (Freedom House's Freedom on the Net Report for 2012 concluded that Internet freedom was threatened in Rwanda. In late 2012, the government approved legislation that would enable security and intelligence services to conduct widespread surveillance of email and telephonic communications.[55]) In Côte d'Ivoire, also in late 2011, the new government of President Alassane Ouattara forcibly arrested three reporters for publishing accounts criticizing his government's lavish spending on ministerial perquisites. In Ethiopia, in 2010 and 2011, journalists were jailed, a newspaper was closed down and four others were fined severely. In 2012, an opposition journalist and prominent blogger who had won the United States' prestigious Pen America's Freedom to Write prize and who had questioned the arrest of other journalists was jailed for 18 years as a terrorist. In Swaziland in 2012, the Editor-in-Chief of the *Swazi Observer* was fired because the newspaper exposed the Swazi Prime Minister's corrupt land deals. The editor-in-chief, King Mswati III's former speech writer, also reported on the travails of Swaziland's emerging democracy movement, but his real offense was to provide facts and figures on a number of shady property transfers.[56] In the new nation of South Sudan, an editor and a writer were imprisoned and their newspaper shuttered for suggesting that the President's daughter was unpatriotic for marrying an Ethiopian. In late 2012, a prominent South Sudanese opinion writer for local newspapers and blogs was shot in the face and killed.[57] In the Sudan, even broadcasts from the Voice of America are jammed. The Sudan periodically bans the BBC's Arabic service and closes down independent local radio broadcasters.[58]

Despite a 2009 power-sharing agreement with the opposition, Zimbabwe's dominant Zimbabwe African National Union-Patriotic Front (ZANU-PF) has systematically refused to share the local air waves, keeping television and radio licenses for itself or its nominees. (In 2011, ZANU-PF finally allowed an independent daily newspaper to re-open after firebombing and shuttering it in 2004.) In late 2011, its illegally constituted Broadcasting Authority of Zimbabwe breached a carefully negotiated agreement between the two leading components of the supposed Government of National Unity allowing independent radio stations to compete with the government-controlled monopoly. Instead, the Authority granted licenses to two ZANU-PF front companies and denied the applications of a host of private, unaffiliated, contenders for the potentially lucrative and influential opportunity to supply news and entertainment to the people of Zimbabwe. An opposition commentator called that action "the final nail in the coffin of media plurality in Zimbabwe." Prime Minister Morgan Tsvangirai called the decision a "national joke." It was the result of the responsible ZANU-PF minister's "outright arrogance and intransigence."[59] More so, it underscored the reliance that authoritarian regimes, like those in Mugabe's Zimbabwe, naturally place on managing the news and minimizing transparency and accountability.

So, apparently, does free musical expression in bars threaten autocracy. In 2012, Mugabe's men prohibited singers from performing openly for fear that their lyrics would embarrass the regime. Free media and free expression threaten the fundamental obscurity and secrecy that enable tyrants and tyrannical governments to mislead and cheat their fellow citizens.

Most Africans obtain much of their news from the radio, urban dwellers from television and the press, and the middle class as much from the Internet. Where news is not allowed to be gathered freely, perhaps in two-thirds of Africa, and where investigative reporting is rare, always struggling, and very occasionally flourishing only in South Africa, Nigeria, Kenya, and Zambia (before 2011), the accountability role that media play so well in the developed world has been effectively neutered. Politicians and officials can take advantage of their positions with greater impunity if there is limited or no public oversight. Outrages can and do occur when the media are intimidated or their struggling workers harassed. At the best of times, the media in Africa are anyway under-resourced and overwhelmed with immediate challenges. Conceivably, new kinds of crowd reporting using mobile telephones and innovative web-based technologies will, a decade hence, deliver the kind of oversight that Africa and its politicians so desperately require.

At present, however, Global Integrity (and Freedom House in the case of Rwanda) reports that Africans suffer from occasional Internet censorship (Ethiopia and Cameroon), poor access to government information (Somalia, Cameroon, Tanzania, and Nigeria), and civil services lacking professionalism (Somalia and Angola).[60] Indeed, since Global Integrity could not survey all of sub-Saharan Africa across these three categories, it would be a fair assumption that poor access to official information and weak civil service performance are the norm across much of the continent. Civil servants are under-motivated, poorly paid, aware of how their political masters profit from corrupt practices, and – except in places such as Botswana and Mauritius – disdainful of the rights of the publics that they are employed to serve. Despite the explicit right of all Africans to seek, receive, and impart information, as enshrined in the International Covenant on Civil and Political Rights and the Declaration of Principles on Freedom of Expression in Africa, only seven African countries have enacted legislation granting their publics access to public (government) information. The national constitutions of most sub-Saharan African nations also recognize the right to obtain official information. Nevertheless, information is regarded in too many places as something to be withheld from citizens, not freely shared. Once again, these are long-standing problems addressed best by leadership and governance reforms.

The business atmosphere

Analogous to informational, bureaucratic, and integrity insufficiencies, sub-Saharan Africa has also long lagged other parts of the globe when it comes to "doing business." The World Bank and the IMF have, since the 1990s, asked: How long does it take to set up a business or to deal with construction permits in the nation-states of the world? How long does it take to obtain electric power, register property, secure credit, and resolve questions of insolvency? How well are investors protected? How well are contracts enforced? How fair is taxation? *Doing Business* also measures the time required for, and cost of, exporting and importing a standardized cargo by sea. On these measures, aggregated as "Ease of Doing Business," Singapore, Hong Kong, New Zealand, the United States, and Denmark headed the list of efficient global countries in 2011. South Africa ranked 35th, the highest place for an African country. Rwanda was 45th, Botswana 54th, Ghana 63rd, Namibia 78th, Zambia 84th, and the Seychelles 103rd. At the bottom of the 183 states rated were Angola, Niger, Haiti, Benin, Guinea-Bissau, Venezuela, Congo (Kinshasa), Guinea, Eritrea, Congo (Brazzaville), the Central African Republic, and Chad, in that order from best to worst. In 2011, in Rwanda, an entrepreneur could open a business in 3 days (the global average is 31), following two procedures. In Namibia it took 66 days and ten procedures. In Angola, next door, ranked 172nd, it took 68 days and eight procedures to achieve the same results. Possibly even more troubling than the delays and cumbersome procedures were the costs to entrepreneurs; in Congo (Kinshasa), ranked 178th, it costs 5.5 times the annual average per capita income to open and register a business. Even Kenyans, where the regulations and bureaucratic obstacles are somewhat less onerous, have to pay a secretarial fee of $220 plus heavy legal bills to commence commercial work.[61]

It takes 586 days in Liberia for a new business to be connected to the national electrical grid. The average for sub-Saharan Africa is 137 days. Rwanda, Namibia, Cape Verde, Ghana and Ethiopia do better, at 30, 55, 58, 78, and 95 days, respectively. But in prosperous Gabon, the number of days for a connection is 160, in relatively well-off Kenya 163, in Malawi 244, and in Madagascar 450. It is hard to be competitive if a new business cannot link itself to stable power for more than a year, or if electricity from the grid is only available intermittently, as in so many African countries. (See chapter 7.)[62]

Many sub-Saharan African countries also tie themselves and their investors up in red tape. An American company had to forgo a $120 million investment in a bathroom products factory because it was only allowed to import specified kinds of paper. It took a year for an airline to be allowed to fly from

Atlanta to Lagos. A survey by the International Finance Corporation (a sub-
sidiary of the World Bank) ranked Nigeria 178th out of 183 global countries
in terms of the ease of transferring (buying and selling) property. In some of
Nigeria's states, governors must personally approve every property transaction – and for a fee.[63]

There are obstacles to intercontinental and intra-sub-continental trade, too,
which impede growth prospects across sub-Saharan Africa. Many occur
between countries, at borders, despite abundant agreements meant to facilitate trade in goods and services among the separate nations of Africa. At the
border between Rwanda and the Democratic Republic of Congo, for example,
there are 17 agencies, each asking for paperwork and, sometimes, payments
from those who are trying to bring goods from one of the countries to the
other. A South African supermarket chain with branches in Zambia spends
$20,000 a week just on permits. "If a firm has to spend a lot of resources on
paperwork . . . if their trucks [lorries] spend a long [time] waiting at the
border because the processing of . . . documents [is slow] . . . then that's
passed on to the consumer in terms of high prices."[64] Concerted efforts to
simplify border procedures and improve regional trade integration with
deeds, not just words, would strengthen commerce throughout the
sub-continent.

The 2011 African Competitiveness Report of the World Economic Forum,
the World Bank, and the African Development Bank ranked South Africa
(54th globally), Mauritius (55th), Namibia (74th), Botswana (76th), and Rwanda
(80th) at the top of its African listings. Burkina Faso, Mauritania, Zimbabwe,
Burundi, Angola, and Chad (134th–139th globally, respectively) were the least
competitive African countries. (Competitiveness here means "the set of institutions, policies, and factors that determine the level of productivity of a
country.") These results, together with those for *Doing Business*, reflect sub-
Saharan Africa's perceived weak regard for corporate endeavors (and "free
enterprise") and its failure to be as successfully productive as similar low- or
medium-income regions in Asia or Latin America. Indeed, only South Africa,
Mauritius, and Namibia score above the North African competitiveness
average of 4.1. (The Southeast Asian competitiveness average was 4.3.)
Botswana ranked above the Latin American and Caribbean average of 4.0,
whereas the sub-Saharan African average for competitiveness was 3.5.
Zimbabwe's poor rating was 3.0.[65]

The findings of the *Global Entrepreneurship Monitor's* (*GEM's*) examination of
a handful of important sub-Saharan African countries in 2010 (the 2011
review only included South Africa) confirm many of the wry conclusions of
the Competitiveness Report and *Doing Business*. The *GEM* measures entrepreneurial attitudes, activities, and aspirations within a country. Its premise is
that any economy's prosperity is highly dependent upon dynamic local entre-
preneurialism. So it analyzes "individual involvement in venture creation,"
not firm-level data.

GEM found that there are abundant entrepreneurs, mostly young ones, in sub-Saharan Africa, as casual observers would have noted. They comprise and populate the informal sector, which thrives and must try to thrive when formal-sector jobs are few and prevailing social safety nets have holes. Most of these entrepreneurs are driven by necessity rather than opportunity, so they are compelled by parlous circumstances, rather than innate drive, to scrabble for gainful pursuits and income. But what is different in sub-Saharan Africa, as compared to Southeast Asia and other parts of the world, is that very few of these individual entrepreneurs go on to establish small businesses. They usually work only for themselves, and inconsistently. Indeed, few stay in business for themselves very long.

In the factor-driven economies of sub-Saharan Africa surveyed by GEM – Angola, Zambia, Uganda, Ghana – as opposed to the efficiency-driven economy of South Africa (and those of Costa Rica, Croatia, Macedonia, and Turkey), only 2 or 3 percent of the entrepreneurs interviewed expected to create much employment for others. South Africans, Croatians, and Latvians, however, anticipated building small firms of 20 or more employees; nearly 20 percent of Turkish entrepreneurs planned to enlarge their activities on that scale or something larger.[66] These differences between South Africa and Angola et al. reflect structural impediments to the scaling-up of entrepreneurship, not a lack of drive on the part of individuals. Chinese employers in Africa claim that Africans are "lazy," but the GEM data show instead that little businesses have a difficult time growing when governance is low, corruption high, the money and banking system worrisome, inexpensive credit mostly unavailable, roads lack maintenance, and Safety and Security are marginal.

Africa is less well banked than it should be. In 2011, only one in five Nigerians had a bank deposit, and only 15 percent of women had their own accounts. (There are many more mobile telephones in sub-Saharan Africa than there are bank accounts.) Bank branches were mostly located in the big cities of Lagos and Abuja, with smaller cities and rural areas being largely unbanked. Even much-touted microfinance banks were more often located in the big cities than in rural areas. Nearly 70 percent of Nigeria's currency circulated outside the banking system. Its ratio of bank deposits to GDP was unusually low for a developing world economy. This problem was compounded by the decisive manner in which Nigeria's banks favor lending to the federal and the state governments, not to small- and medium-sized enterprises or to ordinary consumers. Africa's most populous country therefore operated on a cash-and-carry basis, with relatively little lending outside government. "The contribution of the financial sector," says one knowledgeable critic and former national official, "to the GDP without government deposits is below 15 percent – far below what is obtainable in . . . other countries of similar standing." He concluded that the Nigerian financial sector functioned primarily, and debilitatingly from a developmental point of view, as a channel for capturing government deposits and recycling them primarily to purchase government debt. It was the reverse of what was needed for "vibrant economic growth."[67] Indeed, the weaknesses of Nigeria's financial sector prevent easy relief by individuals or government action from poverty. Credit simply is limited and economic stagnation more the norm than it ought to be in an oil-fueled economy. The Nigerian example is also mirrored more than it should be elsewhere in Africa north of South Africa and Botswana.

Another method of measuring the utilization (and reliability) of financial institutions in nation-states is to assess Contract Intensive Money, using the International Monetary Fund's International Financial Statistics. Contract Intensive Money (CIM) is the ratio of non-currency money to a nation's total money supply, or M2-C. The closer the CIM value is to 1, the more money is likely to be held in the form of bank deposits rather than floating currency. When this happens, individuals regard financial institutions in their country to be comparatively safe and reliable. Doing so also implies relatively more secure property rights and an ability to enforce contracts. Low CIM values suggest little faith in banks and contracts, with individuals preferring instead to hold their assets as currency, or "in mattresses," the African pattern. Whereas most developed countries approach 1 in their CIM scores, most developing countries show ratios from 0.3 to 0.9. In Africa in 2009 those values ranged from 0.37 in Guinea-Bissau to 0.97 in Botswana and Namibia, with an average across Africa of 0.78. South Africa, Swaziland, Mauritius, and Lesotho were near in scores to Botswana and Namibia with values of 0.92 to 0.96, respectively. Nigeria fell in the middle, with a CIM score of 0.86. Clustering near Guinea-Bissau were Chad, the Central African Republic, and the Comoros, the last with a score of 0.60.[68]

The rule of law

Weak, stressed, poorly competitive and corporate-unfriendly low-income polities with weak arteries of commerce – like most of the sub-Saharan ones – further suffer from rule-of-law regimes that are rarely well resourced, hardly ever independent, and only in a few countries capable of imposing their decisions on recalcitrant legislatures or executives. The supremacy of constitutional safeguards, as interpreted by supreme or constitutional courts, has been established in only a few places, such as Botswana and Mauritius (where there still is a final appeal to the British Privy Council), and South Africa, Namibia, and Ghana. In South Africa, the Constitutional Court that President Mandela was so pleased to establish and fill with well-regarded appointees is now very much under threat from the ANC. When that tribunal, or one of South Africa's other higher courts, hands down a ruling that annoys the ANC, one or another leading ANC politician complains that the judges (most of whom are now African) are "counter-revolutionary." Or they are said to be "untransformed." President Zuma has complained of "judicial interference in the functions of the executive branch;" the courts were said to be "encroaching" on the other two branches of government and of attempting to "co-govern" through the courts. Zuma's cabinet in 2011 decided that it would "assess" the courts to decide whether their rulings advanced the goals of "development" and "racial transformation."[69] In other places, judges attempt to fulfill their traditional mandates of fairness and impartiality but, for so many, the pressures from presidents, ministers, security officials, and politicians are relentless. Poorly paid and overworked, they are thus often tempted to lean their judgments one way or another in exchange for appropriate considerations. Along with Zuma and the ANC in South Africa, many of Africa's much more challenged and compromised states seek compliant, not impartial, judges.

The picture is not pretty. In 2012, the World Justice Project's World Law Index rated 97 countries world-wide, including 18 sub-Saharan African ones. It examined eight categories of law in each country, including scores for effective criminal justice, access to civil justice, fundamental rights, and open government. There was no evaluation of judicial independence, possibly because the levels of such independence are difficult to establish. Nor was there a measure showing how well contracts were enforced. In any event, most of the African countries, unsurprisingly, scored below the half-way mark on all eight indicators, some at the very bottom for most. Botswana scored best in the region, although its criminal justice system worked slowly and its correctional facilities were poor. Ghana and Senegal were strong performers. Malawi was praised for its judicial independence, civil justice capabilities, and its relative lack of corruption. But Burkina Faso, Cameroon, Côte d'Ivoire, Ethiopia, Kenya, Madagascar, and Nigeria were downrated because of heavy corruption and limited governmental accountability. South Africa's criminal justice system was called "ineffective." Zambia's legislature and judiciary were deemed "vulnerable to government interference." Uganda had little governmental accountability and Zimbabwe was labeled "among the weakest performers worldwide" across most dimensions of the rule of law.[70] African states with good governance, as minimally indicated by comparatively strong rule-of-law regimes, are more prosperous, more peaceful, and better deliverers of essential services than those with low rule-of-law scores.

In 2009 (and before), the Index of African Governance rated all of the countries of Africa on judicial independence, court efficacy, and contract rights and enforcement. It ranked Cape Verde, Mauritius, Botswana, Ghana, Benin, São Tomé and Príncipe, and South Africa at the very top for judicial independence, and Congo (Kinshasa), the Sudan, Somalia, Chad, Equatorial Guinea, Eritrea, and Zimbabwe at the very bottom. With regard to court efficacy, based on a study of the length of time detainees typically awaited trial, Namibia, the Sudan, Botswana, the Gambia, and Lesotho led the list, with Liberia, Niger, Congo (Kinshasa), Benin, and Burundi bringing up the rear. The Index ranked Botswana, Cape Verde, Ghana, Madagascar, Mauritius, Senegal, the Seychelles, South Africa, and Swaziland as the countries most respectful of private property. The two Congos were at the bottom of this measure, together with Somalia, Eritrea, the Central African Republic, Guinea-Bissau, Liberia, and Zimbabwe. Contract disputes were settled fastest through the courts, the Index reported, in Namibia, Guinea, Mauritania, Rwanda, and Eritrea, and slowest in Djibouti, Gabon, Guinea-Bissau, Liberia, São Tomé and Príncipe, and Angola.

A glimpse of the raw data for these measurements, especially for judicial independence, shows that two-thirds of the sub-Saharan African countries made no pretense of giving independence to its judges.[71] In other words, across Africa's weak and potentially failing states, citizens cannot look to their courts for much by way of real redress in terms of civil remedies or criminal justice. Settling disputes violently, by the law of might, or according to executive preference, still prevails more than Africa's emerging middle class would like. Until the citizens of Africa can all expect the kinds of judicial fairness that by and large prevail in Botswana, Cape Verde, Ghana, South Africa, and Mauritius, modernization and economic development in much of sub-Saharan Africa will remain limited. It will remain hard to attract meaningful foreign direct investment outside of the petroleum and mineral extraction arenas, aside from that which arrives from China. Domestic investment and re-investment will be restrained, too, as long as contract disputes continue to be hard to adjudicate fairly and quickly.

A robust rule of law is essential to good governance everywhere, no less in Africa.[72] Wherever rule-of-law regimes are weak, oversight by media is challenged, and corruption prevails, there are few escapes for the poor. Even the advances that the middle class wants and expects will prove difficult. Opportunities for social advancement will be wasted, if not forfeited. Once again, Africa will look to its more successful countries for guidance on these issues. Where good governance persists, founded originally on the initiative of exemplary leadership, prosperity and rising living standards have followed. The more challenged African countries can catch up, as their middle classes desire, when and only when the new and awakened leadership feels ready to replace the drive for immediate financial enrichment with exemplary service to the public good.

7
The Infrastructural Imperative

To grow economically – as sub-Saharan Africa must if it is to meet the aspirations of its inhabitants (especially the burgeoning middle class) and provide well for them as they swell exponentially in number over coming decades – the large and small countries of the sub-continent must overcome great infrastructural handicaps. Despite energetic construction efforts in recent years almost everywhere in Africa by Chinese state and private firms, most of sub-Saharan Africa still lacks a robust transportation network and sufficient generating capacity to power its existing – much less its future – industrial and consumer requirements. Even if it could rapidly erect electrical plants, transmitting such new supplies over the necessary long distances would present a further difficulty. Sub-Saharan Africa is woefully short of energy and deficient in paved and maintained roads, railways, adequate harbors and airports, land-line telephones (largely obsolete), and the availability of fast broadband Internet access. Sub-Saharan Africa has reached this parlous place in its infrastructural provisioning by failing over decades of misrule to invest and re-invest in these vital components of economic viability. Even large and prosperous countries such as South Africa, Ghana, and Nigeria have fallen way behind the infrastructural demands of their own growth plans. A report a half-decade ago indicated that even the most successful sub-Saharan African states had "outrun" their available power supplies and that many had road and rail networks "inadequate" for the industrial and agricultural growth on which their economic advances depended.[1] Now those inadequacies are being remedied, but possibly too slowly. Moreover, without ongoing Chinese efforts, these nations and many others would find themselves in even deeper energy, transportation, and infrastructural deficit. The task of this decade is to catch up – to prepare the infrastructure of sub-Saharan Africa to meet the needs of the remainder of the twenty-first century.

Energy considerations

The statistics are daunting, and stark. Only 25 percent of sub-Saharan Africa's total inhabitants have regular access to electric power. (About 83 percent of sub-Saharan Africans rely on solid biomass energy sources for cooking and heating.) Only 10 percent of rural sub-Saharan Africans use electric power on a regular basis. Elsewhere, 5 percent of all Asians and 80 percent of all South Americans have that access now, and the gap between continental populations is growing wider. According to the World Bank, only 40 percent of African countries will offer their citizens universal availability of electricity by 2050, long after nearly all of Asia and all of South America will have achieved almost full service.[2] It is hard for citizens, wherever they live, to enjoy the benefits of modern life without regular and nearly full-time access to electric power.

Whereas South Africa provides access to electricity to 75 percent of its people and Nigeria 47 percent, Ethiopia and Kenya have only 15 percent electricity cover, Mozambique 12 percent, and Rwanda 5 percent. In the rural areas of those same representative countries, the percentages of people who receive electricity from the national grid (respectively) are 55 percent, 26 percent, 2 percent, 5 percent, 6 percent, and 1 percent. On a per-capita basis, which is much more telling and instructive for these selected African countries and for sub-Saharan Africa as a whole, South Africa consumes nearly 5,000 kwh per annum, Mozambique 472 kwh, Kenya 151 kwh, Nigeria 137 kwh, Ethiopia 40 kwh, and Rwanda 20 kwh.[3] Those yearly per-capita figures are a proxy for the attainment of modernity. Most other global villagers outside of Africa enjoy this essential amenity.

Rwanda wants to become Africa's Singapore, but – to take an extreme case – its installed power capacity is a minuscule 75 MW. That limited power availability is, as in so many other sub-Saharan African states, a major detriment even to the limited realization of industrialization and agro-processing aspirations. It also severely reduces Rwanda's ambitions to become a Central African transport hub, to reduce the country's dependence on its East African neighbors, and to modernize generally. Electricity is also costly, at $0.18 per kwh (17 times typical American charges).[4] As a result of both shortages and expense, most of Rwanda outside of Kigali is habitually dark.

In 2008, the entire generating capacity of sub-Saharan Africa was a mere 68 gigawatts (68,000 MW), roughly equivalent to that of Spain. Excluding South Africa, with 40 gigawatts on its own, the remainder of sub-Saharan Africa could only count on the availability of 28 gigawatts, the amount then available to Argentinians. Moreover, in 2008, about 25 percent of the 28 GW installed capacity was often unavailable, thanks to aging plants and insufficient maintenance. With the failure over several years of normal rains, hydroelectric schemes also lacked water and, hence, generating ability, especially in Ghana and Uganda.

On a per-capita basis in 2008, sub-Saharan Africa could rely on less than a third of the electrical power available to South Asians. (Long ago, in 1980, the two regions had equal power resources per head.) In 2008, sub-Saharan Africans only enjoyed a tenth as much electrical generating capacity as Latin Americans. What has happened, obviously, is that sub-Saharan African electrical power installed capacities have increased much more slowly than else-where in the world. Indeed, outside of South Africa, per capita consumption of power in sub-Saharan Africa has declined since the last century. Since the era of independence, sub-Saharan Africa's relative share of global energy availability has fallen substantially. The World Bank suggests that energy supplies should grow as fast as a national economy if demand for power is to be met. But sub-Saharan Africa's power capacity has trailed growth rates by about 2 percent a year since 1980. The Bank also indicates that, if African countries were to improve their electrical capacities and availabilities to the level of Mauritius, the best among sub-Saharan polities, the region would grow at an additional 2.2 percent a year.[5]

Consequently, in 2008 sub-Saharan per capita consumption of electricity per year averaged 457 kwh. Without South Africa, that figure fell to 124 kwh. High-income countries consume power at the per capita annual rate of 10,198 kwh. The average across all developing countries is 1,155 kwh. From another vantage point, sub-Saharan Africa constitutes 18 percent of the globe's land mass and 12 percent of its total people but only produces 2 percent of the world's power. The Democratic Republic of Congo, with abun-dant potential hydroelectric resources, today provides electricity to a mere 6 percent of its 67 million people. The national, near-bankrupt, power monop-oly serves only 400,000 people, but 20 large mostly mining enterprises consume 50 percent of the total distributed along antiquated transmission lines. In Kenya, 48 percent of urban and only 4 percent of rural households were connected to the national grid in 2011, but the country hopes to step this up to 100 percent urban connectivity and 32 percent rural by 2015. Tanzania hopes to supply electricity to 63 percent of its urban population and 2 percent of potential rural customers by 2015. Zimbabwe, a country of 10 million people, in 2012 required at least 2,000 megawatts a year of steady electrical power to enable its economy to grow and new industrial projects to proceed. But, heavily in debt to the regional grid, it was only producing 800 megawatts a year from its own plants; its Minister of Finance also asserted that the country needed not 2,000 MW, but more likely 4,000 MW a year to recover from its great loss of income and jobs throughout the first decade of the twenty-first century.[6]

Reliability is another issue. Many sub-Saharan African countries operate their energy grids at less than half their installed capacities thanks to inad-equate maintenance and decades of under-investment. Across the sub-conti-nent, power outages are frequent, in many countries amounting to an average of 56 days a year without electricity. The use of back-up diesel-powered gen-erators is common where and when they can be afforded by businesses or individuals. Load-shedding is often resorted to by suppliers, and has been particularly frequent and damaging, especially in South Africa in 2007–2008. In Zimbabwe in early 2012, some sections of Harare, the capital, and Bulawayo, its second city, endured rolling blackouts almost every day. At least 35 percent of Zimbabwe's installed capacity was not working. Compounding the problem was the refusal or inability of customers, including government departments, cabinet ministers, and citizens, to pay their bills to the government-owned electricity company. President Robert Mugabe and his family owed at least $345,000 of the total millions of dollars in arrears.[7] Rationing of power was common in Kenya, Rwanda, Tanzania, and Uganda in 2011.

Nigeria, the seventh most populous global country now and the seventh-largest oil exporter, typically only produces enough power each day to power a city the size of Britain's Bradford. As a result, Nigeria has long endured intermittent blackouts of electricity in its cities, and even in such vital places as its main international airport in Lagos, which was without power for as long as six hours on many occasions during 2012. Nigeria is the world's largest purchaser of home generators.[8]

Fortunately, beginning about 2010, South Africa and the rest of sub-Saharan Africa realized how far behind their power needs they were. From their own budgets, with assistance from donors, and by enlisting public–private partnerships, they began to invest in the necessary generating capacity. At about the same time, large discoveries of natural gas off the coasts of Africa began to be made, new petroleum resources (offshore and onshore) were found, and the utilization of existing but hitherto unexploited coal deposits started in earnest. Among the largest discoveries of natural gas were those straddling the Tanzanian and Mozambican border, providing ample potential prosperity for both energy-poor countries. Namibia in 2012 found offshore oil and gas. Ethiopia may also have a big gas field under the Ogaden desert, and in 2012 there were rumors that similar deposits of natural gas were available beneath the sands of Somalia. In 2012, a massive oil strike in north-western Kenya also gave hope to another energy-anxious country. South Africa refurbished old coal-burning thermal plants and began constructing new ones. (South Africa holds about 90 percent of the sub-Saharan African 55 billion tons of coal deposits suitable for thermal generating, but Mozambique and Botswana also are exploiting their own supplies. Indeed, the coal fields near Tete, in Mozambique, now appear much more extensive than previously thought.) Botswana constructed a 600 MW thermal plant, Morupule B, near Palapye in 2012. It uses locally mined coal. In 2012, Zimbabwe tried to repair its aging Hwange coal-fired generators, which the government had previously permitted to fail.

These patchwork efforts have been necessary, but insufficient. The cost of oil- and coal-fired electricity is higher than hydro-generation. That reality makes the average expense of power in sub-Saharan Africa formidable – about twice that ($0.13 per kwh) elsewhere in the world. Even so, customers in the region do not pay the full price of power; some countries such as Zambia, Cameroon, Ghana, and Mozambique have long subsidized their copper and aluminum industries. Others subsidize household consumers for political reasons. Thus, in order to compete industrially and to allow its citizens to consume more power, sub-Saharan Africa must find ways to both increase supply and lower average charges.

All of this new attention to the energy infrastructure will eventually make a difference. New thermal installations have become operational since the dark days a few years ago. But those countries such as Ghana and Uganda which suffered acutely in 2006 and 2007 from water shortages and thus an inability to generate hydro-power as thoroughly as before must still depend on rainfall for reliable and less expensive electricity generation. Indeed, new hydro-power possibilities are likely to transform the availability and price of electric power in much of sub-Saharan Africa and to relieve or substantially to alleviate the shortfalls of recent decades. About 90 percent of Africa's power potential is in water flowing down its several major and many minor rivers. But weather fluctuations, climate change variability, and unexpected periods of severe drought may make sub-Saharan Africa's increasing reliance on water-generated electrical energy an unreliable proposition. Additionally, in the tropics evapotranspiration losses are always high. The immense reservoirs behind all of Africa's dams end up causing the forfeiture of vast quantities of water in a water-short environment. Sub-Saharan Africa cannot afford to waste water; nor can it grow without abundant supplies of power, preferably available routinely.

Hydroelectricity and new dam projects

There are massive hydro projects everywhere, most supported by China, a few assisted by Arab wealth funds, and the remainder backed by the World Bank and the African Development Bank. The two largest and potentially most transformative are in Ethiopia and the Democratic Republic of Congo, where water flows are abundant and largely unimpeded.[9]

Ethiopia should have ready for operation in 2015 or later the largest hydro facility in all of Africa. Meant to produce 6000 MW, more than double the output of the Aswan Dam in Egypt, the $5 billion Grand Ethiopian Renaissance Dam will flood 1,700 sq. km of forest along Ethiopia's border with the Sudan and create a reservoir twice as large as Lake Tana. Once built, it will multiply Ethiopia's installed electric capacity fivefold. But Prime Minister Meles Zenawi had not yet secured firm external funding sources at his death in 2012. The World Bank and private consortia have refused to help, and China was hesitating because Ethiopia, a very poor country, had refused to negotiate deals with neighboring countries or with companies capable of purchasing its surplus power. Furthermore, how this serious impoundment of the abundant flow of the Blue Nile will affect water supplies in the Sudan and Egypt is not yet determined, but the downstream neighbors are worried.

Ethiopia already generates power in its south, from two Gilgel Gebe dams on the Omo River, which drains into Lake Turkana. The Chinese are paying $1.75 billion for a third, massive 1,870 MW Gilgel Gebe dam after the World

Bank and other donors rejected supporting it because of severe environmental and social concerns, and are considering a fourth project there. Human Rights Watch claimed in 2012 that Ethiopia was forcibly relocating up to 200,000 nearby local citizens from the Omo River valley in order to construct state sugar plantations 0.25 million hectares in extent using irrigation water from behind the dam, and its new power.[10] China recently constructed the 185-meter tall Tekeze dam, which produces 300 MW, and is finishing a 100 MW dam on the Neshi River. If, along with these other new installations, the Grand Renaissance dam succeeds in powering all of Ethiopia's needs, and earning revenue from exporting surplus electricity, Ethiopia could in theory construct three more dams along the Blue Nile and earn further significant amounts from its fast-flowing and steep-falling water supplies.

There have been dreams of dams along the Nile River in the nearby northern Sudan for centuries. After the Aswan dam was constructed in Egypt during the Cold War, Sudanese governments imagined building their own hydroelectric facilities. Now the rushing waters of the second, third, and fourth cataracts of the Nile in northern Sudan – prime Nubian territory – have all been interrupted by the construction of dams, the massive displacement of people, and the submerging of 500 to 1,000 irreplaceable archaeological sites. The second cataract carries the new 400 MW Dal dam. A large number of Sudanese had to be displaced when the government and China decided to construct yet a further large dam on the third cataract of the Nile. The so-called Kajbar dam has submerged 90 villages, forced 10,000 Nubians to move, and created a 110 sq km reservoir. When finished in 2015, Kajbar will generate 360 MW per year of power

South of both of these edifices is the Merowe dam, costing $1.8 billion and completed by Chinese, French, and German firms in 2010. It is capable of delivering 1,250 MW of electricity when fully operational. Fifty thousand people were displaced to build the dam and its 174-km-long reservoir. Now the Chinese are also slated to build a new dam on the fifth cataract of the Nile. Called Shereik, it is designed to produce 420 MW a year. Together, these four mighty dams will make the Sudan electricity-sufficient, with large supplies for profitable export to Egypt and, conceivably, North Africa and the Middle East. But the people and heritage costs have been immense. Moreover, to keep these new hydro facilities turning, the waters of the Nile must continue to flow smoothly and strongly. Ethiopia's damming of the Blue Nile, upstream, may make the Sudan's investments, and even Egypt's at Aswan, questionable. On the Upper Atbara River in eastern Sudan, the Chinese are building one more facility that will bring power to this long-neglected region near the Red Sea and perhaps produce surpluses capable of powering neighboring Eritrea.

Much farther up the White Nile are two dams in Uganda – the 250 MW Bujagali structure (downstream from Jinja and two existing smaller hydro-generating facilities) and the 700 MW Karuma edifice (south of Gulu as the

Victoria Nile bends toward Lake Albert). At a cost of $1 billion and $2.2 billion (and growing), respectively, both facilities together are intended to erase Uganda's existing 160 MW power shortfall (as of 2012). But Karuma may not come fully on-stream until the end of the decade. When Bujagali is completely operational in 2013, there will still be a small difference between what will then be an even greater demand and installed capacity. With Karuma, Uganda may have sufficient electricity by the end of the decade and beyond, but not for long, as its population numbers soar.

An even larger scheme than the one on the Blue Nile is being contemplated in the Democratic Republic of Congo. The massive Inga dam complex on the Congo River between Kinshasa and the mouth of the river could conceivably be expanded from its current 1,175 MW to at least 39,000 MW, at a cost of $80 billion, but formidable amounts of outside and local finance will have to be located. If its construction is eventually realized, "Grand" Inga would produce three times more power than the giant Three Gorges dam complex on the Yangtse River in China. It would also then be producing fully a third of all of sub-Saharan Africa's power. However, in 2012, only the existing Inga 1 and Inga 2 dams were being operated, and both are busily being rehabilitated after being allowed, during the later Mobutu and the first Kabila presidencies, to deteriorate substantially. As a short-term partial remedy for southern Africa's energy shortages, there also exists a scheme to build Inga 3, a 3,500 MW facility capable, when up and running, of adding meaningfully to the power available through the southern African grid.

Since the 1970s, the Cahora Bassa dam and hydroelectric facility upstream from Tete, Mozambique, on the middle Zambezi River, has produced about 2,125 MW of electricity a year, most of which has been sold to South Africa via a 1,400-kilometer-long high-voltage transmission line. Cahora Bassa also supplies power to Mozambique (with its coal mines and aluminium smelters), to Zimbabwe (which had massive unpaid arrears in 2012), and the Southern African Power Pool. In late 2012, Mozambique was contemplating constructing, with Chinese assistance, the Mphanda Nkuwa dam, downstream from Cahora Bassa. Unfortunately, its critics say that erecting Mphanda Nkuwa will require Cahora Bassa to operate according to its current "destructive release patterns, and make downstream restoration very difficult." The dam could also worsen downstream environmental damage by causing daily fluctuations in river levels, and by reducing the natural flow of river sediments, which are critical to the health of the Zambezi delta. Chinese and Brazilian funding is also being made available for the Boa Maria dam on the Pungue River – the first significant structure on the Pungue, which, like Mphanda Nkuwa, is expected to have severe negative effects on the water flow into and through the Zambezi Delta.[11]

Upstream from Cahora Bassa are 30 dams and large storage reservoirs on the middle and upper Zambezi River and its major Kafue River tributary. Together, they largely have stopped the annual floods on both rivers, created environmental damage, and caused human disturbance throughout the length of the Zambezi basin. The oldest and largest of these hydroelectric facilities is the $600 million Kariba dam spanning the river between Zambia and Zimbabwe at the head of an impoundment reservoir 280 km (174 miles) long. Because the Zimbabwean turbines were maintained poorly by President Robert Mugabe's government in the early years of this century, the Zimbabwean side of Kariba has for many years produced half or less of its capacity of 705 MW. The slightly newer Zambian plant on the northern side of the river produces 614 MW a year.

At a major bend on the middle Kafue River, the Itezhi-Tezhi hydroelectric facility will produce 120 KW a year after new turbines are installed in 2013. Originally, the Itezhi-Tezhi dam was intended only to impound water and then slowly to release it to the Kafue Gorge dam 260 km downstream on the Kafue River. That dam was situated where large river impoundment operations were impossible. The Upper Gorge facility has for decades generated 900 MW of electricity a year. A Lower Gorge scheme, now being constructed by the Chinese, could add another 660 MW to Zambia's overall capacity.

Also in southern Africa, the Kunene River along the Angolan-Namibian border offers potential sites for new hydroelectricity-producing dams. Three installations are proposed, from west to east, at: Baynes, Epupa, and the second Ruacana (one exists already, with an installed capacity of 120 MW). Together with the existing Ruacana installation, they could together produce 200 MW – but not without greatly disadvantaging the local semi-nomadic Himba people and losing (wasting) large amounts of impounded water through evaporation in a country terribly short of potable supplies.

There are existing dams and water diversion aqueducts in the highlands of Lesotho, where the Orange River forms and rushes out of the Drakensberg massif. Not for itself, but to sell energy to South Africa, Lesotho is constructing a further structure – the 165 KW Polihali dam project. It will displace thousands of villagers, substantially reduce the flow of the Orange River, and succeed in supplying large amounts of water to Gauteng Province – South Africa's industrial heartland – without significantly reducing southern Africa's overall energy shortfalls. Nevertheless, the country's Highlands Water Project already meets 90 percent of Lesotho's current power demand as well as sending significant amounts of water to Gauteng. Polihali should supply 100 percent of local needs for a few years, anyway, as well as help to meet Gauteng's apparently insatiable demands for both water and power.

In West Africa, where the terrain is less rugged and water flows are generally more sluggish, there are still a number of hydroelectrical generating possibilities. On the Niger River, at Mambilla north of Abuja in Taraba State in Nigeria, the Chinese and others are spending $4 billion to finance a dam and impoundment reservoir which, when completed in 2018, promises to double the country's existing power supplies by adding 2,600 MW of installed capacity. When the dam is constructed, Nigeria will be less dependent upon petroleum-fired facilities and much more able to offer power to new industries and the growing consumer market.

Although the development of Ghana has in recent decades been severely hampered by energy shortages and energy rationing brought about by low water levels behind the Volta dam, the Volta River Authority has identified 16 possible sites along that river for new hydrogenerating projects. Backed by China, the government is also building the Bui dam on the Upper Black Volta River. It will flood a quarter of a national park, destroy habitat for rare hippos, and bring about the forcible resettlement of thousands of citizens. But, if it rains and if water continues to flow, it promises to add 400 MW to Ghana's erratic electrical supply, beginning in 2013.

Farther south, in Gabon, the Chinese are constructing two hydroelectric dams capable of producing electricity sufficient to power an iron-ore mining operation that will send its production to China via a Chinese-constructed railway and a Chinese-developed port. The first, the Belinga dam, is situated 500 km east of Libreville. The second, the Grand Poubara dam in the country's far southeast, is designed to generate power for a Chinese-run manganese mine.

The Chinese also supported a dam in the Republic of Congo (Brazzaville) across the Lefini River, a tributary of the Congo River. The Imboulou dam, completed in 2012, generates 120 MW and will supply the energy needs of the upper half of the country.

Smaller, local hydro projects are also bound to be important for sub-Saharan Africa. It is at least possible to envisage a time in Africa when power needs will be met more locally than centrally – when decentralized distributed energy generation (hydro and non-hydro) will play a much larger role in satisfying Africa's (particularly rural Africa's) electricity needs than it does at present. Although China alone has 45,000 micro-hydro plants below 10 MW in capacity, sub-Saharan Africa has a mere 150. Yet it has the potential for many thousands of such affordable and helpful local power delivery systems based on river flows. Rwanda, with 36 plants either constructed or planned, has been among the African leaders of micro-hydro installation, along with Kenya, Ethiopia, and South Africa. Ethiopia alone has 12 watersheds currently unexploited for hydropower. Uganda, Mozambique, and Zambia also have many sites with a high potential for development. Malawi is planning 15 projects. Some of these countries will build upon or restore decommissioned operations from the colonial era. China is also involved, and its "Light-Up Rural Africa" program has sought to install numerous pico- as well as micro-hydro plants.

Solar and wind alternatives

Electricity generation from solar installations ought to be another alternative for sub-Saharan Africa. For at least half of any year, most sections of the sub-continent can count on abundant sun and clear skies. Even during the rainy season, the skies often clear and the equatorial sun is powerful. Many African countries enjoy 325 days per year of bright sunlight. Each square kilometer of 80 percent of Africa, to take another measure, receives 2,000 kwh a year of energy from the sun. But solar power has so far attracted limited investment in Africa. For a family home, the installation costs ($500 to $1,000) are prohibitive. Yet many small businesses find purchasing and maintaining photo-voltaic panels less expensive than purchasing kerosene (paraffin); there are successful operations in eastern Zambia which may prove a model for other sections of the sub-continent. In Zambia, too, its high-end tourist industry of bush camps depends almost entirely on solar power. On a much larger scale, there is one major project in South Africa and three small- to medium-size solar plants being constructed in Rwanda, the Gambia, and Sierra Leone. On a smaller scale, there are hundreds of solar-powered pumping stations, especially in the Sudan, and even in Chad. Obviously, the potential for many more small- and medium-sized experiments exists. So does the scaling-up to much larger projects to supply power to national grids.

The South African plant, due to come on-stream in 2013, is meant to be the largest solar capture project in the world. Using an array of mirrors and solar panels, and costing $25 billion, it is intended to supply a full 10 percent of the country's current power needs. Initially capable of producing 1 GW of power per year, it is intended to be scaled up to 5 GW. The solar complex is situated on 9,000 hectares of land in the northern Cape Province, among the driest and sunniest sections of South Africa. It can draw abundant supplies of water for the project from the nearby Orange River. It also has the advantage of accessibility to transmission lines with a ready connection to the national and regional power grids. If this first major solar collection facility can generate electricity at prices competitive with South Africa's existing thermal (coal-driven) and, possibly, its nuclear installations, then the government promises to expand solar installations across the country as a critical forerunner for Africa.[12]

At the micro-level, by contrast, solar power may have become or will shortly become inexpensive enough to provide electricity for families who are beyond national grids. An experiment in Kenya, Malawi, and Zambia uses a solar cell (soon to be supplied in the form of plastic strips) capable of producing 2.5 watts of electricity – sufficient to power a battery capable in turn of powering an energy-efficient light-emitting diode (or two) and a mobile telephone charger for seven hours. (The battery is re-charged via solar cell on day two, and so on.) Employing a payment mechanism analogous to telephone SIM cards, the families in the experiment pay the company supplying the solar cell, battery, and lights little by little (via the "SIM" cards) until they "own" the equipment and can use it for free. Certainly, using solar rays in this manner is less expensive than lighting an off-the-grid home by paraffin and paying to have a mobile telephone re-charged commercially at a location on the grid.[13]

The exploitation of wind power is in its infancy, with projects in the Gambia and Kenya, and an installation north of Cape Town in South Africa. At Darling since 2008 four 50-meter-tall wind towers have been producing power. The success of that wind farm, a collaboratively supported effort by the South African government and several international donors, demonstrates the potential for wind power in at least southern Africa and provides a stimulus to additional wind projects (as yet unplanned) in South Africa.[14] But the continued commercial feasibility of the Darling project depends on selling power to the South African state-controlled electricity generator – Eskom – and to municipalities such as the city of Cape Town at higher prices than normal. In times of austerity, such cost issues put a damper on expanding the utilization of wind for energy.

There is abundant potential, too, especially along the Rift Valley, for generating electricity from underground geothermal energy, but only Kenya fully operates a productive 210 MW plant near Olkaria, south of Lake Naivasha. Olkaria's potential production could be as high as 1,600 MW. Kenya also hopes to produce large amounts of geothermal energy from the sulphurous heart of the Menengai volcano, 180 km northwest of Nairobi. Already, drawing on expertise from Iceland, Kenya wants Menengai's vast steam reserves ultimately to generate 27 percent of the entire country's electrical needs by 2031. But to do so may cost as much as $20 billion for 5,000 MW of capacity.[15] Elsewhere, Ethiopia has a prototype installation, Zambia has several projects in the planning pipeline, and there are investigations of geothermal possibilities in Djibouti, Eritrea, and Uganda. Rwanda is attempting to exploit methane from its neighboring lakes for power generation.

At present, centralized energy provision is the norm in sub-Saharan Africa. In addition, four regional power pools spread the provisioning and costs, distributing power beyond national borders. The Southern African Power Pool, established in 1995, is a grid linking twelve of the countries in mainland southern Africa; that pool essentially shifts Congolese, Mozambican, and South African surpluses (when available) to the smaller and less energy-sufficient countries of the region, plus Angola. The West African Power Pool, created in 2000, tries to tie together the 14 members of the Economic Community of West African States (ECOWAS) and draws heavily on natural gas-generated electricity from Côte d'Ivoire and Nigeria, and hydropower from river flows in Ghana, Mali, Côte d'Ivoire, and Nigeria. That pool has two mutually interdependent sections: one includes the countries from Mali and Senegal to Liberia; the other runs from Niger and Nigeria westward to Côte d'Ivoire. The Central African Power Pool serves 11 countries from Chad to the Congo (Brazzaville) and was started in 2003. The members of this very underdeveloped pool suffer from small and isolated power systems. The East African Power Pool, opened in 2005, runs from Egypt to Tanzania and includes members of the East African Community and the Nile Basin Initiative. This last pool may someday finally realize Cecil Rhodes' dream of linking the Cape to Cairo; he conceived a rail transport tie but Egyptian and East African planners would like to take advantage of Congolese and Zambian power surpluses to supply Cairo when Aswan water supplies are low and vice versa. Many intermediate interconnections have yet to be built, however, so it may be a decade or more before the modern analogue of Rhodes' vision will be achieved.

A shortage of transmission lines and interconnections clogs all of these distribution systems and has in the past prevented one or more of the pools from expanding to meet sudden power surges or unusual and unforeseen crises (such as the theft of critical equipment in the Congo and Zambia in 2008). Indeed, power pools in general, and African power pools especially, suffer at the best of times from: underdeveloped transmission networks and tie lines, non-existent connections, inadequate generating capacities and reserve margins, lack of investment in necessary facilities, inadequate legal frameworks and dispute resolution arrangements, and a lack of trust and confidence among members of the pool.[16] A map of the various existing and contemplated interconnections between countries and grids shows how much still needs to be done to strengthen sub-Saharan Africa's limited ability to share power surpluses efficiently and smoothly.

Sub-Saharan Africa's energy weaknesses remain real. The demand for power will but grow as population numbers multiply dramatically and increased consumer purchasing potential draws investors into the sub-continent. With the completion of the large thermal and hydroelectric projects already mentioned, and with steady rainfall, some shortages will be relieved, but many others will remain because of the poor quality and coverage of the various regional grids. For sub-Saharan Africa to grow economically in the manner that its middle class desires, political leaders will want, for the next decade, to devote every possible spare amount of funding from their own national budgets, and from China and other donors, to the expansion of available supplies of electrical power.

Arteries of commerce: roads and rails

Even with abundant and secure sources of energy – when they are realized – much of sub-Saharan Africa's economic growth prospects will be constrained by road and rail networks that are inadequate for the agricultural and industrial growth on which its individual national futures depend. Harbors are shallow and crowded, international airports comparatively few, and airline connections to the greater world less than required for great surges in growth.

Tourism, especially, is constrained by infrastructural handicaps. One way for sub-Saharan Africa to grow robustly would be by attracting more tourists. In this century, the region, despite its magnificent fauna and avifauna, and notable ancient and natural sites such as Axum, Lalibela, Great Zimbabwe, and Victoria Falls, was the destination of but 4 percent of global tourism.

Only 5 percent of all global air traffic took off or landed in sub-Saharan Africa despite a demonstrated unfulfilled demand; sub-Saharan Africa's annual air traffic increases exceeded increases elsewhere for both passengers and freight. Protectionism – restricting which airlines could fly in and out of many sub-Saharan African countries – and the failure of a number of sub-regional African air transport companies, provided two explanations for shortfalls in air transport opportunities. So did obsolete bureaucratic and visa practices, shortages of hotel accommodation, and perceptions of crime – all of which deter tourists.[17]

Sub-Saharan Africa, compared to the situation in North Africa, or on other continents, lacks paved and well-maintained roads. Thus, Africa's arteries of commerce, essential for business activities of all kinds, for the delivery of fertilizer to rural farmers, for the sale of produce from outlying farms, and for tourism, are a weak point, greatly hindering developmental efforts. Giant Congo (Kinshasa) has dramatically lost road lengths and other transport capacity (even by river). In 2011, Congo (Kinshasa) counted fewer than 1,800 miles of paved roads. The Sudan, and a number of other of Africa's weaker states – even Nigeria – were road-poor per capita and per square kilometer. The wealthier and better-governed states, by contrast, had higher road (and sometimes rail) capacities. Of the geographically sizable countries, Botswana, Namibia, Zambia, and South Africa led the way, but Ghana and Uganda had also managed to retain a reasonably robust road network. In 2012, Congo (Kinshasa), Ethiopia, the Sudan, Burundi, the Central African Republic, and (surprisingly) Tanzania had Africa's fewest paved and fewest well-maintained roads per capita.[18]

Good roads are of vital concern to Africans of all classes. Perhaps more than their leaders realize, sub-Saharan Africans equate good leadership with the provision of adequate roads. "Good governance," wrote a particularly agitated Nigerian commentator, "is only achieved when a leader makes up his mind with good intentions to lead," and to build and maintain good roads. In Rivers State, in late 2011, "we are still keeping our fingers crossed till when the government will repair the roads." In town after town, "the roads are hellish." The Igbo Etche road had been forgotten. So had been the Ada George road: "You may call them streets. Many of them are glorified abyss [sic]. We have kept our eyes open how we live in dungeon in Rivers State because the roads are very bad. . . . Bad roads have held people down. Businesses have been ruined."[19]

Sub-Saharan Africa's road network, combining main and secondary roads, totaled about 1,052,000 km in 2010. There were probably another 492,000 km of unclassified passable dirt connecting tracks and 193,000 km of city roads. Together, all of these numbers add up to a road network of 1,735,000 km.[20] By international standards, sub-Saharan Africa therefore has but a low spatial density of 109 km of classified and 149 km of unclassified roads per 1,000 sq. km of land area. Those numbers mean that sub-Saharan Africa's road spatial density is only 30 percent of South Asia's and 6 percent of North America's. Of the 49 nations composing sub-Saharan Africa, only compact Mauritius shows an internationally adequate road density of 933 km per 1,000 sq. km. Most of the other countries in the sub-continental region show densities below 10.

On a per capita basis, the results are also low by international standards. The average for the entire sub-continent is 2.5 km per 1,000 people, with a broad variation from sparsely populated Namibia's 21 km per 1,000 down to 0.5 km per 1,000 in tightly settled Burundi and Rwanda. Lesotho, Namibia, and South Africa claim only 50 km of primary roads per 1 million inhabitants. But poor Niger and wealthier Uganda each have 1,000 km of primary roads per 1 million people. On average, 64 percent of primary and 17 percent of classified roads are paved throughout sub-Saharan Africa, with South Africa and Botswana having the highest proportions. But the Central African Republic, Chad, and the Democratic Republic of Congo show less than 20 percent of their primary network as paved, and fully 25 percent of all sub-Saharan countries have only paved 10 percent or less of their roads. In South Asia, half of all roads are paved; in North America, two-thirds are. The total paved road network in sub-Saharan Africa amounts only to 0.79 per 1,000 people, half of that of South Asia and one-fifth of the world average.[21]

Road networks exist to facilitate the movement of people and commerce. The more compact the country the easier it should be to provide a high-quality set of paved roads; the more sparsely populated, the more isolated, the more difficult and expensive it is to provide adequately for a country's transportation needs. In Europe, the Americas, and large parts of Asia, the average percentages of paved road km per 1,000 people are 4 times, 8 times, and twice what they are in Africa, respectively. In Asia, 65 percent of all roads are paved. In sub-Saharan Africa, the average km of paved roads per 1,000 people is 3.40, whereas the world average is 7.07. Even among Africa's smaller states by area, some enjoy as little as 1.5 and others as much as 5.8 paved km per 1,000 people. Mainland Botswana, a country with substantial sq. km of desert, in the first decade of this century counted 4.5 paved km per 1,000 people. Namibia, Zambia, and South Africa also rated high on the same scale. But the remaining countries of sub-Saharan Africa were road-poor: ranging from Chad's 0.03 paved km per 1,000 people and the Democratic Republic of Congo's 0.04 figure upwards to Nigeria's 0.20, Kenya's 0.25, and Uganda's 0.53 per 1,000, the peoples of the sub-continent could rely on much shorter paved road lengths compared to the inhabitants of other continents.[22] Fewer than 40 percent of all rural sub-Saharan Africans live within 2 kilometers of an all-season road, "by far the lowest level of rural accessibility in the developing world," and even rudimentary roads and tracks supportive of agricultural development – a "top priority" – are scarce.[23]

Even if we examine paved roads per land area (km per 100 sq. km), only the very small states and island nations show good results. Rwanda's number is nearly 11 paved km per 100 sq. km and Uganda's is 8, but South Africa only shows 5, Ghana 4, Nigeria 3, Côte d'Ivoire 2, Senegal 2, and Botswana 1. At the other end of the scale, the DRC's number is 0.10, the Central African Republic's 0.11, and Angola's 0.62.

These vast disparities per person and per area indicate the many thousands of kilometers of roads that Africa will need to pave and maintain to support its increasing populations and growing industrial and agricultural aspirations. These disparities also reflect policy decisions made by generations of political leaders. Expenditures on roads, now averaging about 2 percent of national budgets, have always lagged well behind minimal needs. Only with Chinese assistance in recent years have some of the vast road construction requirements begun to be alleviated. Even so, what roads there are, paved or not, are poorly maintained. A Zimbabwean cabinet minister publicly decried the state of his finance-starved country's once admirable roads; they were developing Congolese-sized potholes, he told an audience in Harare. Congo (Kinshasa), admittedly, now has a road network that is much smaller and much less well maintained than it inherited at independence in 1960.[24]

These sad numbers tell only part of the story. On the one hand, with a superb road and rail network capable of supporting most of its agricultural and industrial objectives, South Africa's statistical profile belies the overall contribution to development of what is a robust transportation network. By sub-continental standards, South Africa has an excellent rail network, 31,000 km long. It also has 58,000 km of paved roads, urban and rural. Its roads are among the best in Africa even though its per capita and per sq. km ratings are lower than some of its neighbors. South Africa also has the best-run harbors in Africa, and highly rated international and domestic airports.

Wealthy Botswana, next door, also has excellent paved roads, 9,000 km in length, or 26,000 km counting gravel and earth roads. At independence in 1966, Botswana had only a mere 12 km of paved roads, nearly all inside Francistown and Lobatse. (Botswana also has 900 km of railway that traverse its eastern reaches, tying Zimbabwe to South Africa.) Despite immense distances across the Kalahari desert, it is now possible to drive from Gaborone to Windhoek (Namibia) and then on to South Africa's Atlantic Ocean port of Walvis Bay. Another paved route connects urban Botswana to Zambia via a pontoon crossing (soon to be a bridge) over the Zambezi River at Kasane.

In great contrast to these two examples of sub-Saharan countries with road and rail infrastructures capable of supporting economic and agricultural developmental objectives, comparatively well-managed and well-organized Ghana, a much smaller country in area than South Africa and Botswana, has only 8,500 km of paved roadways, far fewer on a per 1,000 people basis than either South Africa or Botswana. It does have two long-used working harbors which need upgrading, and a rail network about the same size as that of Botswana. In 2012, however, Ghana was proceeding with a Rural Roads

Project intended to improve existing feeder arteries as well as major highways.

Uganda, another relatively compact country in sub-Saharan Africa's interior mainland, once claimed the densest road network per capita in Africa. But nowadays its mere 1,800 km of paved roadways translates into one of the least effective road networks on the sub-continent, or 0.53 km per 1,000 inhabitants. Many of the lines on its once efficient railway system have been shut, and the system's full 1,350 km are not always in use. Although both the main railway from Kampala to Mombasa and the parallel road through Kenya to that prosperity-giving port have been refurbished, it still takes an intolerably long four days for goods to be transported to Mombasa from Kampala, and at a high cost per ton: about $100.

Landlocked and densely populated Rwanda depends on the same road and rail route via Uganda to Mombasa, its main port. Even as it attempts to diversify its import and export options via the port of Dar es Salaam in Tanzania and rail and road to that harbor via Mwanza on Lake Victoria, Rwanda's future economic and social achievements are heavily mortgaged by its location in the heart of the Great Lakes region and its consequent sheer distance from every other part of the globe. President Paul Kagame, always thinking boldly, dreams of leapfrogging such geographical bottlenecks by the creation of a major air transport hub in Rwanda, now only a secondary airport mostly dependent on traffic from Nairobi. But with high-quality coffee and coltan and other Congolese mining products its only substantial exports, plus some incoming tourism, Rwanda may not produce sufficient human and freight traffic to justify such a massive investment.

Tanzania's main port at Dar es Salaam has a very narrow mouth and has long been congested. Ships often wait a week or more (as they do outside Apapa, the port of Nigeria's Lagos) offshore before they can enter the harbor and unload. This delay constrains the full operation of the new oil refinery there that is meant to serve up-country Tanzania, Rwanda, and Burundi. Tanzania is also very road-starved. Given its anticipated enormous rise in population numbers, the fact that a country of its size only has 3,700 paved km, or 0.17 per 1,000 and 0.77 per 100 sq km, limits its ability to develop rapidly and effectively. Without newly constructed arteries and better maintained old roads, future commercial growth and agricultural productivity are bound to be compromised. Tanzania's intrinsic impoverishment per capita is reflected in these sobering road numbers.

Mozambique, larger than Botswana and much larger than Ghana, has only 5700 km of paved roads and 25,000 km of unpaved arteries, or only 0.25 km overall per 1,000 population. Its harbors, however, are being dredged and upgraded so that they can welcome larger vessels at Maputo's coal and sugar terminals, at Beira, and at the newer port of Nacala, where exports of sugar and tobacco from Malawi will be delivered via a refurbished rail connection.

Nigeria, sub-Saharan Africa's most populous country by far, has long been weakly served by paved and unpaved poorly maintained roads, by creaky railways, by badly run and inherently dangerous domestic airports and airlines, and by overcrowded and unsafe harbors. Fortunately, Chinese engineering companies began upgrading Nigeria's roads and ports from 2010. Although still lacking good results, with as few as 0.20 paved km per 1,000 people, the road network in 2012 was becoming much more serviceable, especially in the south. These improvements have been less noticeable in the vast northern reaches of the country, where distances are longer and the road network has been weaker in terms of area, but not population. Even so, in 2011, the official Rural Road Access and Mobility Project sadly declared that fully 85 percent of Nigeria's roads were in "bad condition." Only 15 percent of the country's 16,000 km of secondary and tertiary roadway were "motorable." Seventy percent of 132,000 km of local roads were said to be "impassable." As a result, only 20 percent of agricultural production ever reached markets.[25]

For these several reasons, because of the consumption of beer and other alcoholic beverages by drivers, and because of careless driving habits (many African and Nigerian drivers lack properly obtained licenses), the World Health Organization and the government of Nigeria labeled Nigerian roads among the most dangerous in Africa, after Kenya, South Africa, and Eritrea, and not far behind India world-wide. In South Africa in 2011, an average of 43 people a day were killed in traffic accidents, or about 33 per 100,000 inhabitants. About 16,000 lost their lives in the same way in 2007, a peak statistical year – six times Britain's road accident death totals that year, even though there are more British cars on the road per inhabitant. (Findings by the South African Medical Research Council disclose that nearly 60 percent of all drivers killed in motor accidents in South Africa possessed blood alcohol levels over the legal limit; Nigerian driver blood levels would probably equal those of South Africans.)[26]

In many ways, Nigerian (or Tanzanian and Rwandan) road and rail outcomes are metaphors for all of the sub-Saharan African transportation frailties. Many of the smaller and weaker Francophone states, such as wealthy Gabon, resource-rich Guinea, and the impoverished backwater Central African Republic, have excessively limited roadways and significant transportation handicaps to overcome as they modernize and attempt to grow. Côte d'Ivoire, once much better-served than its neighbors with a modern port, effective railways, and ample paved road kilometers, must now rebuild and recover from its devastating civil war. Liberia and Sierra Leone, poorer places, are doing the same. Even the tiny Gambia, autocratically run, has much to do; even (as in the Congo [Kinshasa]) it attempts to rely on improved river transport to connect its people and bring goods to market.

No place in the sub-continent is as desperate, from a transportation point of view in 2012, as the Democratic Republic of Congo. Whereas Kinshasa was once, long ago, connected strongly to its inland cities such as Kisangani and Lubumbashi, and to eastern Goma and Bukavu, by road (or even to Matadi at the mouth of the Congo River), using these routes in 2013 is at best extremely difficult and barely possible. "In Bukavu, once a Belgian colonial pearl at the southern tip of Lake Kivu," reported an acute observer in 2010, "the infrastructure had degraded to the point that there were no roads, or at least none worthy of the word. The 30 kilometers to Bukavu's airport was now a gravelly track, taking at least an hour. The independence square was a muddy blob, the road gone, the central feature of the roundabout long absent."[27] The Belgian-built road network is gone. Even the vaunted river transport system up the Congo has regressed to rudimentary. Only air transport, too expensive for ordinary Congolese – and dangerous – now in no practical manner links the disparate and distant outposts of President Joseph Kabila's empire. When the Congo is better led and much better governed, and much less corrupt – some distant time from now – it might just be possible to knit such a physically vast entity back together, and to project power and good governance from Kinshasa outwards. To begin to do so, however, will depend on the Congo (and the rest of the sub-continent) greatly enhancing its transportation infrastructures (as in Angola, Kenya, and Malawi) from domestic resources or with inputs from China and other major donors.

Everywhere in sub-Saharan Africa it is obvious that all manner of development – rural, urban, national – depends as much on major transportation upgrades, refurbishments, and imaginative new construction as it does on almost any other conceivable input into the economic growth mix. That is why the Chinese (see chapter 9) have been asked to create or re-make so many new roads, to renovate existing rail lines, to modernize ports (like Lobito and Luanda in Angola), and to provide electrical transmission lines and other communication facilities. But Africans will have to maintain those roads and rails, a challenge for coming decades. Africans will also have to obtain funding to expand the capacity and safety of their existing airports (Mali has a new Bamako airport underway), and to build new air facilities for peripheral communities. As in the Congo, if road, rail, and river transport is inadequate, Africans will have to take to the air to strengthen local commerce and to continue exporting perishable commodities. The most forward-looking sub-Saharan African countries have already embraced this transport imperative; more will want to follow. But the decision to do so will be made by a new generation of engaged political leadership.

8
Harnessing Mobile Telephone Capabilities

In the least favored parts of sub-Saharan Africa (and even across its cities), where poverty is common and life is mean, short, and brutish, innovative information technology advances may be able to improve livelihood outcomes relatively economically and efficiently. The increasingly widespread availability of mobile telephone coverage and devices in most parts of Africa, and in many hands, gives new power to persons whose horizons have hitherto been limited by circumstance, isolation, and lack of resources. Mobile telephone technology raises economic productivity. Connectivity is productivity. It lowers transaction and search costs, enables transparency, and improves efficiency. The use of mobile devices makes possible, in other words, the unlocking of Africa's vast human potential and the enhancing of economic growth prospects through the instant communication and reporting abilities that are possessed especially by mobile telephones.

During the tumultuous opening days of the Arab spring (2011) and throughout the weeks and ensuing months of protest in Egypt, Bahrain, Libya, the Yemen, and Syria, SMS texts brought disparate individuals together, accumulated and marshaled crowds, directed groups to this or that location, and – overall – boosted the power of anonymous people versus the state or its military and police proxies. There is no denying the efficacy of texting and social media (especially Twitter and Facebook) in organizing and directing otherwise inchoate masses against the often stolid and otherwise immovable apparatus of the state. "Allez, to the barricades," would have been much more difficult without the ability to arouse previously apathetic assemblies that was offered by mass messages disseminated by mobile telephony.

Although recognizing the importance for political and social change of the use of mobile telephone capabilities in these ways, and of social media more generally, this chapter focuses on the demonstrated ability of mobile telephones to generate the kinds of information that can create behavioral, social, economic, and political progress. Hand-held communication devices have already altered and reformed commercial and social practices throughout sub-Saharan Africa. In future they may also be utilized to enhance individual economic, social, and political freedoms. Mobile telephone capabilities can protect human rights, correct breaches of civil liberties, ensure the fairness and transparency of elections, further improve the flow of commerce (urban and rural), and imaginatively strengthen health remediation measures.[1]

The weaker the state, the greater the need for ordinary citizens to gain access to and control over information that directly affects and impacts upon their lives. Such information, if deployed adroitly, offers a method whereby ordinary citizens can exercise options capable of checking or exposing flaws in the usual comprehensive power of a dominant regime. Whereas the downtrodden never before possessed much leverage vis-à-vis the state or overweening economic concentrations, mobile telephones now offer considerable new decisive technical capacities to create lasting social and economic change.

Innovation is crucial. Mobile telephones permit persons to talk to each other in real time and to send messages inexpensively and rapidly in text form. Mobile telephone devices are versatile. They have been used (extensively in Kenya, where perhaps funds equivalent to 10 percent of GDP have been moved within the M-Pesa system since its inception) to provide a form of electronic banking, to transfer money (even across international borders), to deposit funds in banks (even into interest-bearing accounts – M-Kesho), to pay bills, and to apply for and receive micro-loans. Mobile telephones in Kenya and Tanzania, and increasingly elsewhere in sub-Saharan Africa, provide a full money transaction platform much less expensive and much more reliable than Western Union, the postal service, friends, bus drivers, et al. In Zambia, where only 20 percent of the people have bank accounts, Mobile Transaction International processes nearly $1.5 million worth of payments a month, distributes microfinance loans, and helps to disburse aid for the World Food Programme.

In East and West Africa, text messaging capabilities have brought a critical awareness of market prices to distant (and near) producers and farmers. Ghana's TradeNet matches buyers and sellers of agricultural goods, in four languages. In Senegal, Xam Marse ("know your market" in Wolof) gives farmers real-time text messages that provide full market information, especially the prices of fruit, vegetables, meat, and poultry. Farmers in Niger, Ghana, and Senegal can type in a coded text and receive the prices of market goods immediately. Eight thousand cocoa farmers in Ghana furthermore receive practical information about cultivation practices, crop disease prevention, post-harvest production and marketing, farm safety, child labor, and health issues through their mobile telephones from the World Cocoa Foundation's CocoaLink.[2] Farmers in the Lower Congo or in the Iringa District of Tanzania can discover the prices that their manioc or maize will fetch that day or that week in Kinshasa or Mbeya, hundreds of miles distant. Job opportunities, even distant ones, become known (or rumored) and job-seekers can evaluate the utility of taking long journeys in the hope of gaining employment. A new mobile layaway scheme in Kenya allows women to save for water pumps and other farming devices by sending micro-payments to a prominent NGO working to empower women.

Mobile telephone capabilities have been employed to monitor the making and taking of bribes, and to bear witness to and prevent eruptions of violence. They report medical worries, such as incidents of swine flu; transmit technical knowledge to nurses and doctors (the Democratic Republic of Congo); and send text reminders to patients taking anti-retrovirals or medications for tuberculosis (Kenya, Malawi, and South Africa). Mobile telephones now permit individuals everywhere to be connected to neighbors or distant relatives, even colleagues or relations living overseas. Rural Africans in deprived circumstances can use their new telephones to text or call from a capital city such as Lusaka to distant Chinsali or to London.

Overall, as research by Aker and Mbiti and others demonstrates, the existence and availability of mobile telephones in this decade has brought technological possibilities for the first time to large swaths of Africa (even within some cities) where functioning land-lines were a myth and communication across cities and districts, much less whole countries and continents, was trying, at best, for almost everyone until recent years. The consequent reduction in the monetary costs of communication as well as the opportunity costs of transmitting ideas and propositions and receiving confirmation has improved agricultural and labor market efficiency and enhanced human welfare broadly across the sub-continent. Mobile telephones have become "service delivery platforms," thus creating new ways of improving African lives.[3]

But they have to work. Customers in a number of sub-Saharan African countries give their mobile networks high ratings for call clarity and calls that continue without frequent droppings. But the competitive networks in Nigeria, with a massive subscriber base of 90 million, and in Zimbabwe, provide less reliable service. Users complain. In 2012, Nigerian regulators – in a first for Africa – fined the populous country's four mobile providers a collective total of $7 million. The Nigerian Communications Commission found high levels of dropped calls, lost credit, poor call quality (lots of static), and poor communications with customers. "Nobody tells anybody anything," said a spokesman for the Commission. On their part, the four companies apologized to consumers, and said that they would doubtless face more fines because they were unable, in the short term, to fix the problems for which they were apologizing. Major and constant shortages of publicly available electric power were the main cause of their difficulties, they said, forcing the companies to generate their own supplies of energy. Local governments also interfered with their operations and demanded extra payments.[4]

In Zimbabwe, there have been no fines and no apologies, but calls are constantly dropped and service interruptions are frequent. So are messages telling consumers to "try again" since service is temporarily (sometimes for hours) unavailable. Of the two main providers, one is privately owned, the other government-owned. Calling across networks is unusually difficult, as is calling during storms.

Not yet the Internet

Despite the data-driven conclusion that digitization and growth are highly correlated, the Internet has not as yet transformed the lives of sub-Saharan Africans. The Internet has fewer possibilities to alter African lives because it is more unwieldy to use, especially for illiterates or the marginally literate. But the major drawback to relying on the Internet to spur social, economic, and political change in Africa is the fact that it has been adopted only sparsely. According to the Digitization Index, which tracks 21 measures including speed, coverage, reliability, and utilization of networks and mobile telephones, sub-Saharan Africa scores 36 of 100 through 2010, whereas Western Europe and Asia score near 60 and North America just under 60. Hong Kong has 40 fixed broadband connections per 100 people, Kenya fewer than 1. Senegal's broadband coverage reaches about 30 percent of the population, but only 1 percent use broadband.[5] Overall, only about 5 percent of all sub-Saharan Africans own or have access to a computer. But that number is expanding rapidly and many researchers assert that the Internet, once it is more available and less expensive, will have a transformative impact on businesses, governments, civil societies, and farmers. Until recently, much of interior sub-Saharan Africa relied on comparatively expensive satellite transmissions to feed the local Internet connections. But the 2011–2012 linking of East and Southern Africa to the world-wide web by suboceanic fiber-optic cables has gradually permitted greater as well as faster Internet availability.

In West Africa, too, after the completion of another underwater cable, in 2012 one of the Nigerian fiber-optic providers was expanding its aerial (using existing high-voltage electric power lines) networks into Benin, Togo, Ghana, Côte d'Ivoire, and Senegal. It also links Niger by the same method. A number of other satellite-only broadband states, such as Sierra Leone, Chad, Guinea, and Liberia, were also hoping that new fiber-optic links would end their expensive reliance on slow services. Through 2012 all of Sierra Leone, for example, relied on 155 megabits of bandwidth, less than would serve a small European town. It also cost subscribers 10 times what comparable service cost East Africans and 25 times what it cost average Americans.[6] The New Partnership for Africa's Development (NEPAD) is sponsoring an undersea cable (Uhurunet) and a terrestrial one (Umojanet) to link all of Africa together by broadband fiber-optic means in 2013. Encouragingly, Freedom House reports that the Internet is relatively free of governmental interference in Africa: South Africa, Kenya, and Nigeria rated highly. Only Rwanda, Zimbabwe, and Ethiopia, of the countries examined, scored highly on Internet restrictiveness.[7] Admittedly, mobile phone owners and users can and do download data off the Internet to their mobile handsets, but collecting data in that way is much more expensive than doing so by voice or text.

Mobile phones everywhere

Mobile phone coverage in sub-Saharan Africa has grown at staggering rates over the past decade. In 1999, only 10 percent of the population had mobile phone coverage, primarily in South Africa and Senegal. From 2000 to 2008, according to Wireless Intelligence and the Groupe Speciale Mobile Association, persons owning mobile telephones in sub-Saharan Africa increased from 16 million to 376 million.[8] By 2012 that last figure was well over 500 million, perhaps two-thirds or more of the entire population of the sub-continent. (Individuals sometime share telephones, thus multiplying the number of users. And some individuals own multiple telephones and multiple sub-scriber identity module – SIM – cards.) The wealthier countries of the sub-continent, such as South Africa, Mauritius, Cape Verde, Botswana, and Gabon (and the outliers of Mauritania and the Gambia) show higher rates of mobile telephone ownership and penetration. But even in relatively impoverished places such as Mozambique and Sierra Leone, about 30 percent of citizens own mobile devices. In part, appallingly provided and expensive to purchase and employ land-line telephone service accelerated the adoption of mobile telephones when they became widely available and comparatively inexpensive. Additionally, a long pent-up demand for communication ability was responsible for the rapid migration to mobile telephones by poor sub-Saharan Africans despite the costliness of the devices (half a month's wages in Kenya). But the supply of time allotments provided by purchased cards, with no billing or accounting issues, also facilitated the rapid spread of mobile devices during the first decade of this century. Today, many more people in Africa's poorest places have mobile telephones than have bank accounts.

By the end of 2013, even the most remote villages in sub-Saharan Africa will have mobile telephone coverage, and only a handful of countries – Guinea-Bissau, Ethiopia, Mali, and Somalia – will remain relatively (but not completely) unconnected.[9] In poor and information-hungry Zimbabwe, for instance, a full 8.1 million mobile devices exist in a population estimated at about 10 million in 2012. Coverage in Zimbabwe is 65 percent, including large portions of remote, rural sections of the country. Kenya today has at least 30 million subscribers; there are 74 mobile telephones for every 1,000 Kenyans. (In Kenya, too, 99 percent of all Internet subscriptions are on mobile telephones.) The constraining factor in the spread of mobile coverage has not been the stringing of wire and the placing of poles along roads, for decades the inhibiting issues for land lines, but rather the construction of base stations that depend for their power on solar rays (rarely), reliable electricity supplies (mostly in urban areas and rarely outside such centers), or on diesel-generated electricity. In Nigeria in 2008, one mobile provider had at least 3,600 base stations, together burning 450 liters of diesel fuel every second.[10]

These regional figures mask substantial heterogeneity at the country level. For example, while the lowest rate of subscriptions per 100 persons is found in Africa, countries such as Gabon, Mauritius, the Seychelles, and South Africa show rates of 80 or more. Similarly, while the number of mobile subscriptions per 100 persons averages almost 50 in Asia, countries such as East Timor, Burma (Myanmar), and Turkmenistan all have rates lower than 10.

In most cases, the types of mobile phones adopted are relatively "simple" devices: handsets with only calling, texting, and mobile money capabilities, in some cases limited Internet coverage. Although "smart" phones – namely, those that allow for more sophisticated applications and Internet capabilities – are available throughout Africa, their penetration is primarily in the urban areas. As with the arrival of the earliest mobile phone handsets – which were adopted by urban residents and more educated and wealthier populations – these smarter handsets remain firmly entrenched in specific areas and have diffused within more limited populations. This result is hardly surprising given the expense of sophisticated mobile devices – most smart phones cost well over $50, ranging from 30 to 1 percent of annual per capita incomes in the poorer African states. Whether these smart phones achieve the same level of adoption as the simple phones will depend, in part, upon international and local prices for such handsets, their availability on the local market, the diffusion (and speed) of 2G (and above) services, and their ability to provide content that is useful to poor, remote, and partially illiterate populations.[11]

Mobile devices and social and economic remediation

Mobile phone technology and other informational devices potentially are able to improve access to and deliver core services. Hence, they can improve developmental prospects in at least the weaker states of sub-Saharan Africa. The rapid growth of mobile telephony throughout the sub-continent has introduced a new technological platform that offers several advantages over older and other forms of communication. It enhances access to information in terms of cost, geographical coverage, and ease of use.

Although radios are a major source of information in much of Africa (over 55 percent of sub-Saharan African households listen to the radio at least weekly), they generally provide a limited range of information and offer only one-way communication.[12] A proposed brand-new broadcasting service for Zimbabwe promises mostly music and religion, a little news, and limited political coverage. Even where the press is vibrant (Nigeria and South Africa) and willing to experiment with investigative techniques, its readership is highly urban, relatively expensive, and because of circulation barriers inaccessible to many rural residents and persons of limited literacy. Fewer than 19 percent of individuals in sub-Saharan Africa read a newspaper at least once per week, with many fewer doing so in rural areas. Moreover, in many African states, press and media coverage is government-controlled and highly partisan and partial. Land-line coverage has been limited, with less than one land-line subscriber per 100 people in 2008. Access to other search mechanisms, such as fax machines, email, and the Internet, is similarly restricted. Additionally, gathering what a person needs by travelling to different locations to obtain up-to-date and accurate information not only requires the cost of transport, but also taxes the opportunity cost of an individual's time. Mobile telephones are inherently interactive, too, and whereas traders might prefer to go themselves to a market to obtain commodity prices and gossip about who was selling what to whom, all of that information can be gathered by a judicious employment of telephonic capacities that were unavailable and much more expensive (when available) via land lines.[13]

There are several mechanisms through which mobile phone technology is already affecting the economic, political, and social development of the weaker parts of Africa. First, mobile phones reduce the cost of communicating over long distances. By doing so, the use of such devices can enable individuals to communicate more frequently with members of their social networks, thereby allowing them to seek help when and where it is needed. In countries where credit and insurance market failures abound, the ability to communicate with one's social network can play a crucial role in smoothing consumption problems, enhancing investment, and reducing an individual's (or a household's) risk. Second, mobile phones can improve access to and use of information, thereby reducing search costs, improving coordination among agents, and increasing market efficiency. Such increased communication flows should improve firms' productive efficiencies by allowing them to manage their supply chains better. Third, mobile phones create new jobs (selling SIM cards and so on, and renting out telephones) and address demand for mobile-related services, thereby providing income-generating opportunities in rural and urban areas. Fourth, the introduction of mobile money services – which enable households and firms privately to transfer money via a series of commands – lowers the transaction costs associated with shifting funds and making and receiving remittances to and from elsewhere in Africa or overseas, thus improving households' access to informal private monies, especially in times of crisis. M-Pesa in Kenya (hosted on an Amazon cloud server) has teamed up with Western Union to facilitate the transferring of funds from 45 countries into Kenyan mobile deposit accounts. A platform called CurrencyFair makes the buying and selling of money across borders (whether sending remittances or purchasing foreign exchange) much less expensive than legacy methods through established banks. Fifth, mobile phone technology can be used as a powerful tool to collect and disseminate information – on diseases, droughts, and violence – that can be employed to allow NGOs, governments, and private citizens to organize efficiently. Sixth, as one young entrepreneur has demonstrated, mobile telephones can administer all kinds of surveys, gathering critical commercial and economic information for businesses, the United Nations, and so on – even in Somalia. The same service can also distribute coupons to home owners and shoppers, thus producing market cost-savings as effortlessly as paper coupons do in the developed world.[14] Seventh, as Aker shows, the versatility of a mobile device can be utilized to improve literacy, especially among the young: "Text messaging makes literacy functional." Students, even the least literate, can learn letters and numbers, practice texting them, and then graduate to fuller messages, even to full phrases as they grow more literate.[15]

SMS Texting for change

The unavailability of accurate information provided by and affecting citizens living in unsafe and compromised situations has always limited the ability of citizens to hold their own against, or even to make their wishes known in relation to, the state or agents of the state. Fortunately, the new widespread ubiquity of mobile hand-held devices and inexpensive SMS texting provides major tools capable of effecting meaningful betterment, especially where peoples' pursuit of livelihoods and happiness are inhibited by state neglect or state-imposed constraints.

There are many ways in which life chances in Africa can be improved through access to information flows and through the employment of text-messaging capabilities to hold governments and their agents to account. Many have already been cited above. In addition: (1) Official rules and regulations may be uploaded regularly to hand-held devices by central or local entities, thus offering a new layer of accountability and transparency to transactions between a government and its citizens. Until now, citizens, especially rural inhabitants, often have been kept in ignorance, purposely, to give bureaucrats and bureaucracies enhanced levels of power. (2) Obtaining licenses of all kinds could be arranged through mobile telephones, thus saving time and opportunity costs for citizens and, again, removing arbitrary discretion from bureaucrats. (3) Citizens could complain directly to official ombudsmen or to other designated officials about issues arising in their home areas, say missing street lights or road signs. Likewise, citizens could alert their representatives (if the system were constituency-based and democratic) to problems of particular concern. In South Africa's KwaZulu-Natal, mobile phone text messages and attached videos were deployed by a villager plagued with frequent sewage overflows from a nearby river; once the evidence was shown to the district municipal manager, the main broken pipes were repaired and the overflows prevented. (4) Humanitarian uses are easily available, too. This was the case during the extreme Somali (and northern Kenyan) famine of 2011, when mobile phones enabled concerned Kenyans to donate small sums through a dedicated number provided by one of the mobile telephone providers. Just as 70 percent of Kenyans (and others) now use M-Pesa mobile money techniques to add calling credits, they simply entered tiny or larger sums for famine relief and sent them off. The ease of such transactions, combined with publicity via Facebook and Twitter social media, and knowledge that contributions would be administered by the

Kenyan Red Cross, enabled $10 million for famine relief to be collected in two weeks and $67 million after a month.[16]

These are but a sample of the ways in which SMS texting, now widely available even in the most deprived of African states, can be utilized to improve peoples' lives. Additionally, and more significantly, SMS capabilities can and should be employed: (1) to give citizens themselves a method of combating and reducing prevalent corruption; (2) to curb brutality against persons – the dark excesses of predatory states; and (3) to ensure the fairness of electoral processes.

Hampering Corrupt Practices

In the first case, the prevalence of corrupt practice in a country may not be known exactly. Mobile text reporting can provide a better sense than we now have of the level and pattern of corruption within a state, and of what kinds of persons are giving and taking bribes. Such crowd reporting has its limitations, since verification is difficult and names are usually omitted for fear of defamation suits or other forms of (lethal and nonlethal) retaliation. Yet the accumulation of incidents and the mapping of those occurrences enable patterns to be discerned and pressures to be brought to bear on governments and offenders. (No one favors corruption except those who profit from it.)

Even better than crowd-sourced texting about bribes, as soon as they are witnessed, would be more systematic reporting by trained observers. Results of the two approaches would reinforce each other and permit the aggregated knowledge, in the right hands, to deter, simply because accumulated knowledge existed. Prosecutions are more likely, too, if there are patterns and suspicions which can at last be verified. Certainly, the state and its highest officials, no matter how personally compromised, will be challenged by such new repositories of information.

Several of these approaches have been and are being tried. In India and Kenya, there are "I Paid a Bribe" sites which collect anonymous but telling reports. The Kenyan organizer wants to have a network capable of instantly reporting vote-buying during the 2013 national elections. These are among the powerful new ideas that promise to help reveal who is bribing and being bribed, thus giving ordinary victims of bribery at least some agency. "In the past," said a Transparency International program director, "we tended to view corruption as this huge, monolithic problem that ordinary people couldn't do anything about." He continued: "Now, people [can] . . . identify it and demand change."[17]

Violence Against Persons

In the second case, since violence against persons is the scourge of weak and failed states in Africa, and because such violence is meant to deprive citizens of their own sense of purpose and power, an ability to limit violent acts of all kinds levels the field of power between the helpless citizens and the overweening state (and its agents).

Almost everywhere in the heavily authoritarian states of sub-Saharan Africa, such as Angola, the Congo, the Sudan, and Zimbabwe, ruling classes and governments prey on their own people. Or ruling-party-sponsored militias attack opponents of the government of the day on behalf of the tyrant who is in charge. Sometimes there are military juntas or former generals who, having assumed control, strive to maintain their hegemony through the exercise of force. Whatever the underlying causal factors, innocent civilians are too often caught in the crossfire between state actors and non-state actors, between rebels and soldiers, between marauding militias from different sides, and between one criminal gang and another. Many of the 4 million or so Congolese and the 3 million or so Sudanese who have lost their lives since 1990 in the civil wars of those large entities have been bystanders, not combatants. Likewise, the 40 women who are raped daily in the chaotic conflict zones of the eastern Congo are all presumed to be innocent victims of wars that are resource-driven and ethnically denominated, and largely anomic. In Zimbabwe today, as in so many other similar weak and failed situations, ruling-party thugs attack supporters or presumed supporters of the opposition in order to intimidate them, and in order to demonstrate the long hand of the despotic state prior to national elections.

In these kinds of brutal situations, anecdotal reports of violent outbreaks in remote rural areas, in much more accessible townships, and even in cities have always been available for much later compilation, but not in real time. Too often the data obtained from such monitoring of violence and intimidation have been of a generalized nature, suitable for advocacy, but insufficient for either legal action or election petitions. Better are data that directly implicate behavior or retail incidents that can be shown to affect the election result. To do so requires verifiable and, if possible, material evidence of the kind that can be supplied by trained observers using SMS texting.[18]

The power of verifiable real-time awareness of such depredations, provided by SMS texting, could thus prove significant: (1) people and areas at risk could be warned, and episodes of violence reduced in duration and intensity; (2) allies could come to the aid of victims and could pose a countervailing power capable of limiting the scope of violence; (3) the authorities could be informed, instantly, and police and other official bodies could at least be asked to intervene (even if they refused or were lax); (4) the awareness that the violent actions of desperadoes, militias, criminal gangs, and rogue groups could be reported in real time should serve as a deterrent, conceivably causing tactical and strategic reassessments and the dampening of intensified conflict.

Crowd sourcing by mobile telephone texting is already being employed in some situations to report episodes of violence, and for rape recounting. But as helpful as crowd sourcing might be in these situations, it suffers from one major disability: the reliability of such reports cannot readily be ascertained. Crowd sourcing can offer early warnings, can cause potential victims to flee, and might in certain kinds of circumstances provide enough information for post hoc preventive assessments and retribution. But better information could be obtained in real time, and with much greater potency and more likely deterrent impact, if crowd sourcing were replaced by an SMS reporting mechanism whereby individual observers could transmit to trained middle-men who would in turn send the reports onward to a central collecting depot.

What is envisaged, building on existing initial testing in a context of rural and urban systemic violence (primarily in Zimbabwe), would enable the most unsophisticated victim or observer to transmit a very simply coded message to a local, but trained, person who could vouch for the sender's reliability largely on the basis of proximity and face-to-face personal knowledge. The trained local person could then upload one or more community text messages to a server in the cloud, again using simple codes (with no attributions that could be traced back to the reporter). Her/his information from a community at risk could then quickly and simply be aggregated, mapped, and transmitted to persons and areas in peril, to the authorities (if they were likely to oppose violence), to international bodies such as the United Nations or a regional or sub-regional body such as SADC, and/or to the press and other media, internal or external. Later, too, the incidents could be analyzed and their distribution displayed for all to see.

As an additional form of deterrence, it is possible, because of the verifiable quality of this kind of SMS reporting, to target individual attackers by name. Photographs could even accompany the SMS accounts. Even without photographic evidence, recordings of intimidating statements made at meetings or to groups about to be targeted by militias, etc., could supplement the SMS accounts. In any event, if X were associated with a violent attack at Y, and later at Z, at C, at D, and so on, a case could be made against a specific individual and/or that specific individual could be watched and, sooner rather than later, deterred by his acts being revealed publicly or by community responses. Information supplied by calibrated and credible SMS texts could then be a force capable of countering violence and thus for freeing poor, defenseless, and individually vulnerable citizens in the more dangerous parts of Africa from the scourge of violence.

The border area between the Sudan and South Sudan is tense and conflicted. In 2012, it was rife with external bombing and cross-border violence as South Sudan resisted the Sudanese stranglehold over South Sudanese oil exports and, according to Khartoum, clandestinely supported insurgent groups in the southern sectors of the Sudan that were linked to the South. In such troubled circumstances, here and elsewhere, text-messaging capabilities could be utilized to report the results of Khartoum-directed attacks on communities in Blue Nile, South Kordofan, and Abyei (in the southern reaches of the Sudan). In 2011 and 2012, those suspected attacks were noticed by satellite-provided surveillance. But on-the-ground verification was difficult, if not impossible. If and when SMS texting capabilities reach such affected areas, the existing on-high observation could be buttressed from the ground and the results reported to the UN and both governments, for remedial action.

Ensuring Free and Well-Run Elections

In the third case, even despotisms hold elections in order to enhance their credibility locally and internationally. But despotisms never prefer to lose, so whatever electoral artifices they use are frequently accompanied by intimidation of voters or outright chicanery during and after the polling exercise itself.

Despotisms, autocracies, authoritarian polities, illicit and minority regimes, and the like often employ elections as a means of bolstering their otherwise unlikely legitimacy nationally and internationally. In post-Soviet entities such as Belarus or Turkmenistan – which held an election in 2012 to re-anoint its President (he gained 97 percent of the vote) – the rigged and illegitimate quality of the exercise is readily apparent. But many less tyrannically run but still troubled and tightly controlled African states, such as Zimbabwe, the Congo (Kinshasa), and Rwanda, have used elections to ratify the grip of existing regimes. The manner in which those polls are conducted becomes very critical because democratic forces are pitted against anti-democratic elements. The difference between loss and victory may come in the run-up to an election, on polling day itself, or by rigging the results afterwards. The possibility of blatant chicanery influencing the ultimate outcomes, and thus the fate of a nation and its people, is ever present. In Zimbabwe, for example, the results of the national electoral contests of 2000, 2002, 2005, and 2008 (twice) were all heavily manipulated by the ruling party of President Robert Mugabe. Violent acts against his opponents were also perpetrated on the polling days themselves and during the long pre-electoral phases of each of the campaigns. Over the decade, and especially in the 2008 first balloting, Mugabe's people and his security forces attacked opposition supporters viciously before and on the date of the election, stuffed ballot boxes, changed or attempted to change the counts from each polling station, and then delayed issuing the results for weeks in order to massage the finally released, hardly believable, totals that kept Mugabe in contention for the presidency.

Fortunately, the availability of SMS texting capabilities now provides a series of reporting mechanisms and modalities that could reduce the reach of non-democratic manipulation and could help to preserve the integrity of elections where they really matter: (1) Acts of intimidation and violence against regime opponents well before an election can be reported and remedial responses prepared. (2) On the actual day itself, intimidating practices, violent incidents, voter interference, theft of ballots and ballot boxes, ballot stuffing, and so on can be reported in real time to electoral authorities, to civil society, to national and international observers, to regional supervisory bodies, and to the media. The fact that such anti-democratic acts can be noticed and publicized immediately could deter, if not ultimately rule a contested result invalid. (3) At the end of the specified voting period, results, whether posted or not, can be gathered, uploaded, verified, and announced by bodies independent of questionable governmental commissions, thus creating one or more separate (often called "parallel") paths for results to be ascertained. Falsifying results after the fact can thus be prevented. (4) The Carter Center and other international observer entities have long utilized a so-called "quick count method" to sample voter actions as they leave the polls. Thanks to mobile telephone messaging capabilities, such preliminary representative returns could also be gathered, uploaded to a central station, and leaked or announced in order to strengthen the believability of the official results. These parallel voting methods have already been employed to good effect in Senegal in 2012, in Ghana in 2010, and to some extent in Zimbabwe. In Afghanistan and Uganda, local researchers armed with digital cameras and smart phones have photographed publicly posted election tallies, thus providing a "quick-count" record against which "official" results can be placed and legitimacy ascertained. New off-the-shelf applications are available which could be downloaded to any or all smart phones by ordinary voters in the future.

Creating a Network of Mobile-Trained Observers

Crowd sourcing works well for alerts, but in order to make the most of SMS tracking and reporting abilities, and in order to provide hard-to-dispute evidence of norm and legal infractions, it is important for national and local NGOs (civil society groups) in sub-Saharan Africa to create networks of observers from the community upwards to districts, to provinces, and on to national centers. A single trained aggregator in a remote or a defined urban community or location can rely through face-to-face acquaintance on a network of on-the-ground monitors. They can in turn report upwards to her/him whatever seems out of place or egregious. That intermediate hub person can transmit in simple code to a regional or a central location the collected reports of persons known to her/him. Their credibility can thus be assured, and so can the transmissions that follow. All of these reports can be arrayed instantly and certainly on daily data bases and on maps. The latter capability can provide a rapid method of noticing a pattern of reproachable brutal incidents, pre-electoral intimidations, election-day violence, and so on. Individuals can be named and their depredations tracked from community to community in powerful ways. When it is known that violations of all kinds are being scrutinized, deterrence is possible, even likely. (The experiments in Uganda and Afghanistan showed that cheating was reduced by up to 60 percent.)[19] If not, post hoc retribution is also available. No other method of dealing with the myriad potential abuses that an authoritarian regime can heap on its people is more powerful, potentially, than that contributed by SMS texting capabilities and availabilities. In 2012, Senegalese civil society, backed by George Soros' Open Society Initiative, monitored 11,000 polling stations and text-messaged voting counts to a collation center outside Senegal.

Security of Information Gathering

SMS texting can help to keep dishonest regimes honest and provide information capable of refuting an authoritarian government's distortions of reality. But the text- messaging process itself must be made secure to be credible and to keep participants safe from retaliation. If a chain of transmitters (as above) is created, and if simple codes are employed to disguise the names of informants and relaying personnel, then the potentially weakest link is the place where all of the collected information is retained and analyzed.

There is a need, consequently, for the chain of transmission to end in a cloud, for the servers to which the data are sent to be located outside of the relevant weak or failed African states, preferably in a neighboring strong and democratic state with robust privacy safeguards. This is the method employed in the Ugandan case; data from smart phones were immediately transmitted to servers at the University of California, San Diego. In Senegal, the 2012 vote counts were uploaded to a secure server outside of the country, probably in France. Certain kinds of regimes will retaliate under any circumstances. But SMS respondents can be comparatively free of retaliation if their identities are masked, known only at the first relay point, if the simple codes are strong, and if everything is encrypted and stored externally on secure servers linked to an encrypted cloud.

Mobile Phones and Health Improvements

African states are unhealthy at the best of times. Most lack physicians and nurses. Europe has 3.6 physicians per 1,000 people; the United States 2.3 physicians per 1,000 people; Singapore, Mauritius, and the Seychelles each have slightly more than 1 physician per 1,000; but South Africa has only 0.77 physicians per 1,000, Botswana 0.4, and Nigeria 0.3. All other sub-Saharan countries have fewer than the Nigerian ratio, and Malawi only 0.02.[20] Moreover, the populations of the tropical nations among our 17 suffer from malaria, tuberculosis, schistosomiasis, leishmaniasis, diarrheal complaints, cholera, and much more. As we have seen (chapter3), malnutrition is a common debilitation. For all of those obvious reasons, and more, it is important that mobile telephonic capabilities be employed to improve medical outcomes and life chances.

Already, as indicated above, text messaging can remind patients to take their medicines and retrovirals, can summon people to clinics, and can distribute alerts when epidemics or other crises occur. A flashing light on a smart phone can remind someone to see their physician. Glucose monitoring by diabetics, even in remote areas of Africa, should be possible. In Ghana, mobile technology is even being used to facilitate exclusive breastfeeding through personalized counseling; text-message encouragements and coaching are sent to women in hard-to-reach, low-income areas. Rwanda has distributed free mobile telephones to thousands of community health workers so that they can keep track of pregnant women, send emergency alerts, call ambulances, and offer updates to local clinics on emerging health issues. "Text to Change" in Uganda has been alerting a broad public for more than five years to various medical concerns and issues. One home care service in Kampala sends text messages at least twice a day reminding its cancer, tuberculosis, and HIV/AIDS patients to keep appointments and take their medicines. M-Pedigree, a new drug-monitoring system in Rwanda, Kenya, Nigeria, and Ghana, also permits health workers and consumers to send a text code to a central hotline to verify, quickly, whether a medicine is counterfeit or genuine.[21]

But there is much more to M-Health: smart phones and future improved smart phones will soon be capable of acting also as sensors. In the developed world, and possibly before long even in Africa, distant diagnosticians will receive clinically transmitted or self-sent medical tests and images. The computing power of smart phones can be harnessed to take blood pressures, monitor blood sugar, hear heartbeats, and even (using photographic capacities along with text capabilities) look down throats, into ears, and at body lesions. Individuals, no matter how remote their locations, can tap into ready-made medical support systems. The results of such do-it-yourself medicine, uploaded to smart phones and sent to health providers, can reduce the complications of distance and time that now reduce effective care in countries as poor, under-served, corrupted, and disorganized as are many of those in sub-Saharan Africa.

It may be some time before a simple otoscope is connected to a smartphone, the two being used together to investigate problems in Eustachian tubes. Likewise, even linking a stethoscope to a smart phone and employing both devices in rural areas to "hear" the suspect heart and send the results to a physician in a capital city (from Agadez to Niamey, say) may not happen tomorrow, but it could and will in a few years' time. With support from the Bill and Melinda Gates Foundation, a British innovator has designed a mobile-phone-powered surface acoustic wave device to diagnose malaria remotely. The possibilities for observation, transmission of such information, and a returned diagnosis by text message are vast and potentially uplifting and liberating.[22]

Hand-held devices and the greater good

If the leaders and followers of Africa want to strengthen human outcomes, protect vulnerable populations, enhance the potential prosperity of individuals, and bolster transparency and accountability, then SMS texting provides an essential, powerful, and remarkably innovative tool capable of enhancing information flows and making commercial and agricultural prices and conditions available equally to the poor and the rich. Doing so might help to level existing playing fields and empower the weak against the strong. Medical diagnostic capabilities could be more fully exploited, as could the other medical interventions that SMS texting makes possible. Similar kinds of technological advances could help to redress injustices and ensure the credibility of electoral and other deliberative democratic exercises. Despotism could meet its match. Even bureaucratic obfuscation could be undermined or taken to task. The possibilities are endless, powerful, and exciting.

Fully harnessing this mobile telephonic technological revolution for Africa, however, depends ultimately on national policy decisions as well as on the individual adoption of the devices themselves. In some countries there are still commercial and bureaucratic obstacles to the easy purchase of telephones and SIM cards. Some of the more tightly controlled countries demand that subscribers and even purchasers of air time register each time they add minutes. Some countries have been loath to license mobile telephone providers in order to bolster the profits of state-run monopolies or because of backdoor corrupt dealings. Some countries prohibit the transmission of Internet data to mobile telephones. Some try to eavesdrop on conversations.

But the major advances will come in those countries where leaders embrace the new technologies and introduce them for literacy enhancement in the schools; for health improvements in hospitals, in clinics, and in rural settings and villages; for commercial and agricultural economic boosting everywhere; for reporting on such uncontroversial matters as rainfall amounts, drought incidence, food shortages, infrastructural problems, and needed repairs; and so on. Those outputs and others can also be matched by the ability of mobile telephone messaging systems to receive helpful informational updates from central or provincial governments; from local councilors, teachers, and nurses; from the police; and from any official sources with news to impart.

Every politician in Africa, we venture to say, carries at least one, if not several, mobile telephones. Few politicians are unaware of the power of mobile telephones. They themselves use personal computers or the Internet less frequently and less automatically than they turn to their ever-present telephones. As in so many other ways that the leaders of Africa can act responsibly, if they understand how mobile telephones are capable of improving the lives of their citizens, so they ought to scour the globe to gather and adapt the best possible betterment schemes using mobile telephonic technology and bring them home to Africa. Just as Ushahidi methods were pioneered in Kenya in 2008 and then exported to the world, so whatever works well elsewhere in Africa and outside should be harnessed by the sub-continent's leaders for the uplifting of their fellow citizens.[23] The widespread invention and adoption of the best kinds of mobile telephonic innovations may make it possible for sub-Saharan Africa, with its exploding population numbers, to transform its developmental prospects and leapfrog decades of slower growth.

As in so many other areas of sub-Saharan Africa's growing maturity, political leadership actions and acceptance of innovation matter. The mobile telephone revolution has already swept over sub-Saharan Africa. It will continue, willy-nilly, whatever regimes do. But it will achieve much greater force and direction if leaders explicitly recognize the mobile telephonic potential for positive change, and embrace it fully and publicly.

9
China Drives Growth

"China, its amazing reemergence and its commitments for a win-win partnership with Africa, is one of the reasons for the beginning of the African renaissance," declared the late Meles Zenawi, Ethiopia's acute Prime Minister, in early 2012.[1] He was addressing the opening of that year's African Union summit in a vast new building provided by China.

China's determination to keep growing rapidly at 7 and 8 percent a year in terms of GDP fuels its massive resource input demands – for petroleum, for natural gas, for precious metals of all kinds, for quantities of rare timber, and for agricultural goods. Because the states of sub-Saharan Africa are mineral-rich, because they have land suitable for farming, and because so many coastal African countries are premier oil exporters and potential exporters of natural gas, China needs Africa to fuel its continued industrial expansion; Africa in turn welcomes the rise in commodity prices that flow from incessant Chinese purchases. This happy synergy benefits both parties and, just as sub-Saharan Africa's population numbers are about to explode, it provides significant, sustainable, opportunities for sub-Saharan Africa's own GDP surges.

Sub-Saharan Africa's economic development prospects almost entirely depend on continued Chinese demand. In order to reap the demographic dividend, in order to satisfy the aspirations of its new middle class, and in order to have any hope – however distant – of meeting its Millennium Challenge goals and materially improving the sustainable life chances of its poor majorities, the 49 states of sub-Saharan Africa must depend on China and on Chinese-boosted demand for the underground and undersea resources with which large parts of the sub-continent have been blessed.

"It is the growth of China," Meles has said, "that has increased the prices of commodities, minerals and other products of Africa which had been in secular decline for decades leading to the marginalization of the African economy as a whole." Meles also asserted that, thanks to Chinese companies coming in "in a big way," resources long idle have been developed.[2]

There might be other markets for oil and gas, but at lower prices, and likewise for platinum, copper, cadmium, ferrochrome, iron, manganese, and coltan, but China's large demand has boosted almost all commodity prices – to sub-Saharan Africa's profound advantage. The list of industrially valuable metals that China requires from Africa is long. In addition to the major ones already cited, China buys cobalt, diamonds, gold, nickel, tantalum, titanium, uranium, and zinc.

Were it not for China's factories (and, ultimately, American and European consumer demand), and China's own consumers of electric power and modern amenities of all kinds, sub-Saharan Africa would have had fewer opportunities to attract the capital inflows and other fiscal gains that have accompanied a burgeoning trade with China. Nor, absent China's interest in what sub-Saharan Africa can produce and sell, could the sub-continental region's people have even begun to contemplate joining the global village with heads held high.

The sinews of China's growing and complex relationship with sub-Saharan Africa are extensive and spreading. China has matched its desire to accumulate Africa's resource riches with its willingness to sell very inexpensive consumer goods, provide affordable concessionary loans to countries and corporations, and construct roads, rails, pipelines, refineries, petro-chemical installations, harbors, dams, power plants, transmission lines, sports stadia, political party headquarters, presidential mansions, military barracks, and even a major skyscraper to house the African Union. There is hardly an African country that has failed to benefit in this manner from several or many instances of Chinese largesse: a ring road around Nairobi; a long coastal road in southern Malawi; a new trade-facilitating 100 km motorway between Asossa in Ethiopia and Kurruk in the Sudan; the reconstruction of the Lobito railway from Zambia's Copperbelt to coastal Angola; a refurbishing of the decades-old railway from Zambia to Tanzania as well as double-tracking of the Lagos to Ibadan line and upgrading of the Lagos to Kano rail route in Nigeria; rehabilitating the Takoradi–Kumasi railway in Ghana; a much-needed 339-km railway and toll-road from land-locked Addis Ababa to Djibouti on the Red Sea; a fish landing pier, an industrial research institute, a government office block, and the supply of municipal garbage trucks in Uganda; dams and power plants in more than a dozen places (noted above in chapter 7); an airport and a dam in Mauritius; a bulk water supply scheme in Zambia; the troubled but valuable Sudanese pipeline and an oil refinery in the Sudan; improvements to Tanzania's main port and a $344 million upgrade to and expansion of Ghana's principal Takoradi port; football (soccer) stadia in Angola, Mozambique, Gabon, and Equatorial Guinea; hospitals and water treatment plants in Angola; the stringing of transmission lines and the provision of mobile telephone service in the Democratic Republic of Congo; major assistance with the upgrading of tele-communications and broadcasting facilities in Nigeria and Liberia; and the inauguration or expansion of myriad export processing zones. In the Nigerian case, China delivered an orbiting two-way satellite to Nigeria capable of improving existing methods of accessing Internet broadband and all manner of mobile telephone technology, with the potential to create 150,000 new jobs. China also promises to launch a satellite for Congo (Kinshasa) in 2015.[3] In Angola, a partnership between a Chinese telecommunications equipment company and Angola's premier mobile telephone operator resulted in the launching of Africa's first 4G network. Chinese grow crops in Zimbabwe, Uganda, the Sudan, and Congo (Kinshasa) for export home. China has an extensive import and export relationship with South Africa in many agricultural commodities – principally purchasing wine, wool, sugar, tobacco, and fish meal, and sending South Africa sausage casings, kidney beans, fruit juices, tomatoes, and herbs. In South Africa, too, China is partnering with the local Industrial Development Corporation to produce minibus taxis.[4] From the Republic of Congo (Brazzaville), China purchases oil, and harvests (if that is the best word) old-growth timber from its deep forests. It has supplied aircraft, weapons, ammunition, and military uniforms (plus training) to Zimbabwe and the Sudan. China has even established a promising solar energy equipment industry in Kenya.[5] There are no ends and few limits, in other words, to China's profound engagement with the nations of the sub-continent.

No world power, not even during the official colonial period, possessed an appetite for Africa and the gifts of Africa equal to China's today. China is not a colonizer, and seeks influence and mercantile domination much more than it has political aspirations (or a desire to recruit friendly votes in the United Nations). Its primary drive is mercantilist, not hegemonic (in terms of territory), not ideological (in terms of spreading the Chinese Communist developmental model), and not altruistic (as in ending the slave trade).[6] Thus, even though there may be about 1 million mainland Chinese working in Africa as fishermen in Senegal, bankers in South Africa, copper miners in Zambia, power plant construction supervisors in Botswana, day laborers in two dozen countries, and traders and restaurant proprietors almost everywhere, China is not thinking officially of settling surplus populations in the sub-continent or of trying to export a Chinese way of life. The estimated 250,000 Chinese in Angola alone are active in construction, commerce, oil extraction, and farming. A former official of the African Development Bank believed that more Chinese had come to Africa in the past decade "than Europeans in the past 400."[7]

Nor is China – a latecomer – in direct competition with the United States, Europe, Japan, and India for influence in sub-Saharan Africa. It battles only for control over long-term supplies of critical raw materials. China is not using its engagement with Africa to humble its adversaries, or to score political points. Instead, China has been behaving defensively in order to obtain ready access directly as well as through world markets to the resources that it requires for its own long-term growth and, only incidentally, to boost its economic power as it becomes globally more powerful politically.

China's diplomacy and its foreign assistance program are intended to support its drive to accumulate resources. Unlike the less engaged West, China has established embassies in 39 of sub-Saharan Africa's 49 countries. It has dispatched military attachés to 14 states. It created Confucius Institutes in several national capitals, funded a serious think-tank in South Africa to focus on matters Chinese, encouraged and financed the teaching of Mandarin in several African countries (including Kenya and Zimbabwe), and has provided innumerable scholarships to Africans for study in China. (At the Fifth China–Africa Cooperation summit in 2012, President Hu Jintao promised 18,000 new scholarships and promised to send to Africa 1,500 Chinese medical personnel.) Student exchanges are common. The Chinese Communist Party sponsors frequent people-to-people visits to and from Africa. There have been regular inter-parliamentary exchanges with dozens of national legislatures. Winning and keeping friends is obviously important, and has been effected through intensive party-to-party contact, vigorous wooing of African party leaders and personnel, and extensive hospitality – all in service to the overriding objective of strengthening China's trade and resource capture objectives.

Xinhua, the Chinese state news agency, seeds articles in local African news-papers and spots on local radio broadcasts with reports about and favorable to China. Television viewers can obtain international news from China's CCTV or from CNC World, part of Xinhua. China Radio International offers Mandarin lessons along with "upbeat" accounts of Chinese–African together-ness. "You would have to be blind not to notice the Chinese media's arrival in Kenya," said a top editor of the widely read *Daily Nation*. In late 2012, *China Daily*, the largest English-language newpaper in China, launched *Africa Weekly* to cover China's involvement in Africa and the activities of Africans in China in order to "improve communication between China and Africa." US Secretary of State Hillary Clinton said that "we are engaged in an information war, and we are losing that war."[8]

Chinese President Hu Jintao visited Africa almost yearly from 2003, first as Vice-President. Premier Wen Jiabao toured African countries regularly. In 2012, he opened the cavernous Addis Ababa African Union headquarters and office tower – a "spaceship" dominating the ancient city's largely low-rise skyline. A showcase for Chinese methods and a monument to friendship, it was constructed over three years with $200 million of Chinese funds by the China State Construction Engineering Corporation, largely using Chinese labor. China also pledged to maintain the structure for the AU in future years. China even provided a helicopter landing pad so that visiting dignitaries could be lifted in from the city's international airport at the edge of town. One anonymous delegate to the African Union meeting suggested that the new headquarters building symbolized what the Chinese were "getting out of Africa" as much as it showed what they were "putting in." The building was a "fresh form of dependency."[9]

Investment, trade, petroleum

Without doubt, China has become the largest new investor, trader, buyer, and aid donor in a select number of important sub-Saharan African countries, and a major new economic force throughout the entire continent. Chinese trade with the sub-continental region has been growing at about 50 percent a year since 2003, with some limited slowing of the pace in 2011 and 2012. Total trade numbers increased from $10 billion in 2000, to $50 billion in 2007, to $120 billion in 2011. The US total of all trade in goods with Africa (not just sub-Saharan Africa), in 2011, amounted to slightly more – $126 billion, $93 million of which were imports (mostly of oil) into the US. European Union trade with sub-Saharan Africa was somewhat smaller, at about $82 billion in 2009.[10] The EU received 34 percent of the sub-continent's exports; 16 percent went to the US.

Sub-Saharan Africa's trade with India and Brazil has also grown strongly in recent years, mostly on the back of oil. Trade with India is now worth about $50 billion a year. In addition to oil, India imports gold and diamonds, coal from Mozambique, and uranium from Niger. Sub-Saharan Africa accounted in 2011 for about 5 percent of Brazil's overall global trade total, or $28 billion (up from $4 billion in 2002). Brazil imports oil, coal, iron ore, other minerals, and agricultural commodities, and exports mining equipment, aircraft, and other heavy manufactures. It trains Angolan military personnel and is building roads in Kenya. It gives scholarships to its universities. Brazil has also expanded its embassies; they now number 37 in Africa.[11]

About 40 percent of Africa's exports to Asia are to China; about 30 percent of Asia's exports to Africa are from China. As much as 15 percent of sub-Saharan Africa's total world trade volume is with China. India may someday be as important to Africa's growth as China is now. Until then, Africa above all needs China to prosper.

About 75 percent of all Chinese investment in Africa goes into infrastructural construction activities. More than $50 billion is devoted to the revamping of roads, railways, bridges, harbors, and the like. New dams and hydroelectric installations count for much of the total. According to former British Prime Minister Tony Blair, "If a country in Africa wants something done, such as building a road, they go to the donor community and it ends up . . . [mired] in months of bureaucracy. If you tell the Chinese you want a road, the next day someone is out there with a shovel."[12] Indeed, the Chinese can move with greater speed than others because they are rarely compelled to tussle for tenders; they obtain official contracts easily and produce results, albeit sometimes shoddy, but largely free of competition. Already, Chinese contractors control 37 percent of the sub-Saharan African construction market.

About half of the annual Chinese investments typically are spent in a few unusually resource-rich African nations. But the Chinese have interests almost everywhere on the sub-continent. China focuses on obtaining oils and minerals but also funds agro-processing initiatives, power generation facilities, infrastructure improvements, telecommunications advances, and tourism enhancements in a dozen or more countries ranging from Madagascar to Senegal. China has leased land, too, often in order to grow soybeans and maize for export home to China, thus helping to ensure Chinese food security.[13] Nearly $5 billion a year of Chinese investment funds are devoted to farming projects. China has also purchased part of a major South African bank that now gives preferential loans, sometimes collateral-free, to Chinese companies.

In Zambia, where the total national GDP is only $16 billion, China has already invested well over $2 billion. Trade between the two countries totaled $3.4 billion in 2011. After South Africa, Zambia is the location of China's most extensive investment beachhead in Africa. Zambia relies on copper for 76 percent of its export earnings and 66 percent of government revenues; China is the world's largest consumer of copper and the main reason why global copper prices are high. Three hundred Chinese companies operate in a variety of mining, construction, farming, and other sectors. The big Chambishi copper mine, earlier abandoned by Western companies, and three other copper properties are now owned by Chinese state-approved firms. Chinese companies employ thousands of imported Chinese workers, but also about 25,000 (the Chinese Ambassador to Zambia claimed 50,000) Zambians.[14]

To sub-Saharan Africa, China exports electronic goods, machinery, motorcycles, T-shirts, other clothing, mattresses, sheets and pillowcases, footwear, kitchen utensils, and a host of additional low-value consumer items. Most of these goods are for sale in nearly all African markets. Many, if not all, displace local manufactures and all but high-value or specialized consumer products from within Africa, or from Japan, Europe, and North America. Many local traders complain of thus being undercut; South Africa in 2007 negotiated a quota system so that its own producers would have a chance to compete for consumer sales against the Chinese imports.

The biggest component of trade between China and Africa, naturally, is oil. Indeed, China was originally attracted to Africa because of an awareness of its own energy deficits and long-term needs and because of the realization that newly made discoveries off the coasts of sub-Saharan Africa could supply China with secure sources of "sovereign" oil.

China now consumes 10 percent of the world's oil. Before the 1990s, China relied for energy on abundant locally produced coal and domestic oil reserves. By 1993, however, it had started importing oil. Ten years later, China was the world's second-largest consumer of imported oil, after the United States. It displaced Japan in 2003. China now accounts for about 16 percent of world demand for unrefined petroleum and refined petroleum products. According to the International Energy Agency, China's oil needs will double in this decade and the next, from 10 million barrels per day to 20 million barrels per day. At least two-thirds of that total will have to come from non-Chinese sources – from Iran and Saudi Arabia, from Venezuela, and from the oil-producers of Africa. Because oil prices and supplies are notoriously volatile, and because volatility and potential interruptions of supply worry China, its key drive in recent years has been to ensure oil allotments over which it can exercise direct control, possibly through equity ownership. That is what is meant by "sovereign" oil.

This desire to rely on dedicated suppliers rather than the vagaries of the global market (on which most other large importers are content to depend) has led to China's massive economic thrust into Africa. About 70 percent of Africa's oil now goes to China, 20 percent to the United States. Africa supplies about 31 percent of China's total annual requirements of crude oil and, in 2012, 12 percent of America's.

Until 2012, when South Sudan stopped transporting oil north through the Chinese-constructed and Chinese-patrolled pipeline to Port Sudan on the Red Sea, China exerted "sovereign" control over much of what was then the old Sudan's oil exports (sharing some of it with Malaysia and refining some for local consumption). China entered the Sudan in the 1990s, after Canadian and American companies abandoned their discoveries of rich deposits because of attacks from southern Sudanese insurgents and fear of internal North American consumer and investor hostility. Taking advantage of this with-drawal, China saw a welcome opportunity to secure significant supplies of equity oil on favorable terms. The nature of the authoritarian junta that ran the Sudan, locked as it was in a long war with southerners, concerned China less than the availability of otherwise unallocated oil. After forging strong ties to the junta, verifying the petroleum availability, and constructing a 900-mile two-pronged pipeline from the southern interior (what turned out to be athwart the dividing line between North and South), China began itself extracting oil and then started pumping 40 percent of the Sudan's oil to supply about 10 percent of its own entire oil import requirements. In order to strengthen its hold on those reserves, China built an oil refinery (half of which it owns), invested heavily in several dams and hydroelectric plants, constructed Khartoum's new international airport, pumped funds into the local textile industry, and supplied 88 percent of the arms, ammunition, and aircraft which the Sudanese army used, first, to attempt to quell rebels in Darfur and more recently to attack dissidents in South Kordofan and Blue Nile. China further backed the creation of the Sudan's own arms manufactur-ing industry. China trained the pilots in the Sudan's air force.

China has traditionally been a key friend of the regime that runs the Sudan. When South Sudan stopped shipping oil north to Port Sudan to protest against the Sudan's levying of unusually heavy transit dues, China attempted to mediate in order to keep the South's petroleum flowing (75 percent of the combined Sudan's total), but initially failed. Later, the International Crisis Group detected a determined effort on the part of Chinese diplomats to secure the favor of South Sudan's government, and thus to maintain access to South Sudan's oil, no matter what. China also seemed to promise South Sudan a large loan (supposedly worth $8 billion) to be used for all manner of projects, even for budgetary support – but not (as yet) for a new pipeline to Kenya. According to the Governor of South Sudan's Central Bank, Chinese officials said: "We built one [already]; you use it." The $8 billion would have replaced South Sudan's oil revenues foregone. But, as often with Chinese financing, the central bank governor reported that the real amount tendered was less than $200 million. South Sudan had to seek alternative credit from Qatar temporarily to replace foreign exchange earnings from oil.[15]

China also purchases large quantities of oil from sub-Saharan Africa's other four large producers: Angola, Nigeria, Equatorial Guinea, and Congo (Brazzaville). Angola's oil is light, thus easier to refine, and is therefore a particular and growing favorite of China, but China does not run the oilfield operations there as it does in the Sudan. In exchange for access to Angola's petroleum riches (which an American company shares), China has become a major backer of the wealthy autocrats who run Angola, a considerable lender to their regime, and the key builder of dozens of infrastructural projects – roads, railways, harbors, stadia, affordable housing, and more. Large low-interest loans from China's Export–Import Bank are being repaid over many years by profitable concessions and escrowed quantities of what is, in effect, "sovereign" oil.[16] Equatorial Guinea, Nigeria, and Congo (Kinshasa) also offer quantities of sweet crude, but on the world petroleum market, with China vying with others for its so far very large share of purchases from those countries. In 2012, China lent $3 billion to Ghana in exchange for 13,000 barrels of crude oil daily.

China has not ceased seeking sovereign oil. For that reason its own drilling companies are exploring for oil and gas in deep waters off Mozambique, Congo (Brazzaville), Equatorial Guinea, Gabon, Kenya, and even Nigeria. Promising finds have been located in Indian Ocean waters off northern Mozambique. Other deposits will doubtless be located in 2013.

Foreign assistance

Chinese bilateral financial assistance to Africa comes in many forms, differing strikingly from Western project-focused and socially inclined aid. China gives or lends abundant funds short-term or long-term to support its commodity purchasing and concession accruing endeavors. China makes zero-interest and low-interest concessional loans. It provides outright grants for ministerial office buildings and the AU edifice, for cultural centers, stadia, schools, hospitals, roads, bridges, and agricultural projects. When China proffers grants or loans for various infrastructural projects, and then proceeds to fulfill the resulting contracts itself, using imported Chinese labor, it does so caring only that the governments and key leaders of the countries in question have asked for the office building, stretch of road or rail, or harbor in question. It is largely indifferent to the social or economic results of the Chinese effort. Nor does it concern itself very much with the internal political result of its assistance – the strengthening of the grip of local elites or the enrichment of the leaders who have granted the necessary contracts.

China's aid to Africa "is supposed to be based on equality, mutual benefit, and respect for the sovereignty of the host."[17] Regular loans from the Chinese Ministries of Finance and Foreign Affairs are theoretically unconditional and interest-free, with an emphasis on neutrality and non-interference. China wants to get the job done, expeditiously, so as to enhance its access to desirable commodities. "Mutual benefit" refers in large part to the careful tying of loans to the export of petroleum and minerals. Concessional loans – worth well over $1 billion, to at least 22 African countries – are also linked but are slightly different since they derive from China's Eximbank and the Ministry of Commerce, and a few from the China Development Bank.

Wherever in the Chinese government these funding flows originate, they are managed and coordinated by the Chinese Ministry of Commerce and implemented by its Bureau of International Economic Cooperation. The latter arm of the ministry supervises the firms that are sent out from Beijing or Shanghai to realize Chinese-backed projects in Africa. Farming and fishing initiatives (and most of China's assistance to rural Africa) is organized by the Chinese Ministry of Agriculture. In 2012, for example, China gave $2 million to Mozambique to complete a regional Agricultural Technologies Center. Also in 2012, China and Nigeria together began producing hybrid rice seeds in Nigeria, and Nigeria imported 100 integrated Chinese rice mills for distribution to Nigeria's states. Medical aid, a not insignificant contribution from China to Africa, is arranged by the Ministry of Health. The Ministry of Education supplies scholarships to Africans and sends volunteer teachers to at least 30 African countries. Some of these educators instruct in African universities, some provide special workshops, some give occasional special seminars, and some teach alongside Africans (and American Peace Corps volunteers) in secondary schools.

There is a limited amount of Chinese-created humanitarian assistance, too. It flows out of China's Ministries of Commerce, Foreign Affairs, and Defense. China also established an International Poverty Alleviation Center in Beijing. Among other efforts, it trains African officials and introduces them to poverty reduction projects in China's poor provinces. The Ministry of Health has attempted, additionally, to strengthen the capacity of sub-Saharan Africa to respond to public health emergencies.[18]

The total of all of this assistance is difficult to calculate, not least because of the lack of transparency in Beijing, and within and across the ministries involved. "An accurate number of what China gives is difficult to come up with," according to Yun Sun.[19] Regular loans do not count as developmental assistance, but concessional loans and grants do. Thus, Brautigam concluded that only a puny proportion of the economic transactions between China and the developing world, and Africa, should qualify as "foreign aid," at least in Western terms. The majority of all transactions, whatever the Chinese call them, are for the purpose of facilitating exports beneficial to China. Her calculations show that China's "aid" (straight assistance and concessional lending) in 2010 amounted to about $2 billion, but a further $10 billion had been made available to finance projects, such as the Lobito railway and port in Angola and all of the export processing zones.[20] European, Japanese, and American – $7.8 billion in 2012 – aid totals were far larger.[21]

Debt loads have long saddled sub-Saharan African countries with financial obligations that hindered development and which they could not pay. The World Bank's Enhance Heavily Indebted Poor Countries Initiative (HIPC) was intended to relieve much of Africa of such obligations – to wipe the slate clean so that poorer countries could finally prosper. Have the Chinese now piled needless new borrowing burdens on Africa, and thus set back tomorrow's growth in exchange for the shiny project pottage of today? Or do the Chinese never expect their loans to be repaid and care only and relentlessly about long-term access to Africa's raw materials bonanza?[22] Brautigam asserts that Chinese state lenders and private firms all want to be repaid; nothing is phony. She also says that they lend prudently and are not anticipating forcing African countries back into a debt trap.[23]

Military aid

China has not been hesitant to provide assistance to those sub-Saharan African nations, mostly militarily ruled regimes or autocratic despotisms, that have requested help in the security sphere. Aid in this respect also qualifies under the "mutual benefit" rubric; China is not arming African states to enhance its own sphere of military influence or to pose a distant threat to Western interests. Rather, as with all of China's interactions with Africa, assisting Angola, the Sudan, Zimbabwe, and another dozen or so countries with their arms and training needs benefits the overriding objective of resource extraction. China is content to support the political status quo, whatever it is, and to supply military hardware and other material assistance to buttress existing governments and their defense establishments, however autocratic or dubious in origin or behavior. As Shinn suggests, China's efforts in the security sector "translate into a strategy that encourages a desire to strengthen stability in African countries that sell or have a potential to sell China significant quantities of raw materials."[24] Such transactions also provided substantial profit, in some cases, when China directly sold equipment to the defense establishments of a series of African states.

China is no newcomer to African security questions. In the latter years of the twentieth century, China backed a variety of African anticolonial liberation movements with arms, training, and funds. Some of those ventures were successful; many were not, with more powerful opposing movements triumphing despite their Soviet (and not Chinese) affiliations. There was no end to Chinese support for such military adventures from the 1960s through the 1990s. In the final years of the twentieth century, Russia and China (in that order) provided far more weapons to sub-Saharan African countries than did the United States. Germany overtook both nations in 2002 to 2005, but China remained the third most important supplier of lethal equipment, as well as the major exporter to Africa of small arms and light weapons, sometimes in contravention of embargoes. In 2012, deliveries of major arms from China to sub-Saharan Africa were estimated to have grown from 3 percent to 25 percent of the total volume of arms imports between 1996 and 2010.[25] China constructed arms factories in the Sudan and Uganda. Its equipment fueled both sides of the Ethiopian–Eritrean war, was employed to attack armed combatants and unarmed civilians in Darfur, in the Beja-populated eastern part of the Sudan, and against southern Sudanese insurgents. Ninety percent of the small arms entering the Sudan in 2004 to 2006 were from China. Later it supplied jet aircraft and much else to the security establishment in Zimbabwe, but as early as 2000 it was swapping guns for 8 tons of Zimbabwe's ivory.[26] In this decade, China offers military assistance and training, without formal military alliances, to nearly all of the 49 nations of sub-Saharan Africa. It is the fifth-largest supplier of small arms to the developing world, selling the Chinese version of the AK-47 assault rifle and other lethal materiel to Angola, Benin, Botswana, Burkina Faso, Cameroon, Djibouti, Ethiopia, Ghana, Kenya, Mozambique, Niger, South Africa, the Sudan, Tanzania, Uganda, Zambia, and Zimbabwe. But its fullest bilateral military ties have been to Angola (training, communications upgrades, and hardware); Ghana (communications upgrades, construction of barracks and other military facilities, the transfer of vehicles, and the provision of jet fighters); Nigeria (military buildings, jet aircraft, patrol boats, and communication equipment); South Africa (formal security consultations, arms sales, and arms purchases); the Sudan (all manner of heavy and light arms, jet fighters and trainers, military transport vehicles, and troops on the ground); Zambia (aircraft and medical personnel); and Zimbabwe (the aforementioned jets, all manner of arms, training, communications upgrades, military barracks and a staff college, and consignments of uniforms). In 2012, there were nearly 1,200 Chinese peacekeepers attached to eight UN missions in sub-Saharan Africa. In Darfur, at one point, 100 Chinese engineers were assisting the UN/AU mission there.[27]

On the outer fringes of sub-Saharan Africa, China also joined the US–EU mission to combat piracy off the coast of Somalia. Its frigates were an integral part of the anti-piracy flotilla in the Gulf of Aden and the Indian Ocean between Somalia and the Seychelles. As Shinn rightly observed, Chinese military and security cooperation in this sphere derived from China's self-interested desire to advance its own economic hegemony in Africa and its continued unfettered access to Africa's raw materials.[28] With regard to all of its vaunted assistance to the soldiers of Africa, China's overriding motives are pragmatic, mercenary, and mercantile. Others may label China's activities in this arena cynical; China would not. For China, it makes strategic sense to respond in a reciprocal way, and effectively, to requests to it from the leaders of sub-Saharan Africa. To China, that makes perfect commercial and political sense.

The labor question

Chinese state-controlled, quasi-state controlled, and private commercial operatives in Africa prefer to import their own laborers, sometimes allegedly from Chinese prisons or prison camps. Rather than employing Africans (formal unemployment rates in much of sub-Saharan Africa range from 25 to 80 percent, depending on the country), and thus boosting African incomes and transferring knowledge (even at low technical levels), China insists on using Chinese laborers, not just Chinese foremen or managers.[29] In Angola, China has paid for the construction of new railways and roads but uses Chinese (not local) contractors and workers, thus denying jobs to anxious Angolans. Near Benguela, south of Luanda along Angola's Atlantic coast, a Chinese construction firm in 2009 and 2010 rapidly raised a massive white steel structure (one of four stadia it funded and constructed in Angola) for the Africa Cup of Nations football (soccer) tournament. To do so in Benguela alone, the firm employed 700 Chinese overseers, engineers, and laborers, and 250 Angolans.[30]

In Kenya, in Malawi, in Madagascar, even in Botswana and Mauritius, China relies on its own. In Zambia, where China directly owns coal and copper mines and smelters, it does employ Zambian miners, but primarily to perform unskilled tasks. In Harare, China imported several thousand workers, housing them in dormitories behind barricaded blush pink walls, to construct a staff college for the Zimbabwean military. Others dig diamonds for a Chinese corporation. Very few local laborers were allowed onto the staff college site despite the country's poverty and its stratospheric glut of unemployed artisans and ordinary workers. China has even imported farmers to till the soil, tasks that local Zimbabweans (or Liberians) could do.

This obdurate refusal to do what every earlier entrepreneurial force has done – to employ the locals – is explained away as something "cultural." Chinese feel more "comfortable" relying on their own, who they know will work harder for longer hours than will Africans. They speak the same language and do not need interpreters. Fundamentally, too, Chinese contractors and industrial supervisors believe that Africans are "lazy" or "lackadaisical." They believe in the stereotypical descriptions relayed by their own Chinese contemporaries. They think that they have anecdotal evidence to support such claims. Furthermore, few African states have insisted that their own people should be employed. None has banned immigrant labor from China. African governments seemingly have also wanted to "get the job done" as quickly and efficiently as possible. Or they have refused to curb Chinese firms. Thus, hardly any African government – not even Zambia after the election of President Michael Sata in 2011 – has demanded that Chinese firms should employ greater numbers of Africans, or leave. Earlier, a Zambian Finance Minister had lamented the flood of low-paid, culturally isolated, job-monopolizing and thus local work-depriving laborers imported from China to build his country's roads and mines.[31] Zimbabwe's much-paraded "indigenization" policy specifically exempts China and Chinese investors. In 2012, the China International Mining Group Corporation hence invested more than $21 million to restart Zimbabwe's Bindura nickel mine.

If the sad truth be known, Chinese at all levels believe that their own personnel are more obedient, more reliable, more efficient, and more trustworthy than Africans. Chinese also tolerate unconscionable behavior more readily. As the Zambian case study (below) demonstrates, Chinese corporate CEOs are often willing to cut corners, ignore official safety regulations, pay low wages, and generally push their indigenous workers hard, sometimes beyond comfortable limits. Just as they are accused of behaving badly in factories in Guangdong, in China, managers in Africa care overwhelmingly for productivity achievements and over-fulfilling tonnage or product quotas.

Chinese executives and middle-ranking operatives focus determinedly on their work tasks, and not on social relations. Most Chinese refrain from mingling with their African colleagues or employees. The communities that the Chinese create in Africa around industries, mines, power plants, dams, and other large construction projects are hence "socially thin" and even the imported laborers are often rigidly separated from contact with surrounding local African dwelling areas and villages by barbed wire and other barriers.[32] Chinese firms rarely invest socially in their locales; they discourage fraternization. Chinese workers thus most often socialize among themselves. Even a transplanted fishing community in Senegal keeps to itself and avoids as much of the local interactive scene as it can. So, as much as possible, do Chinese traders and shopkeepers. China, in other words, for the most part is in Africa but is not yet a part of Africa.

According to Rupp, "social relations between ordinary Africans and Chinese are marked by a tension between mutual admiration and mutual loathing." They view each other "with suspicion." They share negative perceptions of each other, possibly because Africans and Chinese rarely interact in intimate ways. The Chinese (Mandarin) characters for "Africa" translate literally as "negative continent." Chinese managers "tend to be aloof" and are hesitant to engage with Africans.[33] It is widely presumed that, since the Chinese who have come to Africa prefer to mingle infrequently with Africans, they must either fear or dislike contact. Many Africans consequently regard their Chinese bosses or co-workers as harboring racist attitudes and behaviors.

The seamy underside of success

Chinese attitudes toward Africa and Africans have naturally generated concern. Yet, for several years, China was able to avoid ferocious criticism of its labor policies; it delivered new or renovated infrastructure on time and on budget. Its supposed emphasis on "efficiency" produced clear benefits for Africans. But then the Chinese were accused of slap-dash practices. A general hospital in Luanda opened with fanfare. But cracks soon appeared in its walls and bricks fell after a few months. Fearing imminent collapse, officials shut it down. Newly tarred Angolan roads washed away after a single rainy season.[34] Tanzania's new main international airport terminal, to be completed by a Chinese concern, was abandoned when local funding could not be raised. But more than 1,000 indigenous families were displaced and relocated. A Chinese newly constructed 130 km road from Lusaka south to Chirundu on the Zambian–Zimbabwean border was swept away when the summer rains fell. Chad's Chinese-constructed oil refinery stands idle because it is too expensive to operate. Chinese oil exploration efforts made a mess in a Gabonese national park and created lakes of spilled crude oil in the Sudan. Gabon has also permitted three separate Chinese concessions to mine vast fields of iron ore from within three different national parks. A Zimbabwean minister accused the Chinese active in the country's eastern diamond-mining field of despoiling the environment. Zambians involved in conservation and tourism allege that the Chinese in their country are sponsors of systematic animal poaching, largely of ivory but also of bush meat. Several Chinese individuals have been prosecuted in Zambia in recent years for poaching offenses, but other hard evidence is lacking.

In northern Nigeria, the landed price of inexpensive cloth and garments imported from China compelled the closure of hundreds of textile factories that could not price their own products low enough to compete successfully. Thousands of Nigerian jobs were lost. Textile traders in Ghana and Togo, mostly women, also suffered through Chinese import competition.[35] In this manner jobs were lost in the indigenous textile and leather manufacturing centers of southern Africa, especially Lesotho, Madagascar, Mauritius, and South Africa. In the centuries-old indigo-dying pits of ancient Kano, the Chinese were reported to be "choking small-scale businesses," according to a local manager.[36] Chickens imported from China are cheaper than local ones in Lusaka's indigenous markets, reducing the profits of local farmers. Cabbage prices have also fallen. Again in Lusaka, the availability of inexpensive new Chinese clothing destroyed the long-existing market for imported second-hand garments. In Cameroon, vendors of inexpensive foods faced relentless competition from Chinese petty entrepreneurs. Also in Cameroon, Chinese sex workers marginalized their local counterparts by charging considerably less. In Angola in 2012, dozens of Chinese suspected violent criminals were forcibly repatriated to China for allegedly being responsible for multiple kidnappings, robberies, blackmail, forcing women into prostitution, and engaging in human trafficking. In Ghana, where supposedly more than 10,000 Chinese nationals have flooded the country to search for alluvial gold, more than 100 Chinese were arrested in 2012 for mining illegally.[37] Dar es Salaam coped with competition from Chinese head-on, by denying trading licenses to Chinese traders and peddlers.[38] Whereas foreign merchants of earlier eras largely remained aloof from daily encounters at the market level, the Chinese are in every African market, creating understandable anxiety and taking customers away from their African rivals.[39]

Overall, the availability of inexpensive commodities from China enables Africans to possess items that were too dear before cheap goods from far away flooded into the markets of the cities, towns, and villages of the sub-continent. Everywhere, consumer goods such as radios, televisions, bicycles, mattresses, and so on are more affordable thanks to China's foray into Africa. But those goods are malignant, too, displacing anything that Africans themselves might have manufactured and driving indigenous traders and shopkeepers to distraction. Furthermore, Africans consider the Chinese products sub-standard and second-class, and probably dumped on Africa because they are not marketable in Europe and America.

In Angola, wrote one indigenous critic, "the Chinese are not investing to develop the country. They have brought more corruption, and, consequently, more poverty." Moreover, "in Angola, the presidential family, government officials and top generals have monopolized the country's resources for their illicit enrichment while paying the Chinese to do shoddy labor."[40]

The Zambian case

Zambians have for many years voiced concerns about the dominant, even bullying, role that China has been playing in its economy, and also in its politics. Michael Sata railed against Chinese firms, contrasting their performance unfavorably with the "old colonial rulers," when he was campaigning in 2006, 2008, and 2011 for the country's presidency. He extolled the British for taking "good care of us," building schools, teaching their language, and bringing us "British civilization." "Western capitalism had a human face," he said. But the Chinese were "only out to exploit us," was his charge. They paid "slave wages," flouted environmental standards, and corrupted African leaders across the continent. "We need investors, not infesters," he also said.[41] But, once he had won the Zambian presidency, Sata evidently decided that he had to be friendly to such a massive partner. He quickly exchanged warm messages with Premier Wen Jiabao and dispatched former President Kenneth Kaunda to provide assurances in Beijing.

"Anti-Chinese feelings in Zambia run high. . . ." Or at least they once did. During a visit to the country in 2007 by President Hu, the University of Zambia, on the main route from Lusaka's airport, was cordoned off by riot police. The police also prevented protesting workers from a factory shut abruptly by the Chinese from voicing concerns. The threat by Copperbelt residents to demonstrate against Hu forced the visiting President to cancel his visit there.[42]

It is not yet clear what Sata will now do to reform Chinese practices and attitudes. In Zambia, Chinese-owned enterprises and their Chinese managers have run roughshod over local laws and regulations. They are known to be tough and unsentimental bosses and to treat their Zambian employees shabbily. In Zambia's copper mines run by Chinese firms, underground workers cannot obtain safety helmets until they have worked for two years. Ventilation in some of these same mines is poor (by southern African mining standards) and accidents are frequent. Supposedly, too, Chinese bosses bribe local union bosses and take them on study tours to massage parlors in China. Obstructionist shop stewards are sacked. Workers who assemble in groups are dispersed, violently. When cases go to court, witnesses are intimidated. In 2010, too, Chinese managers fired shotguns at a crowd of protesting Zambian coal miners, injuring a dozen. But no one has ever been prosecuted. According to a Zambian journalist, "The Chinese . . . can do anything."[43]

Zambians have been mining copper since the 1920s. At one point in the late 1960s, Zambia was the second most productive copper producer in the world. But its nationalization of the mines in the early 1970s coincided with the end of the Vietnam War and a rapid falling of revenues from the precious metal. By the time that the Zambian government reversed course and sold its mines one-by-one to private investors, the copper properties in north-central Zambia had deteriorated thanks to under-investment and general neglect.

The China Non-Ferrous Metals Mining Corporation (CNMC), overseen by China's state-owned Assets Supervision and Administration Commission, purchased the then-shut Chambishi mine in 1998 and transferred ownership to Non-Ferrous China Africa. After spending $132 million, the rehabilitated mine reopened in 2003. Subsequently, CNMC built a copper processing plant, constructed a copper smelting facility, and purchased an open-cast and underground copper operation in nearby Luanshya. The total investment amounts to about $1 billion. Together, these Chinese-controlled copper installations employ 6,000 Zambians. By the end of 2013, they expect to offer jobs to another several thousand local hires.

Zambians, in a country where formal unemployment rates are about 50 percent, welcome the Chinese-provided positions but also note that opportunities at the nearby, better-run Canadian-, South African-, Swiss-, or Indian-owned mines are preferable and better paid. In the Chinese-run establishments, Zambians typically receive more than the national monthly minimum wage of $87, but approximately two-thirds less than what persons laboring in the Canadian- or Indian-owned mines receive. "Workers and union officials who spoke to Human Rights Watch [in 2010 and 2011] said the Chinese . . . operations were the country's worst when it [came] to health and safety." Conditions were also regarded as deplorable in Chinese-run copper mines in the neighboring Congo (Kinshasa).[44] Underground miners employed by the Chinese in Zambia are obliged to work 12-hour, not 8-hour shifts, to put in 78-hour working weeks, and to labor every day of every year. The Chinese mines have copper production quotas to fulfill. Indeed, in 2010, the Chambishi mine had an annual profit of $40 million, having recouped its initial investment with ease.[45]

The Chinese mining operations in Zambia regularly flout official safety laws and procedures. In 2012, the Engineering Institute of Zambia tried to close four Chinese-owned coal mines operating illegally in the country's Southern Province.[46] Generally, Zambian company safety officers are overruled by their Chinese managers. Miners themselves are terminated if they refuse to work in dangerous situations – handling acid or inhaling noxious fumes and dust in poorly ventilated conditions. The Chinese firms have been loath to supply personal protective equipment, standard in other mines in Zambia (and elsewhere in the world). Nor did they regularly provide potable water, despite the parched conditions above- and underground. Often, when injured miners reported to a Chinese-funded hospital near the mine and received medical instructions to cease work for days or weeks, their Chinese shift bosses forced them back to work. "They'll say, 'No work, job is finished . . .' which means you're fired."[47]

Numerous accidents have resulted from conditions and procedures (or lack of procedures) on the laxly run Chinese underground and open-cast mines. Although no deaths have been reported recently (as they were in 2005), there have been many crushed fingers, broken legs and arms, acid burns, lung disease (silicosis) diagnoses, and electrocutions from misplaced cables. "Sometimes when you find yourself in a dangerous position," a Zambian miner told Human Rights Watch, "they tell you to go ahead with the work. They just consider production, not safety. If someone dies, he can be replaced tomorrow. And if you report the problem, you'll lose your job." Another, a person frequently in charge of explosives underground, said that the ventilation was very bad: "As we drill deeper, there is lots of smoke, lots of dust, yet we aren't given respirators. We just have a dust mask. We all have lung problems. I inhale the stuff all the time, because they don't give us a respirator; so my lungs and throat always hurt." An injured underground miner indicated that when someone says a section of the underground mine is unsafe, "the Chinese boss refuses you and says 'You Zambians have no power, just go and work.'" After refusing to remain at work in an area lit up dangerously with welding sparks, a Zambian miner was fired by his Chinese supervisor: "you're not supposed to talk, you're a slave," he said.[48]

The Chinese-owned Chambishi mining properties have largely barred the long-established Mine Workers' Union of Zambia (MUZ) from their compounds. They only allow the weaker National Union of Miners and Allied Workers, formed in 2003, to represent their workers. At the non-Chinese Copperbelt mines, employees are able to establish branches of both unions. International covenants and Zambian law should guarantee the free right to form and join trade unions, but the Chinese owners of the Zambian mines have effectively thwarted such legal obligations. "They say," a miner reported, "if we bring MUZ . . . [it] will cause too much problems advocating for [our rights]. We've tried, but with no success." Moreover, reported an MUZ representative, "The Chinese don't understand the concept of a union. They intimidate those that lead or are part of a union."[49]

Special Economic Zones

In partnership with several African countries, China has pioneered the establishment of seven Special Economic Zones, otherwise called export processing zones. Africans have wanted for many years to attract foreign direct investment to designated enclaves free of taxes and other imposts in order to emulate similar experiments elsewhere in the world. Constructing and opening the new commercial areas presume customs duty waivers, preferential tax rates, flexible hiring and firing, and access to productive labor. Intended to be new growth nodes, these Zones are expected to drive sub-Saharan Africa's economic renaissance. Each Zone – in Ethiopia, Kenya, Liberia, Mauritius, Nigeria, Sierra Leone, the Sudan, and Zambia – is especially linked to purpose-built transport corridors and revamped or brand new harbors. The Zones are intended, too, to help integrate Africa's sub-regions in terms of trade and investment.

The Zones now being completed follow China's own developmental model for its fast-growing southeastern hinterland. The Special Economic Zones in Guangdong and Hainan Provinces played essential roles in spurring the trade awakening and manufacturing upsurge that ignited China's extraordinary growth in recent decades. Technology acquisition and transfer contributed signally to the success of the Zones in China; the African special Zones will also depend on the adaptation of technology and the transfer of knowledge from outside sub-Saharan Africa. At least that is the Chinese model that the Africans intend, or wish, to follow. Indeed, in these nascent African Zones, and elsewhere, nearly 1,000 Chinese firms have brought their operations and their economic goals to Africa. Such Chinese initiatives, together with the activity and attractiveness of the Zones, possess the potential to raise Africa's GDP prospects.[50]

The Zambia–China Economic and Trade Cooperation Zone, to take one example, was designed to bring together world-class infrastructure, expedited customs and administrative procedures, and fiscal incentives that, together, would stimulate foreign investment. It is a "metal hub," attracting Congolese as well as Zambian copper, cobalt, diamonds, tin, and uranium for processing by Chinese firms and then for onward shipment to China. In this case, as well as in the other Zones, one key goal was to maximize and facilitate Chinese access to key resources and to leverage China's local investment particularly. One estimate suggested that 60 Chinese companies were expected to locate within the Zone in Chambishi, next to and around the Chinese-controlled mining property. There they will manufacture televisions, electronic equipment, and mobile telephones. Whether there will be places reserved for purely Zambian concerns and other foreign investors is not clear. China says "no," the Zambian government "yes." Some critics even suggest that the Zambian Zone is but a "pseudo-economic zone" designed primarily to "avoid paying full tax or even the market price on [Zambia's] copper" "and not to boost enterprise generally or to provide Zambia with incentives capable of attracting new foreign investors."[51]

The Mauritian Special Economic Zone was designed to be a "trading hub." Forty Chinese corporations thereby gained preferential market access to the 20 countries belonging to the embryonic Common Market of Eastern and Southern Africa (COMESA), stretching notionally from Ethiopia to Malawi and South Africa, within easy transport distance of South and Southeast Asia. (China lent Mauritius $600 million in 2012.) The Tanzanian hub, in Dar es Salaam, is a so-called "shipping hub," capable of attracting Chinese and other traffic into and out of the Great Lakes region. An Ethiopian hub is expected to focus on shoe manufacturing, eventually using local skins and hides. The late Prime Minister Meles Zenawi wanted Ethiopia "to produce shoes for the world." A senior Chinese manager said that the importing of Chinese workers and inputs would be phased out as Ethiopians become trained shoe-makers and as domestic leather quality improved. The Sudanese zone is supposed to focus on agricultural products.[52]

Human rights concerns

China as an investor or a purchaser of primary products implicitly or explicitly backs the harsh rule of authoritarian governments throughout the subcontinent. As Chinese officials themselves say, China is at best indifferent to the quality of governance in the countries in which it operates. China is thus content to support odious regimes, even propping up some of them, supplying corrupt rents to many, and almost always reinforcing an African regime's least participatory instincts: "China [coddles] dictators, despoil[s] poor countries and undermin[es] Western efforts to spread democracy and prosperity."[53] In the Sudan, in Zimbabwe, and elsewhere, China has supported or is supporting governments sanctioned by or otherwise condemned by the United Nations. "Western-style democratic theory simply isn't suited to African conditions," the Chinese have long believed.[54] There is an underlying official contempt in leading Chinese circles for do-gooding Western notions of how African development should be nurtured politically and economically. For this reason, along with mercenary concerns, China continues to supply small arms and other weapons indiscriminately and in defiance of UN strictures.

China was complicit in the genocide in Darfur and may similarly have aided the Sudanese attacks on South Kordofan and Blue Nile in 2012. Certainly, in Darfur, China could have restrained the Sudanese government from attacking rebels and civilians relentlessly in 2003–2006. It could have used its undoubted economic and military supply leverage to end massacres and mayhem in Darfur, and later against Nubans on the southern border of the new Sudan. China refused, at the height of the Darfur crisis and again later, to put appropriate pressure on the corrupt military junta ruling the Sudan when doing so might well have saved thousands of lives.[55]

China's stated reluctance to intervene on behalf of peace and human rights in the Sudan, or in Kenya after the disputed election in 2007, and its opposition in the UN Security Council and elsewhere to criticism of the Sudan and Zimbabwe, is regarded by human rights advocates as perverse and obstructionist. In 2008, China joined Russia in barring the Security Council from imposing sanctions on President Robert Mugabe's abusive regime in Zimbabwe. But that was China's preference as an authoritarian polity, fearing global critiques of its own actions in Tibet and Xinjiang, and of its harsh treatment at home of non-Han and of religious minorities. Or, conceivably, China genuinely worried that, unless it supported the worst of the worst in Africa, it could lose access to Africa's oil and other raw materials.

Admittedly, in many of the least savory African countries, such as Angola and Equatorial Guinea, China pumps oil alongside US-based multinationals. With regard to the irresponsible behavior that Human Rights Watch observed in Chinese-owned mines, the onus might legitimately fall on the Zambian authorities for failing to enforce their own laws and regulations. Regarding Zimbabwe, where China once again has failed to restrain official abuses or exert a benign influence, it can be accused more of tolerating human rights excesses than of being responsible legally for aiding and abetting repression. A sophisticated analysis of the human rights charges against China also suggests that "evidence for the *direct* commission of human rights abuses by Chinese agents is limited."[56]

The balance sheet

With regard to the development of sub-Saharan Africa, is China a malign force – a modern colonial colossus intent on stripping Africa of its wealth without leaving behind sustainable structures? President Thabo Mbeki of South Africa warned China long ago that it could not "just come here and dig for raw materials and then go away and sell us manufactured goods." His successor, Jacob Zuma, praised China but also cautioned that Africa needed to be careful in entering into new partnerships with "other economies."[57] China has transferred little technology or knowledge to Africa in the past decade, has engaged in little capacity-building, and has paid precious little attention to the strengthening of transparency, accountability, good governance, and the building of effective political institutions – all of which sub-Saharan Africa requires if it is to play a more mature role in world affairs and, crucially, if it is to grow substantially in the decades ahead.

"The Chinese are selfish," a leading Zambian industrialist explained to a dinner audience.[58] China's disregard for the environment, its refusal to follow good extractive industry practices in its petroleum or minerals domains, its slapdash approach to safety issues, its willingness to condone human rights violations in many of the African states in which it is active, and its fundamental disdain for Africa and Africans (despite pronouncements to the contrary) are negative weights on the scale. Even, or particularly, when it enunciates its mantra of non-interference in sovereign nations, whatever their politics, China undermines respect for human rights and transparency as defined by the African Union and even the New Partnership for Africa's Development (NEPAD).[59]

But China is still essential for the sub-continent's continued development. "Without the Chinese," exclaimed a lawyer looking at the ruins of a once Belgian-owned copper mine in Katanga, "all this [would] just be scenery."[60] There would be few profitable global markets for Africa without China. If China vanished from sub-Saharan Africa or, perish the thought, grew much more slowly than it did from 2003 to 2012, the futures of the countries of the sub-continent would be imperiled. The Chinese appetite for what sub-Saharan Africa has underground and offshore drives Africa's rebirth and any hope of realizing a fully blooming African renaissance in this century. Commodity prices would plummet if Chinese demand faltered or if more accessible or less expensive sources of energy were easily obtainable.

Given these realities, and given the unlikelihood of any immediate improvement in the manner in which China and Chinese state corporations and their managers approach Africa and Africans, it behooves the nation-states of sub-Saharan Africa collectively, or in sub-regional groups, to take charge decisively of the Chinese–African relationship in a way that has not yet proved possible. China, with its immense political and economic leverage, has engaged for decades in bilateral bargaining with mostly weak African states. As President Sata's volte-face over Chinese behavior signifies, individually nearly all of the sub-Saharan African states are too weak to bargain effectively with China. Or, in some cases, China has already coopted their leaders.

It is long past time that sub-Saharan Africa turned dealings with China into a multilateral exercise. Neither the African Union, nor sub-regional organizations such as the Southern African Development Community (SADC), the East African Community (EAC), and the Economic Community of West African States (ECOWAS), have as yet articulated clear policies regarding China's role in Africa and how Chinese influence and leverage can best be turned to Africa's advantage. Each of the 49 sub-Saharan African polities now goes its own way, responding to Chinese entreaties (Taiwan has diplomatic relations with four remaining followers – Burkina Faso, the Gambia, São Tomé and Príncipe, and Swaziland) idiosyncratically. The African petroleum producers, the African hard mineral exporters, the African industrial entrepreneurs, the African agro-processors, the African fish harvesters, and other special commercial interests all have specialized concerns. Together, rather than distinctively, they should develop specific, tailored, policies supportive of their endeavors vis-à-vis China.

Additionally, acting together, African states could develop well-articulated rules regarding the importation of Chinese laborers, enhancing African employment; special taxation privileges (or not) for Chinese firms and Chinese state entities; new tariffs honed to increasing trade without disadvantaging African governments; and protection or not (under World Trade Organization guidelines) for domestically produced African goods. Only by making a concerted argument will sub-regional organizations or groups of like-minded African states persuade China and Chinese firms to obey the letter and spirit of local laws, honor African mores, respect African cultural traditions, cooperate with indigenous civil societies, and support those African governments and African ruling elites who seek reforms rather than rents. With a little encouragement, too, China might see that it is in its enlightened self-interest to cease supporting dictatorial regimes. Backing Africa's most reviled despotisms is bad for Africa and bad for China as a world power.[61]

Without concerted African ground rules and improved governance in the receiving countries, China will persist in behaving opportunistically, exploiting weaker nation-states in its relentless quest for resources. It will continue, naturally, to assert its own overweening economic leverage with little consideration for African values and needs. If Africans are to stand on an equal footing with their Chinese guests and entrepreneurs, they need to band together so as to channel Chinese energies and capital in directions that benefit Africa as much as they benefit China. Only by so doing will Africa turn China's massive drive to accumulate Africa's treasures into a mutually sustainable advantage.

These new political stances are essential because – preferably for good but possibly for ill – China *is* transforming sub-Saharan Africa. China provides a much more powerful influence now, and will for at least the next several decades, than the old colonial powers, India, Japan, or the United States. Since so many African countries depend for their economic and social futures on China and Chinese demand, and since the collective well-being of millions of Africans now and for the next half-century depends on commerce with China, putting that relationship on a firm and lasting footing is absolutely essential. For Africa to develop, it needs a responsible, not an exploitative, post-colonial partner.

10
Strengthening Governance

"The biggest obstacle to Africa's development," former British Prime Minister Tony Blair declared in 2012, opening his Africa Governance Initiative, "is governance." It was crucial, he continued, "to have in place a proper system for attracting . . . investment . . . having a legal system that functions fairly and . . . depends on a minimum level of infrastructure." He went on: "This is not only about transparency, that is, honest government, important though that is. It is also about effective government . . . The new Africa needs a new approach from African leaders."[1]

Just as Blair declaimed to an audience of corporate CEOs, sub-Saharan Africa thirsts for improved governance. Only with a strengthened performance by their 49 governments can the nation-states of the sub-continent achieve the developmental, social, economic, and political breakthroughs that their peoples demand. Attracting foreign investment, rewarding indigenous entrepreneurial enterprise, enhancing educational opportunity, upgrading health care and life chances, taking full advantage of the demographic dividend, and creating more secure environments depend on the delivery of adequate quantities and high qualities of political goods to the citizens of the sub-continent.

That delivery – collectively, governmental performance or "effective government" – is what is meant by the term "governance." Blair mentioned some of its necessary components. But there is much more to "governance," and to satisfying consumers of governmental action, than he implied. Moreover, the complex notion that each of us, and every African, expects a bundle of "political goods" as her/his natural entitlement is also essential to set out at length. This notion spans continents and peoples and applies fully (as it has since the Peace of Westphalia in 1648) to the peoples and countries of Africa – whatever their ethnicities, languages, religions, or traditional cultures. It provides a standard by which all peoples and nations (and governmental jurisdictions of all kinds and sizes) can measure performance. Unless the leaders of the new Africa satisfy these performance criteria and thus begin to meet the aspirations of their people, the sub-continent will be slow to mature, slow to take its promised place in the world, and slow to produce what Blair called "effective" government or what an incisive study of national successes and failures calls "inclusive" economic markets and economic and political institutions.[2]

All citizens of all countries desire to be governed well. That is what citizens want from and expect of the nation-states in which they live. Thus, nation-states in the modern world (no less in Africa) are responsible for the delivery of essential political goods to their inhabitants. That is their purpose, and that has been their central legitimate justification since the era of Westphalia. These essential political goods are bundled into five categories: Safety and Security; Rule of Law and Transparency; Participation and Respect for Human Rights; Sustainable Economic Opportunity; and Human Development. Together, these five categories of political goods epitomize the performance of any government, at any level. No one, whether looking to her village, municipality, province, state, or nation willingly wants to be victimized by crime or to live in a society without regulations and laws; to be denied freedom to express herself and to influence decisions; to be without a chance to prosper; and to be held back from access to decent schools, well-run hospitals and clinics, and carefully maintained roads.[3]

Of the five categories of political goods, the paramount one is security.[4] There can be no economic growth or social elevation, and no societal strength as opposed to weakness and failure, without fundamental security. A nation-state's prime function everywhere is thus to secure its territory – to prevent cross-border invasions and incursions; to reduce domestic threats to, or attacks upon, the national domain and the national order; to bolster human security or security of the person by reducing crime – to make its city streets and rural villages safe; and hence to prevent mayhem by roving gangs, non-state actors, or marauding desperadoes. If a nation-state merely controls its capital city, if it cannot project power to the periphery, if it does not have a monopoly of the use of force within its borders, and if it cannot repress would-be secessionists and potential rebels, then the nation-state is insecure and verging on failure. Or it is already failed.

The delivery of other necessary political goods becomes feasible only when reasonable provisions of security are obtained. Good governance next requires a predictable, recognizable, systematized method of adjudicating disputes and regulating both the norms and the prevailing mores of the societies and nation-states under inspection. This second political good implies codes and procedures that together compose an enforceable body of law, security of property and enforceable contracts, an effective judicial system, and a set of norms that validate what is called the rule of law. The practical impact of a strong rule-of-law regime is that it enables citizens to resolve their differences with fellow inhabitants or with an overweening state without recourse to arms or physical coercion.

Each of the globe's nation-states fashions its own rule of law. The English common law and the Napoleonic Code are but two major jurisprudential methodologies, but most sub-Saharan African dispute resolution processes follow those procedural formulae. There are ethnically traditional methods and Sharia-like forms, too. But without some such formalized body of laws, societal bonds weaken, disputes are settled by violent means rather than peaceful parleys, and commerce (and investment) is much riskier than it would be otherwise.

A third political good certifies that citizens are participating freely, openly, and fully in a democratic political process – that they have "voice." This good encompasses the essential freedoms: the right to participate in politics and compete for office; respect and support for national and provincial political institutions, legislatures, and courts; tolerance of dissent and difference; an independent media untrammelled by executive branch surveillance and control; freedom of speech; freedom of assembly and unionization; freedom of religion; and minority rights.

A fearless and un-self-censored media is even more essential than a fully independent judicial system. Few breakdowns of civil order, few state failures, have occurred in countries with an open and active media – with privately run television channels and radio stations and a vibrant press. Without such methods of criticism, the free political space shrinks, accountability is observed in the breach, and rulers and ruling elites can prey on their citizens. Nation-state failure can and often does ensue.

A fourth critical political good and major component of governance is the creation of an enabling environment permissive of, and conducive to, economic growth and prosperity at national and personal levels. This political good thus encompasses a prudently run monetary and banking system, usually guided by a central bank and lubricated by a secure and strong national currency; a fiscal and institutional context within which citizens may pursue individual entrepreneurial goals without let or hindrance, and potentially prosper; and a regulatory environment appropriate to the economic aspirations and attributes of the nation-state. Where a ruling family or clan arrogates to itself most of the available sources of economic growth (from petroleum discoveries, say) and tightly distributes profit-making opportunities only to a select group of cronies and sycophants, a permissive and positive framework is falsified and patrimony readily displaces the possibility of widespread prosperity.

Providing this fourth political good includes the other critical components that help to ensure growth for all: primary are robust arteries of commerce that contribute significantly to the possibility of Sustainable Economic Opportunity. Among these arteries are an extensive road network, preferably paved; railways; working harbors for ocean-going or riverine trade; modern airports; rapid broadband Internet connections to the wider world; and competitive and inexpensive mobile telephone networks.

The fifth political good encompasses the benefits demanded overwhelmingly by the peoples of sub-Saharan Africa: educational opportunity, including the provision of sufficient places in secondary schools and university; and the offering of readily available medical care in clinics and hospitals. The first assumes sufficient classrooms, teachers, and textbooks, plus perhaps computers. The second encompasses such essential health elements as clean water and sanitation, an adequate supply of physicians and nurses, abundant sutures and medicines in medical facilities, and some advanced technical equipment.

Measuring performance

By specifying what governance is and by spelling out the five categories of modern governance in a manner much more precise and specific than Blair attempted, African governments can hold themselves fully to account. Their civil societies equally can scrutinize the regimes under which they work, and so can the United Nations, international lending institutions, and bilateral donors. The overriding purpose is not merely to rank countries against other countries to show which are the well-governed and which are poorly governed. Doing so can be helpful, but even more insightful and informative is the use of this conceptual approach for diagnostic purposes. Not only can we discover which are the better-governed places in sub-Saharan Africa (or anywhere else) but we can also discern which sections of a national governmental apparatus are doing well and which need improvement. On which parts of the nation's government, in other words, should most attention and money be urgently focused?

In order to undertake such an examination thoroughly and carefully, the five categories of political good already discussed must be further refined so that governance can properly be measured. The pioneering Index of African Governance did so by breaking down the five major categories into 57 sub-categories or variables, 22 under Human Development (the fifth political good), 5 under Safety and Security (the first), and so on.[5] The other methodological breakthrough was to attempt to measure objectively rather than subjectively. That is, the Index tried to avoid amassing quantitative scores that were derived from opinions, even if those rendering opinion and passing judgment were experts or other close observers of a national or local scene. The danger of selection bias was palpable and to be avoided. The Index further focused insistently on measuring outputs, not inputs. That is, in evaluating a national or local medical system a country's health budget (an input) matters far less than how that money has been used (or siphoned off) to improve health outcomes. Good ministerial attitudes and fine words matter far less than results. No amount of jawboning can obscure a lack of discernible outcomes.

For the most part, as proxies for several of the otherwise hard-to-measure five major components of governance, the Index employed, for outcomes in the health arena, such internationally standard variables as life expectancy and maternal mortality rates. To help calibrate Sustainable Economic Opportunity, in addition to GDP it employed a nation's kilometers of paved roads and its GINI coefficient standing (an indication of equality of wealth).

For Safety, it counted annual homicides. For Security, it noted the number each year of casualties in civil warfare. Most of these data are assembled annually by such estimable establishments as the World Bank, the International Monetary Fund, the World Health Organization (WHO), the UN Development Program (UNDP), and the UN International Children's Fund (UNICEF). Yet, because nearly all of these resultant numbers ultimately are derived from national statistical offices, and because many of those offices are underfunded and understaffed, the development of reliable data is sometimes compromised. For that reason, the Index checked the internationally collected quantitative sources against local ones by employing a small army of researchers in many national capitals. In some cases Index researchers even themselves measured roads or subjected local numbers to sophisticated checking and recalibration.[6]

The result of this arduous and exacting process was an assemblage of data with which to assess the state of governance within sub-Saharan Africa, country v. country, and not against arbitrary global standards. Countries were scored on each variable, and across several years. For example, within the Sustainable Economic Opportunity category, countries were rated not only on their annual GDP per capita attainment, but on their levels of inflation, the extent to which their inhabitants were equal or unequal in wealth (the GINI coefficient), the integrity of their banking systems ("Contract Intensive Money"), and the length and availability of robust arteries of commerce – such as mobile telephone networks, roads, and railways.

The examination of all of these components of governance, proxies though many plainly are, permits the painting of a full governance portrait of each country in sub-Saharan Africa. Thanks to the successive iterations of the Index, as well as to ratings supplied by the World Bank and individual NGOs, we now know with some significant precision how well and how poorly each part of the sub-continent is governed. We also know which aspects of governance in each country need urgent attention and which are in lesser need of remedial action. Further, we can gather a precise list of sub-Saharan Africa's outstanding governance issues. With them in hand, the political leaders, corporate moguls, and civil societies of Africa can at the very least come to appreciate what they must do to strengthen their individual national governances. They now have the tools with which to improve their governmental performances, as sub-Saharan Africa collectively and its nations individually confront the next decades' consummate challenges – whether demographic, Chinese, in energy, in education, in health, or in other areas.

Good governance

Sub-Saharan Africa in 2013 has three kinds of governments: the clearly well-performing top 10 or 12, the desperately ill-governed bottom 12 or 15, and the middle 22 or so – all ranked according to the above measuring scheme.

The top and bottom categories are easily distinguished and could probably be guessed at without sophisticated quantitative measurement efforts. (Their relative order might be harder to estimate precisely, however.) But the great middle group would be hard to separate out without sophisticated attention to the fifty-seven variables alluded to above.[7]

The best governed sub-Saharan African countries, year after year, are Mauritius, Cape Verde, Botswana, the Seychelles, South Africa, Namibia, Ghana, Lesotho, Tanzania, São Tomé and Príncipe, Zambia, and Benin, in that order in 2012. Except for South Africa, Ghana, and Benin, all are countries with fewer than 3 million inhabitants. Tanzania and Zambia were moved into the top 12 for the first time in 2012. All are countries which score very high on Security; their governments have a monopoly of violence, and project power to all ends of their smallish states. Except for South Africa, all are safe countries, with relatively little crime. Their GDPs per capita are all exceptionally high for Africa. Although South Africa has poor GINI coefficient scores, the others are more equal than most. They all have excellent transport networks. None, bar Zambia, Lesotho, and Botswana, is landlocked. Four are islands or archipelagos. Rule of law is exemplary in each country despite South Africa's official worries about its Constitutional Court. Mauritius and Botswana are the least corrupt countries in Africa, but the others in this top-ranking sample (South Africa excepted) score reasonably well as compared to their sub-continental cohort. They each evince a solid respect for human rights and have good records regarding the media, although South Africa debated questionable legislation in 2012. All have experienced repeated free elections and changes of regime despite the dominance in Botswana by a ruling party and a ruling family. Lesotho has been stable politically only for a decade, and there were troubles in 2012, but its high ranking is still merited.

Our top best-governed polities are literate and well-schooled places. Girls go to primary school and on to secondary school in high numbers; Mauritius and the Seychelles show almost complete schooling coverage of boys and girls through the highest secondary school levels (see chapter 4). Tertiary educational opportunity is readily available, although the smallest of these top ten countries must obviously train their university students elsewhere. Both Mauritius and Botswana, small states by African standards, boast strong local universities. So does Lesotho. Namibia's is less robust, but access to South Africa's many universities is available. The medical facilities in South Africa are the best on the continent but even the smaller states in our top-scoring sample show good medical outcomes despite, in a few cases, high HIV/AIDS prevalence numbers. Botswana has provided antiretroviral medicines to all HIV-positive inhabitants for several years. Clean water and good water-borne sanitary facilities are also more readily accessible in these top countries than they are elsewhere in sub-Saharan Africa.

The performance of these top sub-Saharan African countries across an array of critical variables of governance shows of what the best of the best of Africa are capable. Although the scores of the lower half of these top African nation-states might not vault them into the upper ranks of governance globally, the best top four or five would surely qualify. Moreover, in sub-Saharan Africa taken together, these best 12 set a standard that others – especially the 20 or so countries in the middle ranks – strive to emulate. The new middle class in the sub-continent – especially in upper middle-ranking, relatively prosperous and relatively well-educated countries such as Kenya and Uganda – is aware that there are well-governed places nearby. The citizens of a hulking country like Nigeria, with its underwhelming governance attainments, know that English-speaking Ghana is nearby and producing better outcomes for its citizens than the Nigerian government for its people. In Francophone West Africa, 16th-ranked Senegal has always seemed better-governed than its neighbors. Now, after it celebrated a free and fair election in 2012 and a simultaneous reiteration of its long participatory tradition, Francophone Africans can continue to look to Dakar, and not to neighboring Bamako (Mali), for inspiration and hope.

The special ingredient in each of these well-governed sub-Saharan African states has been visionary, responsible, leadership – a subject for the next chapter. Leadership has invigorated and ensured high-quality governance and created a political culture (a value system) that has enabled strong political institutions to be implanted, to grow, and to flourish. That combination of committed leadership, political culture, and solid institutions has provided the foundations, and reinforced the strengthening, of good governance. Once secure, the habit of good governance with its strong rule-of-law expectations, its internal security, its prudent macroeconomic behavior and open trading regimes, and its emphasis on building infrastructure, providing educational opportunity, and caring for its people's health needs has enabled each of the countries in the top cohort to attract foreign investors and donors, to boost GDPs per capita, and – for the first time – to build modern nation-states, not just states.

Does size make a governance difference? It has probably been easier in the smaller states to construct nation-states from colonial remnants because smaller states (in area and population) are probably easier to lead. Certainly, Singapore shows what can be done in a contained, if very plural, environment. (Being an island may help, too.) But the African raw material in several cases was not that promising. Before independence, Mauritius, with its Hindi-speaking majority and its *mélange* of peoples of different complexions, languages, and religions, had experienced brutal race riots and great internal discord. The Seychelles had to disentangle itself from the pernicious influence of overseas investors with ties to the Mafia. Botswana was, literally, dirt-poor at independence. So was Lesotho, dependent as it still is on exporting labor and water to South Africa. Along with those of Namibia, hardly any of the people of Botswana or Lesotho were educated, even at rudimentary levels. Cape Verde and São Tomé evolved from long centuries of desultory and hard-fisted Portuguese rule, not the most nurturing of colonial environments. So, small they were, but size was not necessarily an easily exploitable advantage.

Among the larger well-governed countries, Benin (once Dahomey) had experienced more military coups d'état than any other African country in the early decades of its post-colonial existence, and had been well accustomed to military dictators before the 1990s.[8] Ghana lived through its own military era as well as years of idiosyncratic despotism. It had gone backwards economically more than any other of these high-ranking countries in the decades after its heady founding in the 1950s. Finally, South Africa had the easiest path to high governance scores: long-standing, if unequal, wealth; a strong educational inheritance; modern hospitals; a robust inherited infrastructure; a long history (however un-rainbow) as a nation rather than a state; and the iconic leadership inspiration of Nelson Mandela, its first independent President. But South Africa's high governance standing had also to overcome the bitter and brutal apartheid legacy, high crime scores (and low Safety ratings), surprisingly high corruption levels, weak performance in the energy sector, and many questions concerning schooling places and health results.[9]

Bad governance

The bottom worst of the worst in the governance listings are mostly obvious poor performers. They include locales such as Somalia, the Sudan, and the Democratic Republic of Congo – all deeply insecure, plagued by civil wars, very unsafe, and dangerous in so many respects for their citizens. None of those places can project power much beyond its capital, although the Sudan certainly sends fighters to strafe its peripherally dwelling citizens and now and then tries to bomb them into submission. Somalia, with its interminably running internal conflict, is a very special case, but its inclusion in a governance index is really a misnomer: Somalia, or at least the southern part of what the African Union considers to be the Somali territory, has no real government and so, rightfully, should not be measured as a government; it cannot perform, so why measure its performance? That said, Somaliland, the northern part of the Somali geographical expression, runs very well. If it were a recognized independent nation, it would probably rank somewhere in the middle of the governance tables. But its semi-autonomous neighbor to the immediate east – Puntland – and (southern) Somalia are lawless, endemically conflicted territories. And they both harbor pirates.

The sub-Saharan African badly governed states in 2012 included its largest, Nigeria, in slot number 43 (on a 52-state scale that also encompassed the 5 north African polities), preceded by Cameroon (#37), Togo, Angola, Congo (Brazzaville), and Guinea, and followed in descending order by Equatorial Guinea, Guinea-Bissau, Côte d'Ivoire, Zimbabwe, the Central African Republic, Eritrea, Chad, the Congo (Kinshasa), and Somalia (the Sudan and South Sudan were not ranked in 2012). Côte d'Ivoire was recovering from a decade-long civil war and a contested electoral result that demanded AU, UN, and French military intervention. As a result, its rule of law, incomes per head, infrastructure, safety, and educational and health systems were all compromised. Good governance had been wanting ever since President Laurent Gbagbo (ousted in 2011) had attempted to disenfranchise his country's northerners in 2001 and had thus motivated a countervailing revolt.

In 2013, the Central African Republic (CAR) was embroiled in civil war, with a northern force capturing a dozen towns en route to Bangui, the capital, in a move to oust long-time President (and former military coup leader) François Bozize. Elsewthere, in early 2013, Joseph Kony and his handful of Lord's Resistance Army marauders were still causing mayhem in sections of the CAR and the adjacent northeast Congo (Kinshasa). Sudanese cattle raiders and elephant poachers were also active within CAR's borders, and in Chad. The Sudan, South Sudan, Chad, CAR, Congo pentagon was as unstable and troubled in 2012 and 2013 as it had been throughout much of this century. In those countries there was very little governance, and very little ability in the capitals of each country to project their power very far outside of Khartoum, Juba, Ndjamena, Bangui, and Kinshasa, respectively. Indeed, South Sudan probably belongs on this least well-governed list, as much because of its failure to perform as a new state across all dimensions as solely because of its insecurity. (The battles over cattle and access to water and grazing lands between the Dinka and the Murle continued in 2013, and there are other internal conflicts as well as its major cross-border one.)

Zimbabwe has no all-out internal war. Its borders are secure. Crime levels are not unusually high. But, despite its supposed government of national unity, there has been an incessant medium-level conflict underway every day between military, police, and organized youth thug gangs all loyal to and paid by President Robert Mugabe's ruling Zimbabwe African National Union – Patriotic Front (ZANU-PF) and supporters of the opposition Movement for Democratic Change (MDC). Intimidation of urban dwellers and villagers, and warnings by the ZANU-PF legions directed at potential MDC backers prior to an expected national election, are the name of the game. Lives are lost, and people are harmed, but without the numbers involved reaching civil war thresholds.

Eritrea has a hot war against next-door Ethiopia that still simmers, but without more than very occasional casualties. Its biggest issue, as for almost all of the other states ranking in places 37 to 52 on the latest African governance list, is its total absence of individual freedom. Eritrea is one of the tightest dictatorships anywhere. No Eritrean enjoys freedom of expression or assembly. The media are rigidly controlled, as are the broadcast media in supposedly democratic Zimbabwe; every Eritrean is subject to close surveillance within the country and, sometimes, abroad. Indeed, in so many ways, governance in Eritrea in 2013 resembles the tight strictures of North Korea, with its thought police, collective punishment, torture, and the absence of individual economic opportunity.[10]

Guinea-Bissau's insecurity and weakness in terms of governance comes from its position as a leading narcotics transhipment point between Colombia and Europe, its penetration by foreign drug cartels, and the violence that has consumed Guinea-Bissau's politics in the wake of its invasion by foreign and local wannabe drug lords.[11] Politicians and prominent military actors are frequently assassinated, possibly for their political views and their political ambitions, but possibly also in order to maintain the dominance of external drug dealers. Guinea-Bissau, even before its 2012 coup, was hardly either secure or safe, so its governance scores in that critical area are appropriately low.

A few of these other badly governed countries in western Africa may also be infiltrated by drug smuggling (as well as arms trafficking and the human trafficking of children and women), but every country among the bottom 13 is wildly corrupt. All sub-Saharan African countries other than Botswana and Mauritius are corrupt, the bad ones much more so than the norm or the median. There is absolutely no transparency in Angola, Equatorial Guinea, Guinea, or the rest – not even in Eritrea. Nigeria is in 2013 attempting with some success to rein in its corrupt traditions after decades, even centuries, of high-rolling fraud and misappropriation, but none of the other states ranked below 37 are interested in, much less capable of, reducing the corrupt practices that pervade every aspect of their national life and influence every deal between powerful people and between the state and its citizens. As chapter 6, above, retails at length, corruption is almost omnipresent in Africa. The badly governed states are where they are in the rankings for many reasons; certainly, being heavily corrupt, lacking rules of law, lacking much in the way of consistent forms of participation, lacking even rudimentary infrastructural provisions, and mostly denying their inhabitants access to educational opportunity and health facilities are reasons sufficient to explain their low standings. The great majority of their inhabitants, and thus millions of hapless and abandoned Africans, are consequently denied the ability to advance socially and economically, or to begin to enjoy the kinds of rewarding lives that their contemporaries in Botswana, Mauritius, Benin, or Ghana have come to take for granted.

Poverty per capita rules all of these dismal places. They are poor because they are badly governed, too, not the other way round. Some of the states in this lowest category have immense resources, like Nigeria and the Congo (Kinshasa). Some have newly discovered petroleum bonanzas, like Equatorial Guinea and Chad. Some, like Guinea, have long squandered the mineral resources with which they were endowed. Angola's rulers have kept their oil rents to themselves. Only the CAR, which has some diamonds, and Guinea-Bissau, which has hardly anything, can claim true destitution of opportunity – of having been dealt a deficient hand by fate. But in every case, even in Nigeria, quality of governance is the intervening variable. Positive leadership has been wanting and therefore good, responsible, governance has not often existed.

Needless to say, throughout this dismal universe of badly governed African states schooling is deficient, where it exists at all. Literacy levels are low (Nigeria excepted), school persistence numbers are poor, teacher training is rudimentary, and expectations of educational advance are very constrained. There are very few university-educated personnel remaining in many of these states, not even in the once advanced Sudan. Medical clinics and hospitals are few, especially in the war zones; physicians and nurses are scarce, and supplies are often wanting. Even potable water is hard to locate, especially in the dry Sahel countries and, sometimes, in the humid reaches of a place like the Congo (Kinshasa). Disease is rife and life expectancies are lower in these bottom 13 states than elsewhere in the sub-continent. Maternal mortality rates are very high. None of these badly governed places, not even the oil places such as Angola and Equatorial Guinea, provide much in the way of social services. Instead, in those two places, but also in Chad (where there are new petroleum earnings), elites largely keep the wealth of their countries to themselves, and distribute little to the bulk of their citizens. Most Angolans are still poor, despite a recent tripling of GDPs per capita in one of Africa's fastest-growing economies. Two-fifths of all Angolans are undernourished. A third of all Angolans are illiterate. Life expectancy is very low, maternal mortality rates high. Corruption is everywhere, transparency and judicial independence nowhere.[12] Those are the rewards of bad governance.

Nigeria deserves its own analysis. Its size dwarfs even the Congo (Kinshasa), and certainly all of the other much smaller polities. It harbors many civil conflicts – in the Niger Delta, in the north, in the Middle Belt between north and south, in Plateau State, and in many cities and towns where different ethnic groups vie for control over resources, or merely over the right to settle. In 2013, the government of President Goodluck Jonathan was attempting to restore order; put down Boko Haram and the Movement for the Emancipation of the Niger Delta (MEND); extirpate or at least reduce the spread of corruption – embezzlement, peculation, nepotism – at both the venal and petty levels; begin to provide efficient social services for its citizens; reconstruct a national infrastructure that has long been in disrepair; and begin to boost the per capita incomes of its countrymen. This tall order, after decades of wild corruption, the backwardness of much of Nigeria's social and physical infrastructure, and deficient electoral and participatory practices explain its low governance ranking. Having a vigorous free press and media, pockets of great entrepreneurial initiative, and abundant (but poorly distributed) wealth cannot compensate, in terms of its intrinsic governance standing for Nigeria's many deficits.

There is much that all of these badly governed states must do to improve their scores. When they can begin to do so – when they can begin to creep up gradually toward the middle of the governance rankings – then, and only then, will their people's prospects advance. One of sub-Saharan Africa's key problems in the decades ahead is how to assist these badly governed, mostly authoritarian, places to learn how to govern themselves more adequately, and thus how to begin to let their downtrodden peoples progress along the road of life chances. Outsiders may be able to assist, but primarily this is a task for Africans themselves.

Middling governance

A number of active and promising sub-Saharan African states comprise the middle of the Governance Index charts. They range from a number that are improving their governance ratings every year and crowding up against the top 12, downward to a set of countries that are in danger of joining the badly governed crew at the bottom of the list.

Just below the top performers on the Index are a set of reasonably well-governed states that, for one or two prominent reasons, have failed over the last six years to break upwards into the ranks of the best-governed. They include: Senegal, Malawi, Burkina Faso, Uganda, Mozambique, Mali, Kenya, Swaziland, and the Gambia (in a 2012 rank of 27). Of Uganda, the International Crisis Group in 2012 bemoaned its "slow and continuing shift from constitutional-style government to patronage-based, personal rule." This shift had been underway for many years, but the Crisis Group recognized with some sadness that Yoweri Museveni, the once-democratic President of Uganda, in 2012 was relying, like his cruel predecessors, on patronage and coercion to maintain control.[13]

Democratic and seemingly stable Mali faltered in 2012 when its junior military officers mutinied and overthrew the government, and the nomadic minority Tuareg, long discriminated against by the Bambara rulers of Mali, fostered an insurgency that quickly captured great swaths of the northern, Saharan, reaches of the country. The Gambia, run by an authoritarian tyrant who calls himself "His Excellency Sheikh Professor Alhaji Dr. Yahya A. J. J. Jammeh," still managed, despite mangled elections, to produce some reasonable scores. In power for 19 years, he has constructed new roads, schools, and hospitals while denying fundamental human rights to opponents, journalists, and any critics who dared to express themselves. He has persecuted witches, wholesale, and advanced unusual ideas about how to cure HIV/AIDS.[14] Rwanda, Swaziland, and Gabon, much more highly rated in earlier Indexes, might substitute in the rankings for Mali and the Gambia in 2013. But Swaziland is an absolute monarchy that in 2011 and 2012 ran roughshod over media and other freedoms, eliminating "voice."

As a whole, this group of second-tier performers illustrates the kinds of improving governance scores and, thus, improving governance attainments of which sub-Saharan Africa is capable. Tanzania, Zambia, Mozambique, and Rwanda, for example, have moved up several places since 2009 following strenuous actions by their leaderships, the dampening of corruption in Rwanda, political participation improvements in Tanzania and Zambia, economic growth and better management in Mozambique, and better health outcomes in Tanzania and Zambia.

It is important to ask, however, why this set of countries is in the second tier and not in the first. Why, for example, is Kenya (#25 in 2012) so far back in the pack, behind impoverished Malawi, poor Tanzania, and autocratically run Uganda? Why is tightly controlled Rwanda, making great developmental strides thanks to determined presidential leadership, still languishing toward the rear of the second tier? Why are Burkina Faso, the Gambia, Gabon, and Swaziland, with their limited or non-existent political participation scores, even in this group at all?

Kenya, after all, is a busy, populous, modern tourist destination and the industrial and transport hub of East Africa, whereas Malawi is a sliver of a landlocked mass, dependent almost exclusively on the sale of tobacco to China. But Malawi has a solid and reasonably independent court system in contrast to Kenya's compromised one. Kenya has experienced far more ethnic tension and violence than Malawi. Kenya's elections in 2007 were rigged and Malawi's were not, leaving serious questions about the integrity of Kenya's democracy and its respect for human rights. Hence, although Kenya's GDP per capita rates are much higher than Malawi's – and higher, for that matter, than those of Tanzania, Mozambique, and Uganda – Kenya's ratings on Security (even before the invasion of Somalia) and Safety, on Rule of Law and Transparency (corruption is far higher in Kenya than it is among its neighbors), and for Participation are lower than those of its peer group and competitors. Moreover, despite its greater wealth, Kenya's prosperity is less equally distributed than that of a number of its second-tier competitors, and its arteries of commerce, per head, are less robust than in comparable countries. Further, despite its progress in educational and health matters, when compared to other second-tier countries Kenya ranks poorly on a per-capita basis. So appearances and anecdotal evidence turn out to be less impressive, when weighing governance, than objective results gathered and expressed quantitatively.

The Gambia was listed in 27th place on the 2012 Index, followed by Niger, Djibouti, Sierra Leone, the Comoros, Mauritania (despite the war in the desert against al- Qaeda), Ethiopia, Liberia, Madagascar (despite an unresolved stand-off between two contenders for its presidency),and Burundi. Djibouti's 2012 score was only 49, so all of the sub-Saharan African countries in this paragraph may be regarded as being poorly governed compared to Gabon (with a numerical score of 53) and countries above it. But they are still a little less desperately governed, according to the latest version of the Index, than those comprising the "bad governance" group discussed earlier.

The difference between Kenya and Sierra Leone in terms of the calibrated scores is only 5 points, a not very significant amount. But between Sierra Leone, ranking 30th, with a score of 48, and Benin, ranked 13th with a score of 58, there are major performance distinctions. If one goes higher, to examine

3rd-ranking Botswana, with a score of 77, serious and significant performance differences emerge. Likewise, to go in the other direction, Kenya's score of 53 is contrasted to those of Guinea and below, where no country score is higher than 42. Thus, there are still major improvements to be made in governance in sub-Saharan Africa. Including Nigeria's 162 million (and growing), the Congo (Kinshasa)'s 75 million, and Ethiopia's 80 million, a significant proportion of sub-Saharan Africa's 900 million people endure excruciatingly weak governance. Large swaths of the sub-continent – the peoples of the badly governed places – are served barely at all by their governments. Others, even those who reside in the Togos, Burundis, and Cameroons of the sub-continent, are only a little better off. Think of how little chance a citizen of a country ranked from Sierra Leone downward has, for example, of receiving any kind of meaningful assistance from her own government. Educational opportunities and health chances are limited. Ignorance and disease are inescapable. Moreover, citizens in such countries can expect to be preyed upon by corrupted elites and functionaries. They lack voice and are often insecure and unsafe. The answer to their plight and to the many problems that plague much of sub-Saharan Africa is more and better governance – as governance is understood and explained in this chapter.

Ensuring better governance

The specific ways in which each government can improve its performance, and its delivery of political goods to citizens, is spelled out in each country profile in the Index. South Africa's lowest scores, for example, are in the Safety area; its homicide levels are among the highest in the world. Obviously, to strengthen its overall score, and thus to provide its citizens with enhanced services – to do better as a government – South Africa justifiably could follow a variety of strategies to reduce its alarming murder (and thus crime) rates. Then, if it were to accept the diagnostic capabilities of the Index – which every country should do – South Africa should next attempt to reduce corrupt practices throughout the nation. It could try to provide better schooling, especially at the secondary and university levels. Those would all be significant changes to "governing as usual," and would doubtless please its citizens as well as enable dramatic increases to be made in its Index scores of governance.

The peoples – the middle classes to the fore – of sub-Saharan Africa all clamour for better governance. No one, except possibly some especially corrupt rent-seekers, wants bad or even mediocre governance. Face-to-face research shows that everyone everywhere, in Africa and beyond, wants safer streets, secure territories, an absence of killings and rapes, predictable rules of law, transparency and accountability, a chance to participate in politics and decision-making, access to better schools and health facilities, and a fair chance to prosper.

Each country of sub-Saharan Africa, following the South African example, can find the low-hanging fruit of positive change. Rwanda can, say, easily improve its media freedom and thus its low Accountability scores. Sierra Leone can focus on its sky-high maternal mortality levels. Angola (and many other states) can reduce its corrupt dealings. Nigeria (and many others) could provide much more electrical power to consumers, as President Jonathan professes to want to do. Road and rail networks could be lengthened and more kilometers could be paved (often by Chinese construction firms). Greater attention could be paid to secondary schooling opportunities in those many countries where hardly any places are available. Where potable water is scarce, efforts could be made to dig more boreholes or to provide better distribution facilities in the region's swelling cities, especially in Harare.

The question is not *can* the countries of sub-Saharan Africa govern themselves more effectively. The question is *how*. Recall that governance is a set of decisions to serve citizens more and more effectively. Governance is not, as is sometimes believed, an approach or an attitude. That is why it can be and has been measured. And that is also why the political leaders of Africa can – as the successive presidents and prime ministers of Botswana and Mauritius have demonstrated year after year since the 1960s – begin dramatically to right the ship of governance.

If Africa is to take advantage of its many potential attributes – its demographical dividend, its innumerable resources and untapped wealth from coltan to petroleum, its pent-up demand for improved services, and its new and capable middle class – it must become much better governed than hitherto. Its political leaders, propelled or encouraged by constituents from the growing middle class, must focus with laser-like intensity on serving their people rather than serving themselves. That is the essence of good governance.

Fortunately, these are not impossible tasks. Botswana and Mauritius have shown how comparatively easy it is to govern well and grow robustly at the same time, the first making the second possible. Cape Verde, São Tomé, Ghana, Benin, Zambia, and other places have learned the same lessons. They and a number of other better performers are making material and nation-building gains for their peoples and are hence in the vanguard of governance progress in sub-Saharan Africa. Radelet and others have observed the "strong and positive relationship between democratic governance and economic performance in Africa." Despite learned debates about that conclusion, in Africa "democratic governments . . . have been successful, while authoritarian governments have by and large been failures."[15]

Note that governance is more than democracy.[16] It is a bundle of political goods that encompasses much more than just democratic values, although those are intrinsic to serious governance. What the new leaders of sub-Saharan Africa therefore are beginning to focus upon, and must continue to so focus, is how they can ready their constituents more and more effectively to take legitimate roles in the world alongside Asians and Latin Americans. That means accomplishing the citizenry uplift that results from improvements in each of the five major categories of governance, and in many (eventually all) of the sub-categories of analysis, some of which overlap worthy Millennium Challenge goals.

The door to the new prosperous, healthy, strong Africa that everyone wants will be opened by keys of enhanced governance. Leaders, not donors, need to forge those keys and to make Africa work in the way it now can and should.

11
Creating Responsible Leadership

"Listen to me . . . I am your leader," declared Nelson Mandela in 1993. "I am going to give leadership. . . . As long as I am your leader, I will tell you, always, when you are wrong."[1] Mandela indeed provided leadership to South Africans, to Africans, and to the world. He offered a clear vision; mobilized his followers behind it; demonstrated abundant emotional intelligence, intellectual honesty, and integrity; behaved inclusively; and gave his followers what all peoples crave – a transcendent feeling of being an integral part of a larger, glorious, meaningful, enterprise.

Although modern Africa has advanced too few national political leaders whose stature, legitimacy, and abilities even approach those of Mandela, the emerging sub-Saharan African middle class now appreciates that leaders with similar attributes are essential if their mostly struggling and sometimes desperate countries are truly to make progress in coming decades. Committed, responsible, effective leaders will preside over the ascendance of modern Africa. By leading well, such politicians can help to deliver enhanced governance as well as material and social rewards to sub-Saharan Africa's 900 million people.

The key ingredients of accomplished leadership in the developing world are now recognized. Mandela; Sir Seretse Khama, the first President of Botswana; Sir Seewoosagur Ramgoolam, the first Prime Minister of Mauritius; Aristedes Pereira, President of Cape Verde; John Kufuor, President of Ghana; Paul Kagame, President of Rwanda; Lee Kuan Yew, Prime Minister of Singapore; and Susilo Bambang Yudhoyono, President of Indonesia – all are among the recent exemplars of African and Asian skilled leadership. Not all led or now lead without flaws. But each strengthened or has strengthened governance in his country and delivered significant quantities and high qualities of political goods to citizens whose lives would have been poorer, less healthy, less well-educated, and (in most cases) less free without their inspired forms of leadership, their (relative) incorruptibility, and their focus on the welfare of their countries and their peoples, not on themselves.

Leaders matter

Imaginative political leadership has the ability to transform embryonic nations, especially in sub-Saharan Africa where institutions are unusually weak and democratic political cultures are as yet largely unformed. Peace, war, economic growth, a relief from poverty, beneficial educational and health outcomes, and a sense of belonging to a worthy national enterprise are all outcomes greatly influenced by the character, skills, and intentions of a nation's leader. Indeed, leaders are more responsible for societal results than has hitherto been realized; the poorer, less stable, and less-educated states are more directly influenced by the quality and decisions of their leaders than are more established, wealthier, states.

Furthermore, the exercise of consummate leadership skills by politicians and statesmen separates endeavors that succeed from those destined to fail. Statecraft depends on such skills. Careful and farsighted leadership are necessary, particularly amid the dangerous or unsettled neighborhoods of sub-Saharan Africa. Stability and peace, or at least the avoidance of cross-border or internal conflict, demands sensible and active leadership. Economic advances follow policies enunciated by the same gifted kinds of leaders, especially in the myriad small, challenged states of Africa. Poverty can hardly be alleviated without a committed political leadership that understands the close connections between macroeconomic prudence, strengthened rules of law, and prosperity. Progress of all kinds depends primarily on forward-looking leadership that appreciates how behaving in that manner accelerates job growth and also creates conditions attractive to foreign investors.

With regard to poverty, at least one knowledgeable and experienced African researcher blames the leaders of Africa for choosing to keep their people poor. Or, at least, his indictment elaborates, for not seizing the kinds of opportunities which would further the economic growth of their countries. They prefer personal power and wealth rather than their people's advancement and – most importantly, said Mills – make bad choices because better choices in the public interest are "not in the leaders' personal and often financial self-interest." Moreover, the international community allowed irresponsible or narrowly focused leaders in Africa to get away with their predations. Donors helped leaders betray their peoples rather than holding them to account; the absence of democracy in much of Africa furthermore permitted leaders to "get away with ruinous, self-interested decisions."[2]

Another distinguished South African observer of the continent suggests that African leaders have sustained and reproduced themselves by perpetuating "the neo-colonial state and its attendant socio-economic systems of exploitation." Referring not entirely to leaders, but to the consequences of decades of irresponsible leadership, Mbeki suggests that sub-Saharan Africa consists of "fossilized pre-industrial and pre-agrarian social formations. . . ." that are "degenerative rather than accumulative."[3] Acemoglu and Robinson likewise argue that European colonialism "threw into reverse" nascent economic modernization and "any possibility of indigenous institutional reform." Thus, the "pernicious institutional legacy" of colonialism in the 1960s "created an opening for unscrupulous leaders to take over and intensify the extraction" of their colonial predecessors.[4] And so a legion of ambitious and canny leaders took advantage of an inherited authoritarian and extractive system and perverted or subverted the representative legacy that the British and French colonizers believed that they had bequeathed to their successors – at least in Africa. But the real test of leadership and character came when a small handful of new leaders rejected autocracy and embraced participation, consultation, and good governance.

There is an important syllogism: wise leaders help to build nations and political cultures. Then their actions enable institutions to take root in the stony soils that underlie many of sub-Saharan Africa's not yet fully realized nation-states. In other words, by shaping political cultures in young or as yet not fully formed states, leaders can breathe life into inherited or dormant institutions. Sometimes they must also motivate institutions from scratch. Overall, leaders influence how governments perform – how they serve or abuse their citizens. Leaders matter.[5]

Although structure and contingency are important variables in considering sub-Saharan Africa's development prospects and its emergence in the twenty-first century as a strong, more vibrant, more accomplished region, the salience of individual agency – leadership – is amply supported by a careful examination of case after contrasting case. The Idi Amins and Jean Bedel Bokassas of Africa's dark past, and the equally dark present's Isaias Afewerki and Robert Mugabe, are malign examples of the force of leadership, just as Mandela, Khama, and the others are telling examples of gifted leadership for good. The conclusion is persuasive, powerful, and sound: that leaders matter as much, if not more, than external influences, internal structures, and institutional constraints. Leaders shape nation-state policy and directly influence the manner in which beneficial results are pursued (or not) across diverse situations and cultures. Human agency has been shown to strengthen or destroy nation-states, to uplift or oppress citizens, and to unleash or to stifle the talents and aspirations of followers and constituents.[6]

Consider the sub-Saharan African case especially: if a Govan Mbeki, a Walter Sisulu, or an Oliver Tambo – not Nelson Mandela – had grasped the leadership of South Africa after the demise of apartheid, would South Africa have avoided a revanchist war, or have so peacefully, even magisterially, achieved independence? In Botswana, without Seretse Khama, ambitious left-leaning nationalists might have taken control in the post-colonial era and have deprived their desert country of its early chance to become so successfully democratic. Or, if Khama had been born a Tanzanian and had risen there to prominence, would Tanzanians now be as poor and corrupt as they are? Likewise, without Paul Kagame, how far would Rwanda now be along the developmental continuum? For both good and ill, Meles Zenawi in Ethiopia, Yoweri Museveni in Uganda, and a host of other "big" leaders put and have put their personal stamp on national political designs. Mobutu Sese Seko's actions, not some abstract impersonal forces, created Zaire and also turned that resource-rich polity into the Congolese failed state that it became. Siaka Stevens systematically destroyed the representative institutions and tolerant political culture of Sierra Leone. Siad Barre's hegemony and clan favoritism gave rise to the anarchic warlordism of contemporary southern Somalia. Who rules, and how they rule, matters.

Or consider two sets of contrasting triads: compare Ghana under Kwame Nkrumah, Jerry Rawlings, and John Kufuor, or South Africa under the very different reigns of Mandela, Thabo Mbeki, and Jacob Zuma. There are clear contrasts in performance, citizen satisfaction, attainment of national objectives, and the provision of governance. If Nigeria under President Goodluck Jonathan succeeds in delivering substantial political goods to its many peoples, then there will be substantial contrasts between the Jonathan era and those of his military and civilian predecessors. Likewise, if Macky Sall in Senegal can govern as a Léopold Senghor reborn rather than another Abdoulaye Wade, his people will be blessed. Joyce Banda, too, now has the unanticipated opportunity in Malawi to overturn the irresponsible leadership examples of Hastings Kamuzu Banda (no relation), Bakili Muluzi, and Bingu wa Mutharika.

An inescapable but counter-intuitive conclusion is that in Africa (as in Asia and elsewhere) the idiosyncratic behaviors of individual leaders have mattered more than colonial legacies, arbitrary borders, inherited national deficiencies, and the like. Such developmental detriments as a regime's wholesale greed and its preference for preying upon and looting its constituents depended and depend upon the designs and integrities of leaders more than they do on imperialism and colonialism. Equally, excellent and reasonably accomplished governance has always emerged from leadership action, not from adherence to a received model. Good governance provides antidotes to ethnic plurality and hostility, geographical constraining factors, tropicality (as discussed in chapter 3), and fluctuating levels of foreign assistance. Leaders now, and throughout post-colonial time, are shaping and have shaped the response of their respective countries to economic dearth and potential wealth, to climatic shifts, to natural disasters, and to threats of war.

Leadership is the employment largely of usually informal means to induce followers and citizens together with the leader to achieve mutual goals and joint purposes. Good leaders do not make people do what they do not want to do. They persuade them. They cajole them. They eschew coercion. They help citizens to maximize their own interests as autonomous individuals. The genius of political leadership melds leadership drives and followership aspirations and beliefs.[7] The task of effective political leadership is to help a nation's peoples to "create and achieve shared goals . . . reinforce group identity and cohesion . . . and mobilize collective work."[8]

In Africa in the modern era, leaders (not parties, not global pressures, not inherited structures) have determined the directions taken by their states and have sometimes, even often, coercively overridden the wishes and interests of their followers. Fortunately, that era is largely coming to an end. Today there is more consultation, more real attention to permitting African groups and individuals to express themselves, more awareness on the part of Africa's middle class of its rights and the importance of those political and social entitlements, greater accountability, and a growing tolerance of dissent and free expression.

Critical competencies

Citizens everywhere, in Africa, Asia, and beyond, seek leaders who are inspirational and who appeal emotionally. They follow leaders who articulate appealing visions, who are courageous, and who are variously intelligent. They are mobilized and empowered by dynamic as well as situationally charismatic persons. But they respond enthusiastically to leaders who exhibit high orders of integrity, who inspire trust, and who appear to labor for all citizens, not just on behalf of narrow ethnic groups or families.

Effective leaders must possess high degrees of analytical and political intelligence. Those twin attributes are their stock in trade. The best leaders are empathetic, demonstrating a "reflexive self-awareness" that amounts to "self-adeptness," or, using another popular and expressive term – emotional intelligence. According to Goleman, "self-awareness," "self-regulation," and "motivation" are crucial components of emotional and social intelligence. Empathy and sustainable social skills are exhibited by consummate leaders. "Sensing what people are feeling, being able to take their perspective, and cultivating rapport . . ." is emotional intelligence.[9] The most accomplished of sub-Saharan Africa's leaders exhibited strong emotional intelligence – not least Mandela. When he visited his former captors, his apartheid persecutors, his political antagonists, or patriotic rugby supporters, Mandela reached out and literally and metaphorically made contact with them, and therefore with his newly empowered rainbow nation.

In addition to emotional intelligence, successful leaders are visionaries who know that being legitimate and projecting legitimacy enables them to mobilize citizens of all backgrounds behind their visions and thus to create a transformational momentum. Stores of legitimacy grow and shrink according to follower perceptions of leader accomplishments (such as raising the economy, reducing poverty, battling crime), but they overwhelmingly depend – in Africa as elsewhere – on whether a country's inhabitants believe that their leaders are trustworthy, have integrity, are personally and intellectually honest, face challenges squarely, and avoid the actuality or the appearance of sleaze. The implied social contract between ruler and ruled, in Africa and everywhere, is that trust, once given, will not be abused. But it very often is, in much of Africa.

Although the relationship between performance and perception is not exact, there are five identifiable competencies that are found in the best of leaders, past and present. I label them "the vision thing," the mobilization momentum, legitimacy, the gaining of trust, and the enlarging of the contours of the national experience.[10]

Transformational political leaders are visionaries. Transactional leaders are not. The first set deals in destinies, dreams, and ultimate purposes, not necessarily practical or immediately realizable goals. They know what they want to achieve, in large sweeps and often without exact specifics. They think they know what their citizens want and value, and are shapers of aspiration. Their role (unlike the transactional leader who thinks more about being re-elected than about reconfiguring and re-energizing his people) is to articulate how and why and in what directions the nation needs to be transformed and how citizens will accordingly be enriched spiritually and materially. At the best of times, leadership visions inspire followers to undergo an inner transformation consistent with the articulated vision.[11] Mandela and Khama (and others) did so dramatically. Others may have intended to so embolden their citizens, but soon their attempts proved flawed.

Accomplished leaders translate their blueprint for the future into a vision to which constituents can readily respond. This enables them to inaugurate the transformational project and to enroll citizens in the dream of a better future. Indeed, as transformationalists, these kinds of leaders (only a handful so far in sub-Saharan Africa) raise the level of consciousness within their states, encourage citizens to embrace national rather than personal or self-interested objectives, and generally project a sense of national empowerment. A transforming leader like Mandela or Khama uplifts the "level of human conduct and ethical aspiration of both leader and led."[12]

Transactional leaders are more common in Africa. They are incrementalists focusing on the mechanisms of statecraft and on perpetuating themselves and their parties in political office. They exchange mutual self-interests with their followers. They operate within existing frameworks. Transformational leaders attempt to alter the framework. Transactional leaders govern, sometimes well, but absent any grand design. Lee Kuan Yew of Singapore described transactional leaders: "If you just do your sums – pluses, minuses, credit, debit – you are a washout."[13]

Mandela conceived a re-configured South Africa capable of overcoming its painful apartheid legacy and of empowering all South Africans, not just the adherents of his victorious political movement, for the national greater good. With decisive gestures, with the gradual unfolding of a comprehensive measure of inclusiveness, and with a bold vision joining black and white together in the new enterprise, Mandela sought to transform his country.

Being actively and genuinely inclusive has been rare among political leaders of sub-Saharan Africa. Inclusive leaders like Mandela and Khama transcend limited conceptions of high office and give all peoples in all quarters of a country the welcome feeling that they belong to the whole – that they as individuals and groups are integral components of a nation being constructed or a broad community being realized. Inclusivity provides respect for those who hitherto might have felt marginalized or rejected. It telegraphs toleration and fairness.

Visionary leaders also listen. They listen hard as well as orate and instruct. Using emotional intelligence, they spend large proportions of their official time taking in, appreciating, and empathizing. At their very best, they encourage deliberation and build consensuses. In other words, they favor deep forms of consultation unlike the examples of recent African heads of state – such as Abdoulaye Wade of Senegal and the late Bingu wa Mutharika of Malawi – who won popular re-elections and then stopped hearing and dialoging with their constituents. Being genuinely democratic and consultative is hard, demanding patience and a forfeit of the "big man" syndrome that has been a default stereotype for so many political leaders of Africa.[14]

Legitimacy is a touchstone. Wade and Mutharika, among many others, lost legitimacy when their personal actions or their political aspirations cast doubt on their believability as leaders and democrats. Too many African leaders have made the assumption that power was theirs by right, to hold forever. Some have behaved arrogantly, forgetting that legitimacy – a people's perception – can be forfeited as quickly as it is obtained. Even Mandela always knew that legitimacy was his to lose in a flash, if he abused the nation's trust.[15]

Legitimacy in the final analysis depends less on competency in office than it does on stewardship: on ethical probity, moral accountability, a refusal to abuse privilege and authority, a dampening of greed, a strengthening of trust, unquestioned fairness, and – hard as it has been for African heads of state – a shying away from the temptations of ostentation and pomposity.

The key components of legitimacy hence are integrity (a refusal to abuse the sacred trust of office for the pottage of financial gain or political ambition), moral steadfastness (not sanctimoniousness), true transparency and accountability, an ability to align means and ends honestly and appropriately, prudence (the art of judgment, of balance, of reality), courage (to know when to act and when not to act, and the ability to stand correctly against appropriate enemies), self-mastery (a primary moral capacity that links leaders to the consequences of their actions), and intellectual honesty (being tough-minded, rejecting easy answers, and questioning assumptions).

When Afewerki and Meles Zenawi, respectively, took their Eritrean and Ethiopian nations to war in 1998 they were being intellectually dishonest and imprudent. When innumerable African leaders took concubines or permitted their relatives and associates to steal from the state, they demonstrated a lack of integrity. Nepotism – the official employment of meritless wives and relatives – the many attempts to overturn constitutional provisions against third presidential terms, and the rigging of elections by authoritarian leaders all abused legitimacy.

Ultimately, great political leaders provide their citizens and constituents with a transcendent sense of belonging to an enlarged enterprise. They offer a sense of purpose capable of enabling persons throughout the state – no matter how small or fragile or large and formless – to boost their individual self-worth. A gifted leader ennobles and uplifts her people. She appeals to a high level of moral and political development in a way that Mandela, Khama, Ellen Johnson Sirleaf of Liberia, and only a few other African leaders have attempted. The role of this kind of head of state or head of government is to "make people feel that they are the origins, not the pawns, of the socio-political system."[16]

"But if there's one thing we've done," said Johnson Sirleaf, "I think we've restored hope . . . to the Liberian people [so] that they can see a future in which they can share, in which they can participate and the Liberians can be proud again to be Liberians. That . . . is our greatest success."[17]

It is the deep responsibility of political leaders in Africa to create a profitable partnership between followers and rulers to strengthen the nation-state. If such leaders can construct a mutuality of responsibility, and if they can persuade citizens to accept and believe in the motives and visions of their leaders, then the national enterprise prospers. Mandela achieved that fusing of vision and national embrace during his brief presidential period, and since. It is the key task of effective and nation-building-focused leadership to foster among citizens a true sense of a larger purpose, what the Chinese from Ming times onward called "the mandate of heaven." Emperors, in China, were merely the instruments of heavenly instruction and were legitimate only to the extent that the people and the emperor were tied together in an all-embracing harmonious enterprise.[18] It will be the responsibility of the next generation of African leaders fully to internalize and act upon the Chinese aphorism, thus enabling sub-Saharan African states to become full nations and to grow economically and socially as their populations expand and their middle-class aspirations intensify.

The Mandelan model

Modern sub-Saharan Africa's two estimable leadership models are those developed by Nelson Mandela and Seretse Khama.

As the quotation with which this chapter began indicates, Mandela as prisoner, as African National Congress (ANC) chief, and as President of South Africa articulated a consistent vision. From the time of his release from 27 years of incarceration in 1990, he knew that, if he were to lead South Africa successfully and responsibly, he absolutely had to win the hearts and minds of his angry followers. He chose to do so by showing courage and exuding integrity. He was conscious of a need to be intellectually honest while tapping into all of his deep wells of emotional intelligence.

Mandela possessed leadership instincts, if not necessarily leadership qualities, from his early years in the Transkei. Descended from one of the key branches of the Xhosa Thembu chieftaincy, he possessed status and an obligation to lead responsibly. He knew that he was destined to play an important role in indigenous politics.[19] At the Thembu Great Place, the site of the chieftaincy, Mandela developed a sense of *noblesse oblige*, a fondness for an appreciation of the best of British style and manners, and a respect for his own abilities that came from being the best boxer, stick fighter, and team athlete, first at primary school in Qunu and subsequently at a Methodist secondary school at Healdtown. There, and later at Fort Hare University College, Mandela stood out as an up-and-coming leader because of his height, warm gaze, imposing appearance and bearing, and quiet self-assurance.

When Mandela arrived in Johannesburg in 1940, fresh from Fort Hare and the Transkei, he fortunately sought out Walter Sisulu, six years his senior. Sisulu, also from Thembuland, was a successful real-estate agent, worldly urbanite, and chair of a local branch of the ANC. "And then one day," Sisulu remembered, ". . . a mass leader walked into my office." Mandela, he said, had "a smile that was like the sun coming out on a cloudy day."[20]

Sisulu helped Mandela to train for the law and to learn politics. By 1948, Mandela was Secretary of the ANC Youth League and a member of the Transvaal [Gauteng] Provincial ANC executive. His vast empathic gifts easily led him into such positions. "He assumed authority easily and early," developing an effective "mask of command."[21] By the early 1950s, when apartheid was destroying the slightly milder forms of segregation that had always permeated South Africa, Mandela emerged as a natural leader. As mobilizer in chief and a member of the ANC's national executive, he took charge of the Defiance Campaign of 1952, a failed but energized attempt to employ massive civil disobedience to push back against growing apartheid legislation. He gained notice and legitimacy, especially after he was jailed under the broadly written Suppression of Communism Act.

From that time onward, and certainly from 1953, Mandela's vision and inspiration were essential to ANC tacticians as the ANC almost overnight became the central pillar of resistance to apartheid's spread. Mandela's embrace of the ANC and its embrace of him transformed what heretofore had been a largely muted parochial voice of protest into a sharply edged defense of justice.

Militant years followed, culminating in the cataclysm of the 1960 Sharpeville massacre, the banning of the ANC, and Mandela's clear emergence as the spokesperson for angry Africans and as one of the key strategists of an increasingly assertive opposition to the ruling white National Party. In 1961, Mandela was ordered by the ANC to go underground, traveling in disguise throughout the country (and later overseas, garnering backers) while clandestinely managing a clever campaign to broaden support among newspaper editors and journalists. Mandela took easily to his new role as a "Black Pimpernel," incipient messiah, and potential martyr.

The ANC began a campaign of sabotage in 1962. When the ANC hideout was raided, and incriminating documents found, Mandela and the other prominent leaders of the ANC were tried under the Sabotage and Communism acts. In a famous speech from the dock at the end of his trial, Mandela freely admitted that the ANC had started a guerrilla campaign in order to scare away foreign capital and to fight for a democratic and free society. "Africans want a just share in the whole of South Africa," he said. "During my lifetime," he continued, "I have dedicated myself to the struggle of the African people. I have fought against white domination. I have cherished the ideal of a democratic and free society in which all persons live together in harmony with equal opportunities. It is an ideal," he declaimed, "which I hope to live and achieve. But if needs be, it is an ideal for which I am prepared to die."[22]

The long years of Mandela's life breaking stones and sewing mail bags on Robben Island followed. He entered this twilight zone knowing that he had to retain his leadership not only of political prisoners like himself from the ANC, but of farther-left adherents of the Pan Africanist Congress and the Black Consciousness Movement, and even of common criminal prisoners. He did so during these testing times by persuading challengers (and there were many) to accept his respectful but principled and, at times, uncompromising relations with his captors; to accept his long-term, mostly non-despairing, mindset with regard to the larger struggle against apartheid; to accept his and Sisulu's belief that a guerrilla war for South Africa could not successfully be fought, Cuban style, within the country, but instead had to be waged from outside; and to acquiesce in a number of his tactical insights and decisions regarding their collective attitude toward hard labor, the timing of hunger strikes, the quality of their food, their behavior toward their jailors, their escape opportunities, and the possibility of his own early release to a "homeland."

Mandela understood legitimacy. He knew intuitively that he needed to gain and keep the respect, and thus maintain the followership, of lesser-ranked prisoners of all stripes. After the Soweto riots of 1976, he had to win over to his style of leadership the brave youths who were dumped in their imprisoned hordes on Robben Island. Was Mandela too moderate, too multiracial, too un-Marxist in his approach to ridding South Africa of apartheid?

Mandela listened and consulted, refusing to confront or instruct. "I regarded my role in prison not just as the leader of the ANC, but as a promoter of unity, an honest broker, a peacemaker. . . . It was . . . important to show the young Black Consciousness men that the struggle was indivisible and that we all had the same enemy."[23] Already, Mandela was a dedicated inclusionist rather than an ideological determinist. He knew, too, that integrity, consistency, and accountability – even in prison – bolstered legitimacy and gave followers a sense of purpose and self-esteem amid their incarceration and abuse. Mandela, not for the last time, created acolytes. His powerful vision kept the anti-apartheid struggle alive during the desolate, seemingly hopeless years.

By the late 1980s, Mandela was the man and the cause with which the National Party government finally learned it had to deal. There could be no resolution, no peace, without Mandela's cooperation. He was 71 when he walked out of his final place of detention, backed by those who had joined him in prison, but still of questionable quality to the township strugglers of the United Democratic Front (UDF) and to those ANC fighters who had spent the dark years attacking apartheid from Zambia, Zimbabwe, and Mozambique. Mandela had to win them over, and to reduce white antagonism, while consolidating his leadership in the face of the National Party's vain search for a soft landing for apartheid.

Mandela had many difficult tasks. One involved shaping the visionary perceptions of his myriad followers, and thus mobilizing them to support subtle, pragmatic, embellishments of an evolving (but still consistent) vision. Mandela proved flexible and adaptive. Indeed, he imposed the rigor of intellectual honesty on himself and his followers over the long-cherished ANC belief in the nationalization of productive resources, which Mandela realized would impede and harm the movement's triumph over apartheid.

Unlike so many other contemporary leaders beyond South Africa's borders, Mandela refused to take on the ostentatious trappings of royalty. Everywhere, Mandela insisted on remaining "an ordinary man."[24] Behaving as the fundamentally warm, decent, polite man that he really was enabled Mandela to rise above the petty struggles of political power and to reach out instinctively to all manner of men and women, embracing them physically or metaphorically. His prudence and self-mastery were important at every stage of this final struggle in winning converts and in controlling the culminating stages of the transfer of power from the National Party to the ANC. Furthermore, without his strong sense of self and his finely honed empathic intelligence, the violent struggle between white and black might well have resumed to the detriment of all and to the destruction of South Africa.[25]

South Africa's electorate overwhelmingly backed Mandela and the ANC in 1994, with the ANC winning 62 percent of the vote, the National Party 20 percent, the Inkatha [Zulu] Front 9 percent, the liberal but white-led Democratic Party (later the Democratic Alliance) 6 percent, and smaller parties the remainder. Mandela knew that, even on the back of such a robust mandate a leader of unquestioned legitimacy, thoroughly forged integrity, and iconic charisma could still be tested by pent-up expectations, by an absence of national coherence, and by the hitherto deferred desires of his long-oppressed supporters.

As president of South Africa from 1994 to 1999, Mandela certainly attempted to create a peace dividend for his long-suffering followers. He elaborated the economic modernization program on which South Africa embarked, inaugurated social improvements, and promoted South Africa's emergence as a middle-ranked world power, on behalf of Africa. Unlike his peers to the north, he insisted on a very liberal and rights-respecting new constitution; on a strengthened rule of law, including a path-breaking American-style constitutional court; and on judicial appointments made uncompromisingly on merit. In this manner he set about propagating a new democratic political culture capable of giving the re-born South Africa a firm basis for its re-established political institutions. In some ways, that was Mandela's greatest leadership gift to his country.

But Mandela also understood that reconciliation between black and white was essential if the rainbow nation were to be glued together so that Humpty Dumpty could never fall and South Africa never again be torn apart. Thus it was that Mandela, the determined inclusionist, deployed his undeniable empathic skills to bridge the color divide and capture the imagination of his countrymen and the world. By his gestures, his symbolism, and his actions, Mandela ensured that all South Africans would feel that they belonged – that they would acknowledge being an essential part of a larger project that promised to uplift them spiritually if not necessarily materially. It was Mandela's natural gift to lead his followers, and to incorporate them and their concerns into his daily pursuits.

In that spirit he visited the chief architects of apartheid or invited them to dine with him in his home. He held a dinner for the former commander of Robben Island and the outgoing head of South Africa's intelligence service. He lunched with the man who had prosecuted him for sabotage. He attended Afrikaans-language church services in Pretoria and went out of his way to meet the wives and widows of his top oppressors and take tea with the widow of one of the principal architects of apartheid.

Acts of conciliation were acts of courage. Forgiveness established Mandela's moral supremacy. It demonstrated his command and his authority. But it was on the sporting field, where South Africans are fervently religious, that Mandela truly knit his disparate nation together. Rugby was the quintessential Afrikaner sport. Mandela first resisted the re-naming of the national team and in 1995 startled and won the hearts of his nation by attending a world championship match between South Africa and New Zealand. When the South Africans unexpectedly emerged victorious after a hard, tense, overtime struggle, Mandela, already wearing a green team jersey and cap, walked ecstatically onto the field to present the trophy to the astounded white South African captain, an Afrikaner. The crowd, and the country, went wild, chanting "Nel-son" over and over: "The only way to beat the tiger [Afrikaners, and whites more generally] was to tame him."[26]

Afterwards, it mattered less exactly how Mandela governed and what were his precise policies. He had successfully positioned himself as the clear leader of all of the peoples of South Africa. He and they together were engaged in a nation-building endeavor capable of supporting, even realizing, Mandela's vision of a united and forward-looking South Africa. Moreover, he made it clear by action and example that so long as he were President, South Africa would be led by someone who accepted individual liberties, due process, and gradualism. No other paths would work for the new South Africa. Indeed, when in 1997 Mandela transferred the presidency of the ANC to Thabo Mbeki, his successor as national President two years later, he characteristically warned him (and the nation), "One of the temptations of a leader who has been elected unopposed is that he may use his powerful position to settle scores with his detractors, marginalize them, and in certain cases, get rid of them."[27]

Khama, nation-builder

Much earlier and in very different circumstances, Seretse Khama used some of the same gifts that Mandela was to employ so successfully. Deftly, gently, persuasively, Khama created a paradigm of African leadership that was unique in his day, impressive subsequently, and path-breaking for the continent. At a time when everywhere else in Africa was jumping to the drum-beat of single-party rule, Afro-socialism, and rationalized autocracy, Khama held to unfashionable notions of democracy, including independent judicial systems, regulated capitalism, free speech and free assembly, and respect for individual human rights. He became Africa's first determined nation-builder. He was an exponent and promoter of a national democratic political culture that ultimately allowed strong national political institutions to rise on the foundations that he laid. As a result of his leadership, and the equally far-sighted leadership of his presidential successors, Botswana now enjoys a strong rule-based democracy, solid institutions, an absence of serious internal strife, effective and well-managed government, and a sense of pride in the national model. Furthermore, Botswana has long been an African cheetah, growing rapidly economically; within the African Union, it is among the two or three wealthiest countries per capita.

As a paramount chief of one of the dominant ethnic groups within traditional Tswana society, the very young Khama might have been able in the 1960s to have followed the path of arbitrary rule pursued by his esteemed African forebears – Kwame Nkrumah in Ghana, Julius Nyerere in Tanzania, Kenneth Kaunda in neighboring Zambia, and many others. Almost without much internal protest, he possessed sufficient traditional legitimacy as a chief and as an early anti-colonialist to have followed their lead – "for the good of Botswana's people." After all, at independence in 1966 his thinly populated stretch of desert bordering on apartheid-driven South Africa and unilaterally independent white Rhodesia had virtually no industry, no hopes of wealth, few literates, and few plans. Khama could have abridged or limited democracy, almost without rebuke. But Khama, from his schooldays in South Africa, from his higher education and enforced exile in Britain, and from inner conviction, was never comfortable with easy answers and authoritarian postures. He was too intellectually honest to pursue tendentious shortcuts. Many of his contemporaries in Africa employed specious arguments to ban opposition movements, to neuter basic freedoms, and to enrich themselves. Khama pursued a distinctly different path.[28]

Whereas South Africa, a country of 39 million people in 1965, was despite apartheid a national entity with a long history of economic growth, advanced arteries of commerce, and a modern infrastructure, Botswana in the 1960s was a forlorn terrain of fewer than 600,000 people scattered across a land mass the size of France. It was among the poorer territories of the sub-continent, with an estimated annual GDP per capita of $50. Its only sources of export earnings were cattle, trekked into South Africa, and mine laborers, sent also to South Africa. There was no public hint of diamonds, hardly any tourism, and no manufacturing. The only paved roads (12 km in total) were within the border settlements of Francistown and Lobatse. In 1966, the new country could count only 22 university graduates and about 100 holders of secondary-school graduation certificates. About 40 percent of primary school teachers were untrained. The chance of eventual prosperity in Botswana appeared to Khama and others to depend exclusively on the long-term health of the country's cattle, a strengthening of the country's pathetic infrastructure, and a major expansion of educational opportunity.

"A wise man is one who can make use of the wisdom of others," Khama declared in 1964 on the verge of winning a popular election in 1965 at the head of the Botswana Democratic Party.[29] That statement alluded first to the fact that he was less a supreme ruler than a coordinator of senior advisors such as Quett Masire, who became his vice-president and later his successor, and a host of local and expatriate senior civil servants, some employed on grants from large American foundations. Khama asserted that his embryonic state should pride itself on a nonpoliticized bureaucracy, not – unlike elsewhere in Africa – on a prematurely Africanized civil service.

On the eve of independence Khama believed that his future nation's destiny was special, even unique. "Our role is not one of violence. We will achieve our independence without it. Our mission [his transformational vision] . . . will be to demonstrate for . . . South Africa that we have a stable African government in which no man is discriminated against on racial grounds and in which the living standards of all are being raised."[30] In other words, similarly to Mandela, Khama was an early inclusionist — a firm believer in being the proto-nation's steward, not an agent of family, lineage, or tribe. Certainly, too, rather than being a "humanist" like Kaunda or a "socialist" like Nyerere, or even being dedicated to Marxism as many in the ANC were (and still are), Khama and Masire were both wedded more to common sense and elemental decency than they were to ideology.

Upon becoming President of independent Botswana in 1966, Khama exuded a sense of calm despite the serious problems of being largely surrounded by South Africa (Namibia was not then free) and Rhodesia; South Africa controlled Botswana's import and export routes and locked the new state into customs and currency unions that prevented much economic maneuverability or autonomous decision-making. He had achieved his country's independence from Britain by demonstrating a quiet vision, by gaining backing for

that vision from his party and his peers and followers throughout the territory, and by a series of principled and adroit advances that slowly made loyal
followers of potential opponents, whether local or colonial. Working closely
with Masire, and slowing him down when Masire wanted to rush forward,
Khama presided over a grand strategy of economic, social, and political
growth in order to lift the people of Botswana out of poverty and out of
dependence.

Khama was aware of the obligation of building a new nation. "The essence
of a democracy," he and Masire believed, "was an informed public" – not a
public being told from on high what to do by its superiors.[31] Without their
mutual vision and Khama's painstaking efforts to knit the disparate country
together, Botswana might have remained a collection of tribal fiefdoms or a
purely cattle economy controlled by big barons like himself. Instead, Khama
knew that the central purpose of any government, especially his own, was to
provide essential political goods and a sense of worthy purpose – to do good.[32]

At his inauguration as President, Khama – looking south to Pretoria and
north to Lusaka, Lilongwe, Kinshasa, Dar es Salaam, and elsewhere in sub-
Saharan Africa – said that he and his administration would "not tolerate
autocracy of any kind." Much later, after visiting North Korea and China,
Khama declared that "Dictatorships and tyrannical systems of government
are hatched in the minds of men who appoint themselves philosophers,
kings, and possessors of absolute truth."[33] He was not one of them. Indeed,
he told an early sitting of Botswana's first parliament that the "histrionics
and fulminations of extremists outside this country will not help Botswana
achieve its destiny." His would, moreover, be a country defined by ideals, not
by color, race, or religion, and certainly not by any "narrow ethnic
criteria."[34]

Khama, in word and deed, was explicit as a leader in attempting to create
a positive ethos – a political culture – on the basis of which Botswana could
grow enduring political institutions. He called them "structures by which
national objectives could be achieved."[35] But a key component of this ethos
was an executive that never acted arbitrarily and always respected the separate powers and prerogatives of the legislature and the judiciary. Khama also
insisted on competency. Diplomats and civil servants were appointed and
promoted on the basis of talent, not in order to distribute perquisites equally
among the country's various ethnic groups. Fortunately, too, Khama was
instinctively consultative; tolerance was a watchword and dissent welcomed.
His commitment to a thoroughly open society was genuine, and enormously
rare in Africa in the 1960s and 1970s.

According to Masire, Khama was "a democrat through and through."[36]
Moreover, as Khama realized toward the end of his life, "democracy, like a
little plant, does not grow or develop on its own. It must be nursed and nurtured if it is to grow and flourish. It must be believed in and practiced if it is
to be appreciated. And it must be fought for and defended if it is to survive."[37]

It is no wonder that, upon returning from state visits to such places as Lilongwe, where Malawian President Hastings Kamuzu Banda was acting every inch the potentate, Khama expressed his annoyance at those of his fellow heads of state who cheated their people.

In addition to embarking upon an unabashed adherence to democratic forms and practices, embedding a strong rule of law, and being inclusive and accountable, Khama made three important, game-changing decisions in the early years of his tenure that were critical in making Botswana the wildly successful nation-state that it has become. (1) By balancing the national budget in 1972 (and thereafter), the infant state showed that it could manage its own affairs prudently and could cease begging Britain for support. (2) In 1976, Botswana created its own currency, the pula, and thus ended its dependence on the South African rand. Doing so gave Botswana control over its monetary and macroeconomic prospects; it also avoided any future importation of South Africa's own inflation or deflation. It greatly enhanced Botswana's independence from the behemoth next door. (3) As diamonds were discovered and their finds exploited in the 1970s, Botswana – led adeptly by Khama and Masire – captured for their people the country's only significant source of real income for decades to come. Instead of nationalizing this source of growing revenue, and revoking mining permits held by South Africa's De Beers Ltd, Khama both asserted his nation's right to its patrimony and also understood that De Beers' had managerial skills and industrial acumen which could serve Botswana's deeper and long-term interests. He forged a full partnership with De Beers, splitting the diamond proceeds 70–30 in the country's favor. Since the 1980s, Debswana, as the partnership was named, has operated on the basis of mutual trust, with revenues from the world's richest gem diamond holdings flowing robustly into the coffers of the state and De Beers.

Even with this unexpected wealth, Botswana under Khama and Masire avoided the resource rent-seeking that has engulfed much of the rest of Africa (usually on the back of oil exports). Botswana has never experienced the dreaded "Dutch disease," with an over-valued currency and the marginalization of all other enterprises. Nor, almost alone in mainland sub-Saharan Africa, has Botswana experienced much corruption.

As early as 1974, Khama noted that Tswanan civil servants and cabinet ministers were as likely to be tempted to pilfer and accept bribes as their counterparts anywhere. But he, like Lee Kuan Yew, knew instinctively that corruption, or the perception of corruption, would doom his young state. Khama was always clear that independence, and positions in government, were not a license for personal enrichment. He insisted that cabinet ministers pay their debts and bank overdrafts promptly. He was even tough on Masire when his close colleague was slow in repaying a large agricultural borrowing. Indeed, Masire reported later that "we worked hard to avoid" corruption and then to punish it severely when discovered. Khama and Masire saw to the prosecution of the few prominent Tswana who profited illicitly from their official positions. One was Khama's cousin, another a senior party official. A third was Masire's younger brother. Khama also insisted, to prevent temptation, that no cabinet minister should hold too much power. Responsibility should be collective, especially for the minister of mines. Full transparency was necessary at all levels, even his own. Appearances mattered if the people as well as his own subordinates were to appreciate that standards were set, and applied to all. For that reason, as well as because of his personal predilections, Khama lived modestly. No cabinet minister flew first-class, unlike their peers across the continent. In the early years of the state, cabinet ministers even drove their own automobiles. They were given few of the trappings of high office. Even Khama's motorcades were short, and accompanied only by a limited security detail. For Khama, being the first modern political leader in his country provided an opportunity to implant alternative African values, to create an open society, and to develop a political culture of democracy. For him, leadership meant guardianship, on behalf of his people. He believed that he was in office to provide a strong moral and practical compass for the nation, and that meant eliminating any germs of corrupt practice and behaving himself with supreme fidelity to principle. Khama would have been ashamed, even mortified, to have behaved in the manner of so many of his neighboring leaders or their successors.

Khama's refusal to condone corruption helped to make Botswana the well-governed and minimally corrupt place that it is – an approach continued by Masire and Festus Mogae, his two immediate presidential successors. Given his and their actions, Botswana for nearly two decades has ranked as the least corrupt country in mainland Africa. In 2012 it ranked 1st in Africa and 30th in the world according to Transparency International's Corruption Perceptions Index.[38]

A searching inquiry by gifted economists concluded that Botswana's impressive economic success was founded on good institutions and respect for private property, not primarily its natural resource wealth. Critically, the country's political elites were constrained by informal (the "ethos") and formal political institutions and assisted by "agency," by the decisive manner in which Khama, Masire, and Mogae had led Botswana. They credited Khama with particularly insightful actions.[39] Without Khama's astute leadership, Botswana might never have developed responsible political institutions or the ability to harness wealth from diamonds for the benefit of all of Botswana's people.

When Khama died young in 1980 the ethos – the political culture of democracy – that he had worked so hard to achieve was mostly a reality. By setting an example of responsible, democratic, incorruptible, national leadership and by implanting in the Botswanan political consciousness a right way and a wrong way of exercising power, Khama launched his new nation into successful political orbit. Without Khama (and Masire), Botswana might have gone the way of so many other 1960s satrapies. Courageous, principled, clear-sighted – but hardly charismatic – Khama provided a leadership model that worked superbly for the infant Botswana and would, even today, serve the rest of sub-Saharan Africa well.

The successor generations

Khama and Mandela were thoroughly democratic in their ideals, their policies, and their actions. They tolerated dissent and welcomed opposition. They fostered new values for leaders, politicians, and the political arena. They created or strengthened the components of governance and raised standards for state performance. Although Khama was much more responsible than Mandela for the delivery of tangible material advances, Mandela offered the promise of such gains. It was enough, during his limited presidential time, that he guided his people from the darkness of apartheid into the bright dawn of a freedom constructed without vengeance and retribution.

Khama's message has withstood the ravages of time, crisis, circumstance, and the personal proclivities of his successors much more robustly than has Mandela's. That is to say, the value framework that Khama pioneered has been sustained far more enduringly than that introduced by Mandela. Botswana is the African country where responsible leadership made a critical difference in terms of human outcomes – improved living standards and its people's enhanced physical and psychological well-being. Although Khama died young, Masire, his successor, had worked closely with Khama and continued to lead Botswana as Khama would have led it. Masire brought Khama's nation-building experiment to a successful conclusion during his long years as President (1980 to 1999).

Masire continued and expanded upon Khama's vision and, in a manner that testified eloquently to the vibrant founding leadership example set by Khama, his own presidency was a model of prudence, self-mastery, and integrity. It focused on quality ends and good means. Fortunately, Masire was the equal of his predecessor's lack of ostentation and remained fiercely combative of corruption. Indeed, when under Masire the country's accelerating wealth from diamonds, beef exports to Europe, and tourism (as well as good management) had begun to swell the national coffers, he demanded powerful new legislative safeguards, greater accountability, and elevated levels of transparency. Masire, like Khama and Mogae, knew that if Botswana's leaders stayed clean, so would the country.

Mogae easily followed the path of his predecessors. By the time that he became President in 1999, Botswana's democratic political culture had been solidly established. Its soaring economic growth trajectory had also delivered tangible benefits to all sectors of the Botswanan population. A nation (not a state) had been created. The political, economic, and social institutions that Khama had implanted and Masire had nurtured were fully established.

Mogae, in the manner of successors elsewhere, could have dissipated the legacy that he had inherited but, when southern Africa was assaulted by new challenges and opportunities – the terrible crisis of HIV/AIDS, Zimbabwean weakness and collapse, South African independence – Mogae, like the best of skilled navigators, was able to steer a sure course that drew upon his country's new institutional strengths and the resilience of its political culture.

In 2009, in accord with local constitutional strictures and custom, Mogae transferred the presidency to Vice-President Ian Khama, Seretse's eldest son. The younger Khama has since demonstrated his seriousness of purpose, his intellectual honesty (in analyzing and promoting solutions both to internal social and to regional political problems), and his internalization of his father's and, by now, national expectations of how their leaders will perform and behave responsibly – with courage, honor, and fidelity to the values introduced and elaborated upon by his three esteemed predecessors.

The returns in neighboring South Africa have been very different. Thabo Mbeki and Jacob Zuma, Mandela's successors, quickly ignored the leadership lessons of his presidency and, as Mandela had forewarned, dissipated much of his legacy. Because of the leadership failings of Mbeki and Zuma, South Africa has increasingly exhibited the weaknesses and leadership insufficiencies of much of the rest of the continent. Neither Mbeki nor Zuma exhibited more than a minimal vision of national renewal and development. They discarded the transformational mantle which Mandela adopted and introduced; both behaved and have behaved as transactionalists only. Neither displayed or has displayed much self-mastery, prudence, or any proportionality. Like most transactionalists, Mbeki, who failed at it, and Zuma, who is ruthlessly consolidating, seem to have been primarily preoccupied not with governing well but in preserving their own power and power bases. Zuma, after several presidential years, remains tarred by allegations of personal and state corruption, dispenses (and withholds) patronage, and in 2012 took a sixth (fourth at one time) wife.

No leadership career illustrates the backward dragging more than Mbeki's. After succeeding Mandela, he soon found his presidency tested severely by a series of calamities to which he was unequal. Each eroded trust within the ruling ANC elite and quickly forfeited the legitimacy with which he had assumed office. First, he chose to deny the importance of the HIV/AIDS epidemic and then attempted to deny that the disease was sexually transmitted. He publicly explored a host of mostly preposterous remedies, thus delaying treatment for myriad sufferers. These years of palpable denial testified to intellectual dishonesty. So did his repeated refusal to acknowledge the seriousness of the crimes against humanity being perpetrated next door in Zimbabwe by President Robert Mugabe, a refusal compounded by Mbeki's flawed mediation of the Zimbabwe conflict and his stubborn unwillingness to advance a democratic agenda there. At home, too, Mbeki proved too willing to condone corrupt practices, although his dismissal of Vice-President Zuma for his alleged complicity in an arms payoff scandal ultimately led to Mbeki's political demise and the elevation of Zuma to the South African presidency. As the *Economist* mused, Zuma has never explained for what he stands.[40] He is no visionary. He is instead the consummate transactionalist, veering like the Vicar of Bray from one patron and one cause to another patron and another cause. He has told one group after another what it wanted to hear. Decisive only occasionally, Zuma has not stanched wildly corrupt practices and "fat cat" power aggrandizement (although his intensely provoked move in 2011 and 2012 against the pretensions of former ANC youth leaguer Julius Malema might argue to the contrary), has neither solved the festering Zimbabwe question nor cosseted Mugabe, nor managed to give his citizens a renewed sense of national purpose or much to appreciate materially. The South African economy continues under his watch to grow slowly, at less than the rate that would begin to lower the country's massive unemployment rate or provide jobs for school leavers. The gap between rich and poor Africans widens rather than shrinks, educational and medical outcomes continue to deteriorate, crime rates remain high, energy stays short, and rule of law is under threat. Mandela's rainbow nation has become less, not more, coherent and less, not more, united. Zuma is but a so-so leader, especially as compared, inevitably, to Mandela and Khama.

Africa's leadership crisis

Responsible, effective, courageous, emotionally and intellectually intelligent leadership is absolutely required if the states and peoples of sub-Saharan Africa are successfully to surmount the stiff and unforgiving contemporary challenges of demographic explosion, educational scarcity, disease proliferation, energy shortfalls, widespread corruption, civil war, food scarcity, and job shortages with which they are confronted. Likewise, gifted leadership is needed if sub-Saharan Africa is going to embrace the abundant opportunities which are presenting themselves as possible responses to weakness: the mobile telephone revolution, Chinese demand for raw materials and agricultural products, the rise of an articulate and aspirational middle class, and a growing popular awareness of the advantage of being well governed and well led.

Clearly there are too few Mandelas and Khamas among the forty-nine heads of state and heads of government that help to determine the fate of sub-Saharan Africa's countries and peoples. There are still despots like Afewerki and Mugabe who run roughshod over their countrymen and women. And, in 2012 alone, there were renewed, if temporary, coups d'état in previously democratic states such as Mali and Guinea-Bissau."We have a deficit in leadership – that is a fact," said Mohamed ElBaradei, the Egyptian reform leader and Nobel Peace Prize laureate, referring to all of Africa. To President Alpha Condé of Guinea, the problem was acute but simple: "As long as the priority of African heads of state is to have bank accounts in Europe, there will be hurdles." Former Botswana President Festus Mogae said that he was disappointed in sub-Saharan Africa's leadership attainments. Many African leaders do well for 10 or 15 years, he noted, "and then something happens."[41]

Fortunately, in 2012, would-be authoritarians like Abdoulaye Wade in Senegal were overturned at the polls and Joyce Banda acceded to the Malawian presidency despite a threatened anti-constitutional cabal to transfer that position from Bingu wa Mutharika, who died in office, to his brother. The importance of responsible leadership is becoming more and more acknowledged.

Although it is clear that effective transformational leadership can make a major difference to human happiness and to human spiritual as well as material attainments, most of sub-Saharan Africa in 2013 is either led by transactionalists – some of whom are steady, capable, and honest, and some not – or by autocrats. Another leadership model prevails when and where national political cultures are weak or nonexistent, when democratic designs are followed only abstractly, and when tyrants manage to ignore or subvert constitutional safeguards. This era's Mandelas and Khamas – persons with vision and integrity – are few, largely as yet trying to prove themselves in difficult national circumstances, or as yet undiscovered.

The majority of today's sub-Saharan African rulers lead less with vision and integrity and more perfunctorily, expressing pedestrian aspirations. They are for the most part limited in leadership skills, no matter how mendaciously they have clawed their way to power and prominence. Although their societies genuinely cry out for a chance at transformation, in so many cases the relevant leaders remain stuck in determinedly self-serving postures. That business-as-usual mode of operation includes a reliance on patronage and corruption, hostility toward free expression and opposition, a mistrust of openness, and a clear partiality to one or more privileged ethnic groups and elites. Political institutions, such as they may be, are abused or devalued (even in South Africa, Nigeria, and Kenya). The executive in such transactional situations remains in control, sometimes reluctantly and tensely sharing power with legislatures, or with the military, but never with the people.

A few of these African transactionalists govern well, but most are less interested in delivering political goods than they are in amassing and keeping power. Today, African transactionalists rule in Benin, the Central African Republic, Chad, Kenya (on both sides of the governing divide), Mozambique, Namibia (despite or because of the absence of strife), South Sudan (now at war), Tanzania (despites its reputation and legacy), Uganda (really an authoritarian state), and Zambia. Malawi's Joyce Banda may emerge from this mold and become a visionary president in the manner of Johnson Sirleaf (below).[42] Other countries not listed are under the control of authoritarians (such as the Sudan's Omar al-Bashir or Equatorial Guinea's Teodoro Macias Nguema Masogo) or democrats singled out in these pages for praise.

Few of the transactional group of national leaders have articulated visions for their countries beyond those involved in the boosting of new economic prospects or routes to growth, although some certainly talk about how best to alleviate poverty, promote literacy, and design infrastructural advances with Chinese assistance. They focus more on managing followers rather than leading them or attempting to uplift and ennoble them. They concern themselves less with improving governance than with re-election and, in some cases, satisfying the avarice of their families and supporters.

Some of these leaders are genuinely popular, but they almost invariably approach the challenges of leadership in Africa tactically, rarely strategically, and their political fortunes rise and fall based on regional or global movements over which they may have little control. They preside more than they lead, and often sweep across their countries from one ceremonial event to another in lengthy motorcades. With their citizens they are fully in an exchange mode: voters seek employment opportunities or agricultural subsidies, schools, clinics, roads, and so on. Citizens also seek honest dealings, fairness, and transparency – often in vain. They may also thirst for transformational inspiration and encouragement, but that is rarely realized. When elections periodically come around, citizens dutifully trek to the polls to vote their ethnic, economic, and social interests, and to re-anoint serving leaders or choose replacements.

Political cultures persist in an embryonic state in these places because vision-lacking leaders are less agents for change than pacers on an executive treadmill. Take, for example, the ten-year reign of Bakili Muluzi in Malawi from 1993. His term, following the despotic rule of Hastings Kamuzu Banda, began with great promise but soon defaulted into the familiar pattern of African disappointment. Economic plans were made but little sustainable growth was achieved. National incomes fluctuated according to the strength and distribution of the annual rains and the price of tobacco, Malawi's main export earner. Smallholder farmers suffered while well-connected businessmen and politicians profited from ties to Muluzi. The President and his cronies also grew wealthy from various staple food and transport monopolies and from the steady escalation of corruption. Some cabinet ministers arranged lavish textbook contracts, with kickbacks, or employed government-owned X-ray machines in their private medical practices. Civil servants and policemen noticed and joined the stampede into rent-seeking. Soon citizens and voters understood that their great hopes of enlightened and uplifting leadership after the dark years of Banda were for nought. All that Malawians gained was a muddled, somewhat watered-down, version of the former regime. Fast forward to Mutharika, Muluzi's choice, who also started out well, was enthusiastically re-elected in 2009, and then began behaving autocratically, battling the press, fighting with the donors on whom his government's budget depended, and plotting to pass his presidency along to his brother.

Another disappointment for voters and civil society has occurred in Uganda, where Yoweri Museveni came to power in 1986 after leading an insurrection that theoretically reclaimed his country for democracy after the abusive years of Idi Amin and A. Milton Obote. But Museveni never became the inclusive leader he promised to be. Nor has he ever granted more than partial democracy to his people, favoring his supporters from the country's southwest kingdom over those of the center and the non-Bantu north. Nor did he do much during his first three terms in office to build a nation. "Our own politicians just care about their own stomachs," a disenchanted voter reported in 2011.[43]

Museveni's much celebrated vision of Ugandan economic and societal advance has since been reduced to a limited and partial gaze. Nor has Museveni been prudent in marginalizing his opponents or limiting political participation among the bulk of Ugandans. Even the usually friendly African Peer Review Mechanism reported that his overbearing influence had progressively reduced democratic gains.[44]

"Some people say that Museveni has overstayed his power," the president told journalists in 2009. But "I have been here for long to solve your problems, not to cultivate in my garden. The problems are so many that I have to keep around." Museveni, like so many other African leaders, believes in his indispensability. "Poor leadership," he said, "is partly due to ignorance."[45] Museveni is certainly strong-willed and he, like others in Africa, has not made (or chose not to make) the transition from conquest to responsible leadership on behalf of an entire nation-state. An original enlarged vision became, through acts of omission and commission, a narrow agenda tailored for Museveni, his cronies, and his military supporters. As the International Crisis Group reported in 2012, he has become more and more authoritarian over time and "the longer Museveni has been in power, the greater the discontent with his rule. Unless he starts to reform . . . pressure will rise . . . [and] will manifest itself in armed revolt."[46]

Rising above the norm

A limited number of contemporary African leaders have attempted in one or more signal ways to emulate the accomplishments and examples of Mandela and Khama. Rising above their otherwise transactional contemporaries, two contrasting but worthy leadership approaches are being pursued by Ellen Johnson Sirleaf in Liberia and Paul Kagame in Rwanda. (Goodluck Jonathan in Nigeria might be added to this tiny list, but it is too soon to be certain.)

On entering office in 2006 Johnson Sirleaf immediately understood that her choices of action were limited by the horrors that had preceded her election. She knew that she had rapidly to engage herself and her followers in a vigorous attempt to build a new nation on the ruins of the tyranny that had preceded her. War-torn Liberia was a looted shell of its former prosperous self. More than 250,000 people had been killed in two back-to-back civil conflicts. Monrovia, its capital, had not enjoyed running water or electric power since 1992. The up-country peoples, less literate and less acquainted with modernity, were alienated from those who lived along the coast and had long ruled them. The newly elected legislature included many of Johnson Sirleaf's sworn enemies, some of whom were hostile to serious political and social reform.

In order to govern and survive, Johnson Sirleaf had to provide a vision of a truly new Liberia, reconstructed, revitalized, and rehumanized. She promised to transform the ways in which Liberians viewed themselves and their national endeavor. She pledged to integrate and to unify her small but divided and fractured state. In order to succeed, she had very quickly to demonstrate to skeptical and long-abused Liberians that she was legitimate – that she had the kinds of integrity and absence of greed that Liberia had rarely known before. Then she had to sell her new vision to cynical countrymen. Gradually and painstakingly, by Mandela-like acts of inclusion and mediation, she showed her people and the world that she possessed leadership competencies sufficient to invigorate a major overhaul of her tiny country. She hustled to deliver basic goods and services, such as electricity and restored roads. She reopened mines and plantations, fought off international drug traffickers, and extended schooling (up by 40 percent from 2006 to 2012) and medical care to remote regions. But among her most telling accomplishments was the development among her peoples of a true sense of national identity.

While knitting her peoples together and forging a new Liberian perspective, Johnson Sirleaf's administration also had to deliver the key political goods of Security and Safety. Fortunately, to help her deliver these critical elements, Johnson Sirleaf's regime was backed for a number of critical early years by 13,000 well-commanded UN peacekeepers, while an American firm trained a new army and police force. No nation-building can occur in an atmosphere of insecurity, so the transition from the anomic tyranny of war-criminal Charles Taylor's era to her own was facilitated by the UN presence.

But the UN could not make the newly restored country transparent. Johnson Sirleaf had to attempt to provide that political good herself, first by discharging senior and allegedly corrupt civil servants and officials, then by cajoling the Liberian legislature to enact new laws and approve the establishment of an Anti-Corruption Commission. Although Johnson Sirleaf has been unable to eradicate what she has called the "debilitating cancer" of corruption, she has shown a determination to combat it relentlessly and civil society has grown vigilant and active.

If anything testifies to the success of her leadership, however, it is the gains that Liberia has made on the economic front. In 2006, Liberia's annual GDP per capita had plunged to about $100. By enticing new foreign investors, including Chinese state-owned firms, she managed to rejuvenate and restore iron mining and the growing and harvesting of rubber, two mainstays of the pre-1980 economy. She has also attempted to create a well-regulated forestry industry. China has reconstructed railways and refurbished roads. By 2012,

Liberia's GDP per capita had at least doubled from its low 2006 base. Absent her vision and her ability to mobilize legions of followers and much external support, Liberia might have stagnated like neighboring Sierra Leone. Her easy re-election in 2011 for a second five-year term testified to the success she had begun to have in forging the re-born Liberian nation. Her dynamic leadership is still a work in progress, and there are many obstacles ahead for her still imperfectly formed nation, but what she has accomplished in trying circumstances is worthy of being compared to the examples of Mandela and Khama.

Paul Kagame also came to power after his country had descended into Dantean hell and been rescued by the post-genocidal liberation army that he had led so decisively and authoritatively. If anything, the challenges that Kagame and Rwanda faced in the 1990s were even more severe than those confronting Johnson Sirleaf. But Kagame had a legitimacy forged in war and, at first, did not require a vision beyond that of restoring good governance, prosecuting those who had persecuted and killed his Tutsi contemporaries, pursuing the Hutu genocidaires who had fled into the nearby Congo, obtaining justice generally, and attempting to seek tentative and then stronger forms of reconciliation.

Since those early days of hard-won victory and consolidation, Kagame has developed a consummate vision to uplift and advance his small, populous, congested, land-locked country. Boosting educational opportunity and strengthening medical care are central, as is the establishment of an effective and fair police force to deter crime and keep citizens safe. But, differing not in rhetoric but in deed from many of his fellow African heads of state, Kagame is attempting to rid Rwanda of the cancer of corruption, a hard and difficult sell amid the rampant corrupt practices in the surrounding states of Burundi, Congo, Kenya, Tanzania, and Uganda: "Corruption . . . is clearly, very largely, behind the problems [that] African countries face. It is very bad in African or Third World countries." It, he says, "has become a way of life in some places."[47] Kagame has made examples of officials high and low who flout his plan to create a non-corrupt society and has also emphasized his own integrity and that of his immediate family and close relatives. Transparency International's Corruption Perceptions Index rated Rwanda in 2012 as the 4th-least corrupt country in sub-Saharan Africa (and 50th globally), after Botswana, Cape Verde, and Mauritius.[48]

The imposition of strong leadership has come at a high cost for Rwandans, however. Kagame's followers and citizens have had to learn to forfeit voice for conformity, to reduce the extent to which their political participation might be exercised in a fully free manner, and to adapt to, if not internalize, a strong leader's singular approach to many if not all aspects of Rwandan life and society. Consultation is not his strongest suit. Nor does Kagame accept competing visions, demanding a level of obedience from citizens that is rare in contemporary Africa and at a level never sought by Mandela or Khama. They led by force of example, reasoned argument, and persuasion.

Kagame, in contrast, asserts that the post-genocidal weaknesses of Rwandan society have compelled him to give direction. Citizens as a consequence are forced to trade autonomy for stability, safety, and the possibility of prosperity.

Kagame and his ruling party were easily re-elected in 2010, but not without bitter criticism of the manner in which opponents of his dominance were prevented from campaigning, in some cases assassinated and exiled, and media freedoms abridged. Nevertheless, beyond the brutalities which have occurred, Kagame remains a visionary with a high order of analytical intelligence. His leadership has already brought real material and spiritual gains to Rwandans. The country and its two peoples grow stronger, prouder, and mostly better governed by the day – a tribute to Kagame's forcefully transformative skills.

Nurturing a new leadership ethos

Across sub-Saharan Africa there have been many more Mugabes and Mugabe-wannabe nation destroyers than there have been nation-builders like Khama, Masire, and Mogae or iconic inclusionists like Mandela. Occasionally, the meteor of a possible responsible leader like Thabo Mbeki, Abdoulaye Wade, or Bingu wa Mutharika has shot across the sky, only to fall to earth in flames. Infrequently, too, there have been well-meaning, appealing heads of state and government who have led in the hopeful manner of Kenneth Kaunda, President of Zambia from 1964 to 1991. But, like Kaunda, they ultimately have known little of the arts of modern leadership and have been prey to persuasive panaceas or formulistic recipes that have turned out to accomplish precious little in terms of advancing their citizens socially, politically, or economically.[49]

The central issue for the peoples and states of sub-Saharan Africa is: How quickly can they now build on the Mandelan and Khaman models, or even on the disparate models of leadership being advanced by Johnson Sirleaf and Kagame? Responsible leaders need to forge a sure path so that African life expectancies grow, civil conflicts end, prosperity spreads, and good governance prevails. That is what the aroused middle class of sub-Saharan Africa craves. It wants enlightened leadership and therefore better governance than that experienced by its mothers and fathers. The African middle class has begun to understand that under-motivated governance by transactionalists – the common African situation – has too often failed to address contemporary social and economic needs in a serious manner. Few of these transactionalists have put the common good ahead of personal or group attainments. Thus the new middle class recognizes that improved, reformed leadership is the route to the better results and global stature that they seek for themselves and their children. There is a new, aroused, belief in the necessity of good governance and full political participation.

How to obtain fulfilling leaders capable of meeting those needs is the key issue of today's Africa. Rigorous exposure to positive examples, and some unabashed competency training may be required to strengthen the ability of a new generation of political leaders to learn how and when to do the right thing – to enunciate and to embody national visions over narrowly secular ones, and to rebuff those who would tempt base instincts. Leadership competencies can be inspired and refined and talents honed.[50] Broad horizons can be substituted for narrow ones, and at least a modicum of the required discipline, prudence, and self-mastery can be learned from the Mandelan and Khaman models.

One young Ghanaian even decided to found a small college to educate future leaders: "Africa can only be transformed by enlightened leaders. Leaders have to be trained and educated right." Ashesi University College's liberal arts curriculum attempts to create "ethical, entrepreneurial leaders of exceptional integrity" – exactly what Africa needs.[51]

As a leading Nigerian politician and businessman wrote about African leadership generally, but particularly the dire situation in his own country:

> It all boils down to the fact that human beings are by nature strategic and just like a thermometer they will adjust their behavior to suit the leadership and their environment. So to change their behavior we have to change the quality and style of our nation's leadership and put in place a clear regime of rewards (for merit and good behavior) and sanctions (for poor performance and misconduct). There is simply no other way to develop a well-ordered, rules-driven, and progressive society.

He continued: the cure for Nigeria's ills are many but foremost is "good leadership by example which gives the people vision, hope and exemplary behavior."[52]

It may not be fanciful to envisage schools for political leaders capable of building the kinds of capacities that are now in short supply. Successful former leaders from Botswana, say, could instruct, as could those responsible leaders who may have served in many countries as Vice-Presidents or cabinet ministers. The important objective would be, by example, exposure to successful models, training in the arts of leadership, and through the reinforcement of peer pressure, to raise a cadre of young and aspiring politicians in a new mold – to help nurture more future Mandelas and Khamas and fewer Mugabes. Africa needs such a new breed of leader to prosper. Without a strengthening of its political guides, Africa may well fail to throw off the shackles of its ill-led past.

Notes

Introduction: A Continent on the Move

1 Steven Radelet, *Emerging Africa: How 17 Countries are Leading the Way* (Washington, DC, 2010), 11–15.
2 Ellen Johnson Sirleaf, "Introduction," in ibid., 3.

1 Myriad Challenges and Opportunities

1 "The New Middle Classes Rise Up," *Economist*, Sept. 3, 2011. See also Witney Schneidman, "Africa's New Middle Class Lures Investment," *Bloomberg News*, August 8, 2011. For mobile telephones, see Jenny C. Aker and Robert I. Rotberg, "Harnessing Mobile Telephone Capabilities for Social Change in Weak and Failed States," unpub. paper, May 2012, 15. See also ch. 8, below. On telephone numbers, see Kalliope Kokolis, "Media (R)evolutions: Global Mobile Trends," World Bank, People, Spaces, Deliberation, April 18, 2012, blogs.worldbank.org/publicsphere/media.
2 George B. N. Ayittey, *Africa Unchained: The Blueprint for Africa's Future* (New York, 2005), xix, 391, 433.
3 George B. N. Ayittey, "After Revolutions, Beware of Crocodiles," *New York Times*, April 6, 2012.
4 See Milton A. Iyoha and Dickson E. Oriakhi, "Explaining African Economic Growth Performance: The Case of Nigeria," in Benno J. Ndulu, Stephen A. O'Connell, Robert H. Bates et al. (eds.) *The Political Economy of Economic Growth in Africa, 1960–2000* (New York, 2008), II, 621–659.
5 Of the many excellent chapters in Ndulu et al. (eds.), *Economic Growth*, I, especially useful for understanding sub-Saharan Africa's "lost years" are Augustin Kwasi Fosu, "Anti-growth Syndromes in Africa: A Synthesis of the Case Studies," 137–174; Paul Collier and Jan Willem Gunning, "Sacrificing the Future: Intertemporal Strategies and Their Implications for Growth," 202–224; Jean-Paul Azam, "The Political Geography of Redistribution," 225–248.
6 See Nkunde Mwase and Benno J. Ndulu, "Tanzania, Explaining Four Decades of Episodic Growth," in Ndulu et al. (eds.), *Economic Growth*, II, 426–470.

7 For an insightful analysis of much of this period, see Michael Bratton and Nicolas van de Walle, *Democratic Experiments in Africa: Regime Transitions in Comparative Perspective* (New York, 1997), 61–148.

8 William J. Reno, "Sierra Leone: Warfare in a Post-State Society," in Robert I. Rotberg (ed.), *State Failure and State Weakness in a Time of Terror* (Washington, DC, 2003), 83.

9 Gervase S. Maipose and Thapelo C. Matsheka, "The Indigenous Developmental State and Growth in Botswana," in Ndulu et al. (eds.), *Economic Growth*, II, 511–546.

10 This is akin to Englebert's concept of "legal command." See Pierre Englebert, *Africa: Unity, Sovereignty and Sorrow* (Boulder, 2009), 223–237.

11 See also Ayittey, *Unchained*, 357–360.

12 Shyam Nath and Yeti Nisha Madhoo, "A Shared Growth Story of Economic Success: The Case of Mauritius," in Ndulu et al. (eds.), *Economic Growth*, I, 369–400.

13 This discussion draws on the material in chapter 2, below, and on Rotberg, "Consummate Challenges for Africa: Demographic Dividends, Governance and Leadership," *Africa Growth Report* (Pretoria, 2012), 172–179. The projected totals, country by country, are explained in the next chapter. They are based on estimates provided by the well-regarded UN Population Division.

14 www.earthtrends.wri.org/text/economics.

15 See "Global Poverty: A Fall to Cheer," *Economist*, March 3, 2012; Annie Lowrey, "Extreme Poverty in Developing World Down Despite Recession, Report Says," *New York Times*, March 7, 2012; National Bureau of Statistics, Nigeria, cited in BBC News, Africa, February 13, 2012. For IMF figures and World Development Indicators data base, see data.worldbank,org/data for 2012 and earlier years.

16 http://stats.uis.unesco.org/unesco/table viewer, 9/27/11; UNESCO as listed in 2009 UNDP Report. Data also available in CIA World Factbook, www.cia.gov/library, for the relevant years. Where 2009 UNESCO numbers were unavailable, 2007 numbers were used.

17 CIA World Fact Book for 2011 and earlier years. Not all figures are year-comparable. US Census Bureau, 2006, in its International Data Base, 2007; www.unicef.org/view_chart, accessed Sept. 28, 2011.

18 UNICEF, *State of the World Children 2009: Maternal and Newborn Health*: www.unicef.org/view_chart, accessed Sept. 28, 2011.

19 Quoted in Adam Nossiter, "For Congo Children, Food Today Means None Tomorrow," *New York Times*, March 1, 2012.

20 www.unicef.org/view_chart, accessed Sept. 28, 2011.

21 www.nationmaster.com; WHO World Development Indicators, 2009; Robert I. Rotberg and Rachel M. Gisselquist, *Strengthening African Governance: Index of African Governance, Results and Indicators, 2009* (Cambridge, MA, 2009), 267.

22 World Bank Indicators, www.tradingeconomics.com, accessed May 9, 2012.

23 International Road Federation, World Road Statistics, www.irfnet.org/statistics. Note that for many countries the IRF numbers are not up-to-date.

See also Rotberg and Gisselquist, *Strengthening African Governance*, 2009, 202–3. Relevant statistics derived from Botswana Central Transport Organization and, for the Congo, from the UN Consolidated Appeals Process: Humanitarian Action Plan, 2007. These numbers, with an explanation of the poor quality of road-length totals, are listed and discussed in Rotberg and Gisselquist, *Strengthening African Governance*, 2009, 201–207.

24 Rotberg and Gisselquist, *Strengthening African Governance*, 2009, 273–275, drawing on UNICEF and WHO. Also www.unicef.org/view_chart, accessed Sept. 28, 2011.

25 US Energy Information Administration, *International Energy Annual* (2008); International Telecommunication Union, *African Telecommunications/ICT* (Geneva, 2008).

26 UN Habitat's numbers for 2010 are very different: the urban world percentage is 50 percent; Europe's 72 percent; sub-Saharan Africa's 37 percent; Asia's 42 percent (Southeast Asia 48 percent, South Asia 32 percent); Latin America and the Caribbean 80 percent — but the percentages are derived from very old numbers, some going back into the early 1980s! www.unhabitat.org, 9/27/11, accessed Sept. 27, 2011.

27 These numbers were obtained with some ingenuity and difficulty from the police establishments in the countries listed. They should be regarded as suggestive only. See the discussion in Rotberg and Gisselquist, *Strengthening African Governance*, 2009, 79–89. For Honduras and the US, see Javier C. Hernandez, "An Academic Turns Grief into a Crime-Fighting Tool," *New York Times*, Feb. 25, 2012, 7.

28 Associated Press, "UN Estimates Cocaine Trafficking in West, Central Africa Generates $900 million Annually," *Washington Post*, Feb. 21, 2012; Walter Kemp, "As Crime in West Africa Spreads, Response Requires Regional Cooperation," *IPI Global Observatory*, March 5, 2012, www.theglobalobservatory.org; "Gang Warfare," *Economist*, Aug. 11, 2012.

29 Estimates are rough and always contested. For a fuller discussion of how deaths in African internal conflicts can best be estimated, see the discussion in ch. 5, below, and Paul D. Williams, *War and Conflict in Africa* (Cambridge, 2011), 23–34.

30 IMF estimates, cited in "Role Reversal," *Economist*, Sept. 3, 2011.

31 Roger Nord, IMF, quoted in Laura Burke, "IMF Says Last Decade Best Ever for Sub-Saharan Africa," VOANews, May 30, 2012, www.voanews.com. See also Charles Robertson and Michael Moran, "Sorry, but African Rise is Real," *Foreign Policy*, Jan. 11, 2013, www.foreignpolicy.com.

32 Steven Radelet, *Emerging Africa: How 17 Countries are Leading the Way* (Washington, DC, 2010), 30–34.

33 Adolfo Barajas, Ralph Chami, Connel Fullenkamp, and Anjali Garg, "The Global Financial Crisis and Workers' Remittances to Africa: Where's the Damage?" IMF Working Paper, January 2010, www.imf.org/external. World Bank, *Migration and Remittances Factbook*.

34 Calestous Juma, *The New Harvest: Agricultural Innovation in Africa* (New York, 2011), 15–19.
35 Freedom House annual rankings. See www.freedomhouse.org. See also Daniel N. Posner and Daniel J. Young, "The Institutionalization of Political Power in Africa," *Journal of Democracy*, XVIII (2007), 127, 131, 138.
36 The Index of African Governance in 2006 to 2009 rated Mauritius as the best-governed country in the African Union. The Seychelles was second, Cape Verde third, and Botswana fourth in 2009.
37 Tony Blair, addressing the opening meeting of the Africa Governance Initiative, London: "A New Approach to a New Africa," March 19, 2012, www.tonyblairoffice.org/speeches/entry. See also Tony Blair and Kate Gross, "From Dependency to Self-Sufficiency," Stanford Social Innovation Review (Winter, 2013), www.ssireview.org/articles/entry/, accessed Jan. 12, 2013.

2 A Demographic Dividend or Just More People?

1 UN Population Division, World Population Prospects, 2010 Revision, esa.un.org/wpp/unpp, 2011, accessed Dec. 12 , 2011. All subsequent population predictions, below, are from this source, unless otherwise noted. Some of these same issues are noted and wisely commented upon by Michel Severino and Olivier Ray (trans. David Fernbach), *Africa's Moment* (Cambridge, 2011), 29–40.
2 UN Habitat, *State of African Cities, 2010*, www.unhabitat.org, accessed 13 December 2011. See also UNFPA, "Planning Ahead for the Growth of Cities," *State of the World Population, 2011*, Foweb.unfpa.org/swp2011/repo2010rts, 77–92.
3 These numbers come from various UN sources and were aggregated in www.mongabay.com/igapo/sub-Saharan_Africa_cities, accessed Dec. 13, 2011.
4 For a fascinating study of one of these cities over time, see Martin J. Murray, *City of Extremes: The Spatial Politics of Johannesburg* (Durham, 2011).
5 See Heinrich Barth, *Travels and Discoveries in North and Central Africa . . . 1849–1855* (London, 1857–1858), 5 volumes.
6 UN Population Division, *World Population Prospects: the 2010 Revision*, http://esa.un.org/unpd/wpp, especially "Population by Five-Year Age Group and Sex, Medium Variant," accessed Dec. 15, 2011.
7 "Hungry Again," *Economist*, July 7, 2012.

3 Tropical Dilemmas: Disease, Water, and More

1 Jeffrey D. Sachs and Andrew M. Warner, "Sources of Slow Growth in African Economies," *Journal of African Economies*, VI (1997), 335–376, and esp. 14.

2 Daron Acemoglu and James A. Robinson, *Why Nations Fail: The Origins of Power, Prosperity, and Poverty* (New York, 2012), 49–50.
3 These calculations and most of the statistics in this section come from John Gallup and Jeffrey Sachs, "Location, Location: Geography and Economic Development," *Harvard International Review*, XXI (1998–9), 57–59. See also John Luke Gallup, Jeffrey Sachs, and Andrew D. Mellinger, "Geography and Economic Development," NBER Working Paper #6849 1998; Sachs, "Tropical Underdevelopment," Harvard Center for International Development Working Paper 57 (Cambridge, MA, 2000); Michael L. Faye, John W. McArthur, Jeffrey D. Sachs, and Thomas Snow, "The Challenges Facing Landlocked Countries in the Developing World," *Journal of Human Development*, V (2004), 31–68. Paul Collier, *The Bottom Billion: Why the Poorest Countries Are Failing and What Can Be Done About It* (New York, 2007), 55, suggests that landlocked countries are "hostages to their neighbors." See also Min Tang and Dwayne Woods, "The Exogenous Effect of Geography on Economic Development: The Case of Sub-Saharan Africa," *African and Asian Studies*,VII (2008), 173–189.
4 Sachs and Warner, "Sources of Slow Growth," 12.
5 Cherian George, *Singapore: The Air-Conditioned Nation* (Singapore, 2000).
6 Angus Maddison, *Monitoring the World Economy, 1820–1992* (Paris, 1995); Jeffrey D. Sachs, "Tropical Underdevelopment," Harvard Center for International Development Working Paper 57 (Cambridge, MA, 2000), 3, 8, 11, 14; Melissa Bell, Benjamin F. Jones, and Benjamin A. Olken, "Temperature Shocks and Economic Growth: Evidence from the Last Half Century." December 2009, www.kellogg.northeastern.edu/faculty/.
7 "East Africa's Climate under the Spell of El Niño Since the Last Ice Age," Aug. 4, 2011, www.eurekalert.org/. See Christian Wolff, Gerald H. Haug, Axel Timmermann et al., "Reduced Inter-annual Rainfall Variability in East Africa During the Last Ice Age," *Science*, CCCXXXIII (August 5, 2011), 743–747.
8 UNICEF, "Climate Change Set to Exacerbate Child Vulnerability in South Africa," Nov. 19, 2011, allafrica.com/stories.
9 African Development Bank, "Cost for 'Vulnerable' Africa to Handle Climate Change Could Reach USD 30 Billion," www.afdb.org/news, Dec. 2, 2011; African Development Bank, "The Cost of Adaptation to Climate Change in Africa," October 2011, www.afdb.org/fileadmin/uploads, accessed July 13, 2012.
10 For one project of tree planting in Niger that is helping to push the desert back, see Burkhard Bilger, "The Great Oasis: Can a Wall of Trees Stop the Sahara from Advancing?" *New Yorker*, December 19 & 26, 2011, 116–121.
11 Patrick Gonzalez, C. J. Tucker, and H. Sy, "Tree Density and Species Decline in the African Sahel Attributable to Climate," *Journal of Arid Environments*, LXXVIII (2012), 55–64.
12 LeeAnne Gelletly, *Africa: Progress and Problems. Ecological Issues* (Philadelphia, 2007), 26–37.

13 Robert I. Rotberg and Rachel M. Gisselquist, *Strengthening African Governance: The Index of African Governance, Results and Indicators, 2009* (Cambridge, MA, 2009), 275.

14 WHO/UNICEF, "Turning the Tap on Water," as reported by Africa Progress Panel, *Bulletin*, V, March 22, 2012, www.app.com. See also WaterAid, an international developmental non-governmental organizations (NGO), quoted during Africa Water Week (April 24, 2012), in VOANews, www.voanews.com.

15 WHO, quoted in *Southern Africa Report*, November 24, 2011. See also "For Want of a Drink," *Economist* special report, May 22, 2010.

16 Bai-Mas Taal, Executive Secretary, quoted at the Sixth World Water Forum, Marseille, in Joe DeCapua, "Africa Major Player at World Water Forum," March 16, 2012, www.voanews.com.

17 Michael Kremer, Sendhil Mullainathan, and Daniele Lantagne, supported by the Bill and Melinda Gates Foundation, produced the conceptual breakthroughs that led to this new method of disinfecting African water. See Alvin Powell, "Willing a Way of Clean Water," *Harvard Gazette*, Feb. 16, 2012, 4. A somewhat similar scheme in India's Tamil Nadu state provides cleansed water to small knots of villagers by using a local entrepreneurial model and very small purification units.

18 A. M. MacDonald, Helen C. Bonsor, B. E. O. Dochartaigh et al., "Quantitative Maps of Groundwater Resources in Africa," *Environmental Research Letters*, VII (April 19, 2012), http://iopscience.iop.org/1748.

19 Jeffrey D. Sachs and Pia Malaney. "The Economic and Social Burden of Malaria," *Nature*, VII (2002), 680–685.

20 All statistics about malaria are from World Health Organization, *World Malaria Report 2011* (Geneva, 2011), iv–xii.

21 Ibid., xi.

22 These numbers are all from Kaiser Family Foundation, US Global Health Policy, Country Data, www.globalhealthfacts.org; see also www.avert.org/tuberculosis, accessed Aug. 12, 2012.

23 See Kaiser Family Foundation, US Global Health Policy, Country Data, URL as above. The African deaths are from 2009 data.

24 Global Health Council, "Neglected Diseases," www.globalhealth.org/infectious_diseases, accessed Jan. 16, 2012. See also the maps in www.thiswormyworld.org.

25 Global Health Council, "Neglected Diseases," www.globalhealth.org/infectious_diseases. For the successful efforts of the Carter Center over many years, see www.cartercenter.org/countries/sudan_health, accessed Aug. 11, 2012.

26 P. Simarro, Abdoulaye Diarra, Jose A. Ruiz Postigo et al., "The Human African Trypansomiasis Control and Surveillance Programme of the World Health Organisation, 2000–2009: The Way Forward," *PLoS, Neglected Tropical Diseases*, V (2011), e1007, www.plosntds.org/article.

27 Conjivaram Vidyashankar, "Pediatric Leishmaniasis," Medscape Reference, www.emedicine.medscape.com/article; Jonathan Berman, "Visceral Leishmaniasis in the New World and Africa," *Indian Journal of Medical Research*, CXXIII (2006), 289–294.

28 Andrew Clark, "Global Drugs Groups Unite to Destroy Tropical Diseases," *The Times*, Jan. 31, 2012.

29 For a close examination of such efforts in Ethiopia, see J. Stephen Morrison and Suzanne Brundage, *Advancing Health in Ethiopia with Fewer Resources: An Uncertain GHI Strategy, and Vulnerabilities on the Ground* (Washington, DC, 2012).

30 "What Has Driven the Decline in Infant Mortality in Kenya?" World Bank Policy Working Paper 6057 (Washington, DC, 2012); "The Best Story in Development," *Economist*, May 19, 2012.

31 Jeannette Strydom, "Pneumonia in Africa: The Silent Killer," Global Health Council blog, Feb. 11, 2011, blog4globalhealth.wordpress.com.

32 James Mullins, "Malawi Breathes New Life into Childhood Pneumonia Care," *Lancet*, CCCLXXX (2012), 717.

33 Emily Simons, Matthew Ferrari, John Fricks et al., "Assessment of the 2010 Global Measles Mortality Reduction Goal: Results from a Model of Surveillance Data," *Lancet*, CCCLXXIX (2012), 2173–2178.

34 Kaiser Family Foundation, URL as above.

35 Jeremie Labbe, "Deciphering a Looming Humanitarian Crisis in the Sahel," ipiglobalobservatory.org, Feb. 10, 2012.

36 For details and numbers, see *The Global Hunger Index, 2011* (New York, 2011), www.ifpri.org/sites/default/files, 7, 48–50.

37 BBC News, Africa, May 8, 2012, www.bbc.co.uk/news/; Samantha Kimmey, "U. S. Moms Die at Higher Rate than Irish, Italian," *Forbes*, May 8, 2012, www.forbes.com; Save the Children, "State of the World's Mothers Report," www.savethechildren.net, accessed May 13, 2012.

38 These numbers mostly derive from Calestous Juma, *The New Harvest: Agricultural Innovation in Africa* (New York, 2011), 11, 13–14.

39 Sachs, "Tropical Underdevelopment," 16.

4 Educating Future Generations

1 Irina Bokova, UNESCO Director-General, Global Education Digest, summary, 2011, www.uis.unesco.org/education/education/pages/ged-2011.

2 These rates are all for the 2005–2010 years, and come from the UNDP, Human Development Report, 2011, hdr.undp.org/en/media/hdr-2011. The data were originally compiled by the Institute of Statistics, United Nations Educational, Scientific, and Cultural Organization (UNESCO).

3 Again, these numbers are from 2005–2010 data, contained in the UNDP Human Development Report, 2011.

4 These data, originally from the UNESCO Institute of Statistics, are listed in Rotberg and Rachel M. Gisselquist, *Strengthening African Governance: The Index of African Governance, Results and Indicators, 2009* (Cambridge, MA, 2009), 235. Numbers were unavailable for some countries, such as Nigeria and the Democratic Republic of Congo. These results are from 2007 and differ little from the UNESCO report for 2009.

5 Ruth Levine, Cynthia B. Lloyd, Margaret Greene et al., *Girls Count: A Global Investment and Action Agenda* (Washington, DC, 2008); Lawrence H. Summers, "Investing in All the People," World Bank Policy Research Paper 905 (Washington, DC, May 1992), 1.

6 www.uis.unesco.org/education/documents/ged2011. In 2012, Malawians protested against the collection of $15 per pupil per year by the central government as a "development fee." Students were being prevented from sitting final examinations until they paid into the national "development fund." Parents and students asserted that the promise of free primary education had been reversed by this measure.

7 Joanna Mantey, "Ghana Lauded for Free Primary School Program," VOANews, Feb. 17, 2012, www.voanews.com. For the African Union numbers, see Gabe Joselow, "Experts Tackling Education in Africa," VOANews, Feb. 17, 2012.

8 *Economist*, Jan. 21, 2012. See also Chrissie Boughey, "South Africa: University Students Can't Read?" *University World News*, Aug. 30, 2009; Andrew England, "Signs of Growing Anger Drive Bid to Curb Poverty," *Financial Times*, Nov. 14, 2011. I am also grateful for discussions with Andre du Toit and others in Cape Town, February 2012.

9 *Economist*, Jan. 21, 2012; "South Africa Fails Pupils on Textbooks – Court," BBC News, Africa, May 17, 2012.

10 "Rectifying Fifteen Years of Good Education Intentions," *Southern Africa Report*, Jan. 26, 2012, 7.

11 Calestous Juma, *The New Harvest: Agricultural Innovation in Africa* (New York, 2011), xx.

12 Lydia Polgreen, "Fatal Stampede in South Africa Points Up University Crisis," *New York Times*, Jan. 10, 2012.

13 These figures are for 2009, as reported by the UNESCO Institute for Statistics, 2010, in stats.uis.unesco.org/unesco/tableviewer. See also David Bloom, David Canning, and Kevin Chan, "Higher Education and Economic Development in Africa," World Bank, Feb. 2006, 3, http://ent.arp.harvard.edu/african_higher_education/.

14 Quoted in Joselow, "Experts."

15 Dalibor Rohac, Eli Dourado, and Hemal Shah, "Six Questions You Always Wanted to Ask About Africa . . . and Answers from Rwanda," (2012) 11, www.li.com/attachments/Rwanda, accessed Feb. 29, 2012.

16 Kofi Annan, "Information Technology Should be Used to Tap Knowledge from Greatest Universities to Bring Learning to All," Aug. 3, 2000, www.unis.unvienna.org/unis/pressrels/2000.

17 Bloom et al. "Higher Education," 17–29.
18 Nico Cloete, Tracey Bailey, Puny Pillay et al., *Universities and Economic Development in Africa* (Wynberg, South Africa, 2011), 4, 44.
19 Ibid., 19, 21, 24, 34. The eight countries studied were Botswana, Ghana, Kenya, Mauritius, Mozambique, South Africa, Tanzania, and Uganda.
20 "Higher Education in Sub-Saharan Africa," www.arp.harvard.edu/ africahighereducation/data, accessed Jan. 30, 2012.
21 "Economics of Higher Education in sub-Saharan Africa," www.arp.harvard. edu/africahighereducation/economics2, accessed Feb. 19, 2012.
22 Ranking Web of World Universities, www.webometrics.info/top 100, accessed Jan. 30, 2012; www.timeshighereducation.co.uk/world-university-rankings/2010–2011/africa, accessed Jan. 30, 2012.
23 Cloete et al., *Universities*, 29.
24 Ibid., 67–68.
25 Ibid., 155–156.
26 Chris Brink and Martin Hall, quoted in Phil Batty, "No Contest," *Times Higher Education Supplement*, Sept. 10, 2010.
27 Cloete et al., *Universities*, 22, 33, 34.
28 Juma, *Harvest*, xxii.
29 Quoted in ibid., 52.
30 International Organisation for Migration, *World Migration Report* (Geneva, 2010, 501); see also Patrick Onsando, "The African Brain Drain: Using Intellectual Diaspora to Manage the Drain, What are the Options?" unpub. presentation to the Association of African Universities, Oct. 2007.
31 Network of African Science Academies, "Brain Drain in Africa," www. nationalacademies.org/includes/nasacbraindrain09.
32 Gumisai Mutume, "Reversing Africa's 'Brain Drain,'" *Africa Recovery*, XVII (2003), 1; www.arp.harvard.edu/africahighereducation/economics2.
33 "Brain Drain in Africa," images.derstandard.at/20080615/factsandfigures. This article employs IOM and UNESCO statistics and includes a solid bibliography of writings mostly from 2000 to 2004. See also William J. Carrington and Enrica Detragiache, "How Extensive is the Brain Drain?" *Finance and Development* (June 1999), 46–49. It listed the Gambia as by far the most prolific sender of professionals to the United States in 1990. Another important paper is R. Loewenson and C. Thompson (eds.), "Health Personnel in Southern Africa: Confronting Maldistribution and Brain Drain," www.medact.org/content/health/documents/, 2005, accessed Feb. 19, 2012; Fitzhugh Mullan, "The Metrics of the Physician Brain Drain," *New England Journal of Medicine*, CCCLIII (2005), 1810–1818.
34 Research by Edward Mills and others, reported by Kate Kelland, "Doctor Brain Drain Costs Africa $2 billion," Reuters, Nov. 25, 2011, news.yahoo. com/doctor-brain-drain-costs-africa/.
35 William Easterly and Yaw Nyarko, "Is the Brain Drain Good for Africa?" *Brookings Global Economy and Development Papers* (March 2008), 21, 25–26, 37.

This is an excellent study of how the brain drain from Africa should be evaluated. See also Mario Cervantes and Dominique Guellec, "The Brain Drain: Old Myths, New Realities," *OECD Observer*, 2011, www.oecdobserver.org/news/fullstory.php/aid/673.

5 To War Rather than to Prosper

1 For the definition of "collapsed," and much more about state failure, see Robert I. Rotberg, "The Failure and Collapse of Nation-States: Breakdown, Prevention, and Repair," in Rotberg (ed.), *When States Fail: Causes and Consequences* (Princeton, 2004), 9–10.
2 For extended discussions of this theory, see Robert I. Rotberg and Deborah L. West, *The Good Governance Problem: Doing Something About It* (Cambridge, MA, 2004). For more on "governance," see ch. 10, below.
3 For the story of Siaka Stevens' destruction of his own state, see William Reno, "Sierra Leone: Warfare in a Post-State Society," in Robert I. Rotberg (ed.), *State Failure and State Weakness in a Time of Terror* (Washington, DC, 2003), 71–100.
4 Vasco Martins, "The Cote d'Ivoire Crisis in Retrospect," *Portuguese Journal of International Affairs*, V (2011), 1–16.
5 For an excellent summary of exactly what went wrong, and how, see Daniel Branch, *Kenya: Between Hope and Despair* (New Haven, 2011), 269–284.
6 Rotberg, "The Failure and Collapse of Nation-States," 3.
7 See Anso Thom, "Africa: Health – Not How Much Money Spent, But How," July 9, 2012, Peoples Health Assembly (held in Cape Town) meeting report citing the work of Fran Baum (Adelaide, Australia) on Costa Rican and US health outcomes and their meaning for Africa, www.allafrica.com/stories, accessed July 10, 2012.
8 The strong nation-states are those that rank highest in the democracy rankings of Freedom House, the human rights reports of the US State Department, the anti-corruption perception indices of Transparency International, the Human Development Index of the United Nations Development Program, the competitiveness indices of the World Economic Forum, and the Doing Business surveys of the World Bank – the Finlands, New Zealands, and Singapores of the world, plus Canada, the United States, and large portions of Europe.
9 Several of these paragraphs draw upon the arguments advanced in Rotberg, "State Failure and States Poised to Fail: South Asia and Developing Nations," in T. V. Paul (ed.), *South Asia's Weak States: Understanding the Regional Insecurity Predicament* (Stanford, 2010), 31–50.
10 The argument in this and subsequent paragraphs parallels that advanced in Robert I. Rotberg, "Is Ethnic Strife Inevitable in Africa?" www.

globalpost.com, Nov. 7, 2010. See also the argument in Gabrielle Lynch, *I Say to You: Ethnic Politics and the Kalenjin in Kenya* (Chicago, 2011), 1–30.

11 Charlayne Hunter-Gault, "Violated Hopes: A Nation Confronts a Tide of Sexual Violence," *New Yorker*, May 28, 2012, 40, quotes "statistics" from the International Criminal Police Organization (INTERPOL) from 2009, suggesting that "a woman is raped in South Africa every seventeen seconds." Half the victims were reputedly under age 18. "One woman in two can expect to be raped at least once in her lifetime." Further, according to the South African Medical Research Council, 2009, one in four men admitted "having committed rape at one time or another."

12 For an excellent discussion of the rough quality of figures for war-induced fatalities, and a caution on counting civil war deaths broadly and in specific conflicts, see Paul D. Williams, *War and Conflict in Africa* (Cambridge, 2011), 23–34. Another instructive examination of what should be considered lethal violence in and outside civil wars is contained in the Geneva Declaration's *Global Burden of Armed Violence, 2011: Lethal Encounters*, www.genevadeclaration.org/fileadmin/docs, accessed Oct. 10, 2012.

13 Compare V. S. Naipaul's coruscating *A Bend in the River* (New York, 1979) to Joseph Conrad's *Heart of Darkness* (New York, 1902). For Mobutu's destruction of the Congo, see M. Crawford Young and Thomas Turner, *The Rise and Fall of the Zairean State* (Madison, 1985); Gabi Hasselbein, "The Rise and Decline of the Congolese State: An Analytical Narrative of State-Making," Crisis States Working Paper 2, November 2007, www2.lse.ac.uk/internationaldevelopment/, accessed Oct. 10, 2012.

14 See also Padraig Carmody, *The New Scramble for Africa* (Cambridge, 2011), 131–138.

15 A 2008 report by the International Rescue Committee is responsible for the first figure. A revision in 2010 by Canada's Human Security Report Project suggests the lower figure. See www.bbc.com, Jan. 20, 2010. For the highest figure, see Laura Heaton, "When a Death Toll Rivals the Holocaust," Enough Project, Feb. 11, 2010, www.enough.com. All death numbers must anyway remain estimates, based on extrapolations and guess-work. But whether the lower or the higher numbers are more accurate, either figure represents an enormous waste of life and unimaginable human suffering. See also Jason K. Stearns, *Dancing in the Glory of Monsters: The Collapse of the Congo and the Great War of Africa* (New York, 2011) for a full narrative of Congolese mayhem during the days of Mobutu and Laurent Kabila.

16 "DR Congo, Too Soon To Walk Away," July 10, 2011, www.refugeesinternational.org, accessed Nov. 1, 2011. For a comprehensive analysis, see Severine Autesserre, *The Trouble with the Congo: Local Violence and the Failure of International Peacebuilding* (New York, 2010), 126–205.

17 "The Civil War in the Democratic Republic of Congo," Africa Knowledge Project, May 30, 2007, www.africaknowledgeproject.org, accessed Nov. 1,

2011. In mid-2012, the International Criminal Court sentenced Thomas Lubanga, one Congolese warlord, to 14 years in prison for recruiting and using child soldiers to wreak havoc in the Kivus.

18 Heather Murdock, "Rapes, Retribution in the Democratic Republic of Congo," VOANews, Nov. 23, 2011, www.voanews.com.

19 Amber Peterman, Tia Palermo, and Caryn Bredenkamp, "Estimates and Determinants of Sexual Violence Against Women in the Democratic Republic of Congo," *American Journal of Public Health*, CI (2011), 1060–1067.

20 Human Rights Watch (Anneke Van Woudenberg), "DR Congo: Rwanda Should Stop Aiding War Crimes Suspect," June 4, 2012, www/hrw.org./news/2012/06/03.

21 See "The Human Impact of War," www.undp.org/cpr/content/economic_recovery, accessed Nov. 1, 2011.

22 Olivier Degomme and Debarati Guha-Sapir, "Patterns of Mortality Rates in Darfur Conflict," *Lancet*, CCCLXXV (Jan. 23, 2010), 294–300. See also Julie Flint and Alex de Waal, *Darfur: A New History of a Long War* (London, 2008), 116–166.

23 But consider the sobering belief that the UN has stopped reporting atrocities in Darfur. See Colum Lynch, "The Silence in Sudan," May 7, 2012, www.foreignpolicy.com/articles/2012.

24 Branch, *Kenya*, 271, 276.

25 On NEPAD, see Todd J. Moss, *African Development: Making Sense of the Issues and Actors* (Boulder, 2007), 193.

26 Admittedly, outside the annual AU summits, the AU's Peace and Security Council can make key decisions on peace and security matters with consensus among only 15 member states. But on the big issues such as Mugabe and Afewerki, or the loss of Mali's north, it has been largely silent.

27 For a much more positive view of the AU's peace-making possibilities, see the Report of the AU Panel of the Wise, *Election-Related Disputes and Political Violence: Strengthening the Role of the African Union in Preventing, Managing and Resolving Conflict* (New York, 2010).

28 "Look the Other Way: The African Union and the Famine," *Economist*, Sept. 3, 2011; Kingsley Ighobor, "Africa's Famine Response – Too Little, Perhaps Too Late," *AfricaRenewal*, December 2011, 5.

29 The AU said nothing, of course, when Teodoro Obiang Nguema tried to give $3 million to UNESCO to establish a prize. UNESCO, embarrassed, rejected the offer in 2011 but accepted it, with African executive board votes, in 2012. Eventually called the Unesco – Equatorial Guinea International Prize for Research in the Life Sciences, it was first awarded in mid-2012.

30 See interview with Amos Sawyer, head of the APRM, by Ernest Harsch, "Peer Pressure Can Be Powerful," *AfricaRenewal* (December 2011), 18–19.

31 See Adekeye Adebajo, *UN Peacekeeping in Africa: From the Suez Crisis to the Sudan Conflicts* (Johannesburg, 2011); Virgina Page Fortna, *Does Peacekeeping Work? Shaping Belligerents' Choices after Civil War* (Princeton, 2008).

32 Former President and warlord Charles Taylor of Liberia was brought to justice in 2012, but by the Special Court for Sierra Leone, not by the ICC. He was sentenced to 50 years in jail for war crimes committed in Sierra Leone by himself and his followers.

6　Accountability and the Wages of Corrupt Behavior

1 Some of the discussion in this chapter draws on the analysis in Robert I. Rotberg, "How Corruption Compromises World Peace and Stability," in Rotberg (ed.), *Corruption, Global Security, and World Order* (Washington, DC, 2009), 1–25.
2 A fuller definition is contained in Joseph S. Nye, Jr., "Corruption and Political Development: A Cost–Benefit Analysis," *American Political Science Review*, LXI (1967), 417–427. See also Laura S. Underkuffler, "Defining Corruption: Implications for Action," in Rotberg, *Corruption*, 27–46.
3 Paul Collier, *The Bottom Billion: Why the Poorest Countries Are Failing and What Can Be Done About It* (New York, 2007), 66.
4 *Economist*, Dec. 3, 2011, 62.
5 Transparency International, Corruption Perceptions Index, 2012, www. cpi.transparency.org/cpi2012/results, accessed Dec. 19, 2012.
6 www.bpi.transparency.org/results, accessed Nov. 25, 2011.
7 "Baby Steps," *Economist*, Aug. 25, 2012.
8 www.globalintegrity.org/report, accessed Nov. 25, 2011.
9 Quamrul Mahmud, "Impact of Corruption on Economic Growth Performance in Developing Countries," www.scribd.com/doc/764/analySEES-Report, accessed Nov. 21, 2011; Kwabena Gyimah-Brempong, "Corruption, Economic Growth, and Income Inequality in Africa," *Economics of Governance*, III (2002), 183–209; Pak Hung Mo, "Corruption and Economic Growth," *Journal of Comparative Economics*, XXIX (2001), 66–79.
10 Human Rights Watch, "Transparency and Accountability in Angola: An Update," April 12, 2010, www.hrw.org/news/, accessed Nov. 27, 2011; Robert I. Rotberg and Rachel M. Gisselquist, *Strengthening African Governance: Index of African Governance, Results and Rankings, 2009* (Cambridge, MA, 2009), 20–1. For more on Angola, see Padraig Carmody, *The New Scramble for Africa* (Cambridge, 2011), 121–124.
11 Human Rights Watch, "Well-Oiled: Oil and Human Rights in Equatorial Guinea," July 9, 2009, www.hrw.org/news/, accessed Nov. 27, 2011. In 2011, the US government started actively investigating the allegedly ill-gotten wealth of Obiang's son and heir apparent, Teodorin Nguema Obiang Mangue. He had a residence and motor cars in California. In 2011, French police seized 11 supercars belonging to his father, in Paris. See Xan Rice, "African Leader's Son in Fight for $32m in Assets," *Financial Times*, June 20, 2012. A warrant for the son's arrest was issued in mid-2012 by

French authorities when Teodorin refused to be interviewed by a magistrate about money laundering and embezzlement.

12 See Adam Nossiter, "US Engages with an Iron Leader in Equatorial Guinea," *New York Times*, May 30, 2011.
13 Josh Kron, "Uganda's Oil Could be Gift that Becomes a Curse," *New York Times*, Nov. 26, 2011.
14 Jackee Budesta Batanda, "Another Case of High-Level Corruption in Uganda," Oct. 31, 2012, transitions.foreignpolicy.com/posts/2012.
15 Quoted in John Eligon, "Diamond Profits Seen as Filling Mugabe Coffers," *New York Times*, Dec. 17, 2011.
16 Robert I. Rotberg, *Beyond Mugabe: Preparing for Zimbabwe's Transition* (Washington, DC, 2011), 6–8; *Southern Africa Report*, Nov. 10, 2011.
17 "He that is Faithful in Small Things Will be Faithful in the Big Things," www.dailynews.co.zw, Dec. 9, 2011. Sata told me that he abhors debts, and did not want the hotel or the Zambian state to end up being stuck with the costs (State House, Lusaka, July 4, 2012).
18 *Southern Africa Report*, Nov. 24, 2011.
19 Jason K. Stearns, *Dancing in the Glory of Monsters: The Collapse of the Congo and the Great War of Africa* (New York, 2011), 321.
20 Marlise Simons, "Hague Court to Decide Where Former Dictator of Chad Will be Tried," *New York Times*, March 13, 2012.
21 Kagame, quoted in Stephen Kinzer, *A Thousand Hills: Rwanda's Rebirth and the Man Who Dreamed It* (New York, 2008), 236; Tutu at the University of the Western Cape, quoted in *Southern Africa Report*, Feb. 25, 2011; Quett Ketumile Joni Masire, "Economic Opportunities and Disparities," in Masire, *Very Brave or Very Foolish? Memoirs of an African Democrat*, ed. Stephen R. Lewis, Jr. (Gaborone, 2006), 239.
22 Mbeki, quoted in Lydia Polgreen, "South Africans Suffer as Graft Saps Provinces," *New York Times*, Feb. 18, 2012.
23 Salva Kiir, letter of May 3, 2012, quoted in BBC News, Africa, June 5, 2012, www.bbc.co.uk/news/world-africa-18326004; BBC News, Africa, June 13, 2012.
24 Daniel Jordan Smith, "The Paradoxes of Popular Participation in Corruption in Nigeria," in Rotberg, *Corruption*, 298. According to one academic study of 166 cases of corruption world-wide, but not only in the developing world, 10 percent was below the norm. Yan Leung Cheung, P. Raghavenda Rau, and Aris Stouraitis – "How Much Do Firms Pay as Bribes and What Benefits Do They Get? Evidence from Corruption Cases Worldwide," NBER (National Bureau of Economic Research) Working Paper 17981, April 2012, 53, table 8B – report that cabinet officials take up to 50 percent of the value of the contracts that they hand out; lower-ranking subordinates capture "only" 20 percent.
25 Described and quoted in Collier, *The Bottom Billion*, 46.
26 Anthony Goldman, quoted in "A Man and a Morass," *Economist*, May 28, 2011.

27 *Southern Africa Report*, March 6, 2009, 5.
28 Huhuonline.com, Nov. 21, 2011.
29 "'Bongo Funded Sarkozy Campaign': Aide," *Yahoo!News*, Nov. 22, 2011. See also Xavier Harel and Thomas Hofnung, *The Scandal of Ill-Gotten Gains* (Paris, 2011), where these quotations originated.
30 Obituary, *The Telegraph* (London), June 8, 2009.
31 International Crisis Group, "Burundi: A Deepening Corruption Crisis," March 21, 2012, www.crisisgroup.org.
32 Transparency International-Kenya, "Kenya Bribery Index 2008" (Nairobi, 2008), www.tikenya.org/documents/KenyaBriberyIndex08, accessed July 12, 2012.
33 Job Ogonda, of Transparency International, quoted in Derek Kilner, "Watchdog Says Graft Could Cause More Election Violence in Kenya," VOANews, March 9, 2009, www.voanews.com.
34 Charlie J. Hughes, "Reporter's Notebook: Sierra Leone," 2009, www.globalintegrity.org/sierraleone, accessed Nov. 25, 2011.
35 Smith, "Popular Participation," 293. See also Daniel Jordan Smith, *A Culture of Corruption: Everyday Deception and Popular Discontent in Nigeria* (Princeton, 2007); Jean-François Bayart, *The State in Africa: The Politics of the Belly* (London, 1993); Jean Pierre Olivier de Sardan, "A Moral Economy of Corruption in Africa?" *Journal of Modern African Studies*, XXXVII (1999), 25–52; Michela Wrong, *It's Our Turn to Eat: The Story of a Kenyan Whistleblower* (London, 2009).
36 *Financial Gazette* (Harare), March 23, 2012.
37 Loren B. Landau and Tamlyn Monson, "Immigration and Subterranean Sovereignty in South African Cities," in Anne L. Clunan and Harold A. Trinkunas (eds.), *Ungoverned Spaces: Alternatives to State Authority in an Era of Softened Sovereignty* (Stanford, 2010), 157–158.
38 "Something Very Rotten," *Economist*, June 23, 2012.
39 See the discussion of Lee Kuan Yew's determination to keep Singapore corruption-free in Robert I. Rotberg, *Transformative Political Leadership: Making a Difference in the Developing World* (Chicago, 2012), 109–112.
40 Rotberg, "Leadership Alters Corrupt Behavior," in Rotberg, *Corruption*, 341.
41 Masire, *Very Brave*, 239
42 Rotberg, "Leadership Alters," 352.
43 Kinzer, *A Thousand Hills*, 235–236.
44 The Fund for Peace, "Unlock (Universal Network of Local Knowledge)," June–August 2010, reports on Liberia, www.fundforpeace.org, accessed Jan. 5, 2011.
45 Simon Allison, "Fellow Nobel Prize Winner Criticizes Ellen Johnson Sirleaf," *Daily Maverick*, Oct. 10, 2012.
46 Quoted in John Eligon, "South Africa Passes Law to Restrict Reporting of Government Secrets," *New York Times*, Nov. 23, 2011.
47 Peta Thornycroft, "New South African Secrecy Law Sparks Outrage," VOANews, Nov. 24, 2011, www.voanews.com.

48 Lydia Polgreen, "Painting Stirs Debate in South Africa," *New York Times*, May 23, 2012.

49 For earlier examples, see Andrew Feinstein, "Hard-wired for Corruption," in his *After the Party: Corruption, the ANC and South Africa's Uncertain Future* (London, 2009), 185–208.

50 Reporters without Borders, 2011–2012 Press Freedom Index, en.rsf.org/press-freedom-index, accessed Jan. 29, 2012.

51 "Eritrea President Denies Stifling Free Speech," VOANews, April 24, 2012, www.voanews.com.

52 Ayesha Kajee, Executive Director of the Freedom of Expression Institute in South Africa, quoted in Mohamed Keita, "Across Africa, Governments Criminalize Investigative Reporting," *Attacks on the Press in 2010: A Worldwide Survey by the Committee to Protect Journalists* (New York, 2011), 17.

53 Jean-Bosco Talla, a Cameroonian journalist, quoted in ibid., 17–18.

54 *BBC News*, Dec. 12, 2011, www.bbc.co.uk/news, accessed, Dec. 12, 2011.

55 Sanja Kelly and Sarah Cook, "Requested Page Could Not Be Found," Sept. 27, 2012, www.foreignpolicy.com.

56 *Southern Africa Report*, Jan. 26, 2012; *BBC News*, July 13, 2012.

57 "South Sudan Blogger and Government Critic Killed," Dec. 6, 2012, www.reuters.com/article/2012.

58 Naomi Hunt, "Africa Overview: Familiar Problems Overshadow Areas of Progress," International Press Institute World Press Freedom Review, May 2, 2011, accessed Nov. 22, 2011 at www.freemedia.at/publications/world-press-freedom-review/; *New York Times*, Dec. 6, 2011, 4; Benno Muchler, "In a Fledgling Country, Perils for the Press," *New York Times*, Jan. 9, 2012.

59 Luke Tamborinyoka, "Granting of Radio Licenses a Farce," Movement for Democratic Change press release, Nov. 25, 2011. Tsvangirai, quoted in Peta Thornycroft, "Zimbabwe's Tsvangirai Slams Pro-Mugabe Media," VOANews, Dec. 19, 2011, www.voanews.com.

60 www.globalintegrity.org/report, 2010, accessed Nov. 25, 2011.

61 www.doingbusiness.org/rankings, 2012, accessed Nov. 25, 2011.

62 Ibid.

63 "A Man and a Morass," *Economist*, May 28, 2011.

64 Paul Brenton, World Bank trade practice leader, quoted in Joe DeCapua, "World Bank: Break Down African Trade Barriers," VOANews.com, Feb. 9, 2012, www.voanews.com.

65 www3.weforum.org/docs, 2011, accessed Nov. 25, 2011.

66 "Job Growth Expectations for Early-Stage Entrepreneurship Activity, 2008–2010," *Global Entrepreneurship Monitor, 2010 Global Report* (Needham, MA, 2010), table 16. I am grateful to one of the *Monitor's* lead authors, Donna J. Kelley, for guidance and assistance. The other authors are Niels Bosma and Jose Ernesto Amoros.

67 Nasar Ahmad el-Rufai, "Money, Money Everywhere," www.huhuonline.com, Nov. 26, 2011.

68 Rotberg and Gisselquist, *Strengthening African Governance, 2009*, 196–7. For the origins of Contract Intensive Money, see Christopher Clague, Philip Keefer, Stephen Knack et al., "Contract Intensive Money: Contract Enforcement, Property Rights, and Economic Performance," *Journal of Economic Growth*, IV (1999), 185–211.

69 Nic Dawes, Judith February, and Zackie Achmat, "Muzzling the Rainbow Nation," *New York Times*, Nov. 30, 2011. See also *Economist*, Dec. 10, 2011.

70 World Justice Project, World Law Index, Nov. 30, 2011, www.worldjusticeproject.org/world-law-index.

71 Rotberg and Gisselquist, *Strengthening African Governance, 2009*, 118–128.

72 See Jennifer A. Widner, *Building the Rule of Law: Francis Nyalali and the Road to Judicial Independence in Africa* (New York, 2001), 214–233.

7 The Infrastructural Imperative

1 Robert I. Rotberg, *Africa's Successes: Evaluating Accomplishment* (Cambridge, MA, 2007), 1.

2 Anton Eberhard, Vivien Foster, Cecilia Briceno-Garmendia et al., "Underpowered: The State of the Power Sector in Sub-Saharan Africa," World Bank, June 2008, www.eu-africa-infrastructure-tf.net/; Blake Clayton, "The Biggest Energy Problem that Rarely Makes Headlines," Nov. 9, 2012, www.forbes.com/sites.

3 "Policy and Regulatory Framework Conditions for Small Hydro Power in sub-Saharan Africa," July 2010, 3, www.gtz.de/de/dokumente/gtz2010-en-hera-euei.

4 Dalibor Rohac, Eli Dourado, and Hemal Shah, "Six Questions You Always Wanted to Ask About Africa . . . and Answers from Rwanda," 10, www.li.com/attachments/Rwanda, accessed 29 Feb. 2012. See also Yussuf Uwamahoro, "Rural Electrification in Rwanda," www.paceaa.org/workshops/Rwanda, accessed Feb. 29, 2012.

5 Rohac et al., "Six," 2.

6 Tendai Biti, personal interview, Harare, Feb. 8, 2012.

7 *Financial Gazette*, March 16, 2012.

8 "A Man and a Morass," *Economist*, May 28, 2011.

9 For a good map showing hydro potentials and hydro projects, see International Rivers, "Hydrodependency in Africa: Risky Business," September 2010, www.internationalrivers.org/en/node/5808.

10 "Ethiopia 'Forcibly Displacing' for Sugar Plantations," BBC News, Africa, June 18, 2012, www.bbc.co.uk/news. See also Xan Rice, "The Money is Welcome But More Controls are Needed," *Financial Times*, June 20, 2012.

11 "Chinese Dams in Africa," www.internationalrivers.org/africa/chinese, accessed March 10, 2012.

12 David Smith, "South Africa Unveils Plans for 'World's Biggest' Solar Power Plant," *Guardian*, Oct. 25, 2010.

13 "Starting from Scratch," *Economist Technology Quarterly*, March 3, 2012.

14 Liane Greef, "Power from the Wind in South Africa," *Africa Renewal* (April 2012), 26.

15 Bjork Hakansson, "Full Steam Ahead to Sustainable Energy," *Africa Renewal* (April 2012), 27; Katrina Manson, "Kenya Pins Its Hopes on Steam Power," *Financial Times*, June 20, 2012.

16 See "Constraints to Pool Development," in UNDESA, "The Challenges of Operationalizing Power Pools in Africa," June 2005, www.un.org/esa/ sustdev/sdissues/energy. On these subjects, see also Christine Mungai, "Sub-Saharan African Power Production Way Below Potential," *The East African*, July 31, 2011, www.theeastafrican.co.ke/news/.

17 Heinrich C. Bofinger, *Preliminary Air Transport Infrastructure Findings in Africa*, World Bank, Feb. 27, 2008; Greg Mills, *Why Africa Is Poor and What Africans Can Do About It* (Johannesburg, 2010), 203–206.

18 Robert I. Rotberg and Rachel M. Gisselquist, *Strengthening African Governance: Index of African Governance, Results and Indicators, 2009* (Cambridge, MA, 2009), 220.

19 Odimegwu Onwumere, "The True State of Rivers Roads," www.huhuonline.com, Dec. 13, 2011. Accessed Dec. 13, 2011.

20 Kenneth W. Gwilliam, *Africa's Transport Infrastructure: Mainstreaming Maintenance and Management* (Washington, DC, 2011), 18. Gwilliam is using World Bank data from 2009 and earlier.

21 Ibid., 21–22, 25.

22 These numbers were compiled from International Road Federation, World Bank, and national sources for Rotberg and Gisselquist, *Strengthening African Governance, 2009*, 210. Note that, where Gisselquist and her country research teams were unable to gather road-length figures from national capitals in 2009, the available IRF and World Bank statistics may be wildly out-of-date. The IRF keeps its data bank up to date only sporadically.

23 Kenneth M. Gwilliam, Vivien Foster, Rodrigo Archondo-Callao et al., "Roads in Sub-Saharan Africa," June 2008, Africa Infrastructure Country Diagnostic, www.eu-africa-infrastructure-tf.net. For the comparison to rural China, see Calestous Juma, *The New Harvest: Agricultural Innovation in Africa* (New York, 2011), 89.

24 Tendai Biti, speaking to the Zimbabwe Economic Forum, Harare, Feb. 9, 2012.

25 Ubandoma Ularamu, National Coordinator, quoted in "85% Nigerian Roads are Bad – RAMP," *The Punch*, Aug. 11, 2011. For safety, see Konye Obaji Ori, "World's un-Safest Roads in Nigeria Unacceptable," *The Africa Report*, Oct. 25, 2011. Re. road safety, it is not clear on what statistical basis the Nigerian authorities declared that their roads were so abysmally unsafe. Consult Claire Provost, "The World's Most Dangerous Roads – Get the Data," *Guardian*, May 11, 2011.

26 "Watch Out!" *Economist*, Jan. 15, 2011.

27 Mills, *Why Africa Is Poor*, 210.

8   Harnessing Mobile Telephone Capabilities

1 This chapter draws heavily on the data and arguments contained in an unpublished paper by Robert I. Rotberg and Jenny C. Aker, "Harnessing Mobile Telephone Capabilities for Positive Social Change in Weak and Failed States," May 2012. Research support for the paper was generously provided by Google Ideas, but without any exercise of influence over the results on Google's part. I am personally appreciative of the initiative taken by Brendan Ballou and Yasmin Dolatabadi of Google Ideas team in this regard, and of their unstinting initial collaborative backing for our research. A shortened version of the unpublished paper appeared as Robert I. Rotberg and Jenny C. Aker, "Mobile Phones: Uplifting Weak and Failed States," *Washington Quarterly*, XXXVI (Winter, 2013), 111–125.

2 Jenny C. Aker and Isaac M. Mbiti, "Mobile Phones and Economic Development in Africa," *Journal of Economic Perspectives*, XXIV (2010), 223; Anna McGovern, "Dialing for Cash: Mobile Transfers Expand Banking," *AfricaRenewal* (December 2011), 21–22; *AfricaRenewal* (August 2011), 35.

3 Aker and Mbiti, "Mobile Phones," 208. This excellent and thorough article cites a variety of research fully supporting their overall argument.

4 "Nigeria Telecoms Rebut Fines," VOANews, May 23, 2012, www.voanews.com.

5 Raul L. Katz and Pantelis Koutroumpis, "Measuring Socio-economic Digitization: A Paradigm Shift", Social Science Research Network, May 29, 2012, http://papers.ssrn.org; N. Czernich, O. Falck, T. Kretschmer et al., "Broadband Infrastructure and Economic Growth", *Economic Journal*, 121 (552) (2011), 505–32. Both cited in "Free Exchange: Silicon Sally," *Economist*, June 2, 2012. The references appear only in www.economist,com/node/21556221, accessed June 10, 2012.

6 www.africa.slow; *Economist*, Aug. 27, 2011.

7 "Nigeria's Phase3 Telecom to Boost Fiber Optics in West Africa," *bikyamasr*, Feb. 23, 2012, www.bikyamasr.com/58298/; "The Freedom on the Net, 2011," *Africa Review* (Kenya), Feb. 23, 2012, www.africareview.com; Freedom on the Net, 2012, www.foreignpolicy.com/articles, accessed Oct. 10, 2012.

8 Many of the statistics in this chapter draw on Aker and Mbiti's summary and compilation of a broad body of research.

9 For 2012 mobile telephone connections and penetration, see GSMA, "Sub-Saharan Mobile Observatory 2012," Nov. 13, 2012, www.gsma.com/public policy/.

10 Aker and Mbiti, "Mobile Phones," 229.

11 Researchers in Kenya find that people will skip a meal or choose to walk long distances (instead of paying for bus fare) in order keep a supply of available minutes in their mobile phone. In other words, mobile phones are an essential, not a discretionary, spending – at least in Kenya: "Vital for the Poor," *Economist*, Nov. 10, 2012. See also Jill Craig, "Keryans Priori-

tizing Mobile Phone Over Food, Transport," VOANews, Jan. 22, 2013, www.voanews.com/.

12 Balancing Act, "Telecoms, Internet and Broadcast in Africa," 16 February 2012, www.balancingact-africa.com/ is the fullest report

13 Research by Aker in Niger and by Muto and Yamano in Uganda shows how the availability of mobile telephonic capabilities greatly improved market efficiencies for grain and banana buyers and sellers respectively. Jenny C. Aker, "Information from Markets Near and Far: Mobile Phones and Agricultural Markets in Niger," *American Economic Journal: Applied Economics*, II (2010), 46–59; Megumi Muto and Takashi Yamano, "The Impact of Mobile Phone Coverage Expansion on Market Participation: Panel Evidence from Uganda," *World Development*, XXXVII (2009), 1887–1896.

14 See Michael Fitzgerald, "Cell Phones Offer Targeted Marketing in Developing Countries," Latitude News, March 13, 2012, www.latitudenews.com.

15 Jenny C. Aker, Christopher Ksoll, and Travis J. Lybbert, "Can Mobile Phones Improve Learning? Evidence from a Field Experiment in Niger." *American Economic Journal: Applied Economics*, IV (2012), 94–120.

16 Kingsley Ighobor, "Social Media for a Social Cause," *AfricaRenewal* (December 2011), 3–4; *Economist*, April 28, 2012.

17 Ben Elers, quoted in Stephanie Strom, "Web Sites Shine Light on Bribery Worldwide," *New York Times*, March 8, 2012.

18 It is possible to use advanced data-mining techniques to note increased activity by mobile telephone users and thus discover – from far away – that trouble is brewing. See Emmanuel Letouzé, "Can Big Data From Cellphones Help Prevent Conflict?" IPI Global Observatory, Nov. 8, 2012, www.theglobalobservatory.or/analysis.

19 Clark Gibson, quoted in "How to Save Votes," *Economist*, on-line, Feb. 28, 2012.

20 "Physicians per 1000 People (Most Recent) By Country," www.nationmaster.com/graph/, accessed May 12, 2012. Another set of physician statistics from the World Health Organization and Eurostat uses 10,000 people as the denominator and reports that the European Union has 34 physicians per 10,000 citizens, Britain 27, the United States 22, Japan 21, South Korea 20, Brazil 17, China 14, South Africa 7, India 6, and Nigeria 4 – all as of 2010, in *Economist*, June 2, 2012. See also ch. 3 for additional data.

21 *AfricaRenewal* (April 2011), 20.

22 See Peter Wayner, "Monitoring Your Health with Mobile Devices," *New York Times*, Feb. 23, 2012; Eric Topol, quoted in "Schumpeter: Now for Some Good News," *Economist*, March 3, 2012; *Economist Technology Quarterly*, June 2, 2012, 18.

23 Ushahidi is KiSwahili for "witness" or "testimony." It was a method of gathering information from many users – crowd sourcing – that was deployed after the 2007 Kenyan elections and has been adapted and used widely in many situations elsewhere ever since.

9   China Drives Growth

1 Meles Zenawi, quoted in William Wallis, "Chinese Put Space-Age Seal on their Role in Africa," *Financial Times*, Jan. 31, 2012.

2 Meles Zenawi, quoted in Andrew Moody and Zhong Nan, "China 'Picking up the Pieces' in Africa," *Weekend China Daily*, April 27, 2012.

3 "Chinese Satellite to Create 150,000 Jobs for Nigerians," *People's Daily* (Beijing), March 16, 2012. For Uganda, see Madina Guloba, Nicholas Kilimani, and Winnie Nabiddo, *Impact of China–Africa Aid Relations: A Case Study of Uganda* (Nairobi, 2010); Centre for Chinese Studies (Stellenbosch University) Weekly China Briefings, Nov. 2, 2012, Nov. 23, 2012, Dec. 7, 2012, www.sun.ac.za/ccs.

4 See Ron Sandrey and Hannah Edinger, *Examining the South Africa – China Agricultural Trading Relationship* (Uppsala, 2009), 18–19; Centre for Chinese Studies, Weekly China Briefings, Nov. 16, 2012, URL as above.

5 Peter Draper, Tsidiso Disenyana, and Gilberto Biacuana, "Chinese Investments in African Network Industries: Case Studies from the Democratic Republic of Congo and Kenya," in Fantu Cheru and Cyril Obi (eds.), *The Rise of China and India in Africa* (London, 2010), 117.

6 But see Chin-Hao Huang, "China's Renewed Partnership with Africa: Implications for the United States," in Robert I. Rotberg (ed.), *China into Africa: Trade, Aid, and Influence* (Washington, DC, 2008), 298.

7 Sanou Mbaye, quoted in "Trying to Pull Together: The Chinese in Africa," *Economist*, April 23, 2011.

8 Andrew Jacobs, "Live from Nairobi, China Puts its Stamp on News From Africa," *New York Times*, Aug. 17, 2012; log.foreignpolicy.com/posts/2012.

9 Wallis, "Chinese," *Financial Times*, Jan. 31, 2012.

10 www.agoa.gov/build/groups/public, 2009, accessed May 8, 2012. For an excellent map representation of China's investment in Africa since 2010, see Mamta Badkar, "Here Are All of the Big Chinese Investments in Africa Since 2010," *Business Insider*, Aug. 13, 2012, www.businessinsider.com/map-chinese-investments-in-Africa-2012-8.

11 Diana Kinch, "Brazil's Africa Relations Now Strategic: Minister," *Wall Street Journal*, May 3, 2012, www.marketwatch.com/story/; Simon Romero, "Brazil Gains Business and Influence as it Offers Aid and Loans in Africa," *New York Times*, Aug. 8, 2012. For more on India and Africa, see Michel Severino and Olivier Ray (trans. David Fernbach), *Africa's Moment* (Cambridge, 2011), 245–9.

12 Blair, speaking at a CEO Africa summit in London and quoted in Sharda Naidoo, "African Countries Want Investment Now, Not Aid Later," March 20, 2012, http://mg.co.za/article/2012-03-20-african-countries-want-investment-now-not-aid-later.

13 But see also the informed commentary in Deborah Brautigam, *The Dragon's Gift: The Real Story of China in Africa* (New York, 2009), 256–257.

14 *Daily Mail* (Lusaka), April 12, 2012.

15 International Crisis Group, "China's New Courtship in South Sudan," April 4, 2012, www.crisisgroup.org; Katrina Manson, "South Sudan Gains a Fraction of $8bn China Loan," *Financial Times*, May 16, 2012.

16 The interface between China and Angola may still be a very shady company called China Sonangol, run by well-connected Angolans and Sam Pa (Xu Jinghua). Sam Pa also has close connections to the Zimbabwe Central Intelligence Organization, with which he digs diamonds in eastern Zimbabwe. See "The Queensway Syndicate and the Africa Trade," *Economist*, Aug. 13, 2011.

17 See Deborah Brautigam, "China's Foreign Aid in Africa: What Do We Know?" in Rotberg, *China*, 207–10. "Mutual benefit" was enunciated at the Forum on China–Africa Cooperation (FOCAC), January 2006, www.focac.org/eng/, accessed March 21, 2012. China went on record then in support of Africa by backing "competent Chinese enterprises to cooperate with African nations . . . on the basis . . . of mutual benefit and common development." For more on the history of FOCAC, see Lawal Mohammed Marafa, *Africa's Business and Development Relationship with China: Seeking Moral and Capital Values of the Last Economic Frontier* (Uppsala, 2009), 8.

18 Chin-Hao, "Partnership," 301.

19 Yun Sun, of the Stimson Center, quoted in Jane Perlez, "With $20 Billion Loan Pledge, China Strengthens its Ties to African Nations," *New York Times*, July 20, 2012.

20 Brautigam, "Foreign Aid," 209. See also her full discussion of the comparability question and other aspects of Chinese assistance in Brautigam, *Dragon's Gift*, 162–88. Rachel Will, "China's Stadium Diplomacy," *World Policy Journal* (Summer, 2012), 36–43 (www.worldpolicy.org/journal/summer2012), says that in 2010 total foreign assistance everywhere amounted to a cumulative $39 billion and US aid to $53 billion since 2000.

21 Alexis Arieff et al., "US Foreign Assistance to Sub-Saharan Africa: The FY 2012 Request," Congressional Research Service (Washington, DC, 2011), www.fas.org/sgp/crs.

22 For China's debt-forgiveness examples, see Chin-Hao, "Partnership," 300.

23 Brautigam, *Dragon's Gift*, 185.

24 David H. Shinn, "Military and Security Relations: China, Africa, and the Rest of the World," in Rotberg, *China*, 155. For further details and updating, see Shinn and Joshua Eisenman, *China and Africa: A Century of Engagement* (Philadelphia, 2012).

25 Centre for Chinese Studies, Weekly China Briefing, Dec. 7, 2012, URL as above.

26 Cited in Padraig Carmody, *The New Scramble for Africa* (Cambridge, 2011), 74.

27 See Kossi Ayenagbo, Tommie Njobvu, James V. Sossou et al., "China's Peacekeeping Operations in Africa: From Unwilling Participation to Responsible Contribution," *African Journal of Political Science and International Relations*, VI (2012), 22–32.

28 Shinn, "Military," 180–183.
29 Deborah Brautigam's excellent blog – "China in Africa: The Real Story," www.chinaafricarealstory.com, accessed April 19, 2012 – contains an important section on Chinese workers in Africa. It provides collected data which amplify, but also moderate, the charge that China brings its own laborers across the ocean. Some of the projects – a sample – that she mentions are relatively light on locals and heavy on Chinese, some are the reverse.
30 Will, "China's Stadium Diplomacy," 36–43.
31 Stephanie Rupp, "Africa and China: Engaging Postcolonial Interdependencies," in Rotberg, China, 76.
32 Ibid., 76.
33 Ibid., 77–78.
34 Rafael Marques de Morais, "Growing Wealth, Shrinking Democracy," New York Times, Aug. 30, 2012.
35 Linn Axelsson and Nina Sylvanus, "Navigating Chinese Textile Networks: Women Traders in Accra and Lome," in Cheru and Obi, China and India, 132–140.
36 Sani Yusuf, a dye-pit manager, quoted in "Nigeria's Northern Capital: The Terror They Dare Not Name," Economist, Jan. 28, 2012.
37 www.ccs.org.za/wp-content, Aug. 31, 2012. See also Cecilia Jamasmie, "Over 10,000 Chinese Rush to Ghana Searching for Gold," Mining.com, Nov. 25, 2012, www.mining.com.
38 "Trying to Pull Together: The Chinese in Africa," Economist, April 23, 2011; Carmody, Scramble, 70.
39 Kweku Ampiah and Sanusha Naidu, "The Sino-African Relationship: Towards an Evolving Partnership?" in Kweku Ampiah and Sanusha Naidu (eds.), Crouching Tiger, Hidden Dragon: Africa and China (Scottsville, South Africa, 2008), 335.
40 Marques de Morais, "Growing Wealth."
41 Michael Sata, quoted in "Chinese–African Attitudes: Not as Bad as They Say," Economist, Oct. 1, 2011; also in Carmody, Scramble, 87.
42 Patrick Mutesa, "China and Zambia: Between Development and Politics," in Cheru and Obi, China and India, 177–178.
43 Quoted in Human Rights Watch (HRW) (Matt Wells), "You'll be Fired if You Refuse": Labor Abuses in Zambia's Chinese State-Owned Copper Mines (Washington, DC, November 2011), 23. For a tough critique of the HRW interview methodology and conclusions, and the HRW response to these criticisms, see the "China in Africa: The Real Story," blog, Feb. 8, 2012, www.chinaafricarealstory.com. Some high-level officials (personal interviews, July 3–4, 2012) in Zambia also question the accuracy of the HRW critique. For earlier criticism of Chinese labor practices throughout Zambia, see Jolly Kamwanga and Grayson Koyi, Impact of China–Africa Investment Relations: The Case of Zambia (Washington, DC, 2009), 3.

44 Kamwanga and Koyi, *Impact*, 3; Rights and Accountability in Development (UK), *Chinese Mining Operations in Katanga, Democratic Republic of Congo* (London, Sept. 2009), 8. Two Chinese mobile telephone companies in the Congo were accused of equally atrocious labor practices – of paying low wages and offering worse conditions. Chinese attitudes and actions even made Congolese trade unionists "sing the praises of Belgian business." See Draper et al., "Chinese Investments, " 115.

45 *Southern Weekend* (a Chinese newspaper), cited in HRW, *Labor Abuses*, 22.

46 *The Post* (Lusaka), July 4, 2012.

47 Boom operator, July 16, 2011, quoted in HRW, *Labor Abuses*, 55.

48 Underground Chambishi miner, November 2010, quoted in ibid., 32; interview with underground boomer operator at Chambishi, Nov. 11, 2010, in ibid., 34; interview on July 15, 2011, in ibid., 57; interview with Kitwe miner, Nov. 15, 2010, in ibid., 59.

49 Forklift operator at Sino Metals, Kitwe, July 13, 2011, in ibid., 88; union representative at the same facility, Nov. 7, 2010, in ibid., 91. See also the conversations recorded in Serge Michel and Michel Beuret (trans. Raymond Valley), *China Safari: On the Trail of Beijing's Expansion in Africa* (New York, 2009), 239–240.

50 See Deborah Brautigam, Thomas Farole, and Tang Xiaoyang, "China's Investment in African Special Economic Zones: Prospects, Challenges, and Opportunities," *Economic Premise* (World Bank), March 2010, 2.

51 Carmody, *Scramble*, 164; an anonymous Zambian parliamentarian, quoted in Michel and Beuret, *China Safari*, 246.

52 Helen Hai of the Huajian Group, quoted on Capital Ethiopia, April 5, 2012, www.capitalethiopia.com; "On the March," *Economist*, June 9, 2012.

53 "A Ravenous Dragon: A Special Report on China's Quest for Resources," *Economist*, March 15, 2008, 13; Centre for Chinese Studies, Weekly China Briefing, Nov. 30, 2012, URL as before. Parts of this paragraph rely on Robert I. Rotberg, "China's Quest for Resources, Opportunities, and Influence in Africa," in Rotberg (ed.), *China*, 11–12.

54 *People's Daily* (Beijing), Jan. 14, 2008.

55 But see Li Anshan, "China's New Policy Toward Africa," in Rotberg, *China*, 38.

56 See Stephen Brown and Chandra Lekha Siriam, "China's Role in Human Rights Abuses in Africa: Clarifying Issues of Culpability," in Rotberg, *China*, 252; Rotberg, "China's Quest," 15.

57 Mbeki, quoted in "Ravenous Dragon," 17; Zuma, quoted in Perlez, "With $20 Billion Loan."

58 Dinner discussion, Lusaka, July 3, 2012.

59 Brautigam offers a spirited and well-argued defense of China's human rights record, setting out a number of extenuating circumstances, but never obscuring the essential nature of China's compromised relations with much of sub-Saharan Africa. See Brautigam, *Dragon's Gift*, 273–304.

60 Paul Fortin, quoted in ibid., 164.
61 Much in these paragraphs draws on Rotberg, "China's Quest," 17–18. But see also Ampiah and Naidu, *Crouching Tiger*, 335.

10   Strengthening Governance

1 Tony Blair, "A New Approach to a New Africa," www.tonyblairoffice.org/speeches/entry/ March 19, 2012.
2 Daron Acemoglu and James A. Robinson, *Why Nations Fail: The Origins of Power, Prosperity, and Poverty* (New York, 2012), 76.
3 This chapter's discussion of governance draws heavily on Robert I. Rotberg, "Strengthening African Governance: Ranking Countries Would Help," *Washington Quarterly*, XXIV (2004), 71–81; Rotberg, "Improving Governance in the World: Creating a Measuring and Ranking System," in Rotberg and Deborah L.West, *The Good Governance Problem: Doing Something About It* (Cambridge, MA, 2004), 3–30; Rotberg, "On Improving Nation-State Governance," *Daedalus*, CXXXVI (Winter 2007), 151–155; Rotberg, "The Meaning of Governance: Ranking Africa," in Rotberg and Rachel M. Gisselquist, *Strengthening African Governance: Index of African Governance, Results and Indicators, 2009* (Cambridge, MA, 2009), 7.
4 This and succeeding paragraphs draw on Robert I. Rotberg, "Good and Bad Governance," in Rotberg, *Governance and Leadership in Africa* (Philadelphia, 2007), 21–24.
5 For details, see the published or web versions of Rotberg and Gisselquist, *Strengthening African Governance* (2007, 2008, 2009). The Index continued after 2010 and is now compiled by the Mo Ibrahim Foundation, under his name. But the original methodology is largely being followed and much of the data contained in recent issues of the Index can be compared against earlier iterations.
6 One of the great unsung needs of sub-Saharan Africa is the rejuvenation of national statistical offices. Such an effort would be worthy of the most farsighted donors. See also Marten Jerven, *Poor Numbers: How We Are Misled by African Department Statistics and What to Do About It* (Ithaca, 2003).
7 Although the original Index measured governance 57 ways, the 2012 Index, now called the Ibrahim Index of African Governance, uses 88 variables. See www.moibrahimfoundation.org/interact/, accessed Oct. 15, 2012.
8 See Victor T. Le Vine, "The Coups in Upper Volta, Dahomey, and the Central African Republic," in Robert I. Rotberg and Ali A Mazrui (eds.), *Protest and Power in Black Africa* (New York, 1970), 1035–1071; Daniel N. Posner and Daniel J. Young, "The Institutionalization of Political Power in Africa," *Journal of Democracy*, XVIII (2007), 128.
9 The Index from 2007 through 2009, and the Ibrahim Index since 2009, have all the details.

10 For a forthright synopsis of Eritrea's many problems, see Dan Connell, "From Resistance to Governance: Eritrea's Trouble with Transition," *Review of African Political Economy*, XXXVIII (2011), 419–433.
11 See Adam Nossiter, "Leader Ousted, Nation is Now a Drug Haven," *New York Times*, Nov. 1, 2012.
12 "Boom Boom," *Economist*, June 30, 2012.
13 International Crisis Group, "Uganda: No Resolution to Growing Tensions," April 5, 2012, www.crisisgroup.org.
14 "Eccentric Gambia Leader Poised to Win Another Term," Jan. 23, 2011, YahooNews, www.yahoo.com/eccentric-gambia-leader/.
15 Steven Radelet, *Emerging Africa: How 17 Countries are Leading the Way* (Washington, DC, 2010), 18, 51, 143.
16 See Rotberg, "Governance Trumps Democracy: Examining the African Experience," in Michael Böss, Jørgen Møller, and Svend-Erik Skaaning (eds.), *Developing Democracies: Democracy, Democratization and Development* (Aarhus, 2013).

11 Creating Responsible Leadership

1 Nelson Mandela, speaking in Katlehong, 1993, quoted in Stanley B. Greenberg, *Dispatches from the War Room: In the Trenches with Extraordinary Leaders* (New York, 2009), 145.
2 Greg Mills, *Why Africa Is Poor and What Africans Can Do About It* (Johannesburg, 2010), 1–2, 10, 12–13, 194, 196, 238, 370. Daron Acemoglu and James A. Robinson, *Why Nations Fail: The Origins of Power, Prosperity, and Poverty* (New York, 2012), 68, make the same point: "poor countries are poor because those who have power make choices that create poverty."
3 Moeletsi Mbeki, *Architects of Poverty: Why African Capitalism Needs Changing* (Johannesburg, 2009), 16–17.
4 Acemoglu and Robinson, *Why Nations Fail*, 116.
5 This section draws deeply on Robert I. Rotberg, *Transformative Political Leadership: Making a Difference in the Developing World* (Chicago, 2012), 2.
6 For the empirical research, see ibid., 7, and the numerous examples scattered throughout the whole of Acemoglu and Robinson, *Why Nations Fail*.
7 Rotberg, *Transformative Political Leadership*, 11. See also Gayle C. Avery, *Understanding Leadership: Paradigms and Cases* (London, 2004), 8, 119.
8 Joseph S. Nye Jr., *The Powers to Lead* (New York, 2008), 18–20.
9 Daniel Goleman, *Working with Emotional Intelligence* (New York, 1998), 318. See also Howard Gardner, *Frames of Mind: the Theory of Multiple Intelligences* (New York, 2004, 2nd edn.), 239.
10 An earlier version of this view is found in Rotberg, *Transformative Political Leadership*, 21.
11 For the original formulation of transformational and transactional, see James MacGregor Burns, *Leadership* (New York, 1978), 20.

12 Rosabeth Moss Kanter, "Leadership for Change: Enduring Skills for Change Masters," A Harvard Business School Class Note, Nov. 17, 2005, 5.

13 Lee, quoted in James Minchin, *No Man Is an Island: A Portrait of Singapore's Lee Kuan Yew* (London, 1990, orig. pub. 1986), 343.

14 See the discussion of "big" men in Todd J. Moss, *African Development: Making Sense of the Issues and Actors* (Boulder, 2007), 37–52.

15 For details and social science research findings, see Rotberg, *Transformative Political Leadership*, 27.

16 David McClelland, *Power: The Inner Experience* (New York, 1975), 260.

17 Ellen Johnson Sirleaf, "A Conversation with Ellen Johnson Sirleaf, President, Republic of Liberia," Council on Foreign Relations, May 25, 2010, www.cfr.org/economics/conversation.

18 See Jiang Yonglin, *The Mandate of Heaven and the Great Ming Code* (Seattle, 2011), 4–6.

19 Nelson Mandela, *Long Walk to Freedom: The Autobiography of Nelson Mandela* (Boston, 1994), 538.

20 Sisulu, quoted in Richard Stengel, "Mandela: His 8 Lessons of Leadership," *Time*, July 9, 2008.

21 Tom Lodge, *Mandela: A Critical Life* (New York, 2006), 8.

22 Quoted in Nelson Mandela, *The Struggle Is My Life* (London, 1978), 155–175.

23 Mandela, *Long Walk*, 424.

24 Anthony Sampson, *Mandela: The Authorized Biography* (New York, 1999), 415.

25 Rosabeth Moss Kanter, *Confidence: How Winning Streaks and Losing Streaks Begin and End* (New York, 2004), 318.

26 John Carlin, *Playing the Enemy: Nelson Mandela and the Game that Made a Nation* (New York, 2008), 4, 16, 17, 95, 113, 163, 193.

27 Quoted in Mark Gevisser, *A Legacy of Liberation: Thabo Mbeki and the Future of the South African Dream* (New York, 2010), 261.

28 Much of this discussion of the Khama example parallels Rotberg, *Transformative Political Leadership*, 69–90, where there is abundant detail.

29 Quoted in Thomas Tlou, Neil Parsons, and Willie Henderson, *Seretse Khama, 1921–1980* (Gaborone, 1995), 223.

30 Khama, quoted in Edwin S. Munger, *Bechuanaland: Pan-African Outpost or Bantu Homeland?* (London, 1965), 2.

31 Quett Ketumile Joni Masire (ed. Stephen R. Lewis), *Very Brave or Very Foolish? Memoirs of an African Democrat* (Gaborone, 2006), 56.

32 Tlou et al. , *Seretse*, 61.

33 Quoted in ibid,, 252.

34 Ibid., 280, 282, 335.

35 Ibid., 271.

36 Masire, *Very Brave*, 103.

37 Quoted in Tlou et al., *Seretse*, 364.

38 Transparency International, Corruption Perceptions Index, 2012, www.cpi.transparency.org, accessed Dec. 18, 2012.

39 Daron Acemoglu, Simon Johnson, and James A. Robinson, "An African Success Story: Botswana," in Dani Rodrik (ed.), *In Search of Prosperity: Analytic Narratives on Economic Success* (Princeton, 2003), 85–88, 104–106.

40 "Zuma's Two Bad Calls," *Economist*, Sept. 4, 2010

41 ElBaradei and Mogal, quoted in Geoffrey York, "Foundation Unable to Handout Ibrahim Prize for Third Time in Six Years," *Globe and Mail* (Toronto), Oct. 15, 2012. Condé, quoted in Liz Alderman, "On Lookout in Davy for Next Growth Story in Emerging Markets," *New York Times*, Jan. 26, 2013.

42 For Joyce Banda's vision of the new Malawi, consult Peter Clottey's interview with her in "President Banda Outlines Her Vision for Malawi," VOANews, Jan. 22, 2013, www.voanews.com/.

43 Quoted in Josh Kron and Jeffrey Gettleman, "Of Irish Soil and Seeking to Take Root in Ugandan Politics," *New York Times*, March 2, 2011.

44 See J. Olaka-Onyango, "Constitutional Transition in Museveni's Uganda: New Horizons or Another False Start?" *Journal of African Law*, XXXIX (1995), 156–172.

45 Daniel Edyegu, "I Am Ready to Live by Sacrifice – Museveni," *The New Vision* (Kampala), Feb. 26, 2009.

46 E. J. Hogendoorn, International Crisis Group, quoted in Douglas Mpuga, "Reform or Face Potential Conflict and Instability, Report Warns Museveni," VOANews, April 11, 2012, www.voanews.com.

47 Quoted in Stephen Kinzer, *A Thousand Hills: Rwanda's Rebirth and the Man Who Dreamed It* (New York, 2008), 236. See also "The Pain of Suspension," *Economist*, Jan. 12, 2013, an article detailing criticisms of Kagame.

48 Transparency International, Corruption Perceptions Index, 2012. See above for URL.

49 Chipimo is much more critical of Kaunda. See Elias C. Chipimo Jr., *Unequal to the Task? Awakening a New Generation of Leaders in Africa* (Lusaka, 2010), 66.

50 There is an excellent discussion of nurturing positive leadership in Nitin Nohria and Rakesh Khurana (eds.), *Handbook of Leadership Theory and Practice* (Boston, 2010), last section, including chapters by Jay A. Conger and Bruce J. Avolio.

51 Patrick Awuah, quoted in Steven Radelet, *Emerging Africa: How 17 Countries are Leading the Way* (Washington, DC, 2010), 125–126. See also www.ashesi.edu.gh, accessed Aug. 18, 2012.

52 Nasir El-Rufai, speech at Patriots for New Nigeria Initiative, Abuja, Oct. 20, 2011, in "Plugging the Leadership Gap – Options for Nigeria," www.huhuonline.com.

Select Bibliography

Acemoglu, Daron, and James A. Robinson, *Why Nations Fail: The Origins of Power, Prosperity, and Poverty* (New York, 2012)

Acemoglu, Daron, Simon Johnson, and James A. Robinson, "An African Success Story: Botswana," in Dani Rodrik (ed.), *In Search of Prosperity: Analytic Narratives on Economic Success* (Princeton, 2003), 85–106

Adebajo, Adekeye, *UN Peacekeeping in Africa: From the Suez Crisis to the Sudan Conflicts* (Johannesburg, 2011)

Aker, Jenny C., "Information from Markets Near and Far: Mobile Phones and Agricultural Markets in Niger," *American Economics Journal: Applied Economics*, II (2010), 46–59

Aker, Jenny C., Christopher Ksoll, and Travis J. Lybbert, "Can Mobile Phones Improve Learning? Evidence from a Field Experiment in Niger," *American Economics Journal: Applied Economics*, IV (2012), 94–120

Aker, Jenny C., and Isaac M. Mbiti, "Mobile Phones and Economic Development in Africa," *Journal of Economic Perspectives*, XXIV (2010), 207–232

Ampiah, Kweku, and Sanusha Naidu (eds.) *Crouching Tiger, Hidden Dragon: Africa and China* (Scottsville, South Africa, 2008)

Andreas, Peter, and Kelly Greenhill (eds.), *Sex, Drugs, and Body Counts: The Politics of Numbers in Global Crime and Conflict* (Ithaca, 2010)

Autesserre, Sabine, *The Trouble with the Congo: Local Violence and the Failure of International Peacebuilding* (New York, 2010)

Ayenagbo, Kossi, Tommie Njobvu, James V. Sossou, and Biossey K. Tozoun, "China's Peacekeeping Operations in Africa: From Unwilling Participation to Responsible Contribution," *African Journal of Political Science and International Relations*, VI (2012), 22–32

Ayittey, George B . N., *Africa Unchained: The Blueprint for Africa's Future* (New York, 2005)

Barajas, Adolfo, Ralph Chami, Connel Fullenkamp, and Anjali Garg, "The Global Financial Crisis and Workers' Remittances to Africa: Where's the Damage?" IMF Working Paper (Jan. 2010)

Bayart, Jean-François, *The State in Africa: The Politics of the Belly* (London, 1993)

Berman, Jonathan, "Visceral Leishmaniasis in the New World and Africa," *Indian Journal of Medical Research*, CXXIII (2006), 289–294

Bilger, Burkhard, "The Great Oasis: Can a Wall of Trees Stop the Sahara from Advancing?" *New Yorker*, 19 & 26 December 2011, 116–121

Bloom, David, David Canning, and Kevin Chan, "Higher Education and Economic Development in Africa," World Bank, Human Development Sector (Feb. 2006), http://ent.arp.harvard.edu/african higher education/

Branch, Daniel, *Kenya: Between Hope and Despair* (New Haven, 2011)

Bratton, Michael, and Nicolas van de Walle, *Democratic Experiments in Africa: Regime Transitions in Comparative Perspective* (New York, 1997)

Brautigam, Deborah, *The Dragon's Gift: The Real Story of China in Africa* (New York, 2009)

— "China's Foreign Aid in Africa: What Do We Know?" in Robert I. Rotberg (ed.) *China into Africa: Aid, Trade, and Influence* (Washington, DC, 2009), 197–216

Brautigam, Deborah, Thomas Farole, and Tang Xiaoyang, "China's Investment in African Special Economic Zone: Prospects, Challenges, and Opportunities," *Economic Premise* (World Bank) March 2012, web.worldbank.org/wbsite/external

Carlin, John, *Playing the Enemy: Nelson Mandela and the Game that Made a Nation* (New York, 2008)

Carmody, Padraig, *The New Scramble for Africa* (Cambridge, 2011)

Carrington, William J., and Enrica Detragiache, "How Extensive is the Brain Drain?" *Finance and Development* (June 1999), 46–49

Cervantes, Mario, and Dominique Guellec, "The Brain Drain: Old Myths, New Realities," *OECD Observer* (2011), www.oecdobserver.org/news/fullstory.php/aid/673

Cheru, Fantu, and Cyril Obi (eds.), *The Rise of China and India in Africa* (London, 2010)

Chin-Hao Huang, "China's Renewed Partnership with Africa: Implications for the United States," in Robert I. Rotberg (ed.), *China into Africa: Trade, Aid, and Influence* (Washington, DC, 2008), 296–312

Chipimo, Elias C. Jr., *Unequal to the Task? Awakening a New Generation of Leaders in Africa* (Lusaka, 2010)

Clapham, Christopher, *Africa and the International System: The Politics of State Survival* (Cambridge, 1996)

— *War and State Formation in Ethiopia and Eritrea*, 2000, www.theglobalsite.ac.uk

— (ed.), *African Guerrillas* (London, 1998)

Clapham, Christopher, Jeffrey Herbst, and Greg Mills (eds.), *Big African States: Angola, DRC, Ethiopia, Nigeria, South Africa, Sudan* (New Brunswick, 2006)

Clarke, Walter, and Jeffrey Herbst (eds.), *Learning from Somalia: The Lessons of Armed Humanitarian Intervention* (Boulder, 1997)

Cloete, Nico, Tracey Bailey, Puny Pillay, Ian Bunting, and Peter Maassen, *Universities and Economic Development in Africa* (Wynberg, South Africa, 2011)

Collier, Paul, *The Bottom Billion: Why the Poorest Countries Are Failing and What Can Be Done About It* (New York, 2007)

Connell, Dan, "From Resistance to Governance: Eritrea's Trouble with Transition," *Review of African Political Economy*, XXXVIII (2011), 419–433

Cranford, Gordon, and Gabrielle Lynch (eds.), *Democratization in Africa: Challenges and Prospects* (London, 2012)

Czernich, N., O. Falck, T. Kretschmer, and L.Woessman, "Broadband Infrastructure and Economic Growth," *Economic Journal*, LXXI (552) (2011), 505–532

Degomme, Olivier, and Debarati Guha-Sapir, "Patterns of Mortality Rates in Darfur Conflict," *The Lancet*, CCCXXV (Jan. 23, 2010), 294–300

Dowden, Richard, *Africa: Altered States, Ordinary Miracles* (London, 2008)

Downie, Richard, and Jennifer Cooke, *Assessing Risks to Stability in Sub-Saharan Africa*, CSIS Report (Washington, DC, 2011)

Easterly, William, and Yaw Nyarko, "Is the Brain Drain Good for Africa?" *Brookings Global Economy and Development Papers* (March 2008), 1–37

Ellis, Stephen, *The Mask of Anarchy: The Destruction of Liberia and the Religious Dimension of an African Civil War* (London, 1999)

—— *External Mission: The ANC in Exile, 1960–1990* (London, 2012)

Englebert, Pierre, *Africa: Unity, Sovereignty and Sorrow* (Boulder, 2009)

Faye, Michael L., John W. McArthur, Jeffrey D. Sachs, and Thomas Snow, "The Challenges Facing Landlocked Countries in the Developing World," *Journal of Human Development*, V (2004), 31–68

Feinstein, Andrew, *After the Party: Corruption, the ANC and South Africa's Uncertain Future* (London, 2009)

Flint, Julie, and Alex de Waal, *Darfur: A New History of a Long War* (London, 2008)

Fortna, Virginia Page, *Does Peacekeeping Work? Shaping Belligerents' Choices after Civil War* (Princeton, 2008)

Fosu, Augustin Kwasi, "Anti-growth Syndromes in Africa: A Synthesis of the Case Studies," in Benno I. Ndulu et al. (eds.), *The Political Economy of Economic Growth in Africa, 1960–2000* (New York, 2008), I, 137–174

Foster, Douglas, *After Mandela: The Struggle for Freedom in Post-Apartheid South Africa* (New York, 2012)

Gallup, John, and Jeffrey D. Sachs, "Location, Location: Geography and Economic Development," *Harvard International Review*, XXI (1998–1999), 57–59

Gelletly, LeeAnne, *Africa: Progress and Problems. Ecological Issues* (Philadelphia, 2007)

Gevisser, Mark, *A Legacy of Liberation: Thabo Mbeki and the Future of the South African Dream* (New York, 2010)

Gonzalez, Patrick, C. J. Tucker, and H. Sy, "Tree Density and Species Decline in the African Sahel Attributable to Climate," *Journal of Arid Environments*, LXXVIII (2012), 55–64

Greef, Liane, "Power from the Wind in South Africa," *AfricaRenewal* (April 2012), 26

Greenberg, Stanley B., *Dispatches from the War Room: In the Trenches with Extraordinary Leaders* (New York, 2009)

Guloba, Madina, Nicholas Kilimani, and Winnie Nabiddo, *Impact of China–Africa Aid Relations: A Case Study of Uganda* (Nairobi, 2010)

Gwilliam, Kenneth W., *Africa's Transport Infrastructure: Mainstreaming Maintenance and Management* (Washington, DC, 2011)

Gyimah-Brempong, Kwabena, "Corruption, Economic Growth, and Income Inequality in Africa," *Economics of Governance*, III (2002), 183–209

Hakansson, Bjork, "Full Steam Ahead to Sustainable Energy," *AfricaRenewal* (April 2012), 27

Harel, Xavier, and Thomas Hofnung, *The Scandal of Ill-Gotten Gains* (Paris, 2011)

Hasselbein, Gabi, "The Rise and Decline of the Congolese State: An Analytical Narrative of State-Making," Crisis States Working Paper, 2 (London, November 2007)

Herbst, Jeffrey, *States and Power in Africa: Comparative Lessons in Authority and Control* (Princeton, 2000)

Herbst, Jeffrey, and Greg Mills, *The Future of Africa: A New Order in Sight?* (New York, 2003)

Hochschild, Adam, *King's Leopold's Ghost: A Story of Greed, Terror, and Heroism in Colonial Africa* (New York, 2006)

Human Rights Watch, "Transparency and Accountability in Angola: An Update," April 12, 2010, www.hrw.org/news

Human Rights Watch (Matt Wells), *"You'll be Fired if You Refuse:" Labor Abuses in Zambia's Chinese State-Owned Copper Mines* (Washington, DC, November 2011)

Hunter-Gault, Charlayne, "Violated Hopes: A Nation Confronts a Tide of Sexual Violence," *New Yorker*, May 18, 2012

Iyoha, Milton A., and Dickson E. Oriakhi, "Explaining African Economic Growth Performance: The Case of Nigeria," in Benno J. Ndulu et al. (eds.), *The Political Economy of Economic Growth in Africa* (New York, 2008), II, 621–659

Johnson Sirleaf, Ellen, *This Child Will Be Great: Memoir of a Remarkable Life by Africa's First Woman President* (New York, 2009)

Juma, Calestous, *The New Harvest: Agricultural Innovation in Africa* (New York, 2011)

Kamwanga, Jolly, and Grayson Koyi, *Impact of China–Africa Investment Relations: The Case of Zambia* (Washington, DC, 2009)

Kanter, Rosabeth Moss, *Confidence: How Winning Streaks and Losing Streaks Begin and End* (New York, 2004)

— "Leadership for Change: Enduring Skills for Change Masters: A Harvard Business School Class Note," November 17, 2005

Katz, Raul L, and Pantelis Koutroumpis, "Measuring Socio-Economic Digitization: A Paradigm Shift," Social Science Research Network, May 29, 2012, http://papers.ssrn.org

Kinzer, Stephen, *A Thousand Hills: Rwanda's Rebirth and the Man Who Dreamed It* (New York, 2008)

Labbe, Jeremie, "Deciphering a Looming Humanitarian Crisis in the Sahel," Feb. 10, 2012, www.ipiglobalobservatory.org

Landau, Loren B., and Tamlyn Monson, "Immigration and Subterranean Sovereignty in South African Cities," in Anne L. Clunan and Harold A. Trinkunas (eds.), *Ungoverned Spaces: Alternatives to State Authority in an Era of Softened Sovereignty* (Stanford, 2010), 153–174

Lemarchand, René, *Burundi: Ethnic Conflict and Genocide* (New York, 1994)

— *The Dynamics of Violence in Central Africa* (Philadelphia, 2009)

— (ed.), *Forgotten Genocides: Oblivion, Denial, and Memory* (Philadelphia, 2011)

Levine, Ruth, et al., *Girl's Count: A Global Investment and Action Agenda* (Washington, DC, 2008)

Lodge, Tom, *Mandela: A Critical Life* (New York, 2006)

Loewenson, R., and C. Thompson (eds.), "Health Personnel in Southern Africa: Confronting Maldistribution and Brain Drain," www.medact.org/content/health/documents/2005

Lush, Allen, and Stephen Ndegwa (eds.), *Growing Africa's Changing Societies: Dynamics of Reform* (Boulder, 2012)

Lynch, Gabrielle, *I Say to You: Ethnic Politics and the Kalenjin in Kenya* (Chicago, 2011), 1–30

Lyons, Terrence, *Ethiopia: Assessing Risks to Stability*, CSIS Report (Washington, DC, 2011)

MacDonald, A. M., Helen C. Bonsor, et al., "Quantitative Maps of Groundwater Resources in Africa," *Environmental Research Letters*, VII (April 19, 2012), http://iopscience.iop.org/1748

Mahmud, Quamrul, "Impact of Corruption on Economic Growth Performance in Developing Countries," 21 Nov. 2011, www.scribd.com/doc/764/

Maipose, Gervase S., and Thapelo C. Matsheka, "The Indigenous Developmental State and Growth in Botswana," in Benno J. Ndulu et al. (eds.), *The Political Economy of Economic Growth in Africa, 1960–2000* (New York, 2008), II, 511–546

Mandela, Nelson, *Long Walk to Freedom: The Autobiography of Nelson Mandela* (Boston, 1994)

—— *The Struggle Is My Life* (London 1978)

Marafa, Lawal Mohammed, *Africa's Business and Development Relationship with China: Seeking Moral and Capital Values of the Last Economic Frontier* (Uppsala, 2009)

Masire, Quett Ketumile Joni (ed. Stephen R. Lewis), *Very Brave or Very Foolish? Memoirs of an African Democrat* (Gaborone, 2006)

Mbeki, Moeletsi, *Architects of Poverty: Why African Capitalism Needs Changing* (Johannesburg, 2009)

Michel, Serge, and Michel Beuret (trans. Raymond Valley), *China Safari: On the Trail of Beijing's Expansion in Africa* (New York, 2009)

Mills, Greg, *Why Africa Is Poor and What Africans Can Do About It* (Johannesburg, 2010)

Mills, Greg, and Jeffrey Herbst, *Africa's Third Liberation: The New Search for Prosperity and Jobs* (Johannesburg, 2012)

Morrison, J. Stephen, and Suzanne Brundage, *Advancing Health in Ethiopia with Fewer Resources: An Uncertain GHI Strategy, and Vulnerabilities on the Ground* (Washington, DC, 2012)

Moss, Todd J., *African Development: Making Sense of the Issues and Actors* (Boulder, 2007)

Mullan, Fitzhugh, "The Metrics of the Physician Brain Drain," *New England Journal of Medicine*, CCCLIII (2005), 1810–1818

Mullins, James, "Malawi Breathes New Life into Childhood Pneumonia Care," *The Lancet*, CCCLXXX (2012), 717

Munger, Edwin S., *Bechuanaland: Pan-African Outpost or Bantu Homeland?* (London, 1965)

Murray, Martin J., *City of Extremes: The Spatial Politics of Johannesburg* (Durham, 2011)

Muto, Megumi, and Takashi Yamano, "The Impact of Mobile Phone Coverage Expansion on Market Participation: Panel Evidence from Uganda," *World Development*, XXXVII (2009), 1887–1896

Mutume, Gumisai, "Reversing Africa's 'Brain Drain,'" *Africa Recovery*, XVII (2003), 1

Mwase, Nkunde, and Benno J. Ndulu, "Tanzania, Explaining Four Decades of Episodic Growth," in Benno J. Ndulu et al. (eds.), *The Political Economy of Economic Growth in Africa, 1960–2000* (New York, 2008), II, 426–470

Ndulu, Benno J., Stephen A. O'Connell, Robert H. Bates, Paul Collier, and Chukwuma C. Soludo (eds.), *The Political Economy of Economic Growth in Africa, 1960–2000* (New York, 2008), 2 volumes

Network of African Science Academies, "Brain Drain in Africa," www.nationalacademies.org/includes/

Olaka-Onyango, J., "Constitutional Transition in Museveni's Uganda: New Horizons or Another False Start?" *Journal of African Law*, XXXIX (1995), 156–172

Osaghae, Eghosa E., and Rotimi T. Suberu, "A History of Identities, Violence, and Stability in Nigeria," CRISE Working Paper, 6 (Oxford, 2005)

Park, Hung Mo, "Corruption and Economic Growth," *Journal of Comparative Economics*, XXIX (2001), 66–79

Peterman, Amber, Tia Palermo, and Caryn Bredenkamp, "Estimates and Determinants of Sexual Violence Against Women in the Democratic Republic of Congo," *American Journal of Public Health*, CI (2011), 1060–1067

Posner, Daniel N., *Institutions and Ethnic Politics in Africa* (Cambridge, 2005)

Posner, Daniel N., and Daniel J. Young, "The Institutionalization of Political Power in Africa," *Journal of Democracy*, XVIII (2007), 126–140

Radelet, Steven, *Emerging Africa: How 17 Countries are Leading the Way* (Washington, DC, 2010)

Reno, William J., "Sierra Leone: Warfare in a Post-State Society," in Robert I. Rotberg (ed.), *State Failure and State Weakness in a Time of Terror* (Washington, DC, 2003), 71–100

Rohac, Dalibor, Eli Dourado, and Hemal Shah, "Six Questions You Always Wanted to Ask About Africa ... and Answers from Rwanda," 2012, www.li.com/attachments/Rwanda

Rotberg, Robert I., *Africa's Successes: Evaluating Accomplishment* (Cambridge, MA, 2007)

— *Beyond Mugabe: Preparing for Zimbabwe's Transition* (Washington, DC, 2011)

— *Ending Autocracy, Enabling Democracy: The Tribulations of Southern Africa* (Washington, DC, 2002)

— *Governance and Leadership in Africa* (Philadelphia, 2007)

— *Nigeria: Elections and Continuing Challenges* (New York, Council on Foreign Relations, April 2007)

— *Suffer the Future: Policy Choices in Southern Africa* (Cambridge, MA, 1980)

— *Transformative Political Leadership: Making a Difference in the Developing World* (Chicago, 2012)

— (ed.), *Battling Terrorism in the Horn of Africa* (Washington, DC, 2005)

— (ed.), *China into Africa: Trade, Aid, and Influence* (Washington, DC, 2008)

— (ed.), *Corruption, Global Security, and World Order* (Washington, DC, 2009)

— (ed.), *Crafting the New Nigeria: Confronting the Challenges* (Boulder, 2004)

— (ed.), *When States Fail: Causes and Consequences* (Princeton, 2004)

— (ed.), *Worst of the Worst: Dealing with Repressive and Rogue Nations* (Washington, D., 2007)

— "Consummate Challenges for Africa: Demographic Dividends, Governance and Leadership," *Africa Growth Report* (Pretoria, 2012), 172–179

— "How Corruption Compromises World Peace and Stability," in Rotberg (ed.), *Corruption, Global Security, and World Order* (Washington, DC, 2009), 1–27

Rotberg, Robert I., and Jenny C. Aker, "Mobile Phones: Uplifting Weak and Failed States," *Washington Quarterly*, XXXVI (Winter, 2013), 111–125

Rotberg, Robert I., Ericka A. Albaugh, Happyton Bonyongwe, Christopher Clapham, Jeffrey Herbst, and Steven Metz, *Peacekeeping and Peace Enforcement in Africa* (Washington, DC, 2000).

Rotberg, Robert I., and Rachel M. Gisselquist, *Strengthening African Governance: Index of African Governance, Results and Indicators* (Cambridge, MA, 2007, 2008, 2009)

Rotberg, Robert I., and Deborah L. West, *The Good Governance Problem: Doing Something About It* (Cambridge, MA, 2004)

Rupp, Stephanie, "Africa and China: Engaging Postcolonial Interdependencies," in Robert I. Rotberg (ed.), *China into Africa: Trade, Aid, and Influence* (Washington, DC, 2008), 65–86

Sachs, Jeffrey D., and Andrew M. Warner, "Sources of Slow Growth in African Economies," *Journal of African Economies*, VI (1996), 335–376

—— "Tropical Underdevelopment," Harvard Center for International Development Working Paper, 57 (2000)

Sampson, Anthony, *Mandela: The Authorized Biography* (New York, 1999)

Sandrey, Ron, and Hannah Edinger, *Examining the South Africa – China Agricultural Trading Relationship* (Uppsala, 2009)

Sardan, Jean Pierre Olivier de, "A Moral Economy of Corruption in Africa?" *Journal of Modern African Studies*, XXXVII (1999), 25–52

Sardanis, Andrew, *Africa: Another Side of the Coin* (London, 2003)

Severino, Michel, and Olivier Ray (trans. David Fernbach), *Africa's Moment* (Cambridge, 2011)

Shinn, David H., "Military and Security Relations: China, Africa, and the Rest of the World," in Robert I. Rotberg (ed.), *China into Africa: Trade, Aid, and Influence* (Washington, DC, 2008), 155–196

Shinn, David H., and Joshua Eisenman, *China and Africa: A Century of Engagement* (Philadelphia, 2012)

Simarro, P., Abdoulaye Diarra, Jose A. Ruiz Postigo, Jose R. Franco, and Jean G. Jannin, "The Human African Trypanosomiasis Control and Surveillance Programme of the World Health Organisation, 2000–2009: The Way Forward," *PLoS, Neglected Tropical Diseases*, V (2011), e1007, www.plosntds.org/article

Simons, Emily, Matthew Ferrari, John Fricks, et al., "Assessment of the 2010 Global Measles Mortality Reduction Goal: Results from a Model of Surveillance Data," *Lancet*, CCCLXXIX (2012), 2173–2178

Smith, Daniel Jordan, *A Culture of Corruption: Everyday Deception and Popular Discontent in Nigeria* (Princeton, 2007)

—— "The Paradoxes of Popular Participation in Corruption in Nigeria," in Robert I. Rotberg (ed.), *Corruption, Global Security, and World Order* (Washington, DC, 2009) 283–309

Southall, Roger, "Alternatives for Electoral Reform in Kenya: Lessons from Southern Africa," *Journal of Contemporary African Studies*, XXVII (2009), 445–461

—— "The Congress of the People: Challenges for South African Democracy," *Representation*, XLV (2009), 173–191

Stearns, Jason K., *Dancing in the Glory of Monsters: The Collapse of the Congo and the Great War of Africa* (New York, 2011)

Stengel, Richard, "Mandela: His 8 Lessons of Leadership," *Time*, July 9, 2008

Strydom, Jeannette, "Pneumonia in Africa: The Silent Killer," Feb. 11, 2011, blog-4globalhealth.wordpress.com

Suberu, Rotimi T., *Federalism and Ethnic Conflict in Nigeria* (Washington, DC, 2001)

Tlou, Thomas, Neil Parsons, and Willie Henderson, *Seretse Khama, 1921–1980* (Gaborone, 1995)

Uwamahoro, Yussuf, "Rural Electrification in Rwanda," 2012, www.paceaa.org/workshops/

Vidyashankar, Conjivaram, "Pediatric Leishmaniasis," 2012, www.emedicine.medscape.com/article

Weinstein, Jeremy, *Inside Rebellion: The Politics of Insurgence Violence* (Cambridge, 2006)

Widner, Jennifer A., *Building the Rule of Law: Francis Nyalali and the Road to Judicial Independence in Africa* (New York, 2001)

Will, Rachel, "China's Stadium Diplomacy," *World Policy Journal* (Summer 2012), 36–43 www.worldpolicy.org/journal/summer2012

Williams, Paul D., *War and Conflict in Africa* (Cambridge, 2011)

Wolff, Christian, Gerald H. Haug, Axel Timmermann et al., "Reduced Inter-Annual Rainfall Variability in East Africa During the Last Ice Age," *Science* (August 5, 2011)

Wrong, Michaela, *I Didn't Do It for You: How the World Betrayed a Small African Nation* (London, 2006)

—— *In the Footsteps of Mr. Kurtz: Living on the Brink of Disaster in Mobutu's Congo* (London, 2000)

—— *It's Our Turn to Eat: The Story of a Kenyan Whistleblower* (London, 2009)

Yan, Leung Cheung, P. Raghavenda Rau, and Aris Stouraitis, "How Much Do Firms Pay as Bribes and What Benefits Do They Get? Evidence from Corruption Cases Worldwide," NBER Working Paper, 17981 (April 2012)

Young, M. Crawford, and Thomas Turner, *The Rise and Fall of the Zairean State* (Madison, 1985)

Index